PANZER
COMMANDER

Hans von Luck, May 1984

PANZER
COMMANDER

The Memoirs of
Colonel Hans von Luck

HANS VON LUCK

Introduction by Stephen E. Ambrose

PRAEGER

New York
Westport, Connecticut
London

Library of Congress Cataloging-in-Publication Data

Luck, Hans von, 1911–
    Panzer commander : the memoirs of Colonel Hans von Luck / Hans von
Luck.
    p. cm.
    Bibliography: p.
    Includes index.
    ISBN 0–275–93115–3 (alk. paper)
    1. Luck, Hans von, 1911–   . 2. World War, 1939–1945—Tank
warfare. 3. World War, 1939–1945—Personal narratives, German.
4. Germany.   Heer—Biography. 5. Soldiers—Germany—Biography.
I. Title.
D793.L83   1989
940.54′13′43—dc19   88–39662

Library of Congress Catalog Card Number: 88–39662
ISBN: 0–275–93115–3
First published in 1989

Praeger Publishers, One Madison Avenue, New York, NY 10010
An imprint of Greenwood Publishing Group, Inc.

Printed in the United States of America

The paper used in this book complies with the Permanent
Paper Standard issued by the National Information Standards
Organization (Z39.48-1984).

10 9 8 7 6 5 4 3 2

To Kai, Clemens, and Sascha
May they always live in peace

Contents

15.   The Start of the Invasion, 6 June 1944   136

16.   "Operation Goodwood," 18/19 July 1944   148

17.   Retreat to Germany, August–November 1944   162

18.   Fighting the Americans, December 1944   177

19.   The Eastern Front: The Last Battle   193

20.   The 21st Panzer Division as "Fire Brigade": The Beginning
       of the End   198

21.   The End   206

22.   Capture and Deportation   212

23.   In the Coal Mines of the Caucasus Mountains   218

24.   *Kultura* and Corruption: The Russian Mentality   227

25.   Punishment Camp: Hunger Strike and the KGB   246

26.   Release   254

27.   A New Start   259

       Epilogue   271

       Selected Bibliography   277

       Name Index   279

Illustrations

Preface

Although names, places, and dates have been carefully checked, this book makes no claim to be history. My memoirs reproduce, rather, the events and experiences that a young German had to go through in a period that changed Europe and almost the whole world.

The Second World War stands in the center. It shows, along with the preceding years, how intolerance, a false ideology, and propaganda can mobilize whole peoples against each other and plunge them into misery.

I dedicated my book to my three sons, born between 1954 and 1970, because I wish to address *those* generations that were born only during or after the war. My son Sascha, the youngest, asked me the other day: "What does 'Nazi' actually mean? Why was Hitler 'bad'? Why did a whole people 'follow' him?" He and his generation must be given answers. Many teachers, even those born only during or after the war, have no answer, or only an inadequate one. Older people, for one reason or another, repress the period.

In countless conversations with the young of Germany, Great Britain, and France, at numerous lectures to young students at American universities, I have found that young people want to clear their minds about a period for which the information they are given is either nonexistent, insufficient, or one-sided.

Thus I firmly resist, for instance, classifying the Russians as "bad" and us in the West as "good."

That is too simple!

The reader will learn that the Russians too love their homeland, as we love ours. That during the war Russian mothers and wives had the same worries as ours. Today young people of the world, and precisely those of former adversaries in the war, understand each other with no problems. I hope that *glasnost* and *perestroika* will make it possible for the youth of the Soviet Union and other East European countries to be given the chance to join hands with young people in the West.

Those of my readers who have had the opportunity to visit the USSR, as athletes, scientists, or tourists, will have discovered that the Russian people are charming, hospitable, and ready to live at peace with all the peoples of our world.

Those who have never been to Russia ought to make good the omission.

I have tried to draw experiences from hundreds of episodes, pleasant and sad; experiences that may help to make it impossible for the events in Germany before and during the war ever to be repeated, anywhere. It is profoundly depressing to discover that since the end of the Second World War more than 150 wars have been, and still are being waged worldwide, whether on grounds of politics, economics, or ideology. It depresses me that only the presence of nuclear weapons, it seems, is capable of preventing a new passage of arms between two power blocs.

The example that young people set us older ones should be followed by all in positions of responsibility: the practice of tolerance, that best of human attributes. All of us should know that one can learn from bad experiences.

I thank all who have helped me to write this book. Without my friend Professor Stephen Ambrose of the University of New Orleans, it would never have been written. He "forced" me to relate my experiences, and constantly gave me the heart to continue.

I thank Major John Howard, my British adversary on D-Day, who as the "hero of Pegasus Bridge" has passed into war history and is today my friend. John tells anyone who asks him: "If you want to know what it was like 'on the other side of the hill,' ask my friend Hans."

I thank Werner Kortenhaus, who is writing the history of the 21st Panzer Division, for the extensive material which he put at my disposal.

My thanks are due to all my fellow prisoners, who shared with me the hard fate of five years of Russian captivity and who are still in touch today through the Camp 518 Association. Many refreshed my memory or, by describing their own experiences, helped to give the reader a graphic idea of our "gulag" life.

All, whether it be my adjutant Helmut Liebeskind, or my orderly and friend Erich Beck, or the many who fought with me on every front for nearly five years, have helped me and are a constituent part of the book.

My particular thanks are due to George Unwin of Surrey, England. Of much the same age as me, George has translated my manuscript into English with fellow feeling, identifying himself with me. My American and British friends who have read his text say without exception, "We can literally hear Hans speaking and understand what he has to say to us."

Last but not least I thank my wife, Regina, for her patience and collaboration. For nearly four years she has allowed me to work on my manuscript, assisted me in my research, and in her spare time made copies of hundreds of pages.

I am deeply moved by the Introduction which Steve Ambrose has written for this book. He has made my experiences his own. I am proud to be permitted to call this remarkable human being, author, and historian my friend.

Introduction

In order to properly introduce Hans von Luck to an American audience, it is necessary for me to first of all write a bit of autobiography, to explain the evolution of my own feelings about Germany and Germans in the Second World War.

I was five years old when America went to war with Germany, living in the small town of Whitewater, Wisconsin. My father joined the Navy and went off to the Pacific. My mother, although she had three boys to raise, wanted to make her contribution to the war effort and took a job in the local pea-cannery. In the spring of 1944 a POW camp was established outside Whitewater. The prisoners, members of the Afrika Korps captured the previous year in Tunisia, were put to work in the cannery. It was there that I got my first look at real live German soldiers.

They were, to me, a terrifying sight. Big men, nearly giants to an eight year old, with blond hair, blue eyes, sharp features, speaking an incomprehensible gutteral language that sounded like the toughest talk I had ever heard. They looked like what they were, highly trained killers. The presence of a half-dozen American guards carrying submachine guns at their hips reinforced the impression that these men, even in their POW clothes and stripped of their weapons, were dangerous to all living things.

Out of fear, and in response to the war news I was hearing over the radio, I conceived a hatred of all things German. In the spring of 1945, I was old enough to go to the movies alone, the cost then was only a dime, a quarter on Saturday nights. The feature changed twice a week, and I saw almost every one of them. So I saw dozens of the Movietone News coverage of the last months of the war in Europe; every one of them, at least in my memory, contained footage from yet another concentration camp uncovered that week. These scenes of Auschwitz, Dachau, Bergen-Belsen, and the others, in their bestiality that went beyond the wildest imagination or the most horrible nightmare, made all the more vivid by being in black-and-white, remain today my strongest image of World War II and its meaning.

I could not believe any human being could be guilty of the cruelty that I saw on the screen, so I read the Germans out of the human race. As far as I was concerned, they were beasts. Later, as I entered high school, the Movietone coverage of the Nuremberg trials, revealing yet more horrors, convinced me that I had been wrong, because even beasts would not descend to the levels of depravity the Germans had reached.

When I was 16 or so, I made a startling discovery. My uncle Fred, who took me hunting and fishing, was a German! My best friend, Ron—we were inseparable— was a German! Nearly all my friends, in fact, and a large number of my relatives, were Germans!

Although Fred's last name was Benz, and Ron's was Vohs, and there were the Muellers and the Schmidts and the others, and although they often used German expressions, and ate bratwurst and sauerkraut and drank lots of beer, I had always thought of them as just plain Americans. But in my junior year, in a civics course, during a discussion of Hitler's seizure of power, the teacher raised the question, Can it happen here? I insisted that it could not, because only the uniquely cruel Germans were capable of embracing such a monster. I said there was an indelible evil strain in the Germans, a bad seed, that gave them, and only them, a capacity for cruelty that was central to the conquest of Germany by the Nazis.

Gently but firmly, my teacher explained to me what a racist attitude I had taken, that I was like Hitler, only I was saying that the German people were the worst while he said they were the best.

"And besides," he concluded, "if what you say about Germans is true, how do you explain the Germans living in America? What about Ron Vohs?" He named some others sitting in the class.

"They are not Germans," I muttered.

"Oh yes they are," he replied, and asked how many in the room came from pure German stock. Eleven of the twenty students raised a hand.

I fretted for years about this problem. How was it that German barbarity never appeared among my most intimate German friends? It became a near obsession with me in my college years.

I sought the answer in history courses, and in dozens of books. I became more sophisticated in the process, going into ever greater detail in my attempt to understand what had happened in Germany. I learned some eighteenth- and nineteenth-century German history, and to appreciate the greatness of German culture, but that only deepened the mystery. How could a people who had produced Beethoven, Goethe, and Remarque produce a Hitler?

I read the explanations—the humiliation of Germany at Versailles, the catastrophic inflation of the early twenties, the threat from the Communists, the effectiveness of the Nazi conspiracy, Hitler's charisma—and I began to understand how the Nazis came to power. I read Hannah Arendt's magnificent and massive *The Origins of Totalitarianism* twice through, and then all the critics of her work, and began to understand how the Nazis took total power.

I read more about Stalin and the Soviet Union, and realized that terrible things had happened there, too, although I still believed (and still do) that what happened in Nazi Germany was worse than anything that had happened in Communist Russia. Ranking monsters is certainly distasteful and probably pointless, but I'll always put Hitler ahead of Stalin or anyone else.

I read everything in English on the Final Solution. I felt that if it could be shown that the bulk of the German people did not know about what was going on in the death camps—a subject often discussed in bull sessions in my fraternity, where many of the members, including my roommate, Dick Lamm, were German-Americans—the Germans would in some measure be redeemed. But I became convinced that to the contrary, every German knew. It was impossible not to know.

I came to the conclusion that my initial instinctive judgment was right, that the Germans were beasts. As to how then to explain why German-Americans did not display any evidence of the fatal flaw in their blood line, I was still stumped.

I went on to graduate school, where I concentrated on the American Civil War, and then to my first teaching post, at the University of New Orleans. There I shared an office with another new Ph.D., Henry Friedlander. Henry was a German Jew who had experienced the full horror and truth of the words Klaus Barbie used when he sent off his victims to the concentration camps, "Where you are going is worse than death."

We became close friends, Henry and I, and he told me his whole story. The most difficult part of it for him to relate was the day he arrived, after a five-day train journey in a closed box car from the ghetto of Lodz, at Auschwitz. He lined up with the other prisoners, for a selection process by an SS doctor. His "examination" consisted of a quick glance. Those who appeared healthy enough to work the doctor sent to the right, toward the factory complex. Those condemned to immediate death he sent to the left, to the gas chambers.

Henry, 14 years old, stood between his parents, clutching their hands. The doctor pointed to the right for Henry's father, to the left for Henry and his mother.

Henry's father grabbed the doctor's arm.

"Joseph, don't you remember me? I'm Dr. Friedlander, we studied together at medical school, we ate together, we worked together."

The SS doctor acknowledged the fact.

"This is my son, this is my wife. For old time's sake, can't you let them come with me?"

The doctor smiled. He cracked his whip against his boot.

"You can have one of them. Choose. Be quick. I've got to keep this line moving."

Dr. Friedlander chose Henry. His mother went to the left. He never saw her again. He survived Auschwitz, thanks to his father, who worked in the prison hospital and thus could steal drugs to sell for food.

There were many such stories. They left me full of rage. My hatred of all things German continued unabated, indeed increased.

Then, in 1971, I met Nick Mueller, another history professor, and established a friendship that has grown and deepened over the years. Nick's parents were German immigrants. His father is a major Luther scholar and theologian, and his mother one of the sweetest, loveliest people in the world. I was brought into the family circle, and through the Muellers finally found an answer to my basic question, What happened to that fatal flaw in the German people when they immigrated to America?

"It is absurdly simple," I recall telling Nick one day. "What happened was that all the good Germans left and came to America."

And so I was able to hold to my prejudices. Although by the 1970s I was a serious student of World War II, I refused to go to Germany. Even though I had learned in my Civil War work that one should never try to write about a battle without first visiting the battlefield and walking over the terrain, I refused to enter Germany. It was only after a great deal of soul-searching, and only due to financial necessity, that I finally bought a Volkswagen car.

George Windell was the professor of German history at the University of New Orleans. We often debated the question of the guilt of the German people. We were simultaneously debating the ongoing Vietnam War (he was for it, I was against). Meanwhile, Vietnam, and most of all My Lai, showed me, to my astonishment and dismay, that American boys too were capable of acts of bestial cruelty.

My arguments with George were often loud. He accused me of racism, I accused him of covering up for the Nazis. He insisted that my insistence on the collective and continuing guilt of the German people could not withstand the experience of getting to know real live Germans in their own country. He chided me for my refusal to go.

"Steve is afraid to go to Germany," George told Nick Mueller. "He's terrified that he might meet a German he would like."

I did finally go to Germany, in November 1983, to meet not just a German, but a German who had fought for the Wehrmacht. Major John Howard, British, the hero of a book I was writing on the capture of Pegasus Bridge on D-Day, was responsible for my going. John insisted that I had to see Hans von Luck, who had commanded the regiment guarding the bridge, and assured me that I would like him. He explained that he and Hans had been brought together as lecturers on the attack and defense of bridges by the Swedish military academy, which every year brought its cadets to Pegasus Bridge. John said that he and Hans had become good friends. Well, I thought, if John Howard can sit down with this ex-panzer commander, so can I.

My wife and I drove from London to Hamburg, where Hans lived and worked as a coffee merchant. We took a hotel room, I set up the tape recorder, and waited. Precisely at the stroke of four P.M., as agreed, there was a knock on the door, and Hans came in.

The immediate impression was of a thin, wiry, strong man of medium height and, despite his white hair, of medium age. But a closer study of his ruddy, weathered face, deeply lined with wrinkles, revealed a man well into old age (he was in fact 72 years old). He had sharp features, a hawklike nose, deep-set, penetrating blue eyes, a jutting chin, a large broad forehead, high cheek bones, and big jutting ears. Although he was dressed in a business suit, it took only the slightest imagination to see him in his desert uniform, buttoned to the high stiff collar, his Knight's

Cross around his neck, a German officer's hat set back on his head, his goggles in place, the dust of North Africa covering him.

We ordered coffee from room service as he spread out his maps of Normandy. His English was accented but perfectly understandable. His manners, and his mannerisms, were those of an Old World aristocrat. He chain-smoked Marlboro Lights. He was eager to tell me of his experiences in Normandy, enthusiastic about my project.

We talked for four hours, with scarcely a pause. I got the details of his actions on the night of 5/6 June 1944, and an outline of his service elsewhere. As a military historian, I was of course fascinated to hear the war stories of the man who led the way into Poland in 1939, who was at the vanguard of Rommel's thrust to the Channel Coast in June 1940, who actually reached the outskirts of Moscow in November 1941, who supervised Rommel's extreme right flank in North Africa in 1942–43, and who commanded the armored regiment that met the first D-Day attack in 1944. His stories of life in a POW camp in the Soviet Union, 1945–50, were gripping and revealing. His frequent expression of his great love for the Russian people, and his sympathy for their plight, was quite genuine, and surprising.

Indeed, much as I was impressed by Hans the professional soldier, I was even more taken, charmed, in fact, by Hans the man. He was kind and open and—I couldn't put the word out of my mind—gentle. In 25 years of interviewing veterans, I had never heard better war stories so well told, nor so full of sympathy for the oppressed, whatever race or nationality. Except for Dwight Eisenhower and John Howard, I had never met a veteran I liked or admired more.

I got to know Hans even better, and to like him even more, in the summer of 1987, when he came to Innsbruck, Austria, to spend a couple of weeks going over the first draft of his memoirs, which I had encouraged him to write. I was teaching at University of New Orleans-Innsbruck, a summer school held in the facilities of the University of Innsbruck by U.N.O. Now in its twelfth year, U.N.O.-Innsbruck (founded by my friend Nick Mueller) attracts students from 25 states. I was teaching a course on World War II, with 45 students. Hans came to class with me each day; my lecturing on the German invasion of Russia, or the war in North Africa, with Hans in the audience, made me feel a little like Forrest Pogue, who, in the early 1950s, gave a lecture on the strategy of World War II and discovered, to his surprise, that George C. Marshall was in the audience (Marshall told the nervous Pogue later he had done a fine job).

I've been a teacher for 30 years. It is what I do best and enjoy most. Nothing gives me more satisfaction than getting 18- to 22-year-olds excited about the past, watching them begin to realize the central importance of events that happened before they were born on their own lives. Nothing makes me prouder than playing a role in making youngsters develop an appreciation of and sympathy for other peoples in other cultures in other times.

I was, therefore, delighted to see the magnetic effect Hans had on American students. We went to a café for coffee each afternoon after class, where Hans would hand around his photographs and explain each one to a rapt audience. Like me, when I was their age, most of the students made no distinction between Germans and Nazis; like me, they could not understand how any decent human being could fight for Hitler. To watch as Hans broke down their prejudices, not through any deliberate attempt to do so, but simply by being himself, made this old teacher, who had dedicated his life to breaking down prejudices, supremely happy. So, too, did watching Hans bring to life for them worlds they would never know: that of the Old World aristocrat in pre–World War II Europe, that of a combat commander in the war, that of an inmate of the Gulag, that of a coffee merchant in post-colonial Africa.

Anyone who encourages young people to think big, set high goals, work hard, and be ambitious, is a friend of mine. Hans did these things naturally, and with great aplomb. He expressed his interest in the American students through a steady stream of questions about their plans, hopes, and lives; he encouraged them to travel and meet foreign peoples and get to know their cultures; he told them they must read this or that; he encouraged them to be open-minded and to withhold judgments until they had seen or studied themselves. Although I'm usually highly possessive about "my" students, I stayed in the background, watching with pleasure as this white-haired old soldier and these young Americans developed a rapport that deepened and broadened as the days went past.

On July 15, Hans celebrated his seventy-sixth birthday. The students held a surprise party for him in the patio of their dorm, complete with a keg of beer. Soon, Hans was dancing with the girls, singing American college fight songs with the boys.

The American students included a number of Jews. Before Hans's arrival in Innsbruck, I had given a lecture on the Final Solution. I asserted that every German had to have known about the concentration camps. I added that nonetheless I thought they would like Hans, and assured them they were free to ask him any questions they liked. One of the Jewish girls said she would find it embarrassing "to the max" to ask him about the concentration camps.

I reassured her, and told her that earlier in the week, while going over the manuscript of his memoirs, in Chapter 14, I had leaned back and said, "Hans, no one in America is going to believe you didn't know about the camps. Don't you want to tell us more here?"

"I never knew," he replied, "not until Dagmar's father was taken away." (Hans relates his wartime romance with Dagmar in Chapters 14 through 27.)

"Well," I had responded, "it's your book. You say what you want to say."

So the Jewish student asked about the camps, and others asked if he didn't have a sense of guilt, or if he didn't wish he had fought on the Allied side. Hans insisted that he had no knowledge of the death camps, he refused to plead forgiveness for his actions in the war, or to deny them, and made it clear that although he had never admired Hitler, he had done his duty as a German soldier proudly and would do so again.

The kids were especially touched by Hans's attitude toward the Russians. Like all young Americans, they have grown up with anti-Soviet propaganda, but are nevertheless intensely curious about life in that vast country. And here was Hans, after five years in the Gulag, telling them about the many friends he made in the USSR, and of the funny and touching characteristics of the Russian people. He insisted that only through mutual understanding and knowledge could world peace be achieved. He urged the Americans to extend their travels beyond Western Europe, to go to the East to see for themselves. He said the Russians were a great and proud people who should never be backed up against a wall, for when it came to defending their Mother Russia, Hans insisted, they would fight like tigers. We all knew that he knew what he was talking about.

At one point I overheard one of the Jewish girls say, "But Hans" (they all called him by his first name), "you are so cosmopolitan. You speak so many languages, know so many people, have been to so many places. You are not German!"

"Oh no," Hans replied, his eyes flashing, "don't ever say that. I am German. Completely, fully, proudly. My Prussian ancestors go back to the thirteenth century; they fought with Frederick the Great. You can't get more German than I am." When she started to protest, he raised his hand. "And there are thousands, millions more like me. Not all Germans were Nazis—we are a diverse people, just like you Americans."

For myself, by that time I thought Hans was more German than Hitler ever was.

Through the days Hans was in Innsbruck, his relationship with the students grew even closer. The climax came on a three-day field trip to Normandy. We took an overnight train to Paris, Hans sitting with students in their compartment, swigging cheap Italian wine from the bottle, telling stories. The next morning, we boarded our chartered bus to drive to Rommel's 1944 headquarters at La Roche Guyon. Hans had been there during the Battle of Normandy and described Rommel to us. Then, on to Pegasus Bridge, just north of Caen, where John Howard joined us. A strikingly handsome, white-haired man with a lively British accent and a kindly, grandfatherlike manner, with a gentleness about him that comes as a bit of a surprise in a man who earned world fame through his exploits as an airborne soldier, John is wonderfully likeable. The sight of John and Hans embracing on the bridge where they fought each other 43 summers past, moved many of the students to tears.

For the next two days, Hans, John, my class, and I toured the invasion beaches. At the American cemetery at Omaha Beach, a number of students asked Hans, while standing among the crosses, how he felt. Hans replied that he was there to pay his respects to these brave young men who had done their duty for their country. We ended up, on Friday night, getting drunk together at an outdoor café in Arromanches, looking out on the British invasion beaches, and having another party on Saturday night in a bistro in Bayeux, where we almost got thrown out for rowdiness.

I've been leading American veterans on tours of World War II battlefields for nearly ten years. Every trip has been rewarding, as I always learn something new from each one of the vets, and enjoyable, as we stay in the best hotels and eat in the three-star restaurants. But I've never had so much fun as in 1987, even though we stayed in a student dorm in Bayeux and ate in cheap cafés, because of the joy I felt, as a teacher, in watching Hans and John expand the horizons and understanding of my students. It was a wonderful thing to see and a privilege to be a part of the scene. I had come a long way from the time, not that many years ago, when I would not even consider shaking the hand of a former Wehrmacht officer, much less talking to one, and least of all, giving him free and full access to "my" students.

I urge those American readers who still believe, as I once did, that all the good Germans are either dead or long ago immigrated to the United States, to give Hans a fair reading. He deserves your attention and respect.

Although these are the memoirs of a professional soldier, they are not written for cadets in a military academy, but rather for a general audience. Hans is a storyteller with a sharp eye for the telling anecdote or incident. For a warrior who was in combat situations almost continuously from September 1939 to April 1945, there is surprisingly little blood and guts. For a man who won his country's highest military decorations for courage, there is surprisingly little boasting about personal exploits. For a man who was a POW doing slave labor, there is surprisingly little bitterness. Instead, there is insight, a marked sympathy for the human condition, good humor, and tolerance and wonder.

These are the memoirs of a German citizen who lived through a time when politics was played with stunning intensity in Germany, by the Left and the Right. His is a country in which politics had a greater impact on ordinary people than anywhere else, ultimately bringing a catastrophe down not only on the heads of the Germans, but of the whole of Europe. But there is precious little on politics in these memoirs. I urged Hans to put in more, but he wouldn't. I tried to find out what his politics were, but couldn't. I finally decided that for all his sophistication, in politics Hans is the simplest of men. It might even be said of him that he is unpolitical. He is for freedom everywhere, and against totalitarianism, whether it comes from the Left or the Right, but beyond that he just doesn't have any politics. I can't understand such an attitude, but there it is.

What we do have in these memoirs is a remarkable life. We begin with the young Prussian aristocrat, following the family tradition by joining the army. We see his training, accompany him on his travels, watch the rise of Hitler, and see the effect of Hitler's policies on the newborn German army. Hans marches us into Poland, and carries us along on the heady string of victories in France and Russia. He tastes defeat, for the first time, in North Africa, but soon is established in a penthouse in Paris, enjoying the life of a conqueror. He gives us the details of his bittersweet wartime romance. Then he learns about defeat again, from the British in Normandy, the Americans in eastern France, and the Russians south of Berlin. We end up in a POW camp in the Caucasus, with Hans working as a coal miner.

In the 1960s, on a state visit to Moscow, Charles de Gaulle went to the monument marking the spot, just outside the city, where the Russians had finally stopped the German advance.

"What a people!" De Gaulle remarked.

"You mean the Russians, of course," a reporter with his party said.

"No," De Gaulle replied, "I mean the Germans. To have come so far."

The Wehrmacht of World War II covered more territory than any army in history, driving thousands of kilometers in every direction, making Hitler the greatest conqueror of all time, even including Napoleon. Hans was a participant, usually in the vanguard with his reconnaissance battalion, on many of these offensives—to the Vistula in Poland in 1939, to the Channel Coast in France in 1940, to the outskirts of Moscow in 1941, from the Egyptian border to Tunis in 1942–43. He provides vivid descriptions of the soldiers he fought against and their national characteristics— Poles, Frenchmen, the British, the Red Army, Americans—along with equally vivid descriptions of the terrain he fought in—the endless steppes of Russia, with their immense fields of snow, the desert dunes of North Africa stretching out seemingly to infinity, the house-to-house fighting in the small villages of Normandy.

Along the way he gives us marvelous vignettes about the people he encountered; the pope (priest) at the Cathedral of Smolensk, the madame at the brothel in Bordeaux, the Bedouins in the desert, his French friends in occupied Paris, and many others.

Famous German generals march through these pages, including Jodl, Kesselring, and Guderian. But the dominant personality, aside from Hans himself, is Field Marshal Erwin Rommel. Hans knew him first in the pre-Hitler era, when Rommel was his instructor in tactics. From 1940 to 1944, Hans spent most of his time commanding the recce battalion for Rommel. He was the general Hans admired most, and clearly Rommel had not only a very high opinion of Hans, but felt nearly as close to him as he did to his own son. Thus Hans is able to describe for us Rommel in action as well as Rommel in contemplation. It makes a fascinating portrait of the general many military historians (including me) would rank as the best of World War II.

But the real hero of this book is the German soldier. Hans's troops, in the 7th Division in France and Russia, and in the 21st Panzer Division in North Africa, Normandy, eastern France, and Germany, never let him down. They were remarkable for their endurance, tenacity, boldness, comradeship, and loyalty.

The German soldier of World War II is universally judged to have been the best soldier in the war. As Max Hastings notes in his masterful *Overlord: D-Day and the Battle for Normandy* (1984), "Whenever British or American troops met the Germans in anything like equal strength, the Germans prevailed."

D. Clayton James, in his study of the American high command, *A Time for Giants* (1987), writes of "how fiercely and shrewdly the Germans could conduct defensive warfare," and observes that American soldiers, originally cocky, grew increasingly wary of "the Germans' superb defensive capabilities." He points out that in Sicily, 60,000 German troops held up 467,000 Allied soldiers for six weeks, at a time when the Allies controlled the skies and the sea around the island, and then escaped to the mainland intact.

Hanson Baldwin remarks in *Battles Lost and Won* (1966), Sicily "proved once again the strength of the German Army and its thorough training and high degree of professionalism." The Allies finally prevailed in Sicily, Baldwin writes, only through the "sheer weight of men and metal."

What were the sources of the German performance? Certainly Baldwin is right to point to training and professionalism. German training was tougher, more realistic, and lasted longer than that of their enemies. German soldiers were in superb physical condition, accustomed to long night marches and the sound of live ammunition whistling over their heads, long before they reached the front lines.

When they got to the front, German soldiers had another advantage—their weapons were superior. Their Polish, French, Russian, British, and American opponents all agreed on that point; in each of those armies, the men would cast aside their own weapons in favor of the German counterpart at any opportunity. In combat situations, this is the ultimate endorsement. The MG–34 was the best heavy machine-gun of the war by every standard—rate of fire, weight of bullet, penetrating power and carrying distance, and above all reliability. The Schmeisser was the best machine-pistol, far superior to the British Sten gun or the American light carbine. The Tiger Royal was the best tank, the 88mm the best dual-purpose cannon (as an antitank gun and as an antiaircraft gun); as the reader will learn, those 88s saved Hans and his men on many an occasion. The quality of German recce vehicles was outstanding, as one would expect from such firms as BMW and Mercedes. In Hans's battalion, the tracked armored cars, the scout cars, the motorcycles with their sidecars, were all the envy of his opponents in the desert, the legendary Colonel Stirling's Long Range Desert Group.

The Germans, though, were not superior in everything, as Hans makes clear. In February 1943, Rommel sent Hans's recce battalion to lead the way through a pass in the Atlas Mountains in Tunisia, a pass named Kasserine. But although the American infantry and armored units, in their first real battle, had taken a frightful licking and were in full retreat, Hans couldn't get through the pass. American heavy artillery stopped him cold. Americans have always put their trust in the big guns. From Washington to Jackson, from Grant and Lee to Pershing, and on to Eisenhower, American generals have regarded artillery as the Queen of the Battlefield. This is a reflection, obviously, of American productive capacity, the ability of American industry to turn out high-quality cannon and to supply virtually unlimited quantities of shells.

The British practice in making war, insofar as possible, is to rely on their wits. They substitute brains for brawn, and in intelligence gathering, most of all in code-breaking, they beat the Germans all hollow. And, except at the very beginning and at the end of the war, American and British aircraft design was superior, and of course the British outclassed the Germans in naval weaponry.

But on the ground, in anything like an equal fight, superior German weapons gave the German soldiers an edge. So did German tactics, especially from 1943 onwards, when the Germans were fighting on the defensive, at which they excelled. In Tunisia in early 1943, Eisenhower noted with dismay that when an American unit occupied a position, the first thing the officers and men did was dig their own foxholes or other shelters, and generally see to their personal safety and comfort. Only later would they lay out their mine fields, put up the barbed wire, clear any obstacles in their fields of fire, zero in their mortars. When American troops were driven from a position, their first reaction was to call over the radio for air and artillery strikes.

In the German army, immediately upon occupying a position and without being told, the German soldiers would lay their mine fields, put up the barbed wire, clear any obstacles in their fields of fire, and prepare their mortars. Only when the unit position was secure would they make themselves secure with foxholes. When German troops were driven from their position, their first reaction was to counterattack, before the enemy had a chance to prepare his defenses. —

Another factor in German performance was the veteran status of the German army. That army was involved in combat from September 1939, to May 1945. No other army fought so long or on so many fronts. Even at the end, when Hitler was calling up boys as young as 14 and men as old as 60 to make up the horrendous losses the Wehrmacht had suffered, there was scarcely a unit so small as a squad in the German army that did not have at least a few old hands in it. Thus, on D-Day, the only Allied units with combat experience were the American 1st Infantry Division and the 101st and 82nd Airborne Divisions. Although England had also been at war from 1939, on D-Day its only veteran units were in the Eighth Army, then fighting in Italy. Almost none of the British units in Normandy had previous combat experience, in sharp contrast to outfits like Hans's battle-tested 21st Panzer Division.

But most of all, as Hans demonstrates time and again, what the Germans had that their enemies never matched, was unit cohesion and, as a consequence, a strong sense of comradeship. From the time of Alexander the Great and Caesar, the great military leaders have known that the way to get citizens to fight is through those qualities. Love of country, patriotism, a cause—these are noble virtues, but people don't fight and die for them. They will fight and die for their units and for their comrades. It comes down to this: no one wants to look the coward before friends, or let them down at critical moments.

The Germans in World War II did everything possible to keep their soldiers together, through training, deployment, combat retreat, even rout (as the Allies discovered in September 1944, when in the "Miracle of the West" the German army that had been routed in Normandy pulled itself together and stopped the seemingly unstoppable Allied offensive at the German border). German units, from squads up to divisions, were like families, instinctively cohesive. This comes through in Hans's memoirs, most notably in the way Rommel kept Hans with him and the core of the 21st Panzer Division together.

In the United States, during the war, it was commonly admitted that the German made a fine soldier, but, it was said, only so long as he had a superior to give him orders. Take away his officers, and he was helpless. But in fact, the exact opposite was the truth. For along with their sense of loyalty to their "family," the German soldiers had an admirable ability to adjust to fluid situations. When half a dozen German soldiers from as many different units came together, in France or Belgium or wherever, German discipline and strong sense of hierarchy asserted themselves. The highest ranking soldier, be he a corporal or sergeant or even just private first class, took command. He would turn the cook and the medic and the tank driver and the gunner and the infantry private into a fighting squad capable of mounting a cohesive defense. The sense of family was restored, and unit cohesion created.

It comes down to teamwork. Infantry and armored combat are above all a matter of teamwork, and no army anywhere, since the days of the Roman legions, has been so successful in establishing and maintaining teamwork as the German army of the first half of the twentieth century. That is why the Germans, twice, came within sight of complete domination over all of Europe.

Teamwork is the most basic theme of Hans's memoirs, both at war and in the POW camp. When Hans came to Innsbruck in July 1987, to go over his manuscript, I repeatedly urged him to substitute "I" for "we," "my" for "our." He almost never would do it. He was part of a team, and can only think of war in relation to his comrades, whether superior or subordinate. In this respect, as in so many others, he was an outstanding officer.

He is also an outstanding human being. From him, I learned that by no means did all the good Germans immigrate to the States. I'm proud to call him my friend.

Stephen E. Ambrose

PANZER
COMMANDER

Prologue

RELEASE

It was a cold winter's day at the end of 1949 in a special camp for prisoners of war in the neighborhood of Kiev; at two o'clock in the morning a barrack door flew open.

"Ganz von Luck," shouted a Russian guard. "*Davai*, to the office."

I still have to smile: the Russians cannot pronounce the *H* sound. How amused we had been a few years earlier when at the shout of "Goggenloge" no one had stirred. Intended was Prince Hohenlohe.

We German prisoners of war had been in Russia since June 1945; since the late autumn of 1948, former members of the SS and the police, and also all those who had fought against partisans, had been collected into a kind of punishment camp. Also included—something none of us could understand—were all staff officers.

Drunk with sleep I stood up. The Russians were fond of interrogations by night. It was easier to extract something from a tired prisoner.

A few weeks earlier, the camp interpreter, a Jewish doctor with whom I had become friendly, had told me what was in the wind.

"I have heard that under pressure from the Western Allies Stalin has agreed to observe the Geneva Conventions and release the prisoners. In the ordinary camps the releases are almost complete, but even here releases will be made. Fifteen percent will be condemned and remain here. We don't want to send home any war criminals. Besides, we need manpower."

Not long after, commissions had indeed arrived from Moscow. At nocturnal hearings, by some system incomprehensible to us, 15 percent had to be sorted out; the rest really would be transported home. A five-person commission from Moscow would make the decision.

And now it was my turn!

My nerves were at breaking point. I forced myself to keep calm. I spoke good Russian; while a prisoner I had been able to improve my knowledge of the language and had often been used as an interpreter. At the office, the commissioners' interpreter, a young woman I knew well, was waiting for me. "I don't understand or speak a word of Russian," I whispered to her. "Understand?" She smiled and nodded; she would go along with my charade.

I was led into a large room and saw in front of me a big, T-shaped table, at the head of which sat the commission. In the middle was a Russian colonel, apparently its leader, an affable-looking man of about my own age, bedecked with orders and with an almost square head. He looked like Marshal Georgi Zhukov, the "liberator" of Berlin.

On either side were civilians, probably a public prosecutor and KGB officers. They looked rather less affable and stared at me with impenetrable expressions. At the other end of the table, about 20 feet away, I took my place with the interpreter.

The hearing began.

"What is your name? Your unit? Where were you in action in Russia?"

The interpreter translated, I replied in German, "I have already said all that at least twenty times for the record."

"We want to hear it again," said the Colonel.

My statements seemed to agree with their documents. They nodded their approval.

Then, "You capitalist, reactionary; *von* Luck is like *von* Ribbentrop (foreign minister under Hitler), *von* Papen (chancellor before Hitler). Everyone with 'von' is a big capitalist and a big Nazi."

After the translation I replied, "I have nothing to do with Ribbentrop or Papen. I have been in the war for more than five years and then five years in captivity. That's more than ten years of my life. I should now like to live in peace with my family, follow a profession. I have neither money nor landed property, so what's all this about capitalist, Nazi, and so on?"

The interpreter translated word for word.

They didn't seem to have anything else to lay at my door. So the Colonel turned to his colleague and spoke openly in Russian.

"What shall we do with the *polkovnik* (colonel)? He's not a member of the SS or the police. At the time of the partisan struggles he was already in Africa. But I hate to let one of these *vons* get away."

One of the KGB officers chimed in, "We can charge him with stealing eggs from Russian villages and thus committing 'sabotage' against the Russian people."

That was the last straw. I knew that even such a minor offense could incur ten to fifteen years in a punishment camp.

I stood up and, as a start, uttered one of the worst Russian oaths. (The Russians and Hungarians are said to have the coarsest of oaths.)

I saw the shocked face of the interpreter and the astonishment of the Colonel and his associates.

Only now and in this way, I thought, would I have the chance of going home.

After a short pause for effect, I spoke accordingly, "*Polkovnik*, you are a colonel like me. (I deliberately used the familiar *du* form of address.) You have done your duty in the war just like me. Both of us believed we had to defend our homeland. We Germans were probably misled by highly accomplished, one-sided propaganda. Both of us have taken an oath."

The Colonel listened attentively.

"It's three o'clock in the morning," I went on. "I am tired. At six we shall be woken up again to start another day of our captivity."

"I know the Russian law. The accused has to prove his innocence and not the court the guilt of the defendant. How shall I defend myself? If you want to keep me here, you'll find a reason all right. So make it brief and then let me go to sleep."

There followed a short whispered conversation between the Colonel and his colleagues. Then the Colonel said, "You speak Russian. Where did you learn it?" His tone was placid, almost benevolent.

"I was interested in the Russian language, Russian music, and Russian writers even as a young man. Long before this wretched war broke out I learned Russian from emigrants. In the nine months of my service in Russia, but above all in the last four and a half years, I have been able to improve my knowledge. I admit it was tactics to let the interpreter translate."

They smiled and my position seemed to me to be a little less hopeless.

Then came a surprising question from the Colonel, "What do you think of Russia and her people?"

"I have seen much and learned much in the years of my captivity. I like your vast country, I like the people, their readiness to help, their love of their homeland. I think I have grasped something of the Russian mentality and soul. But I am not a Communist and never in my life will I be one. I am disappointed by what is left of Marx's ideas and Lenin's revolution. I should like our people to learn to understand each other, in spite of our many contrasts and different ideologies. That is my answer to your question, *Polkovnik*."

It was a gamble, but I felt that in my situation attack was the best form of defense.

"If you are allowed to go home," continued the Colonel, "we know you will become a soldier again and fight against us."

I shook my head and replied, "I should like to get home at last and help to rebuild my bomb-damaged country and establish a democracy and live in peace, nothing else."

At that came the familiar "*Davai*" from the Colonel.

I went back to my barrack. My fellow prisoners crowded around me at once, and after I had described the course of the hearing, they all said the same, "You're mad, that's your undoing. You'll have to stay here." But I judged the Russians differently.

Next morning the interpreter came along. "That was risky, *Polkovnik*, but good. I think you impressed the Colonel. He was a frontline soldier like you and he understands tough talking."

Two days later, in the early hours of the morning, I was called out of bed by one of the guards. My roommates said good-bye to me: "All the best, old man, wherever your journey may take you." In the courtyard prisoners from every barrack were assembling with their few possessions. At a table sat a Russian officer with a list of names, from which he called out one after the other. The man who was called went to the table. There he heard either *"Davai,"* which now meant release, or the fateful *"Niet."*

We saw the stricken faces of those who had been singled out with *"Niet"* and hardly trusted ourselves to look at them. I was the third of our section who had to step up to the table. As the man before me heard *"Niet,"* I patted him sympathetically on the shoulder.

Which word would I hear? It was *"Davai"*!

More running than walking, I hurried to the camp gate. A great stone fell from my heart. We didn't dare look round for fear they might still fetch us back. Did this really mean release?

There I found the interpreter. *"Domoi, Polkovnik,* all the best." I still think of her today, full of gratitude.

Then we marched to the station, where a train was standing ready to take us away. We still didn't trust the Russians. In which direction would it go? But after we had got in, the doors remained unlocked, for the first time in five years. Our joy knew no bounds. We could hardly take it in, that the day we had dreamed of for so many years had now come at last.

— It was bitterly cold. In spite of that we left the doors open a crack, for fear they might be bolted again. We lay pressed tight together and hardly felt the cold. ⟶

A few sang quietly, others imagined the first thing they would eat, what it would be like after nearly five years to be face to face with their own wife or girlfriend. No one was ashamed of his feelings.

We all knew that when we reached home it would be like being born again.

My thoughts went back to my youth, to the security of my parents' house and to the many pleasant years, until Hitler came along and the war began. Of my 39 years I had spent more than 10 at war and in captivity. ⟶

1
Growing Up, 1911–1929

I come from an old military family whose roots can be traced back into the thirteenth century. Monastic records show that my ancestors fought successfully against the Tartars in Silesia in 1213—since that time they have been allowed to bear a Tartar cap in their coat of arms. Family tradition required service in the Prussian army. The name of von Luck crops up several times in the letters of Frederick the Great; two originals hang in the living room of my house in Hamburg. On 29 May 1759, during the Seven Years War, the King wrote to "Lieutenant von Luck" asking him to find out what the Austrian enemy was up to:

> My dear Lieutenant von Luck. I am very pleased with your report but you must now try to find out through your patrols what the officers of the Austrians seen near Hermsdorff were doing there and what they were looking for and asking about, then we will soon see from the circumstances why they were there. This much is certain, when we moved off yesterday, they struck many tents on the Rehorn. It can be therefore that where the heights of Hermsdorff dominate, they have recognized our camp. You will be able to find out about all this from the people of Hermsdorff. I am your affectionate King.
> Reich Hennersdorff 29 May 1759
> (Written by a clerk.)

Added by Frederick II in his own hand:

> His report is very good, only (*illegible*) for spies and when he has them before (him) then he must bring (them) here tomorrow.
> Signed F.

And ten years later, on 13 October 1769, the King informed his "General of Cavalry von Zieten":

> My dear General of Cavalry von Zieten. Reluctant as I usually am to grant my Hussar officers permission to marry, owing to the encumbrance that results, which is too worrying and useless in time of war, I am nevertheless willing this once to yield to the marriage of Cavalry Captain von Luck of your Regiment, for which you sought my consent in your letter of the 11th of this month, and I remain your affectionate King.
>
> Potsdam, the 13th 8 ber 1769
>
> (The letter was evidently written by a clerk to dictation and signed by Frederick II.)

Against the background of this family tradition my father, Otto von Luck, was almost a freak, for he was a naval officer. When I was born, in Flensburg on 15 July 1911, he was with a unit of the fleet, as a lieutenant, in the Chinese port of Tsingtao—on his way into a world which was accessible at that time only to sailors and merchants.

Our house in Flensburg was full of valuable pieces from east Asia. As the remains of this collection I still treasure today a precious Chinese vase and a Japanese tea set which my father had made when I was born. A few years ago a Japanese business friend was very impressed when he drank tea with me from these eggshell-thin cups. "Nothing like these can be made today," he said. "Earlier, the Japanese used to go out in a boat on a quiet lake, before the firing, in order to do the hand-painting free from dust."

After the outbreak of the First World War, and after he had taken part in the battle of Jutland, my father was transferred to the naval school in Flensburg-Muerwik. Among my childhood memories, one of the happiest is playing with my younger brother on the warships lying in the harbor and eating snacks with the sailors in the galleys. My father was an enthusiastic sportsman and was regarded as the best gymnast in the navy.

Our father was a model for me and for my brother, Ernst-August, born in 1913. We loved his sense of humor and his athletic ability. When he came home from work at the naval school, he sometimes came up the stairs to the upper story on his hands, in full uniform, in order to greet us there.

Our generation was born into the First World War. As little children, we lived through its bitter end, the revolution and the difficult years that followed. In contrast to the Second World War, the first took place outside Germany. All we knew of it was the worsening food supply, for turnips in every form became our basic nourishment. We longed for the seamen's diet on the warships.

At the beginning of July 1918, at the time of my seventh birthday, my father died from an influenza virus brought in from East Asia. With him we lost the most precious thing in our lives: a model, a partner, whose influence on us can still be traced today.

The full implications of the end of the war and the revolution of 1918, which began in the navy, were naturally beyond me. I couldn't understand why the young midshipmen, who had been trained by my father, were now being dragged through the streets by shouting sailors who had been our friends. We found it exciting that one or two cadets fled to us and hid themselves in our attic.

Our father's death changed our lives. Our mother had to give up our house. We found a farmer to stay with in the neighborhood. To ensure that we were provided for in the hard times, our mother married again. Our stepfather was a naval chaplain and teacher at a cadet school.

We were now brought up in the "Prussian" manner. Our blond hair was cropped into a crew cut, the beds had to be made army-style. To be late was to be punished. From our stepfather we learned to take care of ourselves, including all household chores. This stood me in good stead later, especially in captivity.

On 1 April 1917, I was enrolled in the Monastery School in Flensburg, one of the oldest schools in north Germany. My stepfather wanted me to go in for the classics, which I have never regretted. Thanks to my study of Latin and Greek, modern languages came very easily to me. My stepfather insisted on my learning the origin of all foreign words. Even at mealtime, the moment I used a foreign word I had to get up from the table, pick up the dictionary, and read out to him the definition of the word employed.

In 1929, at the age of 17, I took my *Abitur*, or graduation examination, which I very nearly missed. The father of one of my classmates always sent his car and chauffeur for us on weekends, as the family lived outside Flensburg. Once we decided to take a diversion to a little seaside resort on the Firth to meet our girlfriends. Wearing our school caps and smoking cigarettes, we were sitting ostentatiously in the backseat when we overtook our headmaster, who was out for his Saturday drive. Not only was smoking strictly forbidden, but on top of that our headmaster had to swallow our dust. He recognized us and the next morning we were summoned to his study.

"You know that smoking in school caps is forbidden. The staff have decided to exclude you from sitting the *Abitur* on account of immaturity."

My classmate seemed unimpressed, for one way or another he was going to take over his father's factory. For me things looked differently, everything was at stake.

Family tradition and my stepfather had decided that I was to embark on a career as an army officer. Out of more than a thousand applicants for only about 140 places in the 100,000-strong army, the Reichswehr, I had been accepted. A postponement of the *Abitur* would have meant the end of my career before it had begun.

So I said cautiously, "Headmaster, I have been accepted by the Reichswehr as a cadet officer in order to serve the Fatherland, true to our family tradition. If you hold me back from the *Abitur* on account of one cigarette, you would be wrecking my career. Can you justify such a thing?"

He seemed moved.

"I would not want that, of course. I will speak to the staff. But you can no longer pass with the mark 'Good.' The highest is 'Satisfactory.' "

I have never understood the logic of this decision. But just to get through the *Abitur* was enough for me.

2
The Reichswehr and My Teacher, Rommel

I was assigned to a cavalry regiment in Silesia, but transferred unexpectedly to East Prussia, to the 1st Motorized Battalion, a bitter disappointment, as the cavalry was the elite force and I loved horses and riding. But we soon realized that the seven motorized battalions in the Reichswehr were to become the nucleus of the later tank force. According to the Treaty of Versailles, tanks and armored scout cars were forbidden. So, very early on, General von Seekt, head of the Reichswehr, entered into a secret agreement with Russia. Under this, young officers of the motorized battalions were sent for three months every year to a Russian training camp in the Urals and instructed on tanks there in the tactics of motorized units. Unfortunately, it was no longer possible for me to go on my course, scheduled for 1933, as the Russians canceled the agreement when Hitler came to power.

It was the beginning of a hard schooling.

Seekt had made of the Reichswehr a "state within the State." It was kept deliberately nonpolitical and it was inculcated with a healthy national consciousness. The "dictate" of Versailles was regarded as a national disgrace; the "Polish Corridor," former West Prussia, which separated East Prussia from the rest of the Reich, as a plundering of German territory.

The economic crisis of the 1930s, the ever increasing number of unemployed (over 6 million in 1932), the ominous growth of the Communist party, and finally the strengthening of the National Socialist party—we paid little attention to all this. Instead, cadres were formed in the Reichswehr which later made it possible to set up the new Wehrmacht in a very short time. Tradition and the oath taken were regarded as sacrosanct and determined the behavior of the officer corps.

Our East Prussian instructors were regarded as particularly severe. The word "drill" was practiced there in its fullest sense. NCOs who sought to compensate for their complexes and their intellectual inferiority by particularly ingenious methods had it in for me and another cadet especially. For the slightest misdemeanor, for instance, we had to clean corridors and lavatories with a toothbrush. Withdrawal of weekend leave was another punishment, as was being chased over the obstacle course. One thing we found particularly macabre was a "test of courage" that our instructor thought up especially for us. One evening we were summoned to his room. He took from his cupboard the upper part of a skull, which was supposed to have belonged to his uncle, and which held exactly one bottle of rum. We then had to drink this receptacle dry. We didn't dare report this petty tyranny to our training officer.

Even if it did us no harm, this kind of "drilling" was still senseless. I decided then and there to treat any young soldier entrusted to me differently, more humanely.

In other respects our training was rewarding and exciting. We had to qualify for all the driving licenses, including that for track-vehicles. This was followed by intensive driving practice with cross-country journeys by day and by night, as well as a four-week course in our motor vehicle workshop. We then had to pass an examination and earn a teaching certificate.

I was particularly proud when I was allowed to be the driver for our company commander for four weeks. He had at his disposal what is today a sought-after vintage model, the super-charged Mercedes cabriolet. Since we were the only motorized unit in East Prussia, I also had the opportunity quite often of driving the divisional commander. Our chances with the girls were naturally also increased because of our car.

As early as 1931 we began to simulate the use of tanks with dummy armor, which we mounted on small private cars.

For us officer cadets, riding instruction was also part of the program. The conclusion of our instruction took place at Neukuhren, a spa on the Baltic Sea, where our horses were quartered on a farm. Each morning before breakfast we rode among the dunes and then down the steep bluff to gallop over the wide, white sandy beach. The years from 1929 to 1932 in East Prussia were among the best of my military career.

In 1931 and 1932, we officer cadets went for nine months to the infantry school in Dresden, to complete our commissioning as junior officers.

Here, in the pearl of Saxony, I met for the first time Erwin Rommel. He was a captain, our infantry instructor and at the same time our most popular training officer. In the First World War he had been highly decorated in the fighting against the Italians with the *"Pour le mérite"* order. He was 42 years old when I met him, tall, strong, tough, wearing a severe uniform with a high collar, but a man with a warm and sympathetic smile. He told us war stories—we hung on every word— and his book *Infantry Tactics* was our bible.   ⌐ check out

In Dresden for the first time I met the Don Cossacks, who even then were emigrants who had had to flee from Russia in 1917. As a further consequence, I took Russian as an optional subject at the infantry school. My teacher, an emigrant from the Baltic, introduced me to the Russian colony. To some extent the emigrants led a miserable existence, but they still kept up their native culture. Prince Obolensky, a charming gentleman of the good old school, was their doyen.

My most memorable experience was at a Russian Easter party with the von Satin family, with whom I had become friendly. Rachmaninoff, the world famous pianist and composer, was Mrs. von Satin's brother. He often came from Paris or Switzerland to visit his family. At this Easter party Rachmaninoff was once again a guest. We ate and drank tea from the samovar, with which preserved cherries were served. Suddenly Rachmaninoff sat down at the piano and called out, "Come on you young people, dance now in honor of our Easter festival."

Who could resist the pleasure of dancing to the accompaniment of Rachmaninoff? With my Baltic teacher I began to read Dostoyevski, Pushkin, and Tolstoy and was fascinated by the beauty and musical quality of the Russian language, which formed a harmony. The two years with my Russian friends and my increasing knowledge of the language helped me to understand something of the Russian mentality, which was to be a valuable aid to me later in Russia.

In 1932, I passed the examination as senior cadet officer, and after a brief spell as guest with my old unit in Koenigsberg, I was transferred to the 2nd Motorized Battalion at Kolberg, a pretty seaside resort on the Baltic coast of Pomerania.

Kolberg, as an ancient trading center, had received its freedom as a city in 1207; in the Seven Years War it was besieged three times by the Russians and in 1761 it was taken. In 1807, Gneisenau, together with the citizens of Kolberg, defended the city successfully against the French. When the Russians were advancing toward Pomerania in 1945, Hitler and Goebbels made use of the Kolbergers' historic deed to inspire the population to even greater resistance. The film that was made about it, *Kolberg*, was shown in every theater.

In 1932 this pleasant town, with its white beaches, the kursaal, and the clubhouse, gave a peaceful impression. The inhabitants were extremely friendly and army-minded, just as the Pomeranians in general were very conservative, so that National Socialism found hardly any support among the predominantly rural population. While Kolberg was enlivened during the summer by visitors, in winter the town fell into tranquil hibernation, and we as the garrison were the only lively element.

In the autumn I was promoted to lieutenant and appointed to train recruits. I thought of the experiences I had gathered in East Prussia and so urged my NCOs to treat the young men humanely and, as Rommel had taught me, to attach more importance to training in the field.

Our unit was now concentrating more and more on its expected conversion into an armored reconnaissance battalion. In 1933, after Hitler came to power, we were suddenly supplied by night, under the strictest secrecy, with the first genuine scout cars, which we were allowed to use for practice purposes, although only by night. Hitler was not risking as yet an open breach of the terms of the Treaty of Versailles. The seven motorized battalions of the Reichswehr now became seven armored reconnaissance battalions of the Wehrmacht, which was to be built up anew. General Heinz Guderian was appointed inspector of the entire armored branch of the army; we "scouts" took over the tasks and the spirit of the cavalry.

We were delighted to see the Wehrmacht expand, and failed to notice the clouds that were gathering over Germany. On brief missions to Berlin we were naturally aware of the change since Hitler had come to power, but Berlin was still the cultural center and offered all the diversions one could wish for.

At the beginning of June 1934, rumors were circulating about high-handed actions by Roehm and some other senior SA leaders. A power struggle set in between the SA and the SS, and between the SA and the Wehrmacht. In the middle of June we were put on alert and received secret orders to march on call to Stettin, the provincial capital, to arrest the SA leadership there—by force if necessary.

On 30 June 1934, the "Roehm coup" began. We marched to Stettin. In a lightning action and on flimsy grounds, Roehm and a series of senior SA leaders were arrested and shot.

With President Hindenburg's death and the final takeover of supreme power by Hitler and his party, our situation changed, though at first this was scarcely perceptible. The SA (Sturmabteilung, or storm troops), with the former Captain Ernst Roehm at its head, seemed to be trying to build up a "second force" alongside the Wehrmacht. The SS (Schutzstaffel, or bodyguard) began to arm itself in secret and to create with the Gestapo an instrument that was to become far more dangerous than the SA and the other Nazi organizations.

With that the coup was over. The SA and other Nazi organizations were tamed and remained so, and no longer represented any danger to the Wehrmacht. We were pleased at this development and never suspected that in the end the SS would emerge as victor from this power struggle even over the Wehrmacht.

3
The Buildup of the Wehrmacht, 1934–1939

IMP

Hitler, at first, met with much approval among the population. He managed, after all, to take more than 6 million unemployed off the streets. He built highways and introduced *Reichsarbeitsdienst* ("National Labor Service"). The Rheinland, occupied by the Allies, was taken over without bloodshed. We felt it was right to lock up the militant Communists, in the course of which the expression "concentration camp" was not yet used. The revocation of the Treaty of Versailles and Germany's withdrawal from the League of Nations seemed lawful and restored national consciousness to the German people. Only a few realized in all this that the highways were laid out on strictly strategic principles and that the Labor Service was a transparent paramilitary organization.

The advantages and disadvantages of having kept the Reichswehr nonpolitical began to appear. We simply did not understand the correlation of events. If, for instance, the leadership of the Wehrmacht had recognized Hitler's aims, the Roehm coup would have been the opportunity to put him back in his place and to demand that the SA and the SS be incorporated in the National Socialist Party as unarmed units. Hitler, however, had seen the danger that could arise from an overpowerful Wehrmacht, and in due time had placed at its head, and the head of its branches, leaders who were acceptable and loyal to him. General Werner von Blomberg, whom we called the "rubber lion" because he was always giving in to Hitler's whims, became commander in chief, and Goering became head of the air force.

The "case" of Colonel-General Werner von Fritsch shows this most clearly. Fritsch was indeed a strong personality who would have asserted himself, we hoped, against Hitler and his SA and SS; but in 1938 he was denounced for supposed homosexual tendencies and degraded to captain. He was killed leading an artillery regiment in the Polish campaign of 1939. Unfortunately it became apparent only afterward that the accusations were entirely without truth. It was macabre that Fritsch was then buried with the highest military honors, since he had been killed in action.

His successor, Colonel-General Walter von Brauchitsch, was also too conservative and anti-Nazi for Hitler. He, and von Blomberg also, were replaced in the following years. The purging of the Wehrmacht leadership began as early as 1934, with the liquidation of General Kurt von Schleichter and the SA officers on the occasion of the "Night of the Long Knives." Before 1933 Schleicher had been chancellor for a short time and had seemed to Hitler extremely suspect.

The "Thousand-Year Reich" had begun.

We did not realize that we had become an instrument of Hitler's policy and had to watch as the churches and the Jews were attacked. Fascinated by Hitler's charisma and his "achievements," young men thronged into the Wehrmacht. Most of them came from the Hitler Youth movement or the Labor Service. Denunciations were the order of the day; officers were betrayed by their recruits, parents by their children, the moment they uttered any criticism of Hitler or the party.

How could a people from whom a Goethe and a Beethoven had sprung become blind slaves of such a leader and fall into hysteria whenever he made a speech, as for instance at the Berlin sports stadium? I believe all people are ready to follow idols and ideals if they become sufficiently emotionalized. Though every epoch brings forth its own idols, the people who cheer them remain the same.

In 1936 I was transferred from Kolberg to Berlin, or more precisely, to Potsdam, the city packed with tradition on the edge of Berlin.

The 8th Armored Reconnaissance Battalion, the third company in which I became a platoon leader, was based in barracks opposite those of the guards. The whole of Potsdam breathed the spirit of Frederick the Great, who had built his palace of Sanssouci there.

The father of the tank force that was now quickly building up was General Guderian. He had studied the British military writer B. H. Liddle Hart and the theories of the Frenchman Charles de Gaulle, and from them he developed the mobile tactics of the German tank force. He saw the advantage of fast and flexible units. At first he had no cooperation from many conservative generals, but we young officers were enthusiastic and felt we were the spearhead of the Wehrmacht.

Guderian visited every single company, observed its training, and afterward discussed his ideas with its officers and NCOs. We realized that in addition to training, material, and modern technique, the spirit that inspired a unit also played an important part.

The first reserve officers came for training. They were for the most part men who had been in the First World War, but also included young conscripts who had ended their period of service as lieutenants of the Reserve. Among these was Franz von Papen, Jr., the son of the former chancellor and subsequent ambassador to Turkey. We had been born in the same year and on the same day and soon became good friends.

The Papens lived in an imposing villa in the elegant Tiergarten district of Berlin, to which I was often invited and where I came to know some interesting people, including the French ambassador, François Poncet. I also met there the daughter of the American ambassador, who was known to have a soft spot for the Russian diplomat.

For me the transfer to Potsdam was fascinating, since I now had the chance of frequent visits to my beloved Berlin. I had already spent three months there in 1932 and had many friends and relations in the city. Berlin, the "cozy" capital of Europe, with its continental climate and its quick-witted people—what more could a young man want?

Theaters, opera houses, renowned artists, couturiers, and newspaper publishers set their mark on this city. German Jews, many of them veterans of the First World War, who were often more German than the Germans, played a leading part in the cultural and economic life of Berlin. When many of them had to flee from Hitler and others disappeared into concentration camps, Berlin became the poorer.

I used to have supper, two sandwiches and a soda from the slot machine, in a snack bar called Quick on the Kurfurstendamm for a total of one mark. At the Majowsky bar I would pay 70 pfennigs for one curaçao and nurse it for the whole evening. The Majowsky was the meeting place of former airmen, such as the stunt flier Udet and the later Air Marshal Erhard Milch, who often bought us poor lieutenants a drink.

I felt happiest in a little pub on the Spittelmarkt, the rendezvous of the Berlin taxi drivers, who drank a quick beer there between fares. The Berlin taxi drivers were famous for their humor and ready wit. I would have exchanged any cabaret performance for their stories of experiences with their fares.

Our training was very intensive and concentrated on two things. On the one hand we were made familiar with the technology and the armaments; on the other we practiced mobile engagements in the field.

My motorcycle escort company, the motorized infantry for the two armored reconnaissance companies, was equipped with the superb BMW 500 machines. They were fitted for the most part with sidecars, which later were even driven via a differential. We slowly developed into true artists on the motorcycle. We drove, also by night, through difficult sandy and wooded terrain and on "open days" were allowed to display our stunts to the public, as for instance a long jump with the motorcycle, for which one of my NCOs held the record at 16 meters. We formed ourselves into a pyramid, in which up to 12 men stood on a single machine, and one number was the "remote-controlled motorcycle." In this a man lay out of sight in the sidecar and from there steered the machine with cables. We were also allowed to take part in official cross-country events. I was on the move every weekend for motorcycle sport (similar to modern rally). At first I drove solo, then with a sidecar, in which I was once going along with my codriver when it so happened that a tree came exactly between the motorcycle and the sidecar. I then had to take a rest for some weeks with a dislocated collarbone. We learned to master our equipment to such effect that we were able to shoot while going along in the field with a machine-gun mounted on the sidecar. In the end I switched to sports cars, which were made available to us, for a team of three, by a motor firm.

New tank units were being formed. Therefore, I was transferred in October 1938 to Bad Kissingen, a spa and health resort near the cathedral city of Wuerzburg, in north Bavaria. After its preceding spa season, Kissingen had already gone into hibernation, so we were very welcome as an enlivening element.

Our first experience was gruesome for us all. It occurred during a night in November, the *Kristallnacht* (Night of the Broken Glass), shameful for the whole of Germany. Heinrich Himmler, his SS, and the SA had taken the murder of a German attaché in Paris by a young Jew as the occasion to destroy and set on fire Jewish synagogues and businesses throughout Germany.

Once again the leadership of the Wehrmacht did not intervene. Hitler had already been able to secure his regime, and surround himself with generals agreeable to him, so that all we could do, operating at the base, was to distance ourselves from these machinations.

The question is still asked today, both at home and abroad, why the Wehrmacht, and especially its officers corps and the generals, failed to confront the gathering strength of National Socialism in good time and put an end, or at least set limits, to its cadres and Hitler's dangerous "playing with fire."

There were, in my view, the following reasons:

—The army of 100,000 men to which we were entitled under the Treaty of Versailles was deliberately trained to be nonpolitical. As a result, the officer corps lacked perspective.

—Hitler's initial successes (the elimination of unemployment and the Communist threat, as well as the repatriation of former German territories to the Greater German Reich) restored self-confidence to the German people and their growing Wehrmacht.

—The young people who were called up for military service were recruited mainly from the Hitler Youth and other National Socialist organizations and were correspondingly motivated, if not fanaticized.

—Most decisively, it seems to me: the oath of allegiance was the creed of the officer corps. Hitler knew this and exploited it shamelessly!

Thus the year 1934 became a turning point. The Wehrmacht came to be abused as a political power factor. After Hindenburg's death, the office of president which he had held was merged with that of chancellor under Hitler. With that the German people, and especially the Wehrmacht, lost its symbolic figure, who was required to stand outside and above politics. On the strength of his personality Hindenburg, or a possible successor of symbolic stature, might have been able to block questionable political decisions.

In spite of many warnings from inside and outside the country, and against its better judgment, the German officer corps stood by its oath, even when that oath had eventually to be taken anew to Adolf Hitler.

Who would have dared as an individual, in 1933 and 1934, to refuse to swear allegiance to Hitler? The military leadership alone might have been able to, had they been politically more astute and not dazzled by Hitler's personality. ✳

Another question that is still discussed to the present day is why the attempt on Hitler's life of 20 July 1944, was not made earlier—at the latest after the start of the march into Russia in 1941. On the one hand, Hitler was so heavily guarded that an attempted assassination was by no means a sure success. And on the other, the officers around Graf Stauffenberg, leader of the conspiracy, felt bound by their oath of allegiance, and it was only the dire situation after the Allied landing in 1944 that moved the group to their "act of desperation." They were aware when they did it that a "legend" could grow up around Hitler, and also that the penalty the Allies would exact would amount to unconditional surrender. But they wanted to try to stop Hitler and avert further suffering for the German people.

Voices that even today in Germany condemn the assassination attempt as a "breach of the oath of allegiance" are to be rejected, for an oath can only be binding so long as it is compatible with the conscience of the individual and freely taken.

4
Europe on the Eve of War: Travels and Experiences

I longed to travel to new places. I wanted to follow the advice of my old mathematics teacher, who said to me, "Travel as often as you can, and see your homeland from outside. Make contact with people of other countries. Only then can you judge your Fatherland correctly."

In the years from 1933 to 1935, when foreign currency was still being allocated, I went to Prague and Warsaw, hence to countries in which I knew no one. Later, after 1937, when only 15 marks per journey were authorized, I visited the western and southern countries of Europe, in which I had friends and could survive quite well even with only 15 marks. My encounters with other people, other languages, and cultures confirmed my teacher's advice.

Prague, the "Golden City," the point of intersection of Western and Eastern culture, impressed me greatly. As did the famous spas of Karlsbad and Marienbad in all their splendor. In Warsaw in 1934 there was no indication as yet of tension. I received a visa without difficulty, although I was a young officer. Warsaw was a very Francophile city. French architects had set their mark on the urban scene with their buildings and many people with higher education spoke French. This made it easier for me to make contact with the inhabitants, and I was able to observe that the Poles had no love either for us Germans or for the Russians.

Further trips to Scandinavia were then followed by trips to France, which quickly became familiar to me. My grandparents had a French governess, so much French was spoken in their house. It was in general considered very chic at that time to *parler français*. Not only the French language, but above all French *savoir-vivre* held a great fascination for me. The charm of the French, and especially the charm of the cosmopolitan city of Paris, were for me as a young man breathtaking. The concierges, the bistros, the yards of bread, the secondhand bookshops on the Seine, the painters on Montmartre—here was the pulse of life. One sat together over wine and discussed the world and all evil seemed so far away.

My trips to England were also a great enrichment for me. The British probably mean even more to us northern Germans, and as a young man I was able to learn much from their tolerance and their sense of humor. Once past the stage of small talk with them, I was impressed by their cordiality and their hospitality. What gave them their confidence, beyond their position as a world power? First of all, their long tradition and their cohesion through monarchy, as well as a democracy developed over centuries.

One little experience always stayed in my mind. A banker with bowler hat and umbrella bumped into a worker in the street. "Awfully sorry," I heard the banker say, as the first to apologize. Unimaginable in Germany.

One day at noon I was in Whitehall to watch the changing of the guard. A man in worn clothes asked me for a light.

"Are you French? You speak with an accent."

"No, I come from Germany." At that, words tumbled out.

"I was a prisoner in Germany from 1917 to 1918. I was well placed with a farmer. Look, here's my war medal. Now I'm a Communist in this damned country that does nothing for me. I've been out of work for months. But with you? Hitler has taken the unemployed off the streets, everything is well organized, everyone can eat."

I didn't want to be drawn into discussion. The changing of the guard came to my rescue. Cuirassiers in their glittering uniforms rode in; the whole splendor of the realm unfolded.

"Look at that," cried the man, now beside me and carried away with joy. He took my arm. "That's where no one can copy us British; that's our monarchy!"

Venice was the dream destination of honeymoon couples, and Rome was the cultural city that everyone wanted to visit. In my classical grammar school I had read so much about Goethe's journeys to Italy that I wanted to follow in his footsteps. So in 1934, with a friend, I planned a three-week trip to Italy. We adapted my DKW car for sleeping, took as our main luggage enough cans of gasoline from Germany to see us at least to Rome and back, and also packed enough food to be as independent as possible.

In Florence we met a lady who invited us to her house for a meal. She led us into a narrow alley and we stopped in front of a house with a grubby facade.

"*Ecco*, we're there. Please come in."

We felt a little uneasy. But we then came into the inner courtyard, and the house that from the outside looked so sad turned out to be a *palazzo* with many art treasures and a dreamlike garden. It was the town house of a *principessa*. We spent a wonderful day in those lovely surroundings.

Rome, with its seven hills, the Villa Borghese, the Piazza Colonna, and St. Peter's Cathedral left us Prussians in endless amazement at so much beauty.

I traveled to Switzerland because we had relations there, the Zeppelins. A particular attraction was skiing. In those days one still used the Kandahar binding, which was equally suitable for climbing with skis and for the downward run. There were no skilifts as yet. One climbed for hours, then descended to the valley in an hour through the untouched powdery snow. The experiences we had on our ski tours were unique; they often lasted days and were broken only by the night's rest in little mountain huts. At that time one could still enjoy the peace and beauty of the mountain world, for there were hardly any tourists.

At the beginning of August 1939, I was once again, to my complete surprise, granted 14 days' leave in Switzerland, although there were already rumors of possible war and complications with the Poles. Perhaps the authorities wanted to show the Swiss and the international public that if an officer on active service was actually allowed to travel abroad there could be no question of war. The two weeks were not up before I was recalled. My division was on alert; all those on leave had to return at once to their garrisons.

"Now there'll be war," said my friends. My attempts to reassure them were unsuccessful. So I drove back to my garrison in Kissingen by the quickest route. There everyone was in high spirits. Although we did not believe Josef Goebbels's propaganda that the Poles were about to attack us, we wanted the corridor and Danzig returned to Germany. We scarcely believed the Poles would resist; we anticipated easy going, as had been the case in Czechoslovakia a year earlier. We were not hungry for war, as the Wehrmacht was not yet ready, and our senior officers all remembered 1918. But we did not believe the British and French would come to Poland's defense.

5
Blitzkrieg: Poland, 1939

The autumn sun shone warmly as our 2nd Light Division under General Stumme moved out of its garrisons. Among its elements was our 7th Armored Reconnaissance Regiment with its two battalions. From a hilltop our eyes strayed back again toward Bad Kissingen and the mountains of the Rhoen, where we used to go skiing.

Officially we were to take part in "grand maneuvers under combat conditions." Although live ammunition was being carried, we were issued only blanks.

Morale of the men was good, my relations with the company excellent. On our eastward march we went through the Sudetenland and continued past Prague in the direction of the Reich frontier in the region of Gleiwitz. Local people greeted us everywhere with flowers and drinks.

"Are you going to Poland?" we were asked.

"Of course not," we replied, "we're going on maneuvers."

On 26 August 1939, we reached the frontier surreptitiously and took up position in a plantation. Suddenly the blank cartridges were exchanged for live ammunition. Now there was no longer any doubt: we were going to invade.

Now I had to show what I had learned, namely, how to defeat our opponent with as little loss to ourselves as possible. I hardly knew what to expect. We still had the feeling of being on maneuvers, and comforted ourselves finally with the thought that we had no need to fear the Poles, since their army was not of great fighting strength or as well-equipped as ours.

In the assembly area I went to each of my men and joked with them. They expressed great confidence in me and believed that their "boss" would see to it that no unnecessary sacrifice would be demanded.

On 31 August came the order. We would attack on the morning of 1 September at 0450 hours.

Our heavy machine-guns were placed in a garden that belonged to a Herr Augustin, who had been living there for some time. His parents owned a textile factory in Lodz, in the middle of Poland.

"Wouldn't you like to come with us?" I asked him. "You speak fluent Polish and could be of great service to us as an interpreter in the questioning of prisoners and to vouch for the proper treatment of the civilian population."

He agreed. No doubt he also hoped by this means to see his parents again. We dressed him in a Wehrmacht uniform; an armband proclaimed him to be a "Voluntary Interpreter."

At daybreak, our air force flew over the frontier, to surprise the Polish air force on the ground, as we were told, and as far as possible dispose of it. This gave us moral support. We heard that our navy was shelling the port of Danzig and that troops were being landed.

We fell in with the armored reconnaissance regiment. The frontier was manned by a single customs official. As one of our soldiers approached him, the terrified man opened the barrier. Without resistance we marched into Poland. Far and wide there was not a single Polish soldier in sight, although they were supposed to have been preparing for an "invasion" of Germany.

I spread my company out. We advanced on foot along a wide front and came to the first Polish village. Still no Polish soldiers to be seen. In the marketplace we were greeted in friendly fashion by the inhabitants, even given refreshments.

Where were the Polish troops?

We still had the feeling of being on maneuvers although we were 15 kilometers inside Poland. Vigilant reconnaissance patrols on motorcycles with sidecars tried to make headway through the thickly wooded terrain, to spy out the land. I had the armored cars follow and continued the advance.

Late on the evening of 1 September we came up against our first opposition. In front of us lay an open, rising tract of land, at the end of which was a village and a forest. Here the Poles had set up a line of resistance on a hill, and opened a heavy fire from machine guns and mortars. Shell splinters hissed through the trees. Branches broke off and fell on our heads. Our stomachs now felt distinctly uneasy. We had often practiced under combat conditions, of course, and had been able thereby to get used to the firing and the landing of artillery shells, as well as the sharp hammering of machine-guns. But that had always been at a safe distance or from bunkers under cover.

Now, we were directly exposed to enemy fire. We could find no cover, nor could we dig ourselves in, since we were supposed to attack. We formed up for the assault. Armored scout cars moved forward, as far and as well as the terrain allowed, so as to give us covering fire from the MG24s.

Suddenly a round of machine-gun fire hit Private Uhl, not far from me. He was dead at once. He was the first casualty in my company, and many of my men saw it. Now we were all afraid. Which of us would be the next? This was no longer a maneuver; it was war.

"No. 1 and No. 2 platoons attack," I shouted, "No. 3 platoon in reserve, the heavy platoon to give fire-cover."

No one stirred. Everyone was afraid of being the next to die. Including me. Anyone who says he was never afraid in his first engagement is a liar.

It was up to me, the CO to set the example. "Everyone follow me," I shouted, and rushed forward with my machine-pistol.

The training prevailed, and they all followed. We gained a little ground, but were then forced to take cover by fire from machine-guns and artillery.

The division worked out a new plan of attack: antiaircraft searchlights lit up the hill during the night. Our scout cars shot at recognized positions with their 2cm tracer bullets. The artillery took up the fire. It was a lurid scene.

At daybreak on 2 September we attacked anew and reached the village and the enemy hill. The Poles had withdrawn. Before us was an image of horror. Lying about in the abandoned positions were dead men and the cadavers of horses. The abandoned houses were still burning. This sight gave us a first impression of the meaning of war. It took some effort to come to terms with the reality.

We pushed forward. The thickly wooded terrain was trackless and made the operations of our scout cars and tanks almost impossible. For two days we had to do without our field kitchens. The vehicles could not get through along the bad roads and in the thick woods.

On our march through villages and small towns we were again presented with the same terrible picture. The air force had done quite a job and deeply demoralized the Poles. In spite of that the Polish divisions fought heroically.

As my orderly Erich Beck later wrote, "We admired our opponents for their national pride and commitment. They demanded our respect. We heard that a Polish cavalry regiment had mounted an attack against our tanks. They had been told that the German tanks were only wooden dummies."

All the bridges had been blown. Our army engineers did a superhuman job of throwing up new ones. Polish snipers had lodged themselves in haystacks and under thatched roofs and now had to be smoked out with tracer bullets. There were fires everywhere.

The cities of Kielce, Radom, and Lodz were our targets in the next few days. The first pockets were formed through pincer movements. We heard from division that the advance along a wide front, from Upper Silesia to the Baltic, was making rapid headway.

On 6 September we eventually came up against strong resistance near a village on the edge of the Lysa Gory. After fierce fighting with few losses we overcame our opponents, whose strength now seemed to be finally broken. Cracow fell on the same day. Powerful units were advancing on Warsaw from the west and northwest.

In Lodz, which was hardly contested any more, Augustin met his parents. I accompanied him. It was a moving reunion. Since the heightened tension they had heard no more of each other. Now the parents had their son back, forever, they hoped. We visited the family textile factory and then went to a café in the market-place. We had coffee and plain cakes, both for us a great pleasure after the first hard days. West Prussia and the ancient city of Danzig were not, it seemed, the only objective. The whole of Poland was apparently to be occupied and wiped out, with the participation, moreover, of the Russians, with whom Hitler had just signed a treaty of nonaggression. We were amazed at how quickly Goebbels's propaganda could change people's minds 180 degrees. Now Russia was our ally!

We were given orders to clear the woods, secure the territory gained, and then hold ourselves ready for the decisive advance on Warsaw.

While searching for a suitable command post for the company, my advance picket found a large country house in the middle of the woods. It had been left untouched by the war. I went there and was greeted by a charming old gentleman who spoke fluent German and English. He had been the Polish ambassador in London and had now retired to his country estate. His house was full of guests. A well-known pianist and other artists had fled there from Warsaw at the outbreak of war in the hope of finding safety. The butler led me to a guest room and asked—a macabre touch— about my luggage.

After I had given the necessary orders to my company and made my report to division, the master of the house invited me to take a little walk.

"Now look," he said, "there's a good friend of mine who lives about twenty miles from here and is married to a German from Silesia. I'm worried about them. Can you find out how they are?"

During our further conversation it turned out that the German woman was a distant relative of mine. It struck me how senseless the war was, and yet there was no escape from it. I promised to find out about his friends.

My host led me to his kennels, where he showed me a litter of young Irish setters. He had brought the mother back with him from England. He picked up one of the puppies and said, "May I give you this to cheer you up in a sad time?"

I took it with pleasure and christened it "Boy."

Then in the evening we all sat around the fireplace in the great hall, which extended to the roof. While the pianist played Chopin, we could hear sporadic gunfire in the distance. There I was sitting among friendly people in a pleasant atmosphere in a country that we had invaded.

I discovered that Poland's most famous animal painter lived in the next town and arranged to visit him the following day. I was very fond of his work and asked him for one of his watercolors that reflected the spirit of Poland. Next evening he brought me the painting. I was enchanted. It portrayed a shepherd in a typical Polish landscape leading a long-suffering little *panye* horse on a halter. The painting survived the war and still hangs in my house today, reminding me of heavy hours, but also of pleasant ones.

That same evening a patrol came and reported that our host's friends were all right. He was visibly relieved.

My commanding officer gave orders during the evening for the further advance on Warsaw. The following morning I left that oasis with my watercolor and Irish setter.

At the briefing for the next advance, my battalion commander told me that on 3 September, France and Britain had declared war on Germany. So far, however, contrary to our fears, they had not attacked. The daily *Army Bulletin* had merely reported some artillery duels and increased aerial reconnaissance. We were relieved. Hitler seemed to have judged both countries correctly. The British, as far as we know, had not even sent an expeditionary force to the mainland.

We now marched on Warsaw. In the eastern part of Poland no operations were carried out by our side. Clearly there were certain agreements here with the Russians. South of Warsaw the two armored reconnaissance battalions took up their positions in a fruit plantation.

On 9 September—after nine days of war—the greater part of Poland, insofar as it belonged to the German sphere of influence, was occupied and in our hands. Only in Warsaw was there still fighting. The remaining, still available elements of the Polish army had withdrawn there to defend their capital after undergoing two weeks of heavy bombing and artillery fire. On 27 September, Warsaw was finally taken. We had seen no further action. Poland seemed unable to offer any more resistance. We were used merely to mop up the territory gained.

On one of my reconnaissance trips, which I made in my cross-country car with my driver Fink and an orderly, I discovered near a village a young Polish woman in uniform. She pointed a machine-pistol at us, but before she could fire we overpowered her.

"Do you belong to a women's battalion, or are you a partisan?" I asked her in French.

Her eyes were full of hate; small wonder after the war imposed on Poland. She led us to a house in which her husband, a Polish officer, lay wounded. I put them both in my car and handed them over to our medical squad, where her husband was immediately taken care of. She then thanked us.

"It's all so sad and hopeless. Why can't you let us live in peace? Now the Russians will come, your allies, and hated by us. But Poland is not lost yet." Her final words, as Augustin told me, were those of the Polish national anthem.

On 17 September, the Russians had marched into eastern Poland. A demarcation line was fixed by German and Russian delegations. One of the interpreters was Boris von Karzov, whom I was to meet later in Russian captivity. Poland was partitioned anew; the bitter history of the country took its course. On 5 October came the victory parade in Warsaw in Hitler's presence. Our division did not have to take part. Among those on the platform next to Hitler was Rommel, at that time still the commander of the units for Hitler's personal protection. During the fighting, however, he had constantly visited the troops and had been fascinated, as he said later, by the use of tank units under General Guderian. Soon after, Rommel managed to persuade Hitler to let him take over a panzer division.

The Polish war was over for us. A few of my men received the Iron Cross II Class, among them the brave leader of the heavy machine-gun platoon. He was promoted shortly after to staff-sergeant.

I was particularly proud of the award to our company tailor. In Bad Kissingen he had always been teased as "our little tailor." Yet during engagements this insignificant man surpassed himself. He was employed, like the company cobbler, as a runner and conveyer of orders between our rear sections and the units in action. Under heavy fire, in which we had to take cover, "our little tailor" came forward with reports and orders at the risk of his life. It was a new discovery for us that the stalwart and robust-seeming men often lost their nerve under combat conditions, while the supposedly weak proved to be strong and kept their heads at precarious moments.

The losses suffered in the nine days of war were comparatively light. Of my platoon leaders, Lieutenant von Fuerstenberg was out of action for a long time with a severe stomach wound. As for our dead, we were able to bury them with dignity and to some extent with military honors.

The ensuing days of rest did us good. I had time to thank all the men in my company. "It was a good thing you made us dig in quickly," they told me. "There's no doubt the hard training saved the lives of a lot of us." Morale was first class. No one thought here, just outside Warsaw, about how things might go later.

I received permission to travel into Warsaw, which I would be seeing again after many years. The outer and industrial districts had suffered badly from the air attacks, but the center had remained to a large extent untouched. There life was returning to normal. The Poles knew how to come to terms, again and again, with the blows of fate. In the café of the largest hotel in the center I obtained my drink as though nothing had happened. One felt that as occupiers we Germans were still more welcome to the Poles than the Russians. Unfortunately, that was soon to change.

At the end of September the division was transferred back to its garrisons in Germany. We marched once more through the Sudetenland to Bad Kissingen.

6
Interim, 1939–1940

Our reception in Bad Kissingen was overwhelming. The Kissingers thronged the roadside and showered us with flowers. Opposite the Kurhaus, already closed, stood our commander, to lead the march-past of our battalion. There was much laughter when my Irish setter, Boy, on the cover of a truck, barked loudly at the band. The civic dignitaries naturally turned up for the reception. These Nazi functionaries sunned themselves in our success, as though the achievement had been theirs.

In the following days everyone was allowed out. Many of the restaurants and bars reopened and supplied free beer. Huber Sepp, the proprietor of the Huber Bar, produced a long-hoarded bottle of Scotch from his cellars. It turned into a long night.

The civilian population, and most of us, thought that with the Polish campaign the war would be over. The French and the British had not attacked. Would there be a second "Munich"? Would the Prime Ministers Daladier and Chamberlain try again to come to terms with Hitler? Perhaps it was wishful thinking, but it seemed that, with the bloodless "Return home to the Reich" of German-speaking territories, the occupation of the Sudetenland and Czechoslovakia, and the "liberation" of West Prussia and Danzig in a blitzkrieg with few casualties, all the goals that redressed the "injustice" of the Treaty of Versailles had been achieved. But I had my doubts. Hitler's hatred of France, against whom he had fought in the First World War, was too deep. The propaganda machine was again going full blast. The names Alsace and Lorraine were also cropping up, territories that had had to be ceded in the wars of 1870–71 and 1914–18, first to Germany and then back to France.

All of us in turn received leave for short visits to our families. We enjoyed those days, but reality soon caught up with us again. The Wehrmacht, especially the armored branch, was being further enlarged. New panzer divisions were being set up from cadres that had to be supplied by us. Our 2nd Light Division was reorganized and reequipped to form the 7th Panzer Division. By an order of 6 February 1940, General Erwin Rommel, my infantry instructor from Dresden, became our divisional commander; he took over the panzer division at Bad Godesberg on the 10th. Much as we admired this man, we wondered if an infantryman could be a commander of tanks.

We soon found out. Rommel had made himself thoroughly familiar with the tactics of tank warfare. A completely new wind blew among us from now on. The division was left with only a single armored reconnaissance battalion, Battalion 37, under Major Erdmann. He now became our commanding officer. Like many other commanders, he had taken part in the First World War. We respected his combat experience and at once felt confidence in him.

The division received new, better tanks. The Mark III with its 5cm gun and the Mark IV with its 7.5cm "stubby" gun were faster, better armed, and better armored. With the three-axled armored scout car and a 3.8cm gun, we received a better reconnaissance vehicle.

We moved from Kissingen to the little village of Heimersheim on the northern fringe of the Rhoen Mountains. Hard training began, which was made more difficult by a very severe winter. Rommel organized field exercises in all weathers, and also by night. He visited every unit daily and insisted that the same units should always work together. Thus tank people, artillerymen, and infantrymen got to know each other and became coordinated. A team was formed within the division, which was later to prove extremely important.

The propaganda increased. Hitler mocked the French. He referred ever more frequently to "Whiskey Churchill" and later to the "Paralytic Roosevelt." Was the ever growing strength of the Wehrmacht intended to deter the Western Allies from making an attack, or did Hitler plan to enter France? We did not know. We relied on ourselves and our modern weapons, which seemed to be superior to those of our opponents.

The first SS panzer divisions were organized. Their nucleus was made up of the *Leibstandarte Adolf Hitler* (Hitler's personal guard) under their commander Sepp Dietrich. We suspected, not without reason, that with the Waffen-SS Hitler wanted to create a counterweight to the army, especially to the conservative officer corps, and we were by no means happy about it. Although Himmler, the "highest SS leader," assumed responsibility for the disposition of the men and their equipment, and through his influence recruited the best people for his Waffen-SS, all SS units were tactically under the control of the army, so it was still a cooperation rather than a rivalry. For want of experienced troop leaders, army officers were transferred to the Waffen-SS as commanders and to their dismay were given SS service ranks.

The severe winter of 1939/40 duly passed. In the meantime the British had begun to move an expeditionary force to northern France. But things still remained comparatively quiet on the western front.

In the middle of February we were transferred to Dernau on the Ahr, hence practically to the western front. Rommel visited every unit. He told us that he was proud to be permitted to lead a panzer division. Guderian, too, came to inspect and talk to us. "You are the cavalry," he told us. "Your job is to break through and keep going." We would thrust in a straight line to the west, to the Belgian frontier east of Luettich (Liège), hence far to the north of the French border.

7
France, 1940

At the beginning of May, we moved west to the Eiffel Mountains. Rommel was in a nearby training area with parts of the division for practice with live ammunition. With the older commanders and reserve officers, who had taken part in the First World War, we discussed what lay before us.

"It won't be a walk-over, as in Poland," we were warned. "The French and the British are quite different opponents."

We younger ones replied that there could not, and must not, be any trench warfare as in 1914–18. Our tank force was too mobile for that, our attitude too positive. We youngsters thought always of Guderian and his flashing eyes when he explained his tactics to us. Rommel, the Alpine soldier of the First World War, had convinced us during our exercises that he had adapted himself to mobile warfare and was the right tank commander for us.

On the evening of 9 May we company commanders were summoned to our commanding officer, Major Erdmann. "Tomorrow morning we march into Belgium. The initial resistance at the frontier must be quickly overcome; the goal of our 7th Panzer Division is the Meuse near Dinant. Along with the 5th Panzer Division, we are part of General Hoth's Panzer Corps, which will advance as spearhead through the Ardennes. Our reconnaissance battalion can take pride in being at the forefront of the division."

At 0532 hours on 10 May we fell in. The Belgian frontier posts withdrew at once or surrendered. Skirting the northern edge of Luxembourg, we advanced due west through the difficult terrain of the Ardennes and without great resistance reached the Meuse north of Dinant on 12 May. From the high ground we could see the valley and, on its western side, further heavily wooded hills. We could also see, however, the broken bridges, which Rommel would have liked to take intact.

We felt our way slowly down into the valley, but at once came under well-directed gunfire and were straddled by heavy artillery.

Rommel appeared among us, as so often in the following weeks, in order to form personally a picture of the situation. He arrived in his armored car, specially equipped with radio gear. "What's going on?" he asked.

"Held up by artillery fire," we replied.

"Show me. Where is the fire coming from?" Standing in his armored car, he studied the opposite bank with his binoculars. He was calm and steady, giving no sign of uncertainty or nervousness. Within minutes he made his decision.

"Stay put," he told us. "This is a job for the infantry."

The May sun was already shining warmly. The river valley lay peacefully below us. Soon we saw elements of the 7th Panzer Grenadier Regiment climbing down the hill, accompanied by army engineers with rubber dinghies. Further south, near Dinant, the 6th Panzer Grenadier Regiment was on the move.

Hardly had the first boats been lowered into the water than all hell broke loose. Snipers and heavy artillery straddled the defenseless men in the boats. With our tanks and our own artillery we tried to neutralize the enemy, but he was too well screened. The infantry attack came to a standstill.

Rommel went to Dinant to see whether the other regiment had been more successful. But there, too, dinghy after dinghy had been sunk.

"Smoke," thought Rommel, but we had no smoke shells. Again came one of Rommel's instant decisions made on the spot: some houses that stood in the right direction for the wind were shot into flames, and under cover of the smoke the attack was begun again.

Like a whirlwind Rommel came back to us, at once organizing covering fire for the 7th Panzer Grenadier Regiment. He personally took command of its 2nd Battalion. With the second wave Rommel was across the river, where it became possible to form a small bridgehead in the teeth of the French, who defended themselves bravely.

During the night the first tanks were ferried over by the engineers. On the morning of 14 May we took up the attack with the infantry.

Rommel was there again; his command post could not hold him. His command tank was hit and the driver put it in a ditch. Rommel was slightly wounded, but hurried forward on foot—in the midst of enemy fire. "Is Rommel immune?" we asked ourselves. It made a strong impression on all the officers and men; his example spurred us on.

From the bridgehead a breakout was successfully made: the way to the west seemed open. Our reconnaissance battalion was put across and we at once set out from the bridgehead into the western advance.

"Keep going, don't look to left or right, only forward. I'll cover your flanks if necessary. The enemy is confused; we must take advantage of it." So ran Rommel's unorthodox orders.

The panzer regiment moved up, and with it a special unit of engineers. Together we managed to make a breach in the French line, one and a half miles deep. Rommel was again right up at the front, driving us on. During the night we were already advancing through the town of Avesnes and next day, the 17th, we reached the River Sambre, where the bridges were intact.

The French were caught completely unawares by our impetuous advance and retreated, to some extent with signs of disbandment.

"La guerre est finie, je m'en fou," we heard, shouted by some French soldiers.

What was up with the famous French army, which in the First World War had fought against us so bravely and on equal terms? In the first place, we thought, the "impregnable" Maginot Line had given them a feeling of complete security; second, they had undoubtedly underestimated our fighting strength and mobility. They did not draw lessons from the blitzkrieg in Poland. In addition, the French will to wage war against us seemed to be very weak, although such outstanding leaders as Marshal Pétain and General Weygand were at the head of the French army.

We had no information about the situation either in the individual sectors of the front or as a whole. We had the feeling of being alone at the head of a division advancing tempestuously. "Forward!" was the cry. By 18 May our panzer regiment was already rolling into Cambrai, that historic town which became famous in the First World War as the place where the British first used tanks and brought about a turning point in the war.

With our reconnaissance battalion we covered the tank advance on the left flank and were thereby involved again and again with the flood of retreating French soldiers, who in their panic mingled to a large extent with the civilian population.

The division closed up. On 20 May the important St. Quentin canal was crossed. That evening we heard that Guderian, with three armored divisions, who had been rushing forward to the south of us, had reached Abbéville on the Somme and was thus only 15 miles from the Channel coast.

Where were the British, whom we were now crediting with more fighting spirit? On the one hand they were tougher than the demoralized French, and on the other they had their backs to the Channel, which separated them from their base on the island. For them, winning was a matter of survival.

On 20 May we reached the area south of Arras. For the first time a division of the Waffen-SS appeared in support of us. We advanced on the La Bassée canal. Rommel wanted at all costs to skirt Arras on the west, so as to cut off the way to the coast for the British who were presumed to be in the area. When our tanks reached and closed the arterial road leading from Arras to the west, a hard and costly battle was about to begin for our division.

I was with my company on the canal, trying to force a crossing. All the bridges had been destroyed. In addition, the French had sunk all the river boats. We were coming under accurate sniper fire from the opposite bank. As I sprang to one of our antitank guns to direct its fire, I received a shot in the right hand. My pistol whirled through the air; several of my fingertips had been shot through and I was bleeding heavily. As my orderly Erich Beck recalls, "I at once fetched an armored car. As I tried to get my boss on to it, he slipped away under my hands. 'My God,' I thought, 'now he's really had it.' But next day he was back among us, with his arm in a sling."

Assault parties had brought in a few prisoners, whom I questioned. After some coaxing, it turned out that the British battalion opposite us belonged to the Grenadier Guards. Its commander was an old friend of mine, with whom I had sat together in the Marlborough Club in London only shortly before the war. How senseless it all was, I thought.

During the night we used rubber boats to cross and, against light opposition, succeeded in establishing a bridgehead on the other bank. Engineers had to construct the pontoon bridge like a snake through the sunken barges and lighters. During the violent crossing of the canal, Rommel stood like a target on the embankment and directed the fire, while next to him men were being wounded and even killed. Once again he spurred us on by his exemplary behavior. Only when Stukas (JU 87 dive-bombers) came into action was the crossing finally successful.

Meanwhile the British had decided, even without the French, to launch a counterattack east of Arras on our right flank. One of our panzer grenadier regiments caught the brunt of it. Our own tanks were already west of Arras at the time. The situation became increasingly critical, so Rommel decided to intervene again personally. To our dismay the British attacked with a new tank which, though slow, was well armored, the Matilda, against which our 3.7cm antitank gun was powerless. Rommel realized this at once and brought up an 88mm battery. He personally directed the 88s shot by shot with the result that over 30 British tanks were knocked out and the enemy withdrew. Rommel never even noticed that one of his orderly officers was killed beside him. The battle for the La Bassée canal and Arras lasted several days and cost the division its heaviest casualties so far.

Rommel's unorthodox tactics horrified the general staff. Even Hitler wanted to stop the headlong forward rush and order a halt to operations. But as Rommel told us, "I must and will turn the favorable situation to our advantage. Our opponents are beginning to fall back and must not be allowed to find a foothold again." We believed him, trusted him, and went along with him.

With two bridgeheads, we pushed forward again at once and on 27 May reached the area south of Lille. The panzer regiment advanced even further during the night and in the early morning was able to block the arterial road from Lille to Dunkirk at Lommé. We suffered from the dust, which covered the vehicles and gave us the feeling of chewing dry biscuits all the time.

On 28 May, Rommel was with his command tank at the command post of the panzer regiment when heavy artillery fire suddenly opened up, which from its direction could only have come from our own artillery. We had probably advanced too fast. Communications were not always so quick. Also with Rommel, to receive fresh orders, was my commander, Major Erdmann.

Erich Beck recalls, "We were just going to have breakfast when a runner came, summoning our boss, von Luck, to Rommel's command post. I needed a little time to pack everything.

" 'Beck, where are you, man?' the boss called, 'I've got to go to the general.'

"Just as we got to the outskirts of the town where we were to meet Rommel, it came under heavy artillery fire. In front of a house lay a dead man. It was our commander, Erdmann. Rommel stood near by brushing the dust from his uniform. Rommel seemed to be greatly affected by this death. He had lost one of his old and reliable commanders. I thought, 'Was it thanks to our guardian angel that we left a few minutes late?' "

Rommel turned to me: "Von Luck, you will take over command of Panzer Reconnaissance Battalion 37 at once. You will receive fresh orders immediately."

I was the second youngest company commander in the battalion.

"General," I protested, "some of the company commanders are older than me. Does your decision stand in spite of that?"

"You're in charge, full stop. If the company commanders obstruct your orders, I will replace them." This again was one of Rommel's unorthodox measures. With him, performance counted for more than rank or seniority.

While securing its right flank, the whole division now advanced on the area west of Lille. The British, after their unsuccessful attempt at a counterattack set off "Operation Dynamo," the beginning of the evacuation through Dunkirk.

On 31 May a French division surrendered in and around Lille. The British managed to get more than 330,000 men back across the Channel to England. We could not understand why we let so many get away.

As our Intelligence reported, the French, after the loss of the area north of the Somme and their divisions in action there, built up a new line of defense, apparently in haste, south of the Somme, which was called after their commander in chief the "Weygand Line." On the north bank of the Somme, meanwhile, our follow-up infantry divisions secured our southern flank. The 7th Panzer Division, the "Phantom Division," as the French had by now respectfully christened it, was give a few days' rest to restore men and material.

On 2 June Rommel was awarded the Knight's Cross of the Iron Cross by Hitler personally, the first divisional commander to receive it. As he presented it, Hitler remarked, "We were all very worried, but success proved you right."

The days of rest did us good. We could bury our dead and our fallen commander Erdmann with dignity and with military honors. The first mail went to our families. I visited my companies and thanked them for their effort. I dwelt longer with my own company, which was now being led by Staff-Sergeant Werner Almus. Rommel had agreed to my suggestion that the company should be led by Almus, who was well known to all the men and NCOs, and not by an officer brought in from the Officer Reserve.

I enjoined all the men to behave correctly toward the civilian population and not play the conqueror. The inhabitants rewarded us for this behavior. Not once did we hear the words *sale Boche* ("dirty German").

During these days medals were awarded with due ceremony. I received the Iron Cross I Class. After the award of the Knight's Cross, Rommel came back from Hitler's advanced headquarters at Charleville and sent for us commanders to issue us new orders. The gist of what he said was as follows.

"The advance movement has led to complete success. Now it is a matter of encircling the British and preventing the bulk of them from retreating to their island.

"The enemy is exposed to annihilation," he went on in his Swabian dialect. "We shall thrust forward across the Somme to the Seine and not bother about our opponents, whom we will overtake or leave behind on our right and left flanks. Our goal is the Seine, which we must reach at Rouen, on the right wing of the Corps. In so doing we shall try to capture the Seine bridges intact. Carry on as before: I have complete confidence in you."

On 5 and 6 June we advanced in "open battle order" across the flat terrain, avoiding the main roads, along which the civilian population and retreating elements of the French 10th Army were moving south. We reached the Somme and took possession of its bridges, surprisingly intact. Always up at the front was the reconnaissance battalion. After us came the tanks, then the grenadier regiments, and the artillery. We no longer bothered about the enemy and had not time to take prisoners. On the far side of the Somme we suddenly came upon resistance, the Weygand Line.

I had the motorcycle escorts break off and attack under covering fire. I was with them myself and was forced to take cover as we came under heavy artillery fire. Then I heard a voice behind me, "Captain, your breakfast." I turned around and couldn't believe my eyes. One of my runners, Lance-Corporal Fritsche, a hotelier from the Saarland, had crawled forward through enemy fire carrying a tray with some sandwiches, which were even garnished with parsley and a paper napkin.

"Man, are you mad? I'm hungry all right, but at the moment I have other things to do than eat breakfast."

"Yes, I know, but a hungry commander gets nervous. I feel responsible for your welfare." And he was off again, back through the fire.

The men around me, who were lying in full cover, just shook their heads and found it quite in order that I was able, somewhat later, to pin the Iron Cross II Class on this man.

With the support of tanks and artillery, the Weygand Line was successfully breached. In only two days we covered about 100 kilometers of open terrain and on 7 June reached the Seine at Rouen. There the Luftwaffe had done quite a job. From afar we could already see huge clouds of black smoke hanging in the sky. From the hills on the southern edge of Rouen we saw the burning oil tanks and the harbor, but also the Seine bridges, every one of which had been destroyed. I reported this to Rommel, who ordered the hills to be held until the arrival of new instructions.

"It will be a hard crossing," we all thought to ourselves.

Next day came the new order: "The division will leave the Seine and turn west, so as to reach the Channel coast north of Le Havre. In the harbors between Le Havre and Dieppe there are said to be British units still, waiting to be evacuated."

On 8 and 9 June we pushed forward in the direction of the Channel coast. The French and British covered the planned evacuation with hastily constructed lines of defense.

At this point, I received from Rommel one of his unorthodox, "mad" commissions.

After my battalion had reached its first objective on the evening of 8 June, and in so doing had thrust at times straight through French columns without bothering about prisoners or resistance on our flanks, just as Rommel had ordered, he appeared at my command post, sat down at a table and studied the map.

"Von Luck, you will fall in tomorrow morning before daylight and push through to the west for about 30 kilometers. There you will reach a hill from which you can overlook the whole terrain. Take the hill and establish yourself there until I arrive with the tanks. Don't look to left or right, only forward all the time. If you get into difficulties let me know."

My intelligence had reported meanwhile that the Allies had set up a strong antitank front 5 kilometers to the west. It was obvious to me that I could not possibly reach the objective with my lightly armed recce battalion. But I knew Rommel, and knew that he set goals as distantly as possible, and that he would not tolerate contradiction but expected his commanders to try and do as well as they could. (I was able to observe again and again—especially in North Africa—how commanders opposed his orders, which often seemed impossible to carry out, and were promptly replaced.) So without raising objections, I said, "General, I have understood your commission. As I see from the map, the hill to be taken is only about 10 kilometers from the coast. Why shouldn't I push on at once to the Channel, then we could at least have a bath?" Rommel laughed; he liked such reactions from his commanders.

So we fell in next morning and, as was to be anticipated, came upon strong antitank defenses, against which we had nothing to throw in. We made only 5 kilometers progress in all. I reported this to Rommel. Shortly after he came to us and satisfied himself personally of the situation.

"I'll have artillery laid on at once and have some tanks push through. Then proceed as before, in accordance with my orders." The eyes of the men around me were shining. They had faith in Rommel and knew that he would give no orders that endangered their lives unnecessarily.

Rommel's tactics worked—we got through and resumed the advance. On 9 June we reached the coast. Rommel sent off his famous signal to headquarters: "Am at sea." Further north lay the little port of St. Valéry sur Mer, in which according to aerial reconnaissance there were still considerable Allied forces. Rommel sent for me.

"I am going to take St. Valéry with the division. You will keep one 88mm battery as support and take the little port of Fécamp south of here and secure the Le Havre direction."

While Rommel advanced with the division on St. Valéry, where he encountered stiff resistance, there began for my armored reconnaissance battalion one of the oddest, indeed almost amusing episodes of the French campaign. With scout car patrols in front, to keep a look-out and protect us against surprise, we marched along the cliff-top road the 30 or so kilometers to the south. We met with no opposition. Here even civilian traffic had petered out.

By the evening of 9 June we were on the hills north of Fécamp. We moved quietly, for no one was supposed to know of our presence. We had to exploit the effect of surprise.

We could see the little harbor, in which lay two British destroyers. They were obviously there for the evacuation. We could see the promenade with pretty villas and a casino, as we supposed. In the harbor and on the streets we could detect a good deal of enemy movement. The French and British seemed to be preparing for embarkation. To our astonishment neither the harbor nor the town itself was secured by outposts on the high ground. No one seemed to be expecting us. The evening sun bathed this pretty resort in a warm light.

Bearing in mind the relative forces and the presence of the two destroyers, I thought of a plan for the following morning, which I explained that evening to the company commanders and the leader of the 88mm battery.

"The hills before Fécamp will be occupied by the motorcycle escorts, the armored scout cars will hold back, so that they can intervene where necessary, the heavy company will secure the motorcycle escorts. The 88s will be positioned on the cliffs in such a way that they can attack the two destroyers, both in the harbor and at sea should they leave it. Everything must be done without attracting attention. No loud commands, no unnecessary vehicle movements."

I sent for Kardorff, my orderly officer. Kardorff spoke fluent French, having attended a French school in Berlin.

"Kardorff, tomorrow morning you will go to Fécamp with a runner and a white flag, ask for the local commander and demand the surrender of the whole garrison. Tell him that the town is surrounded on all sides and that the two destroyers must leave the harbor immediately without taking anyone on board. All clear?"

Early in the morning Kardorff went off. We saw him disappear into the town. Would my trick work? After a short time Kardorff came back.

"The mayor and the French commandant seem to agree, but the British flatly decline."

What now? I couldn't lose face, so had to go on with the game. Toward 10:00 A.M. I sent for Kardorff once more. "Go into the town again and tell the mayor that I should like to spare his beautiful resort. He might care to exert his influence on the Allied commanders in the interests of the inhabitants. There is no escape, only unnecessary loss. If the garrison again declines to surrender, I will open fire on the town and harbor at twelve o'clock with every gun, and call up the Luftwaffe for bombardment."

Kardorff went into the town once more and again came back with a refusal. I sent for the company commanders and the leader of the 88mm battery.

"We shall have to keep our word now and open fire on the town punctually at twelve o'clock," I said.

Apart from the 88s, I had only a 3.7cm antitank gun, the 2cm guns of the scout cars and the normal machine-gun equipment of the motorcycle escorts. So my orders were: "Punctually at 1200 hours fire will be opened from every gun, including signal pistols, to pretend that we're stronger than we really are. The 88s will try to set the destroyers on fire; aim for the gun-turrets and the bridges."

Everybody made preparations. We were in a strange mood. No one wanted to destroy this famous resort. At 11:30, a civilian came up the hill. He held a white cloth in his hand. He was brought before me.

"What's going on in the town, *Monsieur*? Why doesn't your mayor surrender the place?" I asked him. "Tell me where the British are and which buildings are important."

The man said he had been afraid and that was why he had run away. The British were mainly in the harbor, preparing the embarkation. "They're clearing out and leaving us to our fate. Please spare the town. Look, the building over there is the old Benedictine monastery; there in the middle is the old town hall, and there, on the promenade, is our casino."

I put two and two together and asked, "The monastery, is that where the famous Benedictine liqueur is made?"

"Yes, that's the place," he replied.

At that I sent for the commanders again and gave directions, "The monastery, the town hall, and the casino are not to be touched. Concentrate on the harbor and the radio station. The 88s will destroy the radio station first and then concentrate on the destroyers."

Luck was on our side. A few minutes before twelve a squadron of Luftwaffe bombers flew over the town, obviously on their way to England. In addition, one machine dropped three bombs, whether by mistake or to hit the destroyers we didn't know. At the same moment I ordered "Fire!" A somewhat ineffective but nonetheless intensive hail of shots fell on the harbor like fireworks. We all had to laugh as blue, red, and yellow tracer ammunition provided a backdrop.

Suddenly a white flag went up over the town hall: capitulation! The two destroyers left the harbor full steam ahead and began to shoot at our positions. Unfortunately that cost us a few casualties, until the 88s managed to hit one of the destroyers, which continued its voyage under a smoke screen.

I at once ordered cease fire and summoned Kardorff.

"We will both go into the town now and arrange the surrender."

At that moment a couple of Wellington bombers came flying toward us. The 88s opened fire immediately. One machine went down in flames. The crew hung from their parachutes and landed right in my positions.

"You're in luck," I greeted them. "You'll be staying here with me for the time being." We then set off in a scout car on our journey into the town, where the mayor handed me the key to the resort.

"*Monsieur le Maire*, I ordered your town hall, the monastery, and the casino not to be hit out of respect for these historic buildings. *La guerre est finie pour vous*; bring the inhabitants out of the cellars, open the shops. We will pay in genuine currency. Nothing will happen to any of you."

In all those weeks I had seldom seen such a grateful and surprised Frenchman as that mayor. While I stayed with him, I sent Kardorff up the hill to bring the commanders to me. I ordered the southern hills to be occupied, the radio station to be switched off, and feelers to be put out to the south by reconnaissance patrols.

The town was to be hermetically sealed on all sides. Half of every unit was to have a few hours free in turn, to take a bath in the sea and to go shopping. I reported by radio to Rommel that Fécamp had been captured with light casualties, only a half dozen, that many French and British had been made prisoner, nearly 200 men, and that protective measures had been taken to the south.

Rommel radioed back, "Bravo von Luck. You remain responsible for the town. My ultimatum for the surrender of St. Valéry has been rejected. I am preparing bomb attacks and an attack with tanks."

The following day Rommel radioed, "St. Valéry has surrendered. Several generals, including the commander of the 51st Highland Division, and thousands of prisoners taken. The division has one to two days' rest."

We were overjoyed. On the spur of the moment I asked Rommel by radio, "Can you send me the divisional band? The inhabitants are grateful and friendly. In addition I have sealed off the town on all sides, even to German 'visitors,' except for you personally, of course. Have I your agreement?"

Rommel understood a bit of fun; he was in a good mood after his success and consented to both the band and the sealing off of the town.

With the major and my adjutant I now viewed the resort. We first visited the Benedictine monastery, where we were greeted by the abbot. "*Monsieur l'Abbé* (I should have called him *Mon Seigneur*), I heard about your monastery at the last minute before the shelling of the town and at once ordered that no shot was to fall on your building. I hope everything is intact."

The abbot thanked me effusively for our forbearance and asked whether he might show me the monastery. I am somewhat ashamed to admit that the Benedictine liqueur was one of the decisive factors in sparing the monastery. As we descended to the cellars, I could see thousands of bottles and a large number of old barrels.

"Does the famous Benedictine come from these cellars?" I asked innocently.

"It certainly does, and to show our gratitude I should like to offer all your men a bottle." The abbot paled when I told him the strength of my unit, 1,100 men. But he kept his word. Since that day I have always drunk Benedictine with particular respect.

On the afternoon of 12 June, probably for the only time during the campaign, a German band gave a promenade concert in front of the casino. French and German soldiers strolled about together on the promenade and were glad that the battle for Fécamp had been executed so bloodlessly.

I instructed my "hotelier"—the runner with the breakfast—to do some shopping and prepare a meal for that evening in the casino. He was now in his element. Then the mayor appeared with a German U-boat officer, whose ship had been shot up in the Channel. He was the only one to be taken prisoner by the French. "In the excitement of yesterday we forgot that we had this gentleman in our prison," the mayor apologized.

Sitting together at the festive table that evening were the officers of my battalion, the successful leader of the 88mm battery, a German U-boat officer, and the crew of a British Wellington bomber, besides the mayor of Fécamp.

On 15 and 16 June we were set on the march again. Le Havre was left alone and would be taken by other units. Rommel told us that we were now to cross the Seine; the bridges had been rebuilt and substantial bridgeheads secured. Our goal now was the naval port of Cherbourg, which had been developed as a fortress and was to become an important base for our navy.

We crossed the Seine on 17 June and literally "stormed" through Normandy toward Cherbourg. On that day we covered nearly 350 kilometers, our reconnaissance battalion, because of its greater mobility, again forming the spearhead.

Early on 18 June we were at the outer forts of the Cherbourg citadel. Rommel at once called for Stukas, which bombed fort after fort. On 19 June, at a formal ceremony, the French commandant surrendered the fortress. Rommel was very courteous and paid tribute to the garrison. I believe this fair attitude, which he himself always showed toward the defeated enemy, earned him respect—even abroad.

Rommel was already somewhat vain, but we were happy to overlook this. He always had his camera on hand, to photograph the most important scenes. He was taken to task later because he had obviously "improved" the figures for his achievements. In the main, though, it was his unconventional mode of fighting that evoked the criticism of him, and also the envy of some senior officers. According to Rommel's account, the division had taken 97,648 prisoners in six weeks, against losses of its own of 1,600 dead and wounded. Certainly a proud balance.

We did not stop at Cherbourg, but pushed on south at once through Brittany, in the general direction of Rennes and Nantes on the Loire. A captured French captain told Rommel, as I translated, that Marshal Pétain had offered an armistice. In spite of that, we advanced further south so as to control if possible the whole Atlantic coast. St. Nazaire and La Rochelle fell into our hands; practically no resistance was offered any more. The stream of refugees gradually dried up; half of Paris seemed to have fled south to the Mediterranean coast and to Bordeaux. On 21 June the armistice was signed at Compiègne; of its provisos we at first heard nothing.

On we went south. "Bordeaux is our goal," said Rommel. When I arrived with the first elements of my reconnaissance battalion at the Gironde, a river north of Bordeaux, Rommel told us to stop. At a briefing of commanders we heard that Pétain was still in Bordeaux with his provisional government, but would be transferring his seat to Vichy, in the part of France not to be occupied by us.

"You will secure the area by the river with your battalion," Rommel ordered. "Give your men some time to rest. With the armistice the French campaign is over and won."

I posted an armored patrol and some motorcycle escorts at the northern approach to the bridge. My people relaxed and behaved in exemplary fashion toward the inhabitants.

Here I went through the last, this time entertaining, episode of the French campaign. On the second day of our "bridge watch" a runner reported, "Captain, a French colonel with a white flag has arrived and would like to speak to the local commander." I went along, greeted the colonel politely and asked what he wanted.

"*Mon Capitaine*," he said, "General Weygand, chief of the French general staff, requests that an authorized officer be sent to Bordeaux to make arrangements for the withdrawal of the provisional government of Marshal Pétain and the surrender of the city to the Wehrmacht. Your authorized officer will work with General Weygand and the mayor. He will have an office in the district army building and accommodation in the Grand Hotel. Would you kindly settle this question at once with your divisional or corps commander. I am instructed to wait here for your answer."

I winked at Kardorff, "This is a job for us, Kardorff."

I informed Rommel by radio and suggested, "General, I speak good French and have Kardorff as interpreter; I think I should go to Bordeaux."

"Agreed," came Rommel's reply. "I take responsibility and will inform Corps headquarters. The task of the battalion remains unchanged. Hand over to your senior company commander."

I was glad to have something to do and quickly had two scout cars polished up to the nines, equipped with ammunition (who knew what might be happening in Bordeaux?), and manned by our best crews. I settled for my jeep and, besides Kardorff, took the driver and an orderly.

So our little convoy appeared at the bridge, where the French colonel was waiting.

"*C'est moi-même, mon Colonel*; I'm coming to Bordeaux with you."

"*Très bien*, let's go."

The closer we got to Bordeaux the heavier the traffic became. The city seemed to be crammed. Many who still had enough money had fled there from Paris. The Colonel billeted me at the Grand Hotel. Next to me was Kardorff, and rooms there were also made available for the crews of the armored cars. I was somewhat embarrassed to think that other guests had probably been forced to vacate their rooms on our behalf.

"Could we go to General Weygand now?" the Colonel asked, as I returned to the hall.

I agreed and also gave my men quick directions, "The two scout cars are to be drawn up in front of the hotel; the radio post is to be manned day and night. A guard will stand in front of each car with a machine-pistol at the ready. The others will not leave the hotel. No discussion, please, with the inhabitants or the soldiers. Conduct yourself with the utmost propriety."

I followed the Colonel to the local military headquarters, where I was allocated an office. Then, I was received by Weygand. He first expressed his thanks that we had been ready without great formalities to allow the removal of the provisional government under Marshal Pétain to be carried out smoothly. I was naturally very impressed to be face to face with one of the best known French generals, who until only a few days before had been our opponent and regarded by Nazi propaganda as the "archenemy." I tried by my deferential attitude to show him our respect as soldiers, and saw in his tired eyes how heavy that hour must have been for him.

"*Commandant*," he ended the brief audience and gave me his hand, "in two days the French government will be able to leave Bordeaux for Vichy. The Colonel will arrange with you the details of the surrender of the city to the German Wehrmacht."

(I never suspected at the time that Pétain and Weygand would later be accused of "collaboration" with the Germans and marked as traitors to their country. What a bitter end for army commanders of such distinction!)

On the way back to the hotel I was told by the Colonel, "There are no British in the city, but tens of thousands of French soldiers, who have been called upon to hand in their weapons. Whether all have complied with the order, I don't know. We are combing through the whole city."

I had a strange feeling in my stomach and was not sure that we had not overreached ourselves with our little liaison unit. I felt as though I were in a bee hive. I arranged with the Colonel that I would go to my "office" with him the following morning.

On arriving at the hotel, I inspected the guards. A lot of Frenchmen, disarmed soldiers among them, were standing around our armored cars with angry or curious looks.

For the evening meal, tables had been reserved for us on the terrace of the hotel. There, too, we met with hostile looks from many of the guests. I felt somewhat ill at ease. Yet, it was pleasant to sit on the terrace. It was a fine, warm evening. In the harbor lay a neutral passenger ship. Owing to its international status, I could do nothing about it, but I knew that a lot of French people had embarked on it.

I radioed to Rommel that everything was in order and reported the course of events. He told me that Army command, meanwhile, had agreed to our mission. I was relieved.

The following morning, the Colonel took me, as arranged, to the office where journalists and an official of the municipal administration were waiting. The official turned to me, "*Mon Capitaine*, it has already been decreed that no one may leave the city for the north. The disarming continues and should be finished today."

Then the journalists wanted to hear from me, "What time are you setting for the *couvre feu*, the curfew? We suggest ten o'clock. There is a fuel depot outside the city with about 60,000 liters. It is under constant guard. We have emergencies that make it necessary for individual refugees to go to the north, especially to Paris. For that they need a *laissez-passer* from you and a voucher with which they can get fuel at the depot. Doctors and supply vehicles will also need a *laissez-passer*."

I now had to make far more, and more varied, decisions than I had imagined when I took on the job.

I reflected briefly and "made known" as follows, "The curfew at ten o'clock is agreed (we were in the middle of summer after all and it remained light for a long time). I need until tomorrow for a stamp with which gas vouchers and *laissez-passers* can be officially approved. By then I shall be able to tell you which roads may be used without disturbing our troop movements.

"I need a list of doctors and supply agencies which you consider necessary.

"I shall be here from eight o'clock tomorrow morning and count on your continued support."

Motor traffic had dwindled almost to nothing, but some soldiers were obviously carrying on a flourishing black market in army fuel. For the moment, however, I was not worrying about that.

I had to know from Rommel or Army command which roads were not to be used. During the night I was notified by division of a few roads that could be opened to the north.

When I came back to the hotel, I was given some special editions of the local paper in which my function, the location of my office, and the time of the curfew were made known.

After I had eaten my evening meal on the terrace again, the captain of the neutral ship came to see me to ask whether he might put to sea. Once again, I was faced with a problem that could only be solved diplomatically or through Army command. So I made inquiries and received the answer, "The ship must remain in harbor until Bordeaux is surrendered. Further directions will follow."

Since the friendly captain now had to stay in harbor, he invited me on board next day for a long-forgone whiskey, to sit with him in the officer's mess as in times of peace. A pleasant change awaited me.

Next morning I drove to my office—this time unescorted by the colonel. I could not believe my eyes. Waiting for a *laissez-passer* was a line of hundreds of civilians. Waiting in the office itself was a venerable old woman who was introduced to me as Madame Lyautey. She was the widow of the famous Marshal Lyautey, who had played a great part in the subduing of Morocco and was regarded as a popular hero.

"*Mon Capitaine*, I am an old lady who would like to go home. Can you please give me a *laissez-passer* and a gas voucher? I would be grateful to you."

What must have been going on inside this old lady, who had to ask such a favor of a young German who had fought against her country?

I gave her the papers without hesitation, and a leaflet showing which roads she was allowed to use. She thanked me very warmly. I could detect no hate in her eyes, but understanding, rather, for the course of events which neither she nor I could have influenced.

The road map was hectographed and handed out to all recipients of the coveted documents. At my request, a German administrator was sent to the fuel depot to supervise the issue of fuel. The day was filled with handing out documents and answering questions. In this I had strong support from Kardorff and we were both glad when, in the late afternoon, we were able to return to the hotel, then to restore ourselves with a whiskey on board the ship.

Pétain's removal to Vichy was scheduled for the following day. The surrender of the city was also being prepared, so in two days I would be free of my unaccustomed work.

That evening our "Moor" in the hotel had just served coffee.

"What do you think," I asked Kardorff, "should we go somewhere in town and have a drink?"

He thought it was a good idea, so we got into the jeep and drove to the town hall in the vicinity of which we hoped to find a bar.

The town was completely dead. Then it occurred to us—curfew was at ten o'clock, as I myself had ordered. It was now quarter past. What was to be done?

We then spotted a fiacre, at that time the most general means of transport, standing all by itself with the driver asleep on the box.

"*Monsieur*," we shook him awake.

He saw our uniforms and stammered in dismay, "*Mon Général*, I have a family, I fell asleep, for God's sake."

We reassured him, "That's all right, but do you know where one can still get a drink?"

"*Non, Monsieur*, everywhere is closed because of the *couvre feu*, everyone is afraid. There is still a *maison sérieuse* of course, but I don't know if they will be open for you."

We had no idea what a *maison sérieuse* might be, but we were prepared to risk it. So we let ourselves be taken by the driver to our hoped-for drink. The streets became narrower and narrower, the district more and more dubious. Now and then we thought we were being watched from behind curtains. Gradually our situation became uncomfortable.

"Where are you taking us, *Monsieur*?"

"*Voilà*, we're there."

He climbed down from the box and knocked at the door. An elderly lady appeared.

"Please come in, General." (She promoted me just to be on the safe side; one can never tell!)

I impressed upon the driver that he was to wait for us if he valued his life.

No sooner had we stepped inside than we realized the meaning of a *maison sérieuse*. It was a brothel, admittedly in the French manner. The furnishings were of quality, Madame was very kind, and the girls made a good impression.

"*Madame*," I tried to explain our presence, "until the surrender of the town we are the responsible German officers of Bordeaux. We really only wanted a drink, but were caught out by the curfew we ourselves had ordered."

"You are very welcome. Let's drink a glass of champagne to celebrate the end of the war. We women are always the mourners."

After half an hour of lively conversation on the sense and senselessness of the war, we took our leave, not without assuring the old lady that we would recommend her establishment to the local German headquarters. She was highly delighted and gave us her visiting card.

Our driver was asleep again, but he was there, thank goodness.

We trotted slowly back to the town hall, where our jeep was waiting. The driver refused any money. When I paid him liberally all the same, he called out, "The Germans are not half as bad as we've been told. I'll wait for you here, *mon Général*, every evening until curfew, in case you need me." And he trotted off contentedly.

Pétain, meanwhile, had left the city with his provisional government. The ceremonial entry of our division had been fixed for the day after, with a march-past before our corps commander, General Hoth.

I reported back to Rommel and could not help telling him about the *maison sérieuse*, which much amused him.

Our 7th Panzer Division was transferred to the area west of Bordeaux. Further orders were to follow. I managed to get permission from Rommel to move with my reconnaissance battalion to Arcachon, the delightful seaside resort on the Atlantic coast in the lee of the Cap Feret peninsula. There among the dunes I set up my headquarters in one of the pretty summer villas. For a few days we enjoyed bathing in the sea, fresh oysters, which were collected every day from the oyster beds, and the delicious dry white wine. The end of the French campaign could not have turned out better.

8
Interim, 1940–1941

Every war brings with it, through the shifting of theaters of action, longer or shorter pauses, the "periods between campaigns." These pauses are of great value, both for the individual soldier and for the community. Everyone tries to mobilize his mental forces and is ready to suppress negative experiences and assimilate even the slightest positive ones. People encourage each other and strengthen one another in the hope that at some point in time they will be able to escape this constant mortal threat forever.

Probably every soldier finds out in the course of a war that he can only bear the "having to kill" and "being killed" over long periods if he adopts the maxims of the Stoics: learn to endure all things with equanimity. He can only do this if he builds up an immune system of his own against the feelings of fear and sympathy and probably, to a certain degree, even against matters of ethics, moral, and conscience. He cannot afford to question the whys and wherefores of the things that happen around him and in which he, himself, has a part. He must act and apply his whole concentration to that. He learns through a long process of habituation to suppress images of horror, to distance himself from his neighbor in order to remain capable of rational action. If he manages to do this, his chances of survival increase.

These thoughts and emotions were at work in us now after the end of the French campaign. We knew that our families at home were suffering from anxiety about their sons and husbands. We all felt genuine grief for our dead and severely wounded. We thought, also, of the losses we had inflicted on our opponents. Predominant, however, was joy that we had survived thus far.

The navy and the Luftwaffe remained in action; the first Allied air raids on our industrial centers and communication networks made our own country a theater of war for the first time.

Rommel flew to Vienna, his last garrison before the war, for a few weeks' leave, to relax with his wife Lucie and his young son Manfred.

Through close friends on the general staff I learned that Hitler had tried to conclude a separate peace with Britain. To him, the British, besides the Scandinavians and the Germans, of course, were members of the "Germanic race," whom he secretly admired. But he seemed to have completely misjudged Churchill, who, as we gathered from the British news bulletins, was determined to destroy Hitler and his National Socialism.

In July, our division was transferred to the area west of Paris. Rommel came back and told us that "Operation Sea Lion" was being prepared, the invasion of Britain. The 7th Panzer Division was among those earmarked for the operation. This was the start of wearisome weeks and months of preparation. On converted barges and a few special ships, loading and unloading was practiced again and again under combat conditions. But our impression was that the preparations for Sea Lion were halfhearted, as the Luftwaffe was losing the Battle of Britain.

I moved with my reconnaissance battalion to the Parisian suburb of Le Vésinet, which lay on a loop of the Seine west of Paris. Living in the villa opposite was Josephine Baker; our neighbor was the owner of the Lido, which he reopened with a new show immediately after the armistice. Our villa belonged to a Swiss national who wanted to return to Switzerland, as he was unable, for the time being, to do any business in Paris. He saw us as a guarantee that he would one day find his villa again intact.

"I don't know how long we shall be staying here, but don't worry, I'll keep everything in order," I promised him.

He showed me around the villa and the wine cellar.

"Please help yourself as often as you like."

I declined his generous offer with thanks. Finally we agreed on a token price of one franc per bottle of his fine old wines. I particularly enjoyed a 1929 Chambertin.

My men were quartered in a sanatorium. A baroness was the spokeswoman for the citizens of Vésinet. She praised our behavior. Friends were made, but this had nothing to do with so-called "collaboration," which was later to be punished so gruesomely by the French.

July 1940: Paris was on our doorstep. Military headquarters had been set up and entry to the city was permitted only with a special pass. I obtained one of these passes and spent all my spare time refreshing my memory of this unique city and exploring the individual *quartiers*. One evening, I happened to go into *Le Cavalier*, a bar in the vicinity of the Champs Elysées. Its proprietor was Clément Duhour, an Olympic athlete in 1932 and a well-known *chanson* singer and later film producer. We took to each other at once and *Le Cavalier* became my regular bar. There one met no Germans from the ever more swollen administration, who often behaved overbearingly as "victors." They were the ones who had never heard a shot, let alone taken part in the war. It was often embarrassing when drunken members of the military administration sang Nazi songs in the bars, while the French customers would have liked to hear *chansons*. Once, when it became too much for me and physical violence threatened to break out, I called the military police and had the place cleared of rowdy Germans.

At Clément Duhour's, I came to know a number of French artists. I wore civilian clothes to avoid provocation. I also met J. B. Morel there, who is still one of my best friends today. He was an interior decorator and seemed to know everyone and everything in Paris. He was my own age and had fought against me as a lieutenant. He lived in a delightful apartment in the Rue du Dobropol, near the old Tivoli Gardens by the Bois de Boulogne. Through him, I gained access to circles that otherwise wanted no contact of any kind with Germans. One evening he took me to a jazz cellar, in which prohibited black American jazz was played and swing music, unknown to us. There one could only get in by a special knock. "In the Mood" by Glenn Miller and "Down Mexico Way" became two of my favorite tunes; later, in captivity, we were to play them ourselves.

With my special pass and the faithful Mercedes cabriolet, I had no difficulty in roaming about Paris with my new French friends. They were often my guests in Le Vésinet, where we would go out in one of the motorboats lying in the marina for a trip on the Seine, or cross over to Le Peq to eat in the famous restaurant *Le Coq Hardi*.

My men used their "war pay" to buy things for their families which we had long had to do without at home, such as silk stockings, perfume, fine materials, and drinks. Hitler had established an exchange rate that was highly favorable to us.

At the end of August, I received 14 days' leave. That, for me, was a further sign that no one in the leadership planned on a landing in England anymore. I decided to spend the two weeks in Bad Kissingen, my last garrison, to visit friends and settle a few matters. I would take along my orderly and trusted friend Erich Beck, who wanted to go home.

"Beck, get the Mercedes ready. I'm going to take Boy too, the setter, to put him into safe-keeping at home."

"Captain," Beck came to me excitedly, "I've found a brand new Buick in the garage. Couldn't we go in that? No one has ever seen an American car at home."

I let myself be persuaded and actually got papers and army license plates from military headquarters.

In Kissingen, the spa season was well under way, albeit on a restricted scale, and I drove around the district proudly with pretty girls in the much-admired Buick. The setter, Boy, went to a forester in the Rhoen Mountains, where he unfortunately died later of a virus infection while we were in Russia. When we returned to Vésinet after the visit, I decommissioned the Buick and put it back again, clean, in the garage.

In October, "Operation Sea Lion" was called off. Our air force, after heavy losses, had been unable to gain ascendancy. The navy had insufficient capital ships to cover a crossing of the Channel effectively.

How should things continue now, if a landing in England was not possible? We had occupied almost all of Europe, it is true, but uncertainty still hung over the Mediterranean, from which no good news was coming. Through the nonaggression pact with Stalin we had secured our back. But how should we deal with the British?

They had been forced to leave almost all their materiel behind on the mainland and had lost a not inconsiderable number of prisoners. But the mass of the British army was still intact. The materiel was steadily being replaced from America—in spite of the heavy losses inflicted on the British in the U-boat war. The British air force was gradually acquiring superiority. Churchill let there be no doubt that he intended to destroy Hitler and his National Socialism.

After the abandoning of "Operation Sea Lion," our division received orders to move to the Bordeaux area. Movement again at last! I said good-bye to our friends in Vésinet and to my friends J. B. Morel and Clément Duhour.

"Hans," they both said to me, "you can no longer win this war, we know that." Clément even suggested that in an emergency I should take refuge with his mother in the Basque country.

"You'd be safe there; we Basques never betray a friend."

— He meant it well, but for me it was naturally out of the question. After that, he gave me a silver ring with a Basque motto, the French translation of which was engraved on the inside: *Mieux vaut penser que dire* ("It is better to think than to speak"). I couldn't shake off the feeling that the two friends belonged to the Resistance, which was becoming ever stronger. This belief would later turn out to be true. But our friendship was to prove stronger and more important than betrayal and cravings for revenge. —

On our long march to Bordeaux, we stopped for a day's rest at one of the old Rothschild chateaux. There, I was visited by one of my older friends, Siebel. He had been a fighter pilot in the First World War and was the inventor of the "Siebel ferry," which was to save many men in North Africa from being taken prisoner. Siebel mounted old aircraft engines on ordinary ferries and used their propellers to drive them, thus bridging the short link between Tunisia and Sicily in one night.

On arriving in Bordeaux, I couldn't help calling at the *maison sérieuse*. I was greeted effusively.

"*Mon Général*, we have been officially recognized by military headquarters. I am very grateful to you. You will always find friends here and champagne at our expense."

I hope this charming woman did not have to suffer later as a *collaborateuse*.

Further replacements had arrived from home, including the new commander of the battalion, Major Riederer von Paar, who had taken part in the First World War and soon gained our confidence. I took over my No. 3 Company again, which had been led so well by Sergeant Almus. Lieutenant von Poschinger came to the company as a new platoon leader.

I found time to enlarge my collection of French wines and cognacs. In vineyards north of Bordeaux, some of them very small, I bought bottles with a scarcity value which would never come on the market. My collection of old burgundies, cognacs, and armagnacs, some in mouth-blown bottles and with handwritten labels, had now grown to nearly 1,000 bottles, which I was anxious to send to Germany at the first opportunity.

In January 1941, the division was transferred to Germany, to the area west of Bonn. The French chapter was now finally closed. Left behind were reserve units, a swelling military administration, and the Gestapo (the secret state police), with its reign of terror.

My company was billeted in the village of Heimersheim; I myself in a moated manor house from the fifteenth century which belonged to Baron von Boeselager, whose sons were also army officers. In the evening, when I returned from strenuous exercises in the field, we often sat together and discussed the situation. "Old Boeselager" was no follower of Hitler's. He was afraid that the next encounter with Britain could lead to disaster. While we talked, the "old Baroness" sat near us and played patience (solitaire). She encouraged me to try it too because it was so soothing. To please her I let her show me two varieties and found the game by no means so boring and old-ladyish. When I left she gave me a pack of cards. They were to be a great help to me later in the recovery of my inner peace in critical situations. My young officers used to say at such times, "The Boss is playing patience and doesn't want to be disturbed. So things can't be too bad." Even today I still like to play my "soothing patience."

At this juncture I tried to sum up the course of the war so far and consider how it might and should continue.

In two blitzkriegs, Poland and France had been defeated; Denmark, Norway, and Belgium had been occupied. Until the alarming news from the North African theater of war, the Mediterranean area too had seemed to be under control. The Wehrmacht, however, had had to release considerable forces to secure all the territories, especially against a possible invasion by the British at some unforeseeable place.

We still had our back free through the nonaggression pact with Stalin, which had been bought with territorial concessions in Poland and the Baltic. But how could Britain be defeated, who was being supported to an increasing degree by America, whose air attacks on the Reich had started, and who had retained supremacy at sea?

In the long conversations with Baron von Boeselager, in which we looked for a way in which the war might be brought to an end, we found none. We both feared that this war, which had begun so hopefully, would probably last for a long time yet.

At the beginning of February 1941, we were told that Rommel was being sent by Hitler to North Africa. The situation in Tripolitania had become so critical that we were being forced to go to the help of the Italians. Rommel spent a short leave with his family and then had no time left to say good-bye to us. On 12 February 1941, he flew to Rome and by the 14th had arrived in Tripoli, where he personally supervised the disembarkation of the first German unit, the elite 3rd Panzer Reconnaissance Battalion, which I knew well from my time in Potsdam.

We were very sorry to have lost Rommel and met our new divisional commander, General Freiherr von Funk, with some doubts. He was the opposite of Rommel: a general staff officer of the old school, no "trooper" like Rommel. He led "from behind," from his command post, and did not, like Rommel, seek contact with his men. All the same, we unit leaders managed to adapt to him, the more so since he made no attempt to restrict us in our mobility.

The weeks and months went by. The usual routine began: field exercises with imposed complications, training, and the integration of replacements. The war at the time was taking place elsewhere.

From army bulletins, we heard of Rommel's success in North Africa, of his unconventional, and for the British, unexpected, thrust to the east and the recapture of Cyrenaica. We heard of the increasingly heavy air attacks on Germany. These depressed us most. So now, in contrast to the First World War, the civilian population too was being drawn into the war. We were anxious about our families.

Hitler made angry speeches; his Propaganda Minister Goebbels called for the "Final Victory"; and the Jews were pilloried as fiends. Of their fate we heard nothing.

In April 1941, I received a short leave, half of which I spent with my parents. But I no longer felt happy at home. My brother was in action with his whaler somewhere off Norway; my sister was cramming for the emergency *Abitur*; my stepfather was suffering from an incurable intestinal cancer and being cared for devotedly by my mother. He couldn't come to terms with modern warfare and was always making comparisons with the First World War. We were at odds with each other more and more.

The other half of my leave, I spent in my beloved Paris. There, J. B. Morel and Clément Duhour prophesied, again, that the British, alone or with the support of the Americans, would win. In their view, Germany had nothing to set against the inexhaustible materiel of the British and Americans, especially since in Germany industrial areas and communication routes were exposed ever more frequently to air attack. I argued against them, but did not know either how we could win the war.

I then returned to my company and the same old round began again, which is enervating in the long run. The inhabitants frequently asked us what was supposed to happen next. There was great bewilderment. Only one thing was certain: initial euphoria had given way to sober judgment.

I wanted to get my collection of bottles into a safe place and asked Baron von Boeselager if I could leave them with him.

"But of course, I'll sink them in the moat with my own collection. No one will think of looking there."

Later, in Russia, I had a letter from von Boeselager. He had borrowed two bottles of champagne from my stock for his daughter's wedding. He should have taken them all; at the end of the war, the hiding place was discovered by the French occupation troops. "The *sales Boches* stole our wine and cognac. Everything really belongs to us," said the French, as Boeselager told me later. That was the end of my dream of a French wine collection. *C'est la guerre.*

At the beginning of June, suddenly and without warning, our division was entrained in Bonn and, after a journey of two or three days, detrained in Insterburg in East Prussia. The battalion was billeted in the surrounding villages. I used the opportunity to visit some friends on an estate nearby, where some years before, gay and light of heart, I had celebrated the wedding of one of my comrades.

The old woman, who after the death of her husband, now managed the estate alone, greeted me sadly. "How depressing to see you again in these circumstances. How contented we were then and now we are threatened with a long and difficult encounter with Russia. Do you understand it all? What more does Hitler want? The *Lebensraum* so often talked of by him and Rosenberg?"

We walked through the clean stables. It was like saying good-bye to the old Germany. After a meal, my hostess asked me, "Please play something on the piano. Something lively, please, it's got to be something for me to remember." So I sat there by candlelight and played whatever came into my head. The old woman's eyes filled with tears. As I took my leave, her last words were, "Good-bye, may God protect you!" Today, her estate is part of Poland. Unfortunately, I don't know what became of her.

A warm, late spring lay over East Prussia. I thought back to my years as a recruit, to Koenigsberg, the old knight's castle of Marienburg, and the Masurian Lakes. I had grown fond of that little patch of earth with its dry summers and very cold winters with heavy falls of snow. I admired the people who had come there with the Teutonic knights at the beginning of the thirteenth century and in the course of the centuries, through conflicts with Poland, Sweden, and Russia, and not least through the climate, had grown into a tough race. The hospitality of the East Prussians was famous, their dry humor notorious. The wide expanse of East Prussia was a preview of how things would look in Russia.

What did Hitler have in mind? The entry into Russia seemed certain. The mass of the Wehrmacht was concentrated on the eastern frontier. This showed that it would not be a matter of a limited operation, to bring "home to the Reich" the "Baltic provinces," which had once been occupied by the Teutonic knights. Would Hitler declare the nonaggression pact with Russia to be null and void? How would he try to explain this to the people? Goebbels's propaganda machine was going full strength. There was talk, once more, of "subhumans," of *Lebensraum*, which had to be secured for the German race. And, once again, popular opinion was successfully turned around 180 degrees.

The eve of our entry arrived. We were in a strange frame of mind. The vast Russian empire was hidden, as though by a curtain. The huge distances were beyond our mental grasp. The Ural Mountains, which were nearly 2,000 miles away, were merely the end of the European part; behind them lay the start of the endless expanse of Siberia.

We thought of the fate of Napoleon, whose victorious army had foundered in the extent and cold of Russia. We were not actually afraid, but neither were we sure of what our attitude should be toward an opponent whose strength and potential were unknown to us, and whose mentality was completely alien.

The euphoria of the past months had given way to a rather sober view. Even the young ones, who in the years since 1933 had gone through the school of National Socialism, and who had been sworn into the Hitler Youth in the name of their

Fuehrer, had now fallen silent. They doubted that Russia could be defeated with idealism alone.

Would we be able to cope with a "Second Front," as a result of which the first front in the west would be held mainly by reserve divisions? Would Britain be able to exploit the weak spot? In spite of all our doubts and questions, we did what soldiers have done in every age: We set our minds on the present and were ready to do our "duty."

9

The Russian Campaign, June
1941 to January 1942

At 4 A.M. on 22 June 1941, the German Wehrmacht crossed the border into Russia. The Luftwaffe made mass attacks on air fields and railway junctions. On that morning, trains carrying Russian goods were still trundling over the frontier, delivering commodities under the terms of the nonaggression pact. A few days earlier, I had been summoned to my divisional commander, General von Funk. "Luck, you are being attached to 7th Divisional HQ with immediate effect and appointed as my adjutant."

I was reluctant. "General, I don't like leaving my company at this vital moment. Couldn't you find someone else?"

"No," he replied, "the adjutant I asked for has not arrived yet. Besides, we've already lost too many company commanders and are likely to lose a lot more. To that extent, I regard you in a way as a reserve commander."

Gritting my teeth, I said good-bye to my battalion commander and to my men. With Erich Beck and the faithful Mercedes, I reported to divisional HQ. The German troops, with the panzers in the lead, advanced along the whole front and swept over the weak Russian border guards. The Russians seemed to have been utterly surprised by our entry, though our troop concentrations couldn't have escaped them. Our superiority in the air was quite obvious, both in quantity and in quality.

It soon became clear that the Russian air force had only obsolete machines at its disposal, but above all that the pilots did not function nearly as well as our fighter and dive-bomber pilots, or the pilots of our Western opponents. This was naturally a great relief to us, and when Russian aircraft appeared, we hardly bothered to take cover. We often had to smile, in fact, when, for want of bombs, thousands of nails rained down on us from their bomb bays.

We soon came to realize that neither war at sea nor war in the air was suited to the Russian mentality. In the course of her history, Russia had waged war mostly on land and had recruited her army from her rural millions. Russia had never been a sea power to be taken seriously, and her cumbersome military bureaucracy had obviously never given much thought to building up a modern air force. In exchange, however, we very soon had to accustom ourselves to her almost inexhaustible masses of land forces, tanks, and artillery.

Our panzer corps thrust first to the northeast. Its goal was the city of Vilnius, in what was formerly Lithuania. The resistance we encountered was comparatively slight, but already in evidence were the first T34 tanks, later to become famous, which formed the backbone of the Russian tank force. The T34 was an uncomplicated construction. Its armor plates were welded crudely together, its transmission was simple, everything without any great frills or finesse. Damage was easy to repair. In addition, the Russians were masters of improvisation. Thousands upon thousands of the T34 were produced, in factories that lay beyond the reach of our Luftwaffe.

Vilnius was enveloped to the north and south, and captured. We were at once turned east, in the direction of Minsk. As divisional adjutant, many jobs fell to me that were far from being to my taste. It is true I sat in the CO's staff car every evening and learned something of our plans and actions, which General von Funk explained with the help of maps spread out on his table. Though no less efficient, his style of leadership was nevertheless quite different from that of Rommel. I was sent by the divisional commander, more and more often, as liaison officer to the various units, especially when our communications broke down.

We had now reached an area that was typical of the Russian landscape, vast forests and steppes, and roads that we would not even designate as country lanes. After brief downpours of rain, they turned into muddy tracks which were only passable in some places after engineers or off-loaded grenadiers had felled trees to make a wooden runway with the trunks. It was not so much our opponents that held up our advance as the catastrophic roads.

In this impassable terrain, we lost touch one day with our motorcycle battalion. The divisional commander was afraid that it might have been cut off.

"Luck, you're always hankering after something other than desk work. Our motorcycle battalion is not reporting. It must be about here (he showed me the spot on the map). Try and make contact with them and give me an account of the situation. But take care. In this great wooded area, there may still be Russians all over the place."

I had only my Mercedes available and set off with Erich Beck. Without contact with the enemy, but with considerable difficulty on account of the barely passable tracks, I reached the indicated area and did, in fact, find the battalion there.

"Everything is okay here," I was told, "but we seem to have penetrated some Russian units like a thorn, without their full realization. It might be as well if division could free us from this situation. As soon as the Russians know we're here, things won't look too good for us."

I promised to report everything to the divisional commander and ask for immediate help.

I drove back along the same track. Beside me sat Erich Beck with his machine-pistol at the ready. After a few kilometers through dense forest, we came to a clearing. Both sides of the track were full of Russians. They recognized us at once, and I saw them bring their guns to the ready. It was another 30 yards before the track curved away again into the dense woods.

"Beck, duck down and fire to the right and behind me to the left," I shouted, crouched as low as I could at the wheel and pressed the accelerator.

The first bullets were already whistling past us, inaccurately, however, since Beck had forced the Russians into cover by his bursts of fire. Our Mercedes cabriolet, which had certainly never been designed for Russian roads, jolted and bounced over the undulating ground. One shot did strike the car, but caused no great damage.

"Thanks, Beck, and thanks to our car. We certainly had some luck there."

I reported to the divisional commander, who smiled at me over his reading glasses and said, "Well, you wanted a taste of adventure. What more could you ask for? Thanks for your report at any rate. I'll have something done at once for the relief of the motorcycle battalion."

We gradually recognized the Russian tactics: they allowed themselves to be overrun so that they could then, in small groups in our rear, attack our supply lines and following infantry. We learned from prisoners that Hitler's regrettable order, that all commissars were to be killed at once, had turned out to be a boomerang. The Russian reaction had been as simple as it was effective. The commissars, political officers allocated to each unit to keep an eye on the morale of the troops and their commanders, knew of Hitler's order. So they kept their men in check by telling them, "If you fall into German captivity, you will be killed at once. If you take just one step back, we'll kill you." This explained why so many Russians, usually supplied with only a ration of dry bread, allowed themselves to be overrun. But they would not surrender and formed the basis for the ever growing partisan activity. An essential factor was that Stalin, knowing of the Russian's love of their country, declared the war to be a great patriotic war. It was not Nazi versus Communist. We Germans were the attackers destroying the Russian homeland; they were the defenders of "Mother Russia."

Our aerial reconnaissance reported large concentrations of troops west of Minsk and around it, the first large town in Russia east of the former Polish frontier. Our division was to thrust past Minsk to the north and cut off the Russian's retreat to the east. Another panzer corps was to thrust past to the south of the city. The vanguard was made up of the reconnaissance battalion and the motorcycle escorts. Minsk was enveloped in a pincer movement; the first pocket was closed and a large number of prisoners were taken. Our infantry, whose inhuman hardships made us feel sorry for them, followed up on foot and took care of the surrounded Russians. The panzer divisions were at once thrown into action for a further advance to the east. Again we had to fight our way forward through forests and along wretched roads.

For our division, the goal was Vitebsk, a town that lay north of the feeder road Minsk-Smolensk-Moscow. We constantly met with resistance, but the Russians lacked any organized opposition. Our advance had been too rapid for our opponents to have had time to construct effective lines of defense. It looked very like another blitzkrieg.

For the first time in our advance, we came into contact with the local population. We passed through typical Russian villages, in which wooden houses were ranged on either side of the country lane; each included a village church. The churches without exception had been converted into warehouses, but most of them had been plundered. The sparsely furnished houses had a large clay oven in the center, on which, in winter, the whole family slept. Below it stood the oven bench and in front of that a wooden table. In a corner of the room a candle burned, over which hung one or more icons, sacred pictures. In the middle of the village, one found a sauna, which was indispensable for all Russians since washing facilities in the houses were almost nonexistent. Directly linked to the house was a shed for a few cows, which a peasant was allowed to keep for his own use in addition to a small parcel of land for the cultivation of potatoes and maize for his daily needs. Otherwise, the inhabitants worked on the state *kolkhoz* or *sovhoz*, a kind of village or state cooperative. There, it was a matter of fulfilling the "norm," the measure of all purely state concerns.

The condition of the village streets was even worse than that of the roads we had to traverse so far, for here, in addition, the ground had been churned up by the little *panye* horses drawing the farm carts. Here, there was nothing to "requisition" in order to improve the diet of the troops. On the contrary, we gave the women and children chocolate and cigarettes from our ration.

As divisional adjutant, I found time and opportunity to make contact with local people, in the course of which, my knowledge of Russian came in useful. I was astonished to detect no hatred among them. Women often came out of their houses with an icon held before their breast, crying, "We are still Christians. Free us from Stalin who destroyed our churches."

Many of them offered an egg and a piece of dry bread as a "welcome." We gradually had the feeling that we really were being regarded as liberators.

The hot summer was beginning in Russia. It was often broken by heavy downpours of rain, which forced us to take shelter for the night in the houses. Whenever possible, we preferred our vehicles as night quarters, or the ditches beside the road, since we were afraid of vermin.

Vitebsk, like Minsk, was also skirted widely to the north and south. A new, smaller pocket was formed, the elimination of which we again left to the infantry who had, so far, only marched and not yet seen any real action. Then the message reached us that Major Riederer von Paar, the commander of the panzer reconnaissance battalion, had fallen. General von Funk called me in. "Luck, your work with me has been shorter than I expected. You will take over the recce battalion at once; I will have you confirmed as its commander. Thanks for everything. Good luck!"

I called my aide. "Beck, we're off to the front again. Get the Mercedes ready and pack our things. We're driving to the battalion as quickly as possible."

That very evening, we received our combat orders: advance to the east in the direction of Smolensk. Our panzer corps, under General Hoth, approaching from the northwest, and another panzer corps from the southwest, would attack and seek to destroy strong Russian forces reported to be west of Smolensk and around it. My battalion was to form the spearhead and "reconnoiter" to the east and northeast.

We moved out the following morning. We came upon Russian stragglers, who were usually quick to surrender. Word had got around, it seemed, that prisoners would not be shot by us. We made good progress and, just west of Smolensk, struck a wide trail that was not shown on our maps. We soon discovered that the Russians had laid out this trail from Moscow to Minsk as a future highway; as we found out later, it had already been paved with asphalt west of Moscow. This trail became an aid to orientation during the rest of our advance.

Before long, we met with fairly strong resistance, so we veered away to the northeast. The encirclement of Smolensk was literally there on offer. Within a few days, with the help of our air force, we enveloped Smolensk from the north and south and formed a huge pocket, in which there were said to be over 100,000 Russians threatened with capture. With my reinforced battalion, I held and closed the Smolensk-Moscow trail. We were only 400 kilometers from Moscow.

We were given a few days' rest, one of which I used to go to a makeshift collecting camp that had been set up near Smolensk. In it were penned thousands of Russian prisoners in a closely packed space with no protection from the hot sun or the torrential showers of rain. They seemed apathetic, their faces without expression. Their uniforms, which were simple but practical, were dull and further emphasized the impression of a gray mass. Because of the danger of lice, their heads had been close-cropped. They seemed resigned to their fate, for since time immemorial, they had only known oppression. Whether it was the tsar, Stalin, or Hitler, oppression remained oppression. In a pouch, they carried their "iron ration": dry bread. Later, even we would learn to treasure it.

Many of them called out to me for *voda*, water. They seemed to be suffering severely from thirst. Our services behind the lines had not been prepared for so many prisoners. With the best intentions in the world, they were quite unable to look after them and evacuate them quickly. Nor were things much better for the Russian officers. They, too, lay about apathetically. Now and again, someone would start up one of those Russian songs that reveal a corner of the Russian soul. I felt sorry for them, for they too were human beings like ourselves.

In contrast, however, to the way Russians might appear to a foreigner, we also got to know another side of them. They were like children who could tear the wings off a fly one minute, and in the next, cry over a dead bird. They might share their last crust of bread one moment and then hit the same person over the head. They fought with what they had. Once, we came to an abandoned village. A dog ran up to us. He wagged his tail and whimpered. When we tried to stroke him, he crawled under an armored vehicle. Suddenly we heard a bang, an explosion. The vehicle was damaged, but luckily failed to catch fire. We ran up to it and discovered that the dead dog had had an explosive charge concealed in the fur of its back with a movable pin as detonator. When the dog crawled, the detonator tipped over and triggered off the explosion. The dog had been trained to find meat under armored vehicles. Unfortunately, from then on we had to shoot all dogs that approached us.

While the mass of Russian prisoners seemed to accept their fate as the will of God, our own fear of falling into Russian hands was great. We often heard the wounded say, "Please take me with you or else shoot me. I couldn't stand Russian captivity."

Another day, I obtained permission to go to Smolensk to see the old city. I took along my orderly officer and two men as guard. Here, there was, as yet, practically no German occupation since the pocket had formed more to the west of the city and was now being mopped up by the infantry.

Smolensk looked as though it had been abandoned. Destruction in the industrial quarters and of the bridges over the Dnieper was immense. In the midst of the ruins, Smolensk cathedral pointed to the sky. It appeared largely unharmed. I followed the women and the old men and as I entered the cathedral, was deeply impressed by its beauty. It looked intact. The altar was adorned; burning candles and many icons richly embellished with gold bathed the interior in a festive light. As I went up to the altar with my companions, an old man, poorly dressed and with a flowing heard, spoke to me in broken German.

"*Gospodin* officer, I am a pope who used to preach here before the Lenin-Stalin era; I have been in hiding now for many years, scraping a living as a shoemaker. Now you have liberated our city. May I say a first mass in this cathedral?"

"How is it," I asked, "that your cathedral is in such good condition?"

His answer surprised me.

"Immediately after the Revolution, Russians who had emigrated to America in tsarist times bought the church and all its treasures from the Russians who, at the time, were in urgent need of American dollars. The cathedral is American property, which is why everything is—almost—unchanged."

I have never been able to verify his statement, but it was not very important to me. Without referring to HQ, I gave the pope permission to celebrate mass the next day, for which he wanted to bring in an additional pope.

The following day, I went to Smolensk again, having informed the divisional commander in the meantime; as a precaution, I took along an armored patrol.

The sight that met our eyes when we arrived was breathtaking. The square in front of the cathedral was full of people moving slowly toward the entrance. With my orderly officer, I jostled my way forward. Already, there was not a corner left in the cathedral in which people were not standing, sitting, or kneeling. We remained standing to one side to avoid disturbing the service by our presence.

I was not familiar with the Russian Orthodox ritual, but the ceremony that now began drew me more and more under its spell. Invisible behind the altar, one of the two popes began with a monotone chant, which was answered by a choir of eight voices standing in front of the altar. The chanting of the precentor and the choir filled the vast space of the church. The acoustics gave the impression that the chanting came from above, from heaven. The people fell on their knees and prayed. All had tears in their eyes. For them, it was the first mass for more than twenty years. My companion and I were greatly moved. How deep must the faith have been of these poor, oppressed people; no ideology, no compulsion or terror had been able to take it from them. It was an experience I shall never forget.

Our next goal was a town called Vyazma, on the Smolensk-Moscow road, little more than 200 kilometers from Moscow. With the reconnaissance battalion I was to put out feelers to the east and northeast on the northern side of the trail, reconnoiter our flank, and push forward as rapidly as possible.

After about 50 kilometers we encountered stiff resistance. We discovered that the Russians had set up a strong line of defense on the hills east of a wide valley on a tributary of the Dnieper, a few kilometers north of the town of Yartsevo, anchored by T34 tanks and heavy artillery. I reported the situation and the division formed up for a full-scale attack. Fierce tank artillery duels broke out, which lasted for days.

My birthday was 15 July, which I wanted to celebrate in some way or other, as it might be my last. Since we were stuck and unable to move, I invited my fellow commanders to a "meal." My "hotelier," Fritsche, from my own company, was given the job of conjuring something up. On the western hill, within sight of the Russians, lying some thousand yards away, a table was set up and decked with an assortment of delicacies. In the normal way, they would hardly have attracted attention, but here, in Russia, they were rare. With an "organized" bottle of vodka and some bottles of Moselle, we drank to an uncertain future.

The battles at Yartsevo lasted longer than we would have liked. The blitzkrieg seemed to be over. With considerable losses, we finally broke through. Unfortunately, among those who fell was the commander of our motorcycle battalion and I now had to assume command of that, too. Now I was even more the eyes and ears of the division, with four companies of motorized veteran soldiers under my command.

Resistance grew stiffer and stiffer. The Russians now appeared with the T50 tank, which was much better armed and armored. To knock it out from the front, we had to use the 88mm guns. Vyazma remained our goal. Before that, we had to conquer the upper reaches of the Dnieper River.

It was very hot in those August days, but the dry continental heat was quite bearable; it was a hardship only for the infantry following on foot.

While the bulk of the division fought its way slowly forward, my job was to reconnoiter to the north and northeast on our open left flank. There was as yet no continuous front. The tank divisions had thrust forward like wedges and left their flanks exposed. We went through trackless terrain with few settlements, and through never-ending forest. The roads were merely trails for horse-drawn carts.

Once, when I was on foot looking for a route to get around a bridge that was impassable, I came face to face with a Russian soldier. He was standing by a tree and apparently intended us to overrun him. But then, as if in slow motion, I saw him raise his gun and take aim at me. "Either—or", I thought, jerked up my machine-pistol and was the first to fire. The Russian lost his gun and fell to the ground. When I got to him, he was still alive, but not for very long. I shall never forget his eyes. They were full of questioning, "Why?" Here it became clear to me for the first time that "You or me" was decisive. In this, there was no room for feelings. I thought only briefly that this young Russian, too, had a mother and family. I had to leave him there, as so many were left on both sides, with no one to care about them.

After about 50 kilometers we were out of the wooded area. We encountered no resistance. Before us was a little village, which we ventured slowly to approach. The inhabitants came out of their cottages. They seemed to take us for Russians. When I explained who we were, a little old woman came up to me.

"Is it war?" she asked. "What's our little father doing, the tsar?"

It turned out that these people had remained unaware of the Russian Revolution, Stalin, and our war against Russia. Here, time seemed to have stood still. Here, there was no Party functionary. We lingered on in the village for a few hours and tried to explain what had happened in the world since Russia had lost her tsar. As we left, I was given an icon as a present from the village elder, with the words, "Thank you for your understanding. Leave us to live in the future as we have in the past. May God preserve you!"

Our advance became ever slower and more difficult, the resistance ever stronger. The Russians were throwing against us their elite divisions from the Moscow area.

Furthermore, the supply situation was also becoming increasingly critical. Everything had to be transported nearly 1,000 kilometers from Reich territory. My supply officer, who had brought up ammunition, rations, and spare parts with his transport column, told me that depots were slowly being set up and that rail links were being restored.

But time was running out. We were still more than 200 kilometers from Moscow, our first objective, not to mention the "major objective," the Ural Mountains, which lay some 2,000 kilometers further east. On a visit to divisional HQ, I learned something about the general situation.

—Our entry into Russia had been delayed by nearly two months, because Hitler had had to help the Italians in Greece and subsequently deal with growing partisan activity in the Balkans.

—To the south of us Guderian was thrusting forward in the direction of Kaluga, barely 200 kilometers south of Moscow, with the aim of cutting the road connecting Moscow and the Crimea at Tula.

—The Russian winter was at the door and the Wehrmacht was not prepared for it, let alone equipped. Hitler and the High Command seemed to have made no provision at all for a delay until winter. Moscow, said our divisional commander, should be, had to be, encircled as quickly as possible and its lines of communication to the east cut off.

"This war is going to last longer than we would like," said our commander, summing up his sober assessment of the situation. "The days of the blitzkrieg are over."

On either side of the Moscow trail tank units formed up for the attack on Vyazma. Against bitter resistance, the town was enveloped to the north and south, and on its eastern fringe, this pocket too was closed. Losses on both sides were heavy. My faithful Beck was also wounded. Thank goodness only lightly, but enough for a wound badge.

Once again, the pocket had to be mopped up by the infantry, following slowly and weary from its long marches on foot. Panzer units provided cover to the east. Reconnaissance was pushed on to the east and northeast. At every point, we came upon heightened resistance. And yet Moscow lay "within reach."

After the mopping up of the Vyazma pocket, we asked ourselves how Stalin kept producing new divisions, when a million Russians, if not more according to our reckoning, had fallen into captivity. And whence came the thousands of tanks and guns? We heard from a captured Russian officer that in a lightning action, Stalin had evacuated the industrial concerns around Moscow and those further south on the Volga to the east as far as Urals. A unique, logistical achievement.

We stuck without change to our plan of taking Moscow. The fall of Moscow, the heart of the vast empire, should and would have a significant psychological effect on the morale of the people and the Russian army.

While in the north Leningrad was being encircled and in the south an attack to the east was being mounted along a wide front toward Kharkov and the Crimea, our panzer corps was supposed to push forward to the northeast into the area between Moscow and Kalinin, a town on the upper reaches of the Volga, with the aim of crossing the Moscow-Volga canal and thrusting into the rear of Moscow from the north.

It was late autumn before we had fought our way forward through trackless terrain and against bitter resistance to Volokolamsk, a town about 100 kilometers from Moscow. There, the terrain formed a natural line of defense which was well-manned by the Russians. Once again, long pauses ensued; fuel and ammunition had to be brought forward. My two battalions received replacements for the casualties. The young ones had first to get used to the hard conditions. At home, all they had heard about was the "tremendous forward drive" and that "Russia would be defeated in the near future."

Meantime, October had come and we formed up anew for the attack, broke the Russian lines near Volokolamsk and advanced on Klin, a town on the important Moscow-Kalinin-Leningrad highway. After heavy fighting, Klin was taken. With that, Moscow was cut off from Leningrad. Another panzer division reached and took Kalinin. The infantry had moved up, meanwhile, and took over the securing of this critical connecting road.

I was lying just east of Klin. The Moscow-Volga canal was still about 50 kilometers away. I was summoned to division.

"Luck, you will assemble shortly before dawn with both battalions and try to take, intact, the bridge over the canal at Yakhroma. If that comes off, you form a bridgehead on the east bank and wait for the bulk of the division to arrive. You must anticipate powerful counterattacks. Winter is upon us. We must gain our objectives before then."

The divisional adjutant took me aside.

"Luck, strictly between ourselves, you have been asked for by Rommel to take over the 3rd Panzer Reconnaissance Battalion in North Africa. There's an order to that effect from Personnel. The General won't release you at this juncture. He will negate the order and not mention it to you. But I wanted you to know about it."

I was astonished. How did Rommel come to pick me in particular? There must have been enough commanders available at home in the so-called "officer reserve." To exchange Moscow for Tripoli struck me as breathtaking. But as yet, nothing was official; only one thing was immediately before us: the next arduous attack.

The following morning we assembled while it was still dark. It was already distinctly cold. With masked headlights, which gave only a crack of light so that the men at the front and back could at least recognize each other, we felt our way forward along byways. Shortly after dawn, we reached the canal; on the east bank lay the little town of Yakhroma. Of the enemy, there was neither sight nor sound. The advance patrols found the bridge intact and at once drove over to the east bank. Suddenly, we heard some rather haphazard fire from the town and then the sound of motors going away. I followed up immediately with both battalions and occupied the town, which had been abruptly abandoned by the Russians.

I gave out my orders. "The town is to be searched at once; the motorcycle battalion, with the support of scout cars, will see to securing the outskirts of the town. The bridgehead is to be held at all costs." I asked my adjutant to find a house in the center of the town in which to set up my command post and from where I could report to division.

"Welcome to a Russian breakfast," said my adjutant, coming up to me and pointing to a house. To my surprise, we found there a table laid with samovar, bread, butter, eggs, and naturally, cured ham.

"What a nice reception!" I cried. At which the proprietor of the little inn appeared and explained that he had laid breakfast there for the Russian commander. But he had had to leave it all behind when we had appeared in the little town so unexpectedly. Hungry and highly delighted, we sat down to breakfast. That breakfast was to play a surprising role for me later.

Our little bridgehead was not attacked, strangely enough. The division moved up and extended it. Tanks and artillery were brought into action. The way forward, south and southeast to Moscow, seemed to be open.

In our rear, the infantry closed up and took charge of securing the road connecting Moscow and Leningrad. Much later—in Russian captivity—I met "Kobes" Witthaus and when I saw him again, in 1984, he told me, "I, too, was close to Moscow that winter. Our 35th Infantry Division was thrown into the campaign for that road from Kalinin to Moscow. I managed to penetrate with a patrol right into the suburbs of Moscow. There, I was cut off but we were able to remain hidden for two days until we were forced to withdraw by a Russian counterattack."

That, therefore, was how close the German Wehrmacht came to its first objective. In this, our panzer units in the southwest, which were pressing forward vigorously, helped considerably.

At the end of October, winter set in. From one day to the next, temperatures sank far below the freezing point. It began to snow in unimaginable quantities. It made life difficult for us. The one advantage was that the muddy and dusty roads were now transformed into hard-frozen pistes. The snow evened out the ruts and ridges.

The Wehrmacht, as mentioned, was quite unprepared for winter. Along the whole north and central front, almost all troop movements were smothered by the snow. Worst off were the infantry units and our motorcycles, since they were unprotected. To the dismay of us all, the Russians brought in well-equipped ski divisions from Siberia and the far east. Well camouflaged by their white top suits, Russian infantry filtered almost inaudibly and invisibly through our lines of defense.

We sensed catastrophe and thought of Napoleon's fate. At home, reports from Russia were so alarming that measures were immediately introduced to get winter equipment to the front. Goebbels called upon the population "to help the brave men at the front by voluntary gifts. German fellow-citizens, give voluntarily your skis, winter clothing, furs, and warm underwear for your sons and husbands at the front."

As we learned from home, a huge gift campaign began at once. From collecting points, the gifts were passed on up the line. As might have been expected, however, the supply offices and depots were managed so bureaucratically, for the most part, that they were not in a position to distribute the gifts speedily to the right addresses. Thus, some of our tanks got sledges and skis, while the valuable furs were often grabbed, in the first place, by the services behind the lines who, in any case, sat in warm Russian cottages. We helped ourselves as far as we could and requisitioned warm Russian sheepskins to give to our motorcyclists and grenadiers.

To be unprepared for extreme cold had disastrous effects on our tanks and wheeled vehicles. The summer oil was too thin and the cooling water froze at once. We were soon forced to thaw the water in the morning with blow lamps and procure hot water as soon as we got near a village; or else we had to leave the engines running throughout the night. No western or southern European or American can imagine what it means to fight in temperatures of 40°C below zero and in icy gales.

Since I, myself, reckoned to be transferred sooner or later to North Africa, I asked Beck to see to the Mercedes, in which we intended to make the journey home of almost 2,000 kilometers. It was two days before Beck came back from a trip to the supply company.

"The front springs were gone, owing to the bad roads," he reported. "With the workshop platoon, I forged some others for the time being and mounted them at nearly 40°C below. The car ought to stand up to the journey."

Good old Beck; what would I have done without him?

North of Yakhroma, Russian ski units had filtered through between Klin and Kalinin and were threatening to cut us off. "The bridgehead must be given up," said my divisional commander. "We can't hold the front like this. You will disengage from the enemy in the coming night and cover the withdrawal of the division east of Klin on the main Moscow-Leningrad road. Our infantry units are going back to a new defensive position north and south of Volokolamsk, where the division, after fighting a delaying action, will be taken in."

The General looked at me over his glasses.

"Luck, this was to be expected. Hitler has overreached himself. Now we've all got to pay for it, especially the poor infantry and the grenadiers. Give your men all the support you can. Many of them will get into a panic and try to save themselves at all costs. The disengagement—don't talk of retreat—must and will succeed if we all keep our heads. We will lose a lot of materiel, but the main thing is to get the men back. In the hands of God, Luck."

Although catastrophe was looming, I couldn't grasp it. For the first time since the successful blitzkriegs we were going back on disappointing terms. Snow, frost, icy winds, and an opponent who knew this climate and did not give up, had defeated us. The comparison with Napoleon was inescapable. I could see the pictures in my history books, of how the sad remnants of a proud army turned back and crossed the Beresina.

The men, as well as most of our officers, were unaware of the full extent of what was happening. For them other problems took precedence: How can I get my vehicle back in one piece, will enough supplies come up, how can I protect myself against the barbaric cold?

Hitler and Goebbels were still holding forth about the victorious Wehrmacht. My radio operator, who listened to the news now and then on short wave, told me that our retreat was being represented as a straightening of the front.

On 3 December the retreat began. At the rear position at Volokolamsk, so it was said, feverish preparations were being made by the infantry. Little by little individual units of our division disengaged themselves from the Klin-Yakhroma area. With my two battalions I stayed on in the little town and around it. The Russians were not very active there. They preferred the way past us to the north and south. Finally, we too gave up the east bank of the Moscow-Volga canal, while a large fan of reconnaissance tanks kept constant guard to the east, as far as the snow and the road conditions allowed.

In great haste two retreat routes had been cleared of snow. As a result vast mountains of snow were piled high on either side of the road and made any divergence impossible.

Except for intense reconnaissance activity, the enemy made no very strong direct pursuit of us. All the fiercer, however, were the attempts of the Russian air force to attack the backward movements with old biplanes and light bombers. Our own air force was hardly to be seen. The advanced air fields had apparently also been moved to the west, or else the cold and the snowstorms prevented their use.

The effect of the enemy air attacks was devastating. Since no one on the retreat routes could escape, and since the Russians always came from the east, hence from behind, the infantry first caught the brunt of them. The next victims were the horse-drawn supply and artillery units. Before long, the narrow roads were choked with the cadavers of horses and broken-down vehicles. The men fought their further way west on foot and were often attacked in the flank by Russian ski patrols.

Since we formed the rear guard, after a long interval, and since we were able to use our light antiaircraft guns, we were not bothered so much. Once, however, we did come under air attack. Unnoticed and flying very low, some antiquated fighter aircraft crept up on us from behind. Two shots passed between Beck and me and went through the windshield. We were lucky.

West of the great Moscow-Leningrad highway, we too had to use the cleared routes. Only our tanks had made a trail here and there in the deep snow on either side of the roads, by which most of our track and half-track vehicles could circumvent the many obstacles.

It was a grisly sight. Alongside dead horses lay dead and wounded infantrymen. "Take us with you or else shoot us," they begged. As far as space allowed, we took them on our supply vehicles to hastily organized field dressing stations. The poor devils. Protected against the cold with makeshift foot-rags, they were now only a shadow of those who had stormed through Poland and France.

Supplies got through to us only with difficulty, sometimes not at all. The truck drivers had to make their way against the stream of units flowing back. If they failed, there was suddenly no fuel. The best we could do then was to fill up our most important fighting vehicles; the others we had to destroy and leave behind. "Man, horse, and truck by the Lord were struck." The saying here became a reality.

— Only the will to reach safety in the prepared positions kept the men going. Anything to avoid being left behind and falling into the hands of the Russians.—

Our divisional chaplain, Martin Tarnow, in his notes "Last Hours," has described the suffering and death of so many men.

"*Voda, voda* (water): Some wounded men lay in a kind of barn, among them a few Russians. In the face of death there were no longer any enemies. Again and again came the penetrating cry of a Russian: '*Voda, voda.*' I gave him my water-bottle; he drained it in one grateful swig. When I raised his blanket, I saw the blood-soaked bandage. A stomach wound; no hope. We couldn't understand each other, but suddenly he grasped my silver cross. Perhaps he, too, had a cross at home, hanging on the wall of his parent's house? I thought of Christ on the cross, who had once cried out, 'Today shalt thou be with me in paradise.' It was not long before his hand released my cross; he died very quickly. In dying, I believe he was consoled. . . . "

After weeks, which seemed to us an eternity, marked by shared misfortune and hardships endured, we came at last to the prepared position at Volokolamsk, which lay some 100 kilometers west of Moscow. We passed through the infantry positions to where we were to restore ourselves a few miles further to the rear. The primitive peasant huts seemed like luxury apartments to us. Utterly thankful to have escaped the inferno, we lay down on the oven beside the few remaining old inhabitants and wanted only one thing: sleep, sleep, sleep.

The first reinforcements arrived: replacements who were better equipped for the severe Russian winter, vehicles, fuel, provisions that had long been lacking, and mail from home. This reminded us that Christmas, meanwhile, had come and gone and that a new year had begun. What would 1942 bring for us?

In the middle of January, I was summoned to the divisional commander. General von Funk received me in particularly friendly fashion.

"Luck, two important bits of news for you. I had recommended you for the Knight's Cross. A few weeks ago, Hitler founded a new order, the German Cross in gold, which ranks between the Iron Cross First Class and the Knight's Cross. All recommendations for the Knight's Cross have been converted. Yours, too. In the name of the Fuehrer, I have the honor to present you with this new order for bravery in face of the enemy."

I was appalled: a large and clumsy star, with an oversized swastika in the middle of it, to be worn on the right breast. The General smiled.

"Nice and impressive, isn't it? May I congratulate you all the same." His words were full of irony.

We at once coined a new name for this monstrosity: Hitler's fried egg. Except for headquarters' visits, I never wore the order.

"Now for the second bit of news, Luck: you are being transferred with immediate effect to the Africa Korps, to take over the 3rd Panzer Reconnaissance Battalion. I have to confess that this transfer has been on my table since November. I didn't tell you or release you because you couldn't be spared in that decisive phase. Now Rommel is threatening me with the consequences if I don't send you on your way at once. I find it hard to let you go. In spite of our little differences, you were a great help to me as adjutant and as a commander, you have been outstanding. Get everything ready. You can go in your beloved Mercedes. Report, in the first place, to Personnel in Berlin. Drop in here just before you leave. An appropriate movement order will be issued by my adjutant. Thank you, once again, for everything and best wishes for the future."

The news of my transfer came like a bombshell to my officers and men. We had, after all, fought together since the beginning of the war, shared joys and sorrows, and merged into a real team. The morale of the men had picked up again. Although conditions were no better, the days of rest had done some good, nevertheless.

I planned to leave on 25 January 1942. Beck had the Mercedes checked and procured supplies for several days, as well as reserve cans of fuel. As is usual among men, no one showed his feelings when we said good-bye. A few jokes passed between us and then off to divisional HQ, where I took my leave again and was supplied with the movement order: "Destination, Berlin, Captain von Luck is to be given every assistance by all service posts." From my supply section, we collected mail for home and from the doctor, I procured some Pervitin, a stimulant. The last person to whom I said good-bye was Staff Sergeant Kuschel, the RSM of my old company.

I turned to Beck, "We'll drive without stopping until we're out of Russia. We'll relieve each other every 100 kilometers, swallow Pervitin and stop only for fuel."

After about 200 kilometers, we made our first stop for refuelling at a supply unit. "We're not authorized to issue fuel to individual vehicles," said a "silverling," as we called the servicemen behind the lines, because of the silver stripe on their arms.

"Listen," I replied, "I will have fuel within five minutes if you value your life. Besides, the Russians have broken through in our sector and might be here by morning," I lied to him.

Great excitement and in a few minutes, I not only had fuel but also delicacies never seen at the front, such as a bottle of cognac, cigarettes, and tins of meat.

We were disgusted by life behind the lines. The army supply units had soon been followed by the first Party functionaries, who took over civilian control and treated the population, who had often begun by greeting us as liberators, in the manner decreed by the Party and Propaganda Minister Goebbels, as "subhumans of an inferior race."

No one took any notice of us when we appeared, tired and unshaven, in our white-painted car. Every village, every bridge was guarded by old, conscripted soldiers. Only once, when we produced our movement order yet again, did an old reservist ask me, "Sir, have you come from 'up there'? How do things look? We hear nothing definite. I have a son in the infantry. For weeks, my wife has had no news of him. Please tell me the truth, sir. We are very worried." I tried to give the old reservist some reassurance.

From the region of Volokolamsk, we drove west along minor roads that had scarcely been cleared, so as to reach the Moscow-Minsk "runway" as soon as possible, along which progress would be easier.

We could hear the artillery fire of both sides, which grew ever fainter with every mile we covered. And then, there was complete silence. No sound of battle; only a few supply vehicles moving east. Our journey was now almost romantic. We traveled across broad, snow-covered plains, through forests, deep under snow, and through deserted villages. The snowstorm that snatched at our heels covered our tracks in an instant. We drove with the top down, to make it easier to spot Russian planes. Across his knees, Beck had a machine-pistol at the ready. Everything seemed unreal to us. We were traveling through a virgin land that no one could grasp or possess.

Beck and I were lost in thought and enjoying the peace. But we wanted to get on, to put a distance between ourselves and the gruesome experiences of the past weeks, to get out of that country in which we had to leave our comrades.

Finally, we reached the "runway." I had brought maps with us, of course, to avoid losing our way. We grew tired. Pervitin had to help, for we wanted to drive through the night.

On the trail, traffic was brisker and so brought us back to reality. The trail passed north of the cities of Vyazma and Smolensk. I resisted the temptation to revisit Smolensk cathedral. In Smolensk, too, the Nazi functionaries would have made themselves at home.

I decided to go back along the route we had used for our advance. On the one hand, it was familiar to me and on the other, I was curious to see how things looked now. It was no great detour on the way to Berlin.

We drove day and night, taking turns. North of Minsk, we left the trail for Vilnius, the capital of the former Baltic state of Lithuania, which had been pocketed by the Russians in 1940 as one of the Soviet republics, Hitler's "present" to Stalin for the nonaggression pact.

The indicator showed that we had so far covered about 1,000 kilometers. We no longer knew, at that moment, how many days and nights it had been. Gradually, even Pervitin was no help. We were dog-tired and tried to overcome our fatigue by singing or telling each other stories.

"Beck, Vilnius isn't Russia; Lithuania is more part of Europe than of the east. We'll just drive the remaining 200 kilometers and spend the night there."

Now the snow-covered roads had been smoothed by traffic; the Mercedes ran without a sound and like clockwork. Eventually, late one afternoon, we reached our destination. As usual, there was a local German HQ. We came across an understanding reserve officer, who assigned us a room in the Hotel Regina. We threw ourselves onto the beds. For the first time for eight months, a bed and a bath. Only then did we realize that we were no longer at the Russian front. The strain of the past weeks began slowly to fall away.

"Beck, we'll have a bath now, shave off our stubble, and go to the restaurant for a meal. And then, we'll have a really good sleep."

As we entered the restaurant, we felt as though reborn. We thought we were dreaming: officers of the base units were sitting at the tables with women, apparently leading a *dolce vita*. The little band could hardly make itself heard above the loud conversation. No one here, it seemed, wanted to know about the war. We bolted our food in disgust, handed in the voucher provided by HQ, and disappeared to our beds, lacking for so long.

I woke late the following morning.

"Come on, Beck, we're going, as fast as we can, on to Berlin. There's nothing to keep us here any longer."

A further 600 kilometers lay before us. Finally, after two days, via Grodno, Warsaw, and Posen, we reached Berlin.

The Russian chapter was closed.

"The desert calls, Beck."

10
Interim, 1942

Our first goal was Replacement Section 3 at Stahnsdorf, near Berlin, our base until we left for Africa. The replacement sections were responsible for the training of soldiers to make up for losses at the front. They were also centers for the wounded and those on leave who were waiting for new postings. Officers and NCOs who, because of their wounds were no longer "fit for combat service," as it was called, were employed as instructors, so that their experience might be passed on.

I reported to the CO of the replacement section, who was glad to see me.

"There you are at last. Rommel and the battalion have been waiting for you since November. You are to report, at once, to the Personnel Office; there you will receive movement orders and all information."

First, they fixed us up with a bed for the night. I planned to go to the Personnel Office the following morning. But before that, I drove with Beck to the motor vehicle workshop.

"This Mercedes has survived the Russian campaign. Please check it over and remove the white camouflage paint. I'll pick it up again if I come back from Africa." Beck, who was to be quartered in the barracks until our departure, would see to the car and watch over it with Argus eye.

Early next morning, with a jeep and driver from the replacement section, I drove into Berlin. How the city had changed since I was last there. The people seemed cowed and dispirited. The news coming in from the eastern front, the air raids, which were becoming ever more frequent, life on ration cards and the arrogant behavior of Nazi functionaries were sapping the vital energy of the Berliners, who were otherwise so quick-witted and full of zest for life. Air raid shelters of all sorts were to be seen everywhere; at night all the houses and streets had to be blacked out. Berlin seemed like a ghost town.

Friends told me how they crouched night after night on their suitcases, containing their most important papers, an emergency pack by their side, ready to be summoned to the cellars by the air raid wardens at the first warning. Gasoline was rationed; private cars had almost disappeared. The Kurfurstendamm, once so pulsating, and Unter den Linden, were now given over almost entirely to the vehicles of notables, the Wehrmacht, and Party organizations.

At the Personnel Office, I found after much searching, the head of the department responsible for North Africa.

"Welcome home! Now first of all, have a good rest and acclimatize yourself. Here's your allocation to a small hotel on the Kurfurstendamm and an order to the army clothing department for you and your orderly to draw your tropical equipment. Where do you want to spend your leave? I'll have the appropriate movement orders made out."

I protested vehemently. "I know that I've been asked for by Rommel since November. But my divisional commander didn't inform me or release me. I should like to go to Africa as quickly as possible."

"I know, I know," he replied. "Rommel's HQ has already been informed that you have only just got back from Russia and need a rest. Report to me at the end of March. On 1 April, you'll be sent on your way. So, where do you want to spend the next four weeks?"

There was obviously nothing I could do about it, so I asked whether I could go for two weeks to my mother and two weeks to Paris.

The officer smiled.

"Paris is not bad," he said. "But things aren't quite so simple. I must, after all, be able to justify the journey."

"I have a lot of friends there and know Paris from before the war; in addition, the city commandant is a former commander of our 7th Panzer Division, whom I would like to see again."

"That's fine, for a commander of Rommel's former division, we can certainly manage something. You can collect your movement orders tomorrow."

So, as I really couldn't leave for Africa immediately, I made the best of the situation. When I got back to Stahnsdorf, I at once put in a request for four weeks' leave for Beck, too.

Before I went to my mother in Flensburg, which is on the border of Denmark, I wanted to see a few friends, of whom I had heard nothing since the outbreak of war. I went to Gisela von Schkopp. She was still living in Potsdam, where we used to be garrisoned. It was her marriage to "dashing Bernhard," as he was called, that we had celebrated so light-heartedly at the manor house in East Prussia. She told me that she had had no news of her husband for several weeks. He, too, was at the eastern front. We had a meal together and brewed some coffee from beans I had commandeered from a depot on the way back from Russia. But we had no time to enjoy it, for at that moment we heard the bark of the antiaircraft guns and the wail of the air raid sirens. For the first time, I now shared the experience of an Allied air raid on our homeland.

"This is what it's like now, almost every night. Come down to the cellar," Gisela called out to me.

"No, I'm not going into the cellar for anything. I feel better in the open air, where I can see what's happening; I can take cover if necessary, if bombs should fall even on Potsdam."

I went outside. It was a lurid scene. The long, white fingers of the searchlights probed the sky. In the distance, one could hear the drone of the bombers and the bark of the antiaircraft guns. The raid was on Berlin, not Potsdam, which had no strategic significance for the enemy. I fetched Gisela from the cellar.

"Come and see! What a spectacle! But how many houses will fall in ashes and rubble, how many innocent people will be buried in their cellars?"

It dawned on me how much harder things were, in fact, for the civilian population in comparison to us at the front, for they were helpless and passive in face of the air raids. I understood also, why our wounded, when they had recovered, were so keen to get back to the front as quickly as possible.

I arranged meetings with the wives of my friends, who were all on active service. I gave them some real coffee from my supply. Coffee was more precious than gold, for all supplies were reserved for the troops. Civilians had to make ersatz coffee from barley or substitutes.

As I was one of the first, apart from the wounded, who could give some account of the eastern front, I was questioned closely. To avoid disheartening my friends still further, I veiled the truth.

The fate of these women moved me greatly. Many of them had married and started a family and then their husbands had fallen. They had become widows without ever leading a proper married life. For that reason, I had resolved at the outbreak of war, not to marry until the war was over. Although there had been bonds and relationships which made me think of marriage, I still kept to my resolution.

The night life of Berlin had almost disappeared. Werner Fink, the great cabaret artist, still kept his *Katakomben* open. But his biting humor was not to Goebbel's taste. He only avoided the threat of arrest because Hermann Goering had a weakness for him and arranged for him to be called up into the Luftwaffe.

Despite all the pleasures of seeing my friends again, there was nothing to keep me long in Berlin, so I went to my mother's in Flensburg.

Although Flensburg was a naval base, it was not bombed. On 9 July 1941, my stepfather, who had been nursed devotedly by my mother for years, died of intestinal cancer. It was weeks before the news reached me in Russia. My younger brother, a keen whaler, had been called up into the navy and was sailing about in his minesweeper, a converted whaling vessel, somewhere off the coast of Norway. Only my sister, Anneliese, was still at home to give my mother a hand. At the end of 1942, she was "conscripted" to Holland and posted to the staff of the military commander of Holland. Our seven-room apartment was considered too big and several rooms were requisitioned for refugees.

My mother was very brave and concealed her anxieties about her children. She was so pleased to see me again, and with the real coffee I had brought, besides a few tins of army food.

The pleasant days in the company of my mother came to an end. I then went back to Berlin to collect my Mercedes. With movement orders, the tank full of gas and some of my stock of coffee in my baggage, I set off.

Like Berlin before, Paris, too, now proved a disappointment. Supplies had become more difficult. The city was swarming with administrative personnel. The Gestapo, too, had already spread its net over France.

At HQ, I was at once given a room in one of the many requisitioned luxury hotels on the Champs Elysées. J. B. Morel and Clément Duhour were very delighted to see me again. From British and underground sources, they knew our situation on the eastern front better than I did and gave us no great chance of winning the war. All the same, I spent some happy hours in Clément's bar, Le Chevalier. I went there only in civilian clothes. One met no Germans there. I paid a visit also to Le Vésinet, where we had been stationed after the French campaign in 1940.

I left Paris somewhat earlier than planned. I no longer felt so at home there as before. What had the war done to the city? C'est la guerre; the French had come to terms with it and were already reckoning with the fact that we would lose the war.

At the replacement section, I found that Beck had already returned. For him, too, there had been nothing to keep him at home for very long. It was now the middle of March 1942. The severe winter was over and we thought we had become sufficiently acclimatized to go to Africa.

Beck and I went to the Army clothing depot to collect our tropical equipment. What we were "fitted" out with there defies description. One could see that Germany had no longer any colonies since 1918, and so had no idea of what was suitable for the tropics. We need only have asked our allies, the Italians, but no, the commissariat had designed the tropical equipment strictly in the Prussian mode: khaki-colored, tight-fitting uniform of close material with a linen belt and high lace-up boots. In addition, a pith helmet, which, according to long-standing opinion, was essential wear in the tropics. Along with the other pieces, shirts impermeable to air, a brown tie, etc., we acknowledged receipt of our equipment and returned to the barracks to stage a fashion show.

Wounded men from North Africa, waiting there for reposting, told us how they, like many others, had carried on a lively trade with the Italians in order to exchange at least some of their equipment for the more appropriate Italian uniforms.

They told us also of the first actions in the desert, of Rommel's rapid advance, by which he had surprised the British, and of the conditions of desert warfare, such as the heat, the sandstorms, and the cold nights.

Finally, it was time to go. We were given our movement orders, and on 1 April 1942 we boarded the Berlin-Rome express coach, with a sleeping compartment of our own. To the clatter of the wheels, we both thought back to our return from Russia in snow and ice. How quickly things changed!

A night in Rome, which seemed quite unaware of the war. From the German liaison officer we learned that we were to go on to Brindisi by rail and from there, fly in a supply plane via Crete to Derna, which lay in Cyrenaica.

What would await us? We were highly expectant, almost eager for adventure.

11
North Africa, 1942: Rommel, the Desert Fox

From Brindisi, we flew to Crete, the island on which our paratroops had descended the year before, among them, Max Schmeling, the idol of German boxing. We relished the warmth of spring.

Then, on the morning of 8 April 1942, we took off for North Africa in our Junkers 52, known affectionately as "Auntie Ju." I was allowed to sit in the cockpit.

"We have to fly low over the sea," the pilot told me. "In spite of our air superiority, there are always a few Spitfires or Hurricanes buzzing about the Mediterranean. They come from Malta, which for some reason, quite beyond me, has not been attacked and occupied by now."

At that moment, I was not thinking of the war or of what might lie in store for me. I was too taken up with the idea of getting to know a new continent.

Suddenly the machine was pulled higher.

"We were lucky," laughed the pilot. "We shall soon be landing in Derna."

The outlines of Africa emerged before us: the narrow coastal strip cultivated by the Italians, with its date palms, olive groves, the whitewashed houses of the colonists, and the long, asphalt ribbon of the Via Balbia. Behind it shimmered the desert.

"That's the stony desert," the pilot informed me, "about 200 to 300 kilometers deep, before the start of the Sahara proper, with its huge white dunes. These level plains, broken frequently by rocks and hills of gravel, have been the scene of the fighting for the past year or so."

I had read books about the desert and the Bedouins, those nomadic people who, for more than 2,500 years, had wandered across the deserts of Arabia and Libya, living according to their own laws and with no form of state. Already, I thought

I could feel something of the longing that is said to strike all who once set foot in the desert. I hoped I would find time to savor this new environment and its people.✳

Leaving a huge cloud of dust behind her, Auntie Ju landed gently on the sandy runway. The midday heat took us aback even at that time of year. What a contrast to the icy snowstorms of Russia.

"I'm Lance-Corporal Manthey," a man in a faded uniform introduced himself. "Major von Luck, I presume?" His pure, Berlin accent was music in my ears and took me back to my years in Potsdam. "I've come to pick you up. They're expecting you."

Beck and I felt like greenhorns in our new, brown, tropical outfits. We stowed our gear. "Thanks for collecting us, Manthey, but what do we want with our thick coats in this heat?"

"You'll need them all right. It's bloody cold at night. I'll get you something Italian as uniform; they know what's practical down here."

The windshield of the jeep was folded flat and covered over to prevent reflections from the sun.

"I'm to take you to Rommel first, before we go to division and our battalion."

Everyone there spoke only of "Rommel," not of the General, so popular was he with his men; he was one of them.

During the journey, Manthey told us of the battles of the past year, as he had experienced them. He spoke of the "father" of the reconnaissance battalion, Lieutenant-Colonel Freiherr von Wechmar, his popularity, his successes, and of how proud von Wechmar was to have been the first to land on African soil in 1941. "Our battalion is the apple of Rommel's eye," he added proudly. It occurred to me that I wasn't going to find things easy.

We left Derna in an easterly direction. Rommel's HQ must lie somewhere among the olive groves.

"One of us must look out for aircraft. They usually come from behind." Beck took this on.

Suddenly, we turned off the road. No path, no track was to be seen. Tire marks were always removed at once—as camouflage. Suddenly, we stopped. Rommel's HQ. All the vehicles were well dispersed and camouflaged. In the middle, stood a monster of a truck.

"That's the 'Mammoth.' We took it from the British and converted it into Rommel's command car."

I spotted some eight-wheeled scout cars. This was the new, fast, reconnaissance vehicle, which we hadn't had yet in Russia.

I was rather keyed up. After all, I hadn't seen Rommel since the French campaign in 1940. An orderly officer took me to him. He had a deep suntan covering his sharp features, giving him a wonderfully healthy look. He was at the peak of his career, clearly enjoying his world-wide reputation. He was in a high mood and clearly glad to see me.

"I am reporting on transfer to the Afrika Korps, Colonel-General," I said.

"Glad you're here," he replied. "I've waited long enough. Unfortunately, I've had to send Wechmar to Germany, he became sick. You are taking over my pet battalion, let it be a credit to you."

Then, typically, he came straight to the point, "You've come at just the right moment. I'm preparing a new offensive to forestall the British. Your battalion will play an important part in it. My chief of staff, Gause, will brief you. Then report to your division. How's my old 7th Panzer Division, was it bad in Russia?"

I gave him a brief account and was dismissed. It was the start of a new phase.

General Gause, Rommel's chief of staff, with whom I would have much to do, gave me a summary of the situation. He then added, "Rommel is very disappointed at the indifference of the upper leadership. Hitler and the High Command see North Africa as a 'secondary' theater of war. For the British, however, it is decisive. In addition, he is exasperated by the slack conduct of the sea-war by the Italians. In March, for instance, instead of the requested 60,000 tons of materiel, only 18,000 arrived."

In Rommel's view, the chance of victory in Africa had already been missed. Despite heavy losses through our U-boat campaign and despite a 12,000-mile-long sea route, sufficient supplies for the British were getting through to the front.

That didn't sound very encouraging. Nevertheless, Rommel seemed to be set on turning the tables, once again, in his favor. He hoped to take Tobruk by an unexpected thrust and be able to advance far into Egypt, provided he could forestall the British.

I took my leave.

"Manthey, we've got to go to division now (it was the 21st Panzer Division) and then on to the battalion."

"Very well, Major. You seem to be well in with Rommel for him to greet you personally," said Manthey.

I told him a few things about Rommel.

"Well, yes," he said, "it certainly is unusual to bring someone here from Russia. Our commander, von Wechmar, was a great guy. His son Ruediger has also been with us now for a couple of weeks, as a young lieutenant. That's tradition. You'll be all right, Major."

Divisional HQ was well camouflaged under palms and olive trees. General von Bismarck greeted me in friendly fashion. He had been my commander in East Prussia in 1930, at the start of my military career. Like so many who were serving in the desert, he looked emaciated. The pitiless heat by day, the icy cold at night, the sandstorms, the millions of flies, and the hard battles had left their mark.

"A hearty welcome to you, Luck, we haven't seen each other for twelve years. You're entering upon a fine inheritance. Wechmar and his battalion have done great things and are Rommel's favorite unit. After your service in Russia, you've got some adapting to do. Familiarize yourself with conditions as quickly as you can. We shall probably be opening a decisive offensive before long. Best of luck!"

The general-staff officer briefed me on the situation. The task of the 3rd Panzer Reconnaissance Battalion was to reconnoiter in the far south, prevent or report any outflanking move by the enemy, and form the spearhead in any attack.

"The British, meanwhile, have strongly fortified their Gazala position," he continued. "There is a vast minefield with about 500,000 mines stretching from the coast to Bir Hacheim, a water hole south of Tobruk, originally developed by the Italians. Bir Hacheim is held by French troops under General Koenig. Behind this defensive barrier, the British are preparing to go on the offensive as soon as they can bring up enough materiel. And that, apparently, is what Rommel means to forestall.

"So we've got to be extremely vigilant, to ensure that the British don't attack around the south of Bir Hacheim deep in our flank. To look out for that and to prevent it is your job, Luck, among other things."

We left the green of Cyrenaica for the south. Manthey knew the track. Normally one traveled in the desert only by compass, the most important instrument, carried by everyone. Behind us, we raised a huge cloud of dust, which engulfed us whenever we had to brake abruptly.

The desert shimmered. In the far distance, it was often hard to tell whether the shimmering "something" was a vehicle or merely a camel's thorn bush.

Suddenly, visible only a few meters in advance, we came to a *wadi*, one of the many dried-up watercourses, in which my new battalion was lying, well dispersed.

Captain Everth, who had been leading the battalion, and a few other officers were there to greet me: correctly, but with a certain reserve, as it seemed to me. Von Wechmar, the "old man," would be hard to replace.

We went to the command car, a converted Opel "Blitz" truck. As Everth explained to me, all vehicles were fitted with special oil filters against the dust. Many of the trucks had treadless tires, so that they left no distinctive track in the sand. Besides the new eight-wheeled scout cars, I spotted some tracked motorcycles, 750cc BMWs fitted with two narrow tracks in place of the rear tires. They had been developed especially for the desert.

I asked all the officers to gather together so that I could meet them. Once again, I felt out of place in my new tropical outfit, for all the other officers wore faded uniforms, of which they were very proud, or loose Italian trousers and shirts. (Good old Manthey organized something similar for me, too, in the next few days.)

"I know your battalion from prewar days, when I was in Potsdam," I began. "There was a healthy rivalry between our two battalions as to which was the better or the more prominent. But we also took part together in a number of rallies. It is an honor for me to succeed your beloved and seasoned Commander von Wechmar. I have only my experience from the French campaign and from Russia. I have much to learn here and would be grateful for any help you can give me. I should like to go out on reconnaissance with one of your patrols as soon as possible, to familiarize myself with conditions."

I greeted each of the men individually with a handshake; the ice appeared to have been broken.

I learned that on the British side we were usually up against the Royal Dragoons, the 11th Hussars, and the dreaded Long Range Desert Group led by the legendary Lieutenant-Colonel David Stirling. The British used the better-armored but slower

Humber scout car; we the faster, nimbler eight-wheeler. Meanwhile we "understood" each other. The prevailing atmosphere was one of respect and fair play.

I got used to the Fata Morgana, the mirage, which looked so hopefully like a lake, but which on approach dissolved into nothing. I had also to get accustomed to the ferocious sandstorm which the Italians called the "Ghibli." It usually lasted for a day, but sometimes for three. One could see it coming. The sky grew dark, the fine sand penetrated every pore and made any movement, let alone any military operation, impossible.

I learned to travel by compass and at the onset of darkness to find my way back to the battalion with mutual light signals. The reconnaissance trips into the desert held a great fascination for me.

In the weeks that followed, things remained fairly quiet. Individual British patrols put out feelers to the south. But they were intercepted by our own, wide-ranging patrols. In this, our fast eight-wheelers were particularly valuable.

By the beginning of May 1942, I felt myself "integrated." I had visited and gotten to know all the companies and had been out with several patrols. I had grown accustomed to the rhythm of daily life. We used to drink half a liter of fluids in the morning, nothing during the day, then the "second half" in the evening. Supplies came up every few days, usually in convoy, to avoid being intercepted by the British.

One even got used to the cold nights. We didn't take off our tropical coats, and thick, nonregulation scarves, until well into the morning when the heat had slowly worked through them. This was the thermos principle, which we had learned by observing the Bedouins. But the millions of flies were a real torment. Only when one got deeper into the desert did their number diminish.

The heat during the day gradually became unbearable. Everyone sought out a little patch of shade. Some men really did fry eggs on the overheated armor-plating of the tanks. It was no fairy tale; I have done it myself.

The peak period for the massive downpours of rain was over, but when it did rain, the little *wadis* were filled in minutes with three-foot deep flash floods that carried all before them. I once saw how the truck, with our field kitchen, which had failed to get out of the *wadi* fast enough, was swept along some hundreds of yards by such a wave.

On our reconnaissance trips, we sometimes came upon a Bedouin family. Only the Bedouins knew where to dig in order to reach the underground, sweet-water lake. In some *wadi* or other, they would dig out a water hole, guide the water along hastily dug channels, plant their millet, and stay until they could reap the harvest. The corn would be loaded onto camels, the water hole filled in, and a day later, every trace would be gone. The Italians managed to locate a few of these water holes, construct wells and so use them as vital supply points. Bir Hacheim was one such water hole.

I once managed to make contact with a Bedouin family. They seemed to be on the point of departure. The women ran into the tents at once when we approached. No stranger was permitted to see them. The family sheik came up to us. We indicated that we were Germans.

"We didn't want to disturb you, still less, drive you away. We regret that we are causing you inconvenience here in your ancestral land. Aren't you afraid of the war, of the mines, and so on?" In a gibberish mixture of German, Italian, and a few scraps of Arabic, I tried to make myself understood.

"We always know where you are and move away whenever things get dangerous," replied the sheik. "We have many places where we can find water and cultivate our millet. We are glad to greet you as Germans. We don't like the Italians, who have occupied our country, any more than the British, who are oppressing our brothers in Egypt and the other Arab countries. One day, you will all have disappeared again and the desert will belong to us again. Allah be with you, we like you!"

It was strange that the Bedouins not only venerated Kaiser Wilhelm II and Bismarck (who were thought by many of them to be still alive), but approved of Hitler's campaign against the Jews because of their own antipathy. We avoided all talk with them about the Jewish question.

Suddenly, on 24 May 1942—I had been in Africa now for seven weeks—we were summoned to division. General von Bismarck briefed his commanders.

"Rommel has decided to attack. The British are receiving fresh supplies every day. One can predict when they, themselves, will start an offensive. Our supplies are coming in too slowly and they are coming through the harbors of Tripoli and Benghazi instead of through Derna. This means that everything has to be brought up along the one coastal road, a distance of up to 2,000 kilometers.

"The British may know about our offensive and when it will start. It seems our reports and radio communications are being intercepted. But they don't know where the main thrust will come."

Von Bismarck then gave us combat orders and stressed the fact that, by means of a vast night march, Rommel planned to move the whole of the Afrika Korps around the south of Bir Hacheim and swing it north, so as to cut off Tobruk and thrust eastward to the Egyptian border. A feint attack in the north on the Gazala position was to deceive the British.

My panzer reconnaissance battalion, acting independently on the right wing, was to advance around Bir Hacheim, giving it a wide berth, and block the coastal road east of Tobruk, as well as secure the right flank of the Afrika Korps by means of patrols.

We assembled during the night of 26/27 May 1942. It was pitch-black. Only the stars of the clear southern sky were to be seen. The exact compass bearings were known to every vehicle. These had to be strictly observed, so that the thousands of vehicles traveling through the dark night would not get mixed up.

It was a ghostly scene. Each man could just see the vehicle to his front or side. We drove at reduced speed so as to avoid raising too much dust and thus lose contact with our neighbors. We pushed on slowly through the night. After a while, we knew we were south of Bir Hacheim, though we couldn't see it.

Far to the north we saw the flashes of the Italian artillery fire. As we heard later, on the Gazala front Rommel had sent captured British tanks and trucks fitted with old aircraft engines across the terrain to simulate a tank attack. The attack on the Gazala position was mounted by Italian divisions under a German general.

The British didn't seem to have spotted us. In the early morning of 27 May my battalion, on the right wing of the 15th panzer division, turned north in the direction of Knightsbridge on the Trigh Capuzzo, a track parallel to the Via Balbia, which we soon reached. We were in the best of spirits; the surprise appeared to have worked. It was only a few kilometers to the Via Balbia, our objective. It looked as though the British in the Gazala position and in Tobruk were going to be encircled.

Toward midday on 27 May I suddenly saw a British tank column approaching from the east. They were new tanks that we had never seen before. (Only later did we discover that the tank in question was the American Grant, a tank superior to our Panzer IV.)

Suddenly some of the Grants turned south and opened fire on my advanced units from a range that was too great for our 5cc antitank guns.

I stopped the advance at once and ordered the setting up of a defensive front to the north. To coordinate the use of our defensive weapons, I left my command tank and ran to the antitank guns. Shells were bursting all around. I suddenly felt a powerful blow to my right leg and fell at once to the ground. A shell had hit an armored car and a piece of shrapnel had cut my upper right thigh. Blood welled out from my trousers. I lost consciousness for some seconds. A scout car came alongside, picked me up, and took me a few hundred yards further back to our doctor. A bad wound. I was angry and in despair. Had my time in North Africa come to an end already?

"You are lucky in your bad luck, Major," said the doctor after his examination. "You've got a hole the size of a fist in your right groin. Another few centimeters and you would have lost your manhood, but no vein or bones or nerves have been hit. Which is just as well, as I would never have been able to apply a tourniquet on the spot. There's no question, you must go to the nearest field dressing station for treatment."

That was easier said than done, for in the meantime the Afrika Korps had obviously encircled the British in the Gazala position, but it had not taken Tobruk. On the contrary, we ourselves were now encircled. To get out of the envelopment from the east was hardly to be thought of. With the help of morphine injections I managed to resume command in my jeep, free to some extent from pain.

"Captain Everth, in case I can do no more, you will take command. I'm trying to establish radio contact with Rommel, to hear how things stand and what orders are being given."

Thank goodness the connection with Rommel went through. The situation was extremely dangerous. At Knightsbridge, southwest of Tobruk, the attack by the Afrika Korps had petered out under fire from the British artillery and the relays of attack by the royal Air Force. So too had the frontal attack by the Italians in the north.

I managed to set up a defensive front to the east. Luckily for us, the British attack from the east was directed more against the two panzer divisions of the Afrika Korps. The British assumed that Rommel would try to break out to the east. That was the basis of their dispositions in the days that followed. Rommel now made one of his rash decisions: He ordered the Afrika Korps to escape from the encirclement, not to the east, but to the west, through the mine fields of the Gazala position. My orders were to guard against a breakthrough by the British from the east and prevent a possible outflanking movement in the south.

For five days I sat in my jeep—still under morphine—until in the morning of 1 June Rommel succeeded with the help of the army engineers in clearing passages through the mine field and in releasing the whole of the Afrika Korps from its encirclement, although many vehicles had to be abandoned for lack of fuel. We were the last to disengage from the enemy and reassemble behind the Italian lines.

My wound did not look good.

"I can no longer take responsibility," said our doctor. "You must now go to Derna as quickly as possible, to our casualty clearing station."

I realized that I couldn't go on as I was, but hoped that in Derna they would soon get me fit for duty again. With heavy heart I handed over command to Everth and, close to tears with anger and disappointment, let myself be driven to Derna by good old Manthey and my faithful Beck. An examination by the Germans revealed to my dismay that the wound was not only severe but that during the five days in the jeep, and from the dust of a Ghibli storm, it had become infected.

"You must go to Germany at once, an Italian hospital ship is in harbor. It will take you to Europe tomorrow." That was the doctor's lapidary verdict. Deeply disappointed, I was carried on to the ship the next day. Adieu, Africa, but not for long.

The ship was a large liner, painted white and identified as a hospital ship by a large red cross. I heard later that the ship had been sunk on its way back to Africa, supposedly because it had taken on war materiel. I was put in a little cabin, and there I raged at my fate. The following morning we cast off for Sicily.

As my wound was severe, I was one of the first to be taken to the operating theater, which was run by an Italian surgeon and his team, who, as a nurse told me in a whisper, came from one of the best Italian clinics. The bandages were taken off, the pain grew worse, the more so as I had had no morphine since the day before. "We can't have you becoming addicted," my doctor had said. "The wound is not serious, thank goodness. We'll clean it up a bit first and go on from there."

It was then decided to perform a small operation and I was told that the limited anesthetics were needed for very severe cases. "Clench your teeth, please," I was instructed, short and sharp. While two sisters held me tight, the doctor, who seemed to me like a butcher, began to cut away at my wound. I cried out like an animal and thought I would faint with pain. Then I heard a voice.

"Please stop a moment." Beside me stood General von Vaerst, commander of the 15th Panzer Division. "What's up with you, Luck, why are you shouting so?" I explained the situation to him and asked him to insist on an anesthetic. At his intervention the doctors agreed, so that the rest of the procedure was bearable.

General von Vaerst told me that he too had been wounded not far from me. General Gause and Colonel Westphal of Rommel's staff had also been hit. The last he heard from Rommel was that the Afrika Korps, after its successful breakthrough to the west, was being marshalled anew to continue the offensive.

After my wound had been treated, I sat with von Vaerst during the short crossing to the mainland. We discussed Rommel's chances of breaking through into Egypt despite inadequate supplies. In Naples I was examined again and pronounced fit to travel.

Next morning an Italian hospital train bore me north. Although I couldn't stand, I still enjoyed the journey across the north Italian plain and over the Alps. The sun shone, the countryside looked peaceful, and there was nothing to show that Italy too was at war. Our treatment by the accompanying doctor and nurses was exemplary. After the hardships and battles in the desert, I was overtaken by a pleasant feeling of tranquility.

At the Austrian border we were transferred to a German hospital coach, which was coupled to an ordinary train, and we finally ended up in Esslingen, a small industrial town near Stuttgart. There were now only three of us, including a young reserve officer from my own battalion. The municipal infirmary, lying romantically in the hills on the outskirts of the town, had been declared a military hospital. Until we arrived it had contained wounded from the eastern front only.

So far Esslingen had been largely spared by the war, apart from the fact that there too the inhabitants could subsist only by buying food stamps. In addition, there was nothing to be had anymore. It was a good thing I had been able to provide myself with enough coffee and cigarettes before leaving North Africa, for these were more in demand than gold.

I now made every effort to get back on my feet as quickly as possible. After a few weeks I was able to walk on crutches and then, cautiously, with a stick. My mother and sister came to see me from Flensburg. It was an onerous journey right through Germany, since the air raids were continually disrupting rail junctions or causing long delays. My uncle came also, from Stuttgart, and we enjoyed the warm sun on the terrace, with real coffee and substitute cakes.

North Africa seemed far away. All the same, I was glued to the radio every day to hear news from the theater of war. We had been in the hospital just two weeks when the special announcement came that Rommel had taken Tobruk, on 21 June 1942, and that South African General Klopper had surrendered the fortress. Nearly 30,000 prisoners had been captured and much war materiel had fallen into German hands, including considerable supplies of fuel, which the Germans needed so urgently. This was followed by the announcement that Rommel had immediately turned east and crossed the Egyptian border, on 23 June. Rommel, at the age of fifty, was made a field marshal. He commented to his wife that he wished Hitler had given him another division instead.

We three "Africans" were naturally the cocks of the walk. When things looked bad on the Russian front, with the encirclement at Stalingrad beginning to loom, Rommel's exploits in North Africa at last offered people a ray of hope again. Nevertheless they sensed very well that the war would last a long time yet and result in heavy losses. So Hitler and his Propaganda Minister Goebbels didn't fail to put an undue value on Rommel's exploits, even though they treated our theater of war in the desert as of only secondary importance.

After about three weeks I had recovered sufficiently to be able to move about quite well with my stick. Bad Kissingen, my last garrison before the war, was not all that far away. I was able to persuade the medical superintendent to transfer me there until my recovery was complete. I wanted to recuperate in the neighborhood of my old friends and in the atmosphere of the spa. So one Sunday morning I was taken by ambulance to a clinic that had been requisitioned for convalescent frontline soldiers.

As it was Sunday, only one nurse was on duty. She put me in a nice room with a view of the park.

"I'll bring you some supper right away. I hope you'll be comfortable with us. The medical superintendent will see you in the morning." With these words she left me to my fate.

There was no telephone in the room. How was I to make contact with my friends? The clinic could not keep me. I found a broomstick and hobbled secretly out of the house to the Huber Bar, only a few hundred yards away.

When I entered the bar in my faded tropical uniform—it was still early in the evening and only a few customers were sitting about—Huber looked dumbfounded.

"No, it can't be! Our old friend Luck is here. My God, where have you sprung from? You've been wounded. Make room for our Major there! Come to the table of honor." Sepp Huber and his wife could hardly regain their composure, they were so delighted.

"Here's my last bottle of whiskey, which I've kept all these years for a special occasion. We'll crack it now." The bar slowly filled and before long I was the center of a large circle and had to give an account of myself. Everything seemed unreal to me. There I sat as in the last year before the war, as though nothing had happened.

Toward midnight Huber closed the bar. Only a few customers were left. Then I suddenly realized with a shock that I didn't have a key to the clinic. What was to be done? "Absence without leave," "endangering recovery," etc., passed through my mind. "You can stay with us, Major," said Huber. "As an African veteran you'll have no problems here in Kissingen."

Then someone knocked on the door.

"Let me in, please," came a peremptory voice from outside. It was one of the spa doctors whom I used to know well and with whom I had spent many an evening at Huber's.

"I heard you were in Kissingen. Things soon get around here. I came over right away and am very glad to see that you're more or less all right. How long have you been here? What hospital are you in?"

"I'm glad to see you too. Let's drink to that." I gave him the name of my clinic and pointing to my broomstick told him how I had got to Huber's. "But I haven't got a key. That's the problem that's bothering me."

My doctor friend slapped his thigh and burst into laughter. "My dear friend, I'm the doctor in charge of the clinic." I must have turned pale, for he went on, "That's all right, I've got my key on me. I'll take you there and tomorrow I'll see if I can get you a key of your own."

Things could not have turned out better.

July went by. I was well on the way to recovery. It was thought that I would be passed as completely fit for duty by the end of August or the beginning of September.

Over the weeks, equipped now with a proper cane instead of the broom handle, I visited all my old friends. To my astonishment the spa orchestra still played every day in the park. A peaceful world, if it were not for the daily bulletins from the eastern front and the reports of air raids on our cities. I was determined to make the most of my enforced leisure and suppress the unpleasant things, as all frontline soldiers do whenever they have the chance.

In the meantime news came over the radio that Rommel had penetrated far into Egypt and had come to a halt near El Alamein, about 100 kilometers west of Alexandria. From telephone conversations with our Replacement Section near Berlin and from what was said by men who had come back from Africa, I learned that shortage of supplies through logistical failure was the main cause. I could well imagine how angry Rommel would have been at so little understanding at the Fuehrer's HQ and so little support from the Italians.

During my time in Kissingen I often went to my old barracks, where I met many wounded men from my old Reconnaissance Battalion 37, which had been in action on the eastern front. A number of my people had fallen and left behind family and friends in Kissingen. The battles in the winter of 1941–42 and the rearguard actions had left the men washed out. No one believed anymore in a quick finish. I was naturally envied for my posting to North Africa. Many ordinary soldiers asked me to give their regards to Rommel.

Even the mayor and most of the functionaries, who were all members of Hitler's Party, now saw things in a more sober light and wondered whether our march into Russia had not been a mistake. The propaganda tirades that Goebbels delivered regularly over the radio were insufferable. The talk was always of "subhumans," the "Lebensraum" ("living space") that was vital for Germany, and of "faith in our beloved Fuehrer." No one dared to express his doubts openly; the network of informers was too large and too dangerous.

At the beginning of September 1942 I was pronounced "fit for limited combat duty." I went to my mother's for a week and then to the replacement section near Berlin. There I met a number of officers and NCOs who had been severely wounded and were now employed as instructors for the replacements. I even found my faithful Mercedes standing in the garage, repaired and spick-and-span. I used it a few times to go to Berlin to visit friends.

Berlin was suffering most from the air raids and from the stringency of the food situation. The faces of the Berliners, who were once so cheerful and quick-witted, had grown gray. With their sense of reality they had no illusions.

There was nothing more to keep me in Germany. I wanted to rejoin my unit. At the Personnel Office I finally received my movement orders in the middle of September. I was to report to the German liaison office in Rome and then fly to Tobruk via Sicily.

Over the Alps to Rome I duly went, and from there straight on to Sicily. This time I flew in a vast Blohm and Voss flying boat, which was used for transporting materiel. Again we flew low over the water; the British air bases on the island of Malta were not far away. It was fascinating to lift off from the sea and land on the water, leaving a huge cloud of spray behind us. From the air I saw the town of Tobruk and its harbor, which had been hotly contested and badly damaged. Then we were down, alighting by a sunken British freighter.

Moments later I was standing on the dock, breathing in the hot desert air that was so familiar to me. Now in September it was even hotter by day than in the weeks when I was wounded. A car took me with my aluminum trunk to Rommel's HQ, which lay somewhere in the desert near Mersa Matrui.

"We've had some hard but successful battles, Major," the driver told me. "Now there's a lull on the Alamein front. Who will be the first to start things up again?"

I had no idea where my battalion lay; without doubt deep in the desert.

And then I was with Rommel. I reported my return fit for duty and congratulated him above all on his being made a field marshal and on his successful actions.

"I'm glad you're here again," Rommel told me. "Captain Everth has stood in for you very well and achieved great distinction with the battalion. For that I was able to present him with the Knight's Cross. Unfortunately he too has caught one of these insidious tropical diseases. He's only waiting for your return to be posted back home. It's essential for me to have treatment too. You've come just in time to say good-bye to me. I'll be back as soon as I can. Best of luck and have yourself briefed by Gause (chief of staff)." I took my leave and went to General Gause for briefing.

"It's good that you're here, Luck. We were beginning to think you might not be able to come back."

Gause too looked tired and emaciated. It had been particularly hard for him to make the right decisions when Rommel was "leading from the front" and out of reach, often for days on end. He put me briefly in the picture, especially about the thrust into Egypt, which for lack of fuel and supplies had come to a halt at Alamein—only 100 kilometers from Alexandria. He told me of Rommel's deep disappointment over the slack conduct of the war by the High Command of the Wehrmacht, meaning Hitler, and over the halfhearted efforts of the Italians to ensure adequate supplies.

"The Field Marshal struck me just now as disappointed and depressed," I interjected. "Is that to do with his health or also with what was probably the last, unsuccessful attack on Cairo at the end of August? I wasn't able to hear much about that in Germany."

"With both," replied Gause. "His state of health really is a cause for concern. Rommel needs rest and quiet. But you know what he's like. He won't leave his theater of war, especially not in the decisive phase that's coming. Then, to add to it, came the profound disappointment over the offensive at the end of August." (Our rank and file, with their gallows humor, called it the "six-day race," after the popular six-day bicycle race in the Berlin stadium.)

"We knew that Monty (General Bernard Montgomery) was preparing a decisive offensive," Gause continued, "but wouldn't start it until he had received all the materiel he needed for complete success. Rommel hoped to forestall him with an offensive of his own and be able to turn the tables on him yet again. The last chance was at the end of August, at full moon. Marshal Cavallero had promised him that several tankers would arrive before then, and Kesselring had promised 500 tons of fuel a day by airlift.

"On 31 August, the fuel was still not there; now Rommel *had* to start. Severe sandstorms prevented the superior RAF from being used (our own Messerschmidt fighters stood on the airfields with no fuel). On 2 September, a mere 900 tons of fuel arrived out of the 5,000 announced; 2,600 tons had been sunk, 1,500 were still in Italy.

"Next morning the storm had subsided. Now—almost in flyover formation—the RAF launched wave after wave against the Afrika Korps, which was thrusting north behind the Alamein position. A British division, which up to then had not been spotted, had occupied a range of hills with a front to the south. The two, together, brought the attack to a standstill.

"Because of the missing supplies and the almost 100 percent air superiority, the attack came to nothing. The reconnaissance group, which included your own battalion, had been sent east at the very beginning, in order to march at once on Cairo, about 100 kilometers further east, as soon as the Afrika Korps had reached the coast behind the British. The group was hit particularly badly by the air attacks and suffered heavy losses.

"In the night of 2 to 3 September, Rommel decided with a heavy heart, to break off the attack and withdraw from the rear of the British position. On this retreat, Brigadier Clifton of the New Zealand Division was taken prisoner and brought to Rommel. His fate was remarkable.

"Whenever possible," Gause went on, "Rommel likes to talk to prominent opponents. So, too, with Clifton, to whom he first expressed his admiration for the fight his division had put up. He did complain, however, about the atrocities that had been carried out on German prisoners. 'That's the Maoris,' Clifton replied, 'original inhabitants of New Zealand, who fight as ferociously as the Sikhs from India. I deplore it.' Clifton had fought against us in 1940 in France and said now that they were sure of victory in the end. Inwardly, Rommel, too, was already convinced of this. Shortly after, Clifton escaped through a lavatory and was picked up alone in the desert with only a water-bottle in his hand. Rommel couldn't meet his request to be sent into German captivity and not to the Italians. Rommel regretted that all prisoners in North Africa, at Mussolini's wish, had to be handed over to the Italians."

(It became known later that Clifton, after making eight vain attempts to escape, managed to get to Switzerland on the ninth—despite being wounded.)

"During his conversation with Clifton, Rommel mentioned that the Allies, too, would have to get used to the idea that the danger in the future would come from the east, from Russia.

"So, Luck, now you know why Rommel is so disappointed."

(Weeks after Rommel's unsuccessful offensive, the rumor was still going around that an Italian general had betrayed Rommel's plan to the British. Admittedly, this had never been confirmed, but in 1985 Steve Ambrose introduced me to Mrs. Jean Howard at a lunch with General Sir Nigel Poett of the British 6th Airborne Division at the Army-Navy Club in London. Jean greeted me with enthusiasm.

"Hans von Luck, what a pleasure to meet you personally. I know all about you and your activities in North Africa. I was one of the team at Bletchley Park [then under the name of Jean Allington, Hut 3 BP] that managed to break the German code, in what we called the Ultra operation. We intercepted all radio messages on the German side, so that our command in London, and in Africa, had fairly complete information about German plans. I knew you from 1942, when you first arrived in North Africa. I'm pleased to meet the Major of those days personally."

Only then did I realize why the British had always been so well informed about our actions and how convoys with supplies, or the activity of our Luftwaffe, could have been disrupted so accurately. Ultra was a godsend to the British, a catastrophe for us.)

"Rommel intends to see Hitler in Germany," Gause then went on, "and make it clear to him, quite bluntly, that without adequate supplies, the war in North Africa cannot be won.

"In addition, we know from our sources that Churchill was in Cairo at the beginning of August and that on the twelfth, Montgomery took over command of the Eighth Army. A new wind seems to be blowing among our opponents. They will, undoubtedly, be working on an offensive, which this time could be decisive.

"For the moment, however, the British have consolidated their Alamein position firmly with over 800,000 mines, and with replenished divisions and strong tank divisions behind them.

"Now for you: your battalion has once again hit the jackpot. It's lying in the Siwa Oasis, about 300 kilometers south of Mersa Matruh in the Qattara Depression. I was down there yesterday with Rommel and General Fritz Bayerlein. Truly a paradise, which is quite out of keeping with our battlefield here in the desert. But we must maintain a presence down there. The danger of being outflanked to the south of the Alamein position is too great.

"I don't begrudge you this pleasant assignment, after the tough actions and heavy losses of the past months.

"You will have to fly there in a JU 87 (a dive bomber). The runway is too short for other machines and the distance too great for the Fieseler Stork." (The Stuka crews vied with each other for these flights.)

"You will come directly under me, so for the time being, you are detached from the units of the 21st Panzer Division. Captain Everth will brief you in detail before he has to go home, unfortunately also on health grounds.

"I wish you all the best. Enjoy your time down there, before the balloon goes up again."

With that, I was dismissed and taken at once to the airfield of the JU 87. The most interesting part of my time in Africa was about to begin.

I was taken to Captain Hamester, a squadron leader.

"I have the good fortune to be permitted to fly you to Siwa. We use these flights to try out our missions deep into the desert and to drop bombs or ward off British fighters, if we happen to come across British units. That's why we go in a flight of three machines. I'm sure you've heard of our nosedives and our demoralizing sirens. As a landlubber you should find it interesting."

"I've heard from my friends," I replied, "who flew Rommel to Siwa only yesterday, how lovely this oasis is and that for them, the highlight was to swim in Cleopatra's Bath."

"We'll be flying down tomorrow morning," Hamester went on. "You'll have to fly as rear gunner. We only have a two-man crew. You'll know the 2cm cannon, of course, from your scout cars."

On 23 September 1942, Rommel flew to Germany to undergo treatment and to meet Hitler. On the same day, I boarded Captain Hamester's JU 87. I squeezed myself into the rear seat, with my tropical chest stowed vertically between the pilot and me. I donned headphones and microphone.

The flight lasted about an hour. We flew at a height of about 3,000 feet. The stony desert, with its little outcrops of rock and camel's thorn bushes, lay peacefully below us. If I turned round, I could see the sandy desert with its high dunes lying in the distance like a vast trough of the sea. Even camel paths were discernible and the tracks of our reconnaissance vehicles winding through the desert. Or were they the tracks of the Royal Dragoons or the Long Range Desert Group?

There, ahead, was the sharp drop to the Qattara Depression. In front, to the left, I could see the oasis, with only a single winding track leading down to it. ("That would be easy to block," passed through my mind.)

We landed and were directed to a group of palms, where the three machines found cover.

"Welcome to paradise!" I was greeted by Captain Everth, newly decorated with the Knight's Cross. "We're glad to see you back again, fully restored. One of those stupid tropical diseases has got me too, so I've got to go back to Germany sooner or later."

My battalion was quartered in tents, well dispersed under palms. "We've deliberately kept ourselves somewhat apart from the Arabs, to avoid disturbing the daily life of these proud sons of the desert," Everth told me. "May I suggest that we first do a tour of the oasis? In the course of it, I can tell you something about this lovely little spot and about our own task." I agreed at once.

I felt as though I were in a fairy tale from the *Thousand and One Nights:* blue skies above me, hot sun, and endless groves of palms with ripening dates. Little water courses ran through the oasis. In the south, right by the last palms, the huge white dunes heaved up like a sea of waves. In the north, the 150-foot high escarpment, which dropped vertically. In the east, the Qattara Depression, a dried-up salt lake, which stretched 300 kilometers to the east, to a point about 100 kilometers southeast of Alamein.

"The Qattara Depression is impassable," explained Everth. "Only in the dry season is there a little track which can be used by light vehicles. We have to watch out there, in case Tommy tries to surprise us with his Long Range Desert Group.

We are lying about 300 kilometers south of Mersa Matruh. Only 50 to 70 kilometers of the Alamein line are manned. In between, is No Man's Land, hence, an open field of operations for both sides."

I had already heard of Siwa at school, of its palace and Cleopatra's Bath (51 to 30 B.C.). In former times, an "Oracle" was said to be in Siwa, and visited, besides others, by Alexander the Great. Siwa, originally called Ammonion, came under Egyptian rule in 1820. This was now represented by three officials: the doctor, the commissioner, and the postmaster.

The inhabitants, numbering about 5,000, were originally Bedouins who became settled there, and since that time, have no longer mixed with other tribes. Despite inbreeding, they are healthy. Because of this, the Senussi, on their flight from the Italians out of Libya, were allowed to stay in Siwa only for a short while and then had to move on further east. Every extended family had a sheik at its head, the greatest family, a chief sheik, a *primus inter pares*.

While the Egyptian doctor had his raison d'être, the commissioner was less popular, as he was responsible for tax collecting. The postmaster was completely useless, for no one there could read or write. So he found himself a lucrative sideline, as a trader. He had his moment of glory when Rommel visited Siwa a few days earlier and the sheiks presented him with an envelope bearing a set of Siwa stamps, duly cancelled, a philatelic rarity.

We came to Cleopatra's Bath, in which the crews of the Stukas were amusing themselves. I found myself before a well with a diameter of about 30 feet. The water was so clear that one could see the bottom some 20 feet below. There, several carbonated springs bubbled forth. The water had a constant temperature of 18°C and promised to be wonderfully refreshing. Everth invited me to come with him that evening: "We had to draw up a timetable so that all the men could enjoy this treat."

Not far away stood Cleopatra's former palace, where she is supposed to have spent some time every year in relaxation. One could still see the remains of the great blocks of stone; how they got there no one knows. The water from Cleopatra's well, and from some smaller wells in the neighborhood, was led by an ingenious system into the gardens of the sheiks, which were thus kept watered throughout the year.

"Now we'll go into the 'town' as we call it. I must first introduce you, by Arab custom, to the chief sheik, who will bid you welcome as a guest," Everth explained.

On arriving in the "town," we went through a gate in the high wall of the garden of the chief sheik. The sight took my breath away. Here the greenery and the flowers made one forget one was in the desert. Innumerable little ducts ran through the luxuriant garden. Gorgeous vines and bougainvillaeas climbed up the mud walls. Between exotic plants were little beds a yard square, so-called Chinese beds, in which corn and vegetables were planted, to produce tenfold yields. In between stood citrus, pomegranate, and olive trees. And towering over all, were the date palms.

At the end of the garden stood the low, whitewashed house of the chief sheik, who greeted us with a deep bow. We returned his "salaam" and asked to be received by him. He led us into the inner courtyard, which was spread with valuable carpets. By Arab custom, no women were to be seen. We squatted, cross-legged, on the carpets, which very soon gave me cramps in the calves, as I was not used to this way of sitting. The sons offered us cooled fruit juices, for alcohol was strictly forbidden. Besides, we were still in Ramadan, the month of fasting, in which nothing was eaten during the day.

"Welcome to you, Germans," the chief sheik greeted us. "Having had the great honor, a few days ago, of a visit from your famous Marshal Rommel, I now bid you welcome, Major, as the new commander of our oasis. You know that we admire you Germans and wish you success in this war. I have asked Rommel to greet the great sheik, Bismarck, highly honored by us (thank goodness he didn't mention Hitler). Unfortunately, the war cuts us off from Cairo and Alexandria. We can't sell our produce or buy necessities, so that tea, our main drink, has gradually run out."

The chief sheik was an imposing figure, tall, with a dark face and fine-cut features. A white beard gave him a dignified appearance. His burnoose was of the finest white material.

"When we celebrate the end of Ramadan in a few week's time," he said, dismissing us, "you must be our guest."

We drove to the airfield to say good-bye to the Stuka crews, who disappeared to the north in a great arc and with a waggle of wings, to return again to their hard service on the Alamein front.

Everth and I went back to the command post, to the cleverly outfitted Opel Blitz, which was comparable to a modern motor caravan. Everth then gave me a detailed account of the battalion's tasks and equipment.

"Supplies for the battalion seldom come by land, since, for that, convoys have to be assembled to guard against British patrols or raiding parties. Supplies of things like food, fuel, and ammunition, are usually dropped by Stukas or Heinkels, which at the same time make use of these flights for reconnaissance. Since we can buy cereals here in the oasis, Rommel has given us a bakery platoon, which bakes our bread and also fresh rolls sometimes on Sundays.

"A few days ago, we were sent an Italian Ghibli, comparable to our Fieseler Stork, with a nice pilot and the necessary spare parts. This aircraft saves us costly patrolling trips either to the north, out of the Qattara Depression, or in the direction of the Giarabub oasis in Libya, the only tracks leading out of the oasis."

I now had a rough idea of what was to be done and resolved to make the most of what would probably be our short time in Siwa. Next morning, my dip in Cleopatra's Bath was wonderful; and on a trip through the oasis, Everth told me more of its special features.

"A few decades ago, King Faid decided to make the unique beauty of the oasis accessible to tourists and to organize appropriate safaris. At that time, Siwa was so infested by millions of mosquitoes of a dangerous variety, that no one could visit the oasis without at once coming down with malaria. By order of King Faid, scientists developed an insecticide, which was put in the water channels and so prevented them from breeding. Within a few years, the mosquitoes were eradicated."

Meanwhile, the day was drawing to a close and we were being offered a natural spectacle: the setting sun colored the steep slope of the Qattara Depression blood-red and plunged the whole oasis into a blue-green light. The sight was overwhelming.

Next day, I made my first round-flight in the Ghibli. I then realized the extent of the oasis, saw the vast, untouched dunes beneath me, in the north, the escarpment, and in the east, the barely marked track through the dried-up salt lake, which was no longer frequented by the camel caravans.

In the course of the next two weeks—we had, as usual, no contact with the enemy—some of our seasoned officers left us: Captain Everth flew to Germany, sick, and would not be coming back; von Fallois, my predecessor's adjutant, was replaced. Captain Kiehl had already been leading Rommel's "battle group" successfully for some time.

Except for a few of the old hands, who remained to the end, there were new company commanders, platoon leaders, and orderly officers. Among them was Lieutenant Ruediger von Wechmar, my predecessor's son, today the German ambassador in London. Captain Meyer became a new company commander; until 1983, he was the German ambassador in Luxembourg. Lieutenant von Mutius was new. Later he was to bring off an adventurous escape from Tunisia. He is living today in Brazil. As reserve officer, we received Lieutenant Wenzel Luedecke, who was cheerful and always ready for some fun; up to then, he had been an assistant director with UFA film producers, and today, he is the proprietor of an audio-synchronizing firm in Berlin. I would have much to thank him for later.

Left to me of the old stock, were Captain Bangemann and—as my ever calm and reliable adjutant—First-Lieutenant Bernhardt. We managed this drastic change in the corps of officers without difficulty, thanks to the marvellous team spirit and tolerance characteristic of this unusual battalion and all its men.

After about a week, General Stumme announced that he would be visiting us. He, too, wished to "satisfy" himself about our mission, but no doubt wished also to see something of the paradise of Siwa. Accompanied by my corps of officers I greeted Stumme on the runway. While the aircrews were taken to Cleopatra's Bath, we went through the usual program for visitors: trip around the oasis to the Queen's Bath and former palace, followed by a call on the chief sheik and the postmaster.

We began to feel like tour guides—and this in a theater of war where the final decision was imminent. But that is the way of war. In between tough engagements and murderous battles, there is time for relaxation, for regeneration. And all this in the knowledge that it could be one's last day.

During the discussion of the situation that followed, Stumme left us in no doubt that the decisive battle was imminent. "According to our information, the British are receiving large quantities of war materiel, which is being landed at Suez and then brought up to the front at once. Montgomery is behaving like all British commanders: if by means of materiel men can be spared, then that is what is done.

"We, unfortunately, are not in that happy position. The supplies that are reaching us don't cover, by a long way, the minimum we need. My greatest worry is the almost complete air superiority of the British, which in the desert, without cover, represents a mortal danger. We have far too few fighters, and those few are for the most part still grounded without fuel.

"I have just asked Rommel, once again, to bring all his influence to bear on Hitler and Goering to see that we are provided, as quickly as possible, with fuel, more tanks, 88mm guns, and fighter aircraft.

"Your task in the coming British offensive," Stumme concluded, "will be to guard our open southern flank and prevent any attempt to circumvent us."

12

The Retreat from El Alamein

All was still quiet at the front—it was now October 1942—and especially in our oasis. The daily flights of the Ghibli revealed nothing out of the ordinary in our sector.

Our days in the singularly beautiful oasis of Siwa were undoubtedly numbered. The reports of British preparations for an offensive were accumulating. I worked out a plan to enable the rear sections, including the bakery platoon, to march in the direction of the coast without being threatened by the British advance.

In addition, I discussed with the company commanders the two possible ways in which we might go into action: either via the winding road to the north, or to the west via the Giarabub oasis, veering north from there. I was well stocked with fuel and ammunition. All the water canisters were filled. We had to figure that, after the coming offensive, the confusion would be so great that in the early days the delivery of supplies in the depths of the desert was not something we could count on.

In the middle of October, according to our information, the British had 1,000 tanks at their disposal, including 400 of the new, superior, American-made Shermans, against which we could put up just 200. Opposing the 195,000 British, including their allies, who were all fully motorized, we had on our side 24,000 men. In the middle of October, we received only 44 percent of the minimum supplies for the next eleven days. Our tanks were furnished with fuel for a mere 300 kilometers. In addition, the air superiority of our opponents was complete. Our few fighters, which likewise suffered from lack of fuel, could not compete.

On 23 October, the expected inferno broke forth with 1,000 guns and sustained attacks by the RAF. Montgomery opened concentrated fire on our positions and, in doing so, blasted a hole in our mine fields.

My battalion was put on the alert.

"Counterattack by 15th Panzer Division planned for tomorrow," Gause informed us. "You will hold yourself ready for counterattack or to protect southern flank." The orders came in a radio message from Gause (which was intercepted by Ultra at Bletchley Park. This was told to me in 1985 by Jean Howard.) The fact that all our actions were known at once to the British, represented for us a further catastrophe.

Next day, we received more alarming news: General Stumme, on a visit to the front, had come under a sudden concentration of fire and died, presumably of a heart attack. Rommel had broken off his treatment at once and returned to Derna— still not well—on 25 October. That put fresh heart into our people.

Our counterattack was ineffective. Under the hail of bombs and the rockets used for the first time by the British fighters, and in face also of a defensive line of tanks, it broke down. But the Afrika Korps and the Italian divisions offered fierce resistance to the British offensive. Up to 29 October, Monty was unable to force a break-through, although our positions were exposed ceaselessly to the attacks of the RAF and heavy artillery fire. The bombers and fighters came in flyover formation, as though it were peacetime, even by night, when the whole battlefield was lit by flares.

Monty regrouped. During the night of 1 to 2 November 1942, a second offensive began. With 400 tanks and strong artillery and air support, he launched an attack on a narrow sector of the northern front against an unfortunate, inferior Italian division and forced a breakthrough. The division was wiped out after the majority of the Italians had been wounded or killed.

Rommel pulled out the 21st Panzer Division, which had been stationed in the south, and threw it against the point of breakthrough. At the same time, I received orders to fill the gap and support the XX Italian Corps, which was left on its own.

That same day, 2 November, in accordance with our prearranged plan, I ordered the supply sections, including the bakery platoon, to go to our supply center in Cyrenaica. To maintain vital contact for our supplies, I gave them a radio armored car.

Before dawn—on 3 November—we left the Siwa oasis. We arrived in the area of the XX Italian Corps, which, for the moment, had not yet come under strong attack, except from the RAF.

I was able, thank goodness, to keep in constant touch with Rommel's HQ. I was informed that Rommel would shortly be giving the order to retreat, since our front, which had been broken through at several points, could no longer hold out against the superior enemy and the constant air attacks. By giving up Cyrenaica, Rommel planned to reach Tripolitania and set up a line of defense there. In so doing, it seemed to him important to bring to safety, over a distance of nearly 2,000 kilometers, as many units as possible, especially the battered, nonmotorized Italian infantry divisions.

In the midst of these considerations, a briefly worded order from the Fuehrer reached Rommel at midday to the effect that there was no other choice for our soldiers but victory or death. With that, any retreat was forbidden by the highest authority.

As he told me a few weeks after the event, Rommel wavered between doing his duty of absolute obedience to the oath he had taken, and the reality at the front, with the threatening destruction that implied of the whole Africa Army. That same afternoon of 3 November, he decided to pass on to his commanders the Fuehrer's order to hold fast; the men, however, were not to be informed. Rommel was sorely frustrated, but for the present, he obeyed.

On the morning of 4 November, after strong artillery preparation, the British launched an attack against the Afrika Korps. By using 200 tanks, including many of the superior Shermans, and against bitter resistance from the 20 tanks left to us, deep breaches were made. But the Afrika Korps still held out and inflicted considerable losses on the enemy, mainly with our 88s. While the enemy could replace his losses immediately, we lacked any replacements of tanks, heavy weapons, and ammunition.

Then, however, toward ten o'clock, after renewed heavy artillery fire and relays of attack by the RAF, the British moved against the front of the XX Italian Corps, which, with its poorly equipped defensive weapons, stood no chance of stopping the attack. I tried to give the Italians as much help as possible, but with my armored reconnaissance vehicles and their equally weak antitank guns, any help I could offer was more moral than effective.

It was heart-rending to have to witness how the Ariete Division (our most loyal allies) and the remains of the Trieste and Littorio Divisions, fought with death-defying courage; how their tanks (the "sardine tins" so often mocked by us) were shot up and left burning on the battlefield. Although I was engaged in actions myself, I kept in contact with the XX Italian Corps until it was almost surrounded.

At about 1530 hours, the commander of the Ariete Division sent his last radio message to Rommel: "We are encircled, the Ariete tanks still in action." By evening, the XX Italian Corps had been destroyed. We lost good, brave friends, from whom we demanded more than they were in a position to give.

The British now stormed through a breach 20 kilometers wide and threatened a southern outflanking of the Afrika Korps, which was fighting desperately in the north. At that, Rommel decided to begin an immediate retreat and thus ignore Hitler's order. Of the 750 or so tanks, which the Africa Army had at its disposal before the British offensive, only 12 were still available to us.

I received orders to disengage from the enemy and transfer, in the first place, to the area between Siwa and the Giarabub oasis, which was already in Libyan territory west of Siwa. My task was to reconnoiter in every direction and report, or prevent, any outflanking attempt south of the movement of retreat.

In the morning of 5 November, I reached an area north of the Siwa and Giarabub oases without coming into contact with the enemy. Our patrols were positioned in a wide fan, with observation to the east, the southeast, and the south. Sandstorms and heavy downpours of rain set in, making many tracks almost impassable for the elements of the Africa Army that were now falling back.

Next day, we had our first contact with the enemy, with British patrols that had been sent out, it seemed, to explore the possibility of a southern outflanking; but they proved easy to repulse.

On 7 November, in the depths of the desert, a patrol putting out a long feeler to the east, discovered General Ramcke, the commander of the paratroop division, which had been in action on the right wing south of Alamein. General Ramcke was brought to us in a scout car. He looked emaciated and asked to be taken, at once, to Rommel. His paratroops—an elite unit—had been through an adventurous time.

I at once sent a radio message to Rommel:

"General Ramcke, with 700 men and all weapons, has been discovered by us; he himself is with me at the command post." Rommel replied that he had been very worried about the paratroops and had almost given them up. I was to have the General taken to him at once and to convey his men to him with available vehicles.

I shall never forget the sight of Ramcke's men coming toward us, exhausted, out of the desert. For reasons of space, they had left everything behind except for weapons and water, but their morale was astonishing.

In the morning of 8 November, Rommel appeared at my command post—east of the Egyptian-Libyan border—and gave me a review of the general situation. The Africa Army had been in full retreat toward the Libyan border since 4 November. We were resisting the vigorous British advance with our last resources. The fuel that had been landed in Benghazi had come too late or not even reached the German panzer divisions; as a result, some of the last tanks had had to be blown up. At that moment, only four tanks were ready for action; the burden of defense was falling, therefore, mainly on the 88s.

Rommel spoke of the terrible scenes that were taking place on the coastal road. Pursued by British tanks and covered inescapably by carpets of bombs, vehicles were left standing in flames, while the men tried to save themselves on foot. Owing to these insurmountable obstacles, the supply trucks were hardly able to make progress.

Rommel's intention was to hold open the border passes into Libya and channel through them—directed by pickets of officers—the greater part of the Africa Army.

I could see the profound disappointment in Rommel's face.

"Through Hitler's crazy order to hold out, we lost a vital day, which cost us losses that cannot be made good. I can't hold Cyrenaica, so with the remains of the Afrika Korps, under General Bayerlein, I shall cross southern Cyrenaica, despite the rains and the sandstorms, in order to set up a first line of defense at Mersa el Brega (just short of Tripolitania).

"I have information," Rommel continued, "that the British, by means of reconnaissance detachments and scout cars, are trying to explore and prepare a southern outflanking of the whole Afrika Korps. This is a deadly danger. So I'm going to send you the Voss Reconnaissance Group, (Panzer Reconnaissance Battalion 580 under Major Voss and Panzer Reconnaissance Battalion 33 under Major Linau). You will then be strong enough to prevent any outflanking." Rommel seemed unbroken. But one couldn't fail to notice how disillusioned he was at being left in the lurch in this way by the highest authority. What had become of Rommel's proud Africa Army? How depressing it must have been for him to have to give up in a matter of days all that had once been conquered in unprecedented operations.

All of us now felt that we had to stand by "our Rommel."

Major Voss and Major Linau appeared with their battalions; the panzer reconnaissance group of the Africa Army was formed under my command. From Voss I heard more of the appalling events unfolding at the coast.

"It was terrible to have to see how the Italians, and our own people, hung in clusters on the few vehicles that were still intact," Voss reported. "Some of the remaining tanks were on tow, as they were out of fuel. The supply vehicles could hardly make their way forward against the retreating masses. Worst of all was the helplessness in face of the RAF, which covered the one asphalt road with bombs and machine-gun fire, not only by day but also by night."

I divided up our operational territory so that it could be watched over without a break by our three battalions.

Next day, Gause sent us, in addition, a Fieseler Stork, that well-tried, light aircraft for reconnaissance and communication, which was now to be very useful to us, since we had had to return the Italian Ghibli. My adjutant or I went up in the plane once or twice a day to gain a general view of the terrain or of possible enemy movements. This saved fuel for our reconnaissance vehicles.

On 5 November, the remains of the once proud Africa Army crossed the border into Libya; in ten days, on 13 November, our weary, decimated units reached Mersa el Brega. At the cost of terrible losses, 1,000 kilometers had been covered; the 21st Panzer Division had four tanks left.

On 8 November HQ informed me that the Americans had landed in Morocco and Algeria and there was a danger that the Africa Army could be shut in on two sides. As a result, German Luftwaffe units landed in and around Tunis on 9 November and paratroops on the 11th; to follow were the 10th German Panzer Division and an Italian division. The 5th Panzer Army was formed.

The news of the American landing alarmed us, although we were still a long way from Tunisia. There were rumors that the French, with a task force from Chad, were on the march through the desert in the direction of Tunisia, in order to cut us off via the south.

Some days later Rommel's HQ informed me that I was to be sent an Italian armored reconnaissance battalion, the Nizza. At first, I was not very pleased, as I had no great opinion of Italian weapons or morale. They duly arrived, well spread out and apparently still at normal fighting strength. Their commander, a tall, fair-haired Major, presented himself. As he told me later, he had been given the posting "for disciplinary reasons," because of an affair with a member of the royal house. The officers and men came exclusively from the north. They were proud Piedmontese and Venetians. They wanted to show that they knew how to fight.

"May our patrols go on reconnaissance with yours?" I was asked by the commander and his officers. "That would be the best way for us to learn."

I inspected their armored cars and weapons. "More sardine tins," said our men, who were standing around inquisitively. Indeed, the equipment didn't even approach the standard of that which we had had at the start of the Polish campaign. It was hopelessly inferior to the British Humbers and antitank guns. And yet, the Italians wanted to be sent into action at the front.

In the difficult weeks that followed, my feelings wavered between admiration and pity for these brave men, who despite heavy losses, didn't give up and so remained to the end, our good friends.

We have, without doubt, often done our Italian allies an injustice. Frequently mocked by our men as "spaghetti-eaters," they were regarded, on account of their combat performance, as more of a burden than a help. We failed to consider that their weapons and armored cars were far from corresponding to the standard of those which we or our opponents employed in North Africa.

The Italians have a cheerful, amiable disposition; they are of a different mentality from us Germans. It is said of them that they "work to live," whereas, we are supposed to "live to work." There is no doubt that the Italians are outstanding engineers, designers, and road-builders; they have given the world the most beautiful operas and they are the best interpreters of classical music. The past culture of the Romans still marks these people today, and it has influenced all other modern cultures. Charm, gaiety, and a Mediterranean climate, always exercise their fascination on visitors to their beautiful country.

All these qualities and characteristics determine, therefore, the features of the Italian soldier. He doesn't take war with deadly seriousness and ends it for his part when he considers it to be hopeless. Hitler's pathetic, cynical maxim, "the German soldier stands or dies," is, to the Italian, profoundly alien.

It is against this background that the active service and performance of our allies is to be seen. So much more highly did we value the service of the Nizza Battalion, whose officers and men fought bravely beside and with us to the bitter end.

The lack of replacements of weapons, ammunition, and fuel, the supply problem now had a catastrophic effect on the retreat. It was not only that many tanks and combat vehicles had to be towed back or blown up; at times parts of the German Panzer Korps faced the attacks of the British tanks and the RAF with no fuel.

Our reconnaissance battalion was greatly indebted to its supply officer: time and again he managed to organize the fuel that was vital to us, and deliver it to us through the desert in small convoys. Only once was a convoy caught between British lines and destroyed, as was reported to us by the accompanying radio car.

For us that meant water rationing; half a liter of water per man per day—for ten days on end. Half a liter to drink, without thinking of washing and shaving. This measure was necessary, since without water—in the depths of the desert—we would have been hopeless. In spite of great privation, we endured the ten days.

From 6 November, my reconnaissance group—at this time deep in the desert— operated at first from the Giarabub oasis, which lay about 250 kilometers south of the coast.

The stony desert here was not as flat as it was further north, where it permitted large-scale military operations. The further south we moved, the more mountainous the terrain became. In places, ridges with cliffs, scoured by the wind, ran from north to south and thus formed an obstacle that could hardly be overcome. Then, further south, the sandy desert began, with its high, impassable dunes. Long-drawn *wadis* offered cover and thus protection against surprise attacks.

By day, it was very hot and at night, so cold that everyone was glad to have his coat and scarf on hand. Again and again, we were hit by sandstorms or deluges of rain.

Contact with the enemy was resumed. We came upon our old "friends," the Royal Dragoons and the 11th Hussars, with whom we had already been involved during our advance on Alamein. Although we knew we were covering and shielding the withdrawal of the Africa Army to the west, we had no feeling of being in flight. We operated to all quarters of the compass with the object of maintaining contact with the enemy and getting a clear idea of his intentions. Prisoners had to be taken, in order to learn from them something of the enemy's plans.

Our armored patrols developed their "net" tactic: in flat terrain, with a range of sight of more than 15 kilometers, our very fast eight-wheelers formed a large circle, into which they lured the British Humbers and scout cars, in order to close the net from two sides. This tactic usually worked, though we sometimes lost isolated scout cars through the more powerful cannons of the Humbers.

The first prisoners were brought in to me. Some of them greeted me with: "Glad to meet you again, Recces." The British obviously kept their sense of humor in all eventualities. After the usual small talk, we knew that the main job of the two British battalions was to prevent us from trying to interrupt Montgomery's supply routes by an attack from the depths of the desert.

Much more interesting, however, was something a young officer said, which he regretted as soon as he had opened his mouth. The Long Range Desert Group, under Major Stirling, had the task of finding a route for a whole British tank division, through the mountainous country further to the south. From then on, the "hunt for Stirling," as we called it, began. Sometimes, we found vehicle tracks which could only have come from his scout cars. But time and again, this clever unit managed to evade our clutches.

A couple of weeks later, a patrol succeeded in catching one of the Long Range Desert Group's command cars, which had lost its way. In the vehicle, we captured a map on which was marked the exact route across a mountain range, by which a whole British tank division might have attempted a wide outflanking of our prepared positions on the coast. Thanks to this map, Rommel was able to save parts of the Afrika Korps from the threat of encirclement.

In time, we got to know the names of the commanders of the two British reconnaissance battalions. I, too, was often addressed by prisoners. "You are Major von Luck. We'd have been glad to catch you."

While the Africa Army was putting every effort into fighting an orderly with-drawal action on the coast and then straight across Cyrenaica, we, with our four battalions, were able to operate freely for three weeks unmolested by tank and air attacks.

We quickly developed a certain routine. Toward five o'clock in the afternoon the reconnaissance patrols broke off their operations in order to reach base in good time; in the treeless desert with no landmarks it was impossible to find one's way back to base in the dark. To avoid betraying our position, light signals were used only in an emergency. The two British battalions carried on in the same way, so that from 1700 hours, all reconnaissance and combat activity was suspended, to be resumed again the following morning as soon as it was light.

"We could really agree to a cease-fire with the British from 1700 hours until the next morning," I said, more as a joke, to those around me.

"Why not?" I was supported by Lieutenant Wenzel Luedecke, the reserve officer who had worked at the UFA film studios as an assistant director. "After all," he went on, "the British have a sense of humor. We ought to suggest it to them."

Chance came to our aid. One evening, when all our patrols were back, I received a visit from my intelligence officer.

"The Royal Dragoons are on the radio," he said, "and they would like to speak to you."

"Hallo, Royal Dragoons here. I know it's unusual to make radio contact with you, but Lieutenant Smith and his scouting party have been missing since this evening. Is he with you, and if so how are things with him and his men?"

One of our patrols had indeed managed to take some prisoners. It turned out that they were Lieutenant Smith and his party.

"Yes, he is with us. All of them are unhurt and send greetings to their family and friends." Then came the brainstorm. "Can we call you, too, or the 11th Hussars, if we have anyone missing?"

"Sure, your calls are always welcome."

It was only a matter of days before we had arrived at a "gentlemen's agreement":

—At 1700 hours, precisely, all hostilities would be suspended. We called it "tea time."

—At 1705 hours, we would make open contact with the British, to exchange "news" about prisoners, etc.

In fact, from a distance of about 15 kilometers, we could often see the British get out their Primus stoves and make their tea. The agreement was kept by both sides, until we were forced by events to give up the connection in Tunisia. The prisoners we took often had to stay with us for several days, until the next supply convoy arrived and was able to take them away with it. We gave them whatever we could spare from our rations.

One evening, when our radio stations had tuned in once again to the Belgrade transmitter and we heard the song "Lilli Marlene," some of the prisoners joined in.

"Over there we listen to 'Lilli Marlene' every evening," they said. "There's already an English version. Monty has strictly forbidden it, but we like the song and its sentimental words." The French and the Americans also listened to it, as we found out later. Somehow, it made things easier.

Our "five o'clock tea agreement" had some remarkable consequences. One evening, a patrol came back with two men and a jeep captured in the desert. A tall, fair-haired, young lieutenant and his driver were brought before me. The lieutenant was the snobbish, arrogant type of Englishman. Very correctly, he gave me his service number only, no other details.

I tried to get into conversation with him and told him of my visits to London, of my friends, including a captain in the grenadier guards. He gradually thawed and turned out to be the nephew of one of the owners of Player's cigarettes. My officers made a whispered suggestion and I had to laugh.

"Lieutenant, what would you say to our swapping you and your driver for cigarettes? We're a bit short at the moment."

"Good idea," he said.

"How many cigarettes do you think you are worth, what should I suggest to your commander?"

His answer came without hesitation: "A million cigarettes, that's 100,000 packets."

My radio officer made contact with the Royal Dragoons, and I passed on our offer.

"Please wait, we'll come back to you at once," was the reply. Then, after a few minutes, "Sorry, we're a bit short ourselves, but we could offer 600,000 cigarettes. Come in, please."

To my great astonishment, I received a flat refusal from the young lieutenant.

"Not one cigarette less than a million, that's final!" was his answer. So the young man had to pay for the high value he set on himself with captivity.

A week later, shortly before dark, our doctor disappeared behind a rise for the indispensable "spade trip."

"Doctor," I called out to him, "don't go too far, it'll soon be dark." He didn't seem to hear me and went on.

When he hadn't come back after half an hour, we began to be worried. The doctor was not only very popular; with his tropical experience, he was vital to us. We sent out some men and fired the prearranged light signals. The doctor remained missing. Had he lost his way, or had he been caught by the British?

"Yes, we've got your doctor. He ran straight into our patrol on its way back. This time, we have a suggestion. The Japanese have cut our communications with the Far East. We can't get quinine anymore and are suffering badly from malaria. Can we exchange your doctor for some of your synthetic Atebrin? Come in, please."

"Please wait," I replied.

A moral issue now presented itself: Which was more important, to weaken the fighting strength of the British through malaria, or to get our doctor back? I quickly made up my mind.

"Okay, we'll do business. How many packets do you want for the doctor?"

We agreed at once on a quantity that we could spare and arranged the exchange for the following morning. From either side, a jeep with a white flag drove between the lines for the ceremonial trade.

"An expensive spade trip, Doctor. Good to have you back."

Rommel, to whom I related this on one of his visits, was understanding. "That's what I thought about the British. I'm glad you can practice this fair play here in the desert; on the coast, it's just a matter of survival."

Only once was our "agreement" unintentionally broken. One evening, a patrol returned to base from its operation with a British supply truck. The leader of the patrol was a young lieutenant who had joined us from Germany only a short time before.

"Major," he reported proudly, "the truck is full of corned beef and other tins, beer, and cigarettes."

"When and where did you capture it?" was my first question.

It turned out that he had captured the truck toward 1730 hours, hence *after* the agreed time.

"Are you mad, you know the arrangement? This will not be the end of the matter."

The lieutenant was astonished. "But these are things that are really useful to us, and which will be denied to the British. War is war."

I had an idea of what would happen and at once sent off a radio message to Rommel. "Have impression that British patrols intend to outflank us in the south. Suggest moving south."

Rommel agreed and sent word that another small unit would take over my position the following day. I briefed the leader of the unit on the situation in my area and warned him expressly against British patrols, which would appear suddenly and try to take prisoners among us. In the afternoon, I moved south.

What I had suspected promptly occurred. In the evening, toward 1730 hours, a British detachment raided the unit, captured *two* trucks, and disappeared into the darkness. A gentleman's agreement was, after all, a gentleman's agreement.

The end of our "agreement" came later, somewhere in the depths of the Tunisian desert. For some days, we had lost contact with the two British battalions. Then, an orderly came to my command car one evening.

"There's a Bedouin here who wants to talk to you, Major."

With a deep bow, the Bedouin came in. "Salaam, I have a letter for you. I will wait for an answer."

A Bedouin with a letter, here, deep in the desert, where by rights no one could find us? The Bedouins always seemed to know where we were. I opened the letter.

> From C.O.,
> Royal Dragoons.
>
> Dear Major von Luck,
>
> We have had other tasks and so were unable to keep in touch with you. The war in Africa has been decided, I'm glad to say, not in your favor.
>
> I should like, therefore, to thank you and all your people, in the name of my officers and men, for the fair play with which we have fought against each other on both sides.
>
> I and my battalion hope that all of you will come out of the war safe and sound and that we may find the opportunity to meet again sometime, in more favorable circumstances.
>
> With the greatest respect.

I sat down at the table and wrote a similar note to the Royal Dragoons.

"Give this letter to the man from whom you received the one to me," I told the Bedouin. "Say to him, 'Many thanks,' but don't betray where you found us."

Heavy downpours of rain set in, which gave us time to consolidate the Mersa el Brega position. The deluges of rain were a hindrance, not only to us, but also to the two British battalions. We couldn't use the *wadis*, which gave us cover, for torrents of water, three feet deep, were carrying all before them. We were now stationed south of Agedabia, not far from the border between Cyrenaica and Tripolitania.

On 20 November, I was ordered to go in the Fieseler to Rommel, who, for a short time, had his HQ near an airfield.

Rommel looked exhausted. His uniform was worn and dusty. The hard withdrawal actions, his deep disappointment, and his illness, not yet fully cured, had left their mark on him. He greeted me briefly. Instead of giving me fresh orders, for which I had flown to see him, Rommel took my arm, "Come, we'll go for a little walk." General Gause nodded to me, as if pleased to be able to divert Rommel somewhat. We strolled along the edge of the airfield.

"I no longer know how to cope with the supply problem," Rommel began. "A few days ago, an Italian destroyer with 500 tons of fuel turned west and unloaded at Tripoli instead of here in Benghazi. Kesselring has now promised me fuel by airlift. The first fifty JU 52s are on their way here."

In the distance, we could hear the drone of engines; also, however, the rattle of antiaircraft cannon. Out of the fifty machines, only five landed shortly afterward; the rest had been shot down over the sea. How could the British have known about them? We know, today, that it was Jean Howard and her friends in Bletchely Park at work. Rommel was extremely frustrated and stamped his feet.

"Luck, that's the end! We can't even hold Tripolitania, but must fall back on Tunisia. There, in addition, we shall come upon the Americans and, possibly, also the French, who are supposed to be marching with a combat group from Chad through the desert on southern Tunisia. What I was afraid of weeks ago will then occur: our proud Africa Army, and the new divisions that have landed in northern Tunisia, will be lost. First, the loss of Stalingrad, with 200,000 battle-tried men; now we're losing Africa too, with elite divisions."

I was much disturbed. "Field Marshal, we still have a chance. The men are behind you, their morale is first-class. If we can get sufficient supplies, we're bound to pull it off."

Rommel smiled, "I know, and I'm proud of the men. But the supplies will not be forthcoming. Hitler's HQ has already written off this theater of war. All he requires now is that 'the German soldier stands or dies.'

"What we need is to create a German 'Dunkirk'; that means flying out as many officers, men, and specialists as possible to Sicily, while leaving the materiel behind. We need the men for the decisive struggle in Europe."

"How will you ever put that to Hitler?" I asked.

"After consulting Kesselring and the Italians, I shall fly to Hitler at Rastenburg and make my opinion clear to him, beyond all doubt. My word still counts for something; I am still respected among the people and by my men. I don't believe anymore that we shall get what we need in further divisions, aircraft, and supplies, in order to turn the wheel yet again."

His face was lined, his shoulders drooping. He was the picture of dejection.

"Luck, the war is lost!" he said.

I was appalled. Was everything to have been in vain?

"We're still deep in Russia," I protested. "Half Europe is occupied by us. Bitter though the loss of North Africa will be, we can carry on the fight in Europe and bring about a change of fortune."

"Luck, we've got to seek an armistice, precisely because we still have a lot of pawns in hand. If possible, an armistice with the Western Allies. We still have something to offer. This assumes, of course, that Hitler must be forced to abdicate; that we must give up the persecution of the Jews at once and make concessions to the Church. That may sound Utopian, but it is the only way of avoiding further bloodshed and still more destruction in our cities."

What had brought Rommel to this complete reversal in his attitude to Hitler and the war? Without doubt, his great disappointment at being left on his own, as well as the disregard for his ideas and the importance of this theater of war. We walked back slowly to his HQ. Once again, Rommel took my arm.

"Luck, one day you will think of my words. The threat to Europe and to our civilized world will come from the east. If the peoples of Europe fail to join forces to meet that threat, western Europe will have lost. At the moment, I see only one warrior' prepared to champion a united Europe: Churchill!"

I was deeply impressed by Rommel's words.

As General Gause told me at the beginning of December, Rommel had a decisive conference with Marshals Kesselring and Cavallero on 24 November. On 28 November, he flew to Rastenburg in East Prussia to see Hitler. The crucial meeting had the opposite effect of that for which Rommel had hoped: Hitler regarded Rommel as sick and run-down and his report on the situation as greatly exaggerated. He angrily refused to even consider evacuation of the Africa Army.

Goering maneuvered himself into the foreground and promised Hitler that he would give the war in North Africa the decisive turn with his Luftwaffe. Goering had been angry with Rommel ever since the latter had remarked that the Goering divisions and the Waffen-SS were merely "praetorian guards" and should be incorporated in the army.

Rommel went back to "his" men, although it was suggested that he should take treatment for his tropical disease. All he brought with him was empty promises of support.

On 13 November, after all its stores and installations had been destroyed, Tobruk was taken by the British without a struggle. Much blood had been shed there, on both sides, during the previous eighteen months.

The retreat, through southern Cyrenaica, was a masterly achievement by Rommel. Except for a great deal of materiel, we suffered hardly any losses.

The fuel problem had become increasingly critical; of the 250 tons promised by air transport, only 60 had arrived. With that, we could cover just 150 kilometers and had to avoid getting into any battles. Thankfully, the heavy rain that had set in also prevented the British from pursuing us. Italian destroyers with fuel on board turned west; the Afrika Korps was again left standing without fuel. With the last reserves, we managed to bring the motorized panzer units behind the Mersa el Brega line.

Rommel was reckoning on a strong flanking attack around the salt lake south of Mersa el Brega. I had to reconnoiter with greater intensity in this area. At the same time, my reconnaissance group was broken up; the two Voss and Linau battalions were sent north. Only the Nizza Battalion remained with us.

Gause called us again, "Through lack of fuel, we cannot engage in a battle with the British at or south of Mersa el Brega. Everything points to a strong British attack."

From 6 December, the nonmotorized German and Italian elements were moved to Tunisia, which was not easy, owing to shortage of petrol. The supply problem became ever more critical.

Time and again, whole divisions or sections were left immobile. It was only thanks to great combat experience and outstanding morale, that it was somehow contrived, again and again, to release them from encirclement, as soon as some fuel could be organized.

I had to give up the Fieseler Stork again; it was needed at HQ. I had to draw the net of patrols much tighter. Thank goodness our air reconnaissance to the south was intensified. In the course of it, we came to be attacked by our own fighters, who didn't expect to find us so far south. During air attacks, everyone had to leave his vehicle and lie flat on the sand 20 to 30 yards away. The radio operator often stayed voluntarily at his post, to send off our reports.

Our aerial reconnaissance reported that, to the south, a strong column, probably a complete British tank division, was preparing to outflank the Nofilia position. On 17 December, I moved my battalion north, where, with other elements of the Afrika Korps, we launched an attack in the flank of this division. Together, we were able to knock out 20 British tanks with our 88s and for the time being, avert the danger.

While the remains of the Africa Army were fighting for their lives on the coast and suffering constantly from shortage of fuel, we went back into the desert. The danger of a fresh attempt to outflank us remained too great.

South of the Buerat line, we came across our British "friends" again and the old ceremonial of the "five o'clock agreement" was resumed. But we also stumbled on the tracks of the Long Range Desert Group, tracks that led to the west. General Gause sent word that the British had apparently been forced to make a pause, since they had to reorganize their supply routes. But another outflanking attack was expected from the legendary Lieutenant-Colonel Stirling. Our task: to reconnoiter more intensively as far as south of Homs-Tripoli, with particular attention to an almost insurmountable north-south mountain range between Homs and Tripoli.

13
The End in North Africa, 1943

One afternoon, shortly before Christmas, toward four o'clock, I decided to drive to a hill some 12 kilometers to the south in the hope of getting a good view from there. Unthinkingly, I took a light-armored car without radio; I intended, after all, to be back by five o'clock. I ordered my driver to set off.

I could detect nothing unusual and was setting off on the return journey, when I discovered, right between me and my battalion, a fairly large British patrol, which seemed to be settling there for the night. Fortunately, I was not spotted and at once withdrew a little to the south and then to the west. The terrain was difficult and I needed time to distance myself from the British. Meanwhile, it was getting dark and there was no chance of reaching my battalion. So there I was, with no radio, but at least with my compass.

By the last light of day, I saw a *wadi*, in which I decided to hide for the night. As I came to the edge of it, I found a Bedouin family there with their camels and several tents. With a white cloth, I drove toward the Bedouins, who now all ran together, and made myself known as a German. In a gibberish of Italian and Arabic, I outlined my situation and asked for hospitality for the night.

"Come, German, you are our guest. Nothing will happen to you and tomorrow you will be guided back to your people safe and sound. We, too, are moving off tomorrow, to the south, until you and the British have gone away."

As always, the women stayed in the tents and risked only surreptitious glances at the strangers. The family elder led us to the fireplace and we squatted round it. A low fire was maintained with camel's thorn wood and over it hung three kettles from iron forks. The Arab tea ceremony then began.

In one kettle, sugared water was boiled, in another boiling water was poured over the tea leaves, and in the third kettle, the tea and the sugared water were mixed. The procedure was repeated continuously until, in the end, a strong, almost viscous tea was transferred to a pot. Little porcelain bowls in brass beakers were handed around and the most astonishing part of the ceremony then took place. The family elder took the porcelain bowls in turn, held the spout of the teapot close over them, and as he poured, lifted the pot straight up, so that, in the end, the stream of tea was flowing into the bowl from a height of over three feet, without spilling a single drop. I was told later that in this way, the tea became mixed with air, bringing out its full aroma. It was said to be the pride of the Bedouins to be able to pour tea accurately into the little cups from the back of a camel.

So there we sat, together, the Bedouin family, my driver, and I. Meanwhile, night had fallen and the whole sky was covered in stars; among them, one could recognize the Southern Cross. We were enveloped in an uncanny, beneficent peace. Without saying much, the men in their burnooses sat round the glimmering fire, which turned their faces a ruddy brown. I suddenly had the feeling that we might have been sitting there thousands of years before, or thousands of years hence, so timeless did it seem to us.

For a few hours, we wrapped ourselves in our coats; the night was cold. Shortly before dawn, the Bedouins struck their tents. The family elder came to say good-bye.

"German, we are moving on now, to the next water hole. You must now travel on this camel-track, here, for three hours (camel-hours), then you will find another track that branches off to the right. You travel on that for five hours, till you come to a hill. From there, you will see your friends. The British will not see you. We wish you the blessing of Allah, that you may return safe and sound to your country."

A handshake and he moved off with his camels into the desert.

I have never understood how the man knew our position and that of the British so accurately.

I converted the camel-hours into "scout-car hours," took compass bearings, drove cautiously along the indicated tracks and came right on my battalion!

There, great agitation had reigned. Shortly before dark, patrols had been sent out, which had found their way back to the battalion only by means of light-signals—without finding me. Finally, the Royal Dragoons and the 11th Hussars were asked if they had taken me prisoner.

"Sorry, unfortunately, no. We would have liked to greet your commander here!"

Christmas 1942 arrived but we had no time to celebrate. In any case, how? Deep in the desert, without a tree or a bush, and in the heat of day, our thoughts turned to home, where our families were having to endure air raids and food rationing.

On 31 December, New Year's Eve, Rommel came to see me unexpectedly in his Fieseler Stork. He briefed me on the situation and his plans.

"Luck, some time or other, Tommy is going to launch another attack and outflank the Buerat position in the south. I need the remains of the panzer divisions in the north. The reconnaissance group will be reconstituted; in the next few days, Linau and Voss will join you, and you will get back the Fieseler Stork, which will help you to reconnoiter.

"I am very concerned," Rommel went on, "that the Americans, with their vast potential in weapons, might make a thrust from the Atlas Mountains and cut us off at Gabes from the 10th Army in northern Tunisia. Marshal Bastico shares my view that we cannot allow the Africa Army to be destroyed at Buerat.

"I have suggested transferring the remains of the 21st Panzer Division to southern Tunisia, to rest them there and to ward off a possible American attack."

Rommel then repeated what he had outlined to me some weeks earlier.

"I still think that, in view of the disastrous supply situation and the state of our men, who are certainly experienced but far from fresh, we can no longer turn this war around let alone win it. So I should like to get as many men and as much materiel as possible to Tunisia. There, the opportunities for defense are better and— this is my main concern—as many men as possible can be saved by the short route to Sicily.

"Now to you," Rommel continued. "With the reconnaissance group, you will secure for me the whole area south of Homs and Tripoli. The British must, on no account, take us in the rear."

Until the middle of January 1943, things remained quiet. On 13 January, the 21st Panzer Division was transferred to the Mareth position in southern Tunisia, and rested. As yet, the Americans were showing no signs of an eastward move from the rugged Atlas Mountains.

Voss and Linau arrived with their battalions, so did the Fieseler. We kept watch in a broad fan to the south; contacts were resumed with our "friends" on the other side. Very much to my surprise, my battalion was transferred to the area southwest of Tripoli for a few days, to be restored to strength. Major Voss took command of the rest of the reconnaissance group.

The quiet spell in a palm grove did us good; replacements of men, ammunition, and fuel arrived. I used the opportunity for a brief visit to Tripoli. In the bar of the Ouadan Hotel, the Italian barman served me a cocktail. "I shall probably have to serve the next one to Montgomery," he said. The Italians took things more lightly.

On 13 January, I was back with the reconnaissance group. On the 14th, with massive artillery and air support, the British moved against the Buerat position. They then made a strong thrust south of the Buerat position toward Tarhunah-Homs, hence, practically against Tripoli already.

My reconnaissance group, along with elements of the 164th Division and the paratroops, were at once sent in to counter this move. Despite considerable losses in tanks, the thrust was continued fairly successfully toward Garian and Azizia. With that, the British were already southwest of Tripoli. Thanks to the Long Range Desert Group, a complete tank division had found a route over a rugged mountain terrace. The Homs-Tarhunah position was in great danger. To avoid annihilation, Rommel had it evacuated.

On 20 January, we heard, even far to the south, the rumble of explosions in Tripoli. As I discovered later, through the superhuman efforts of the supply units, about 95 percent of the stores were moved to safety from Tripoli, in the direction of Tunisia, all harbor and supply installations were blown up and the food depots handed over to the Italian mayor.

On 23 January, the British occupied Tripoli without a fight.

A few days later, as we were covering the disengagement of our units southwest of Tripoli, a patrol reported: "Gathering of high military personnel about six to eight kilometers to the northeast, believe Monty identified, strong protection with tanks and scout cars."

I went there at once and scanned the scene with binoculars. It really did seem to be Montgomery, and, much more sensationally, Churchill appeared to be with him, wearing a safari helmet. It was too far to open fire with our weapons; 88mm guns and artillery were not available. I, at once, sent a radio message to Gause: "Churchill and Monty believed located at great distance, no action possible." Actually, I thought about what Rommel said about Churchill and held my fire.

Later, I heard that it could well have been Churchill, who, on his way to Casablanca, had stopped off to see Monty and his troops. However that may be, we never saw Hitler in this theater of war, or even senior officers of the High Command of the Wehrmacht (the OKW).

In January, Lieutenant-Colonel Stirling of the Long Range Desert Group, was finally captured.

"Nice to meet you," was his first remark, "I shall be glad to spend a few days with you and perhaps meet your famous Marshal Rommel." He was taken to HQ under heavy guard; a day or two later he promptly escaped. After a mistaken "deal" with Bedouins, however, he was handed back to us.

The British paused to organize their supplies. By an immense effort, continually harassed by the RAF, we were able to bring all our units over the Libyan-Tunisian border to the Mareth position.

With the reaching of Tunisia, the reconnaissance group was again dissolved; I also had to relinquish the Fieseler again, unfortunately.

I received orders to stop, or at least report, any approach by British units south of Mareth. I was to pay particular attention to the track that led north from the desert fort of Foum Tataouine. That was where the French column was expected, which, in an unprecedented feat, was supposed to strike from Chad through the Sahara, against our southern flank. It failed to reach Tunisia in time.

I sent a liaison officer to Rommel's HQ to learn something about the situation and about intentions for the future in our struggle in Tunisia. On his return, he told me that Rommel seemed to be planning an attack through the American-held passes in the Atlas Mountains, in order to score a hit against the completely untried Americans, and thrust north in their rear. Reconnaissance Battalion 3 was to hold itself ready for this operation.

Shortly after, an orderly officer arrived from Rommel with an antiaircraft platoon and one of light artillery.

"Major," he said, "your task is as follows: since Rommel considers it possible that the British may attempt a wide, out-flanking movement from the south, or that the French combat group may turn up, your reinforced battalion is to advance on

Fort Foum Tataouine, capture the French garrison, and from there, reconnoiter to the south and southeast. If no enemy is observed, your combat group will return at once to the Mareth position. You will set off for the south tomorrow morning; radio contact must be maintained without fail."

Well spread out, we made good progress at first, until a British reconnaissance plane flew over us, circled, and flew off again. That was sinister. I sent off a radio message to Gause: "Expect air attack on my combat group, can you alert our fighters? Progress toward Foum Tataouine otherwise good."

Then they came: flying out of the sun and low over the ground, the Hurricanes attacked, protected by Spitfires, which kept watch high above them.

No special orders were needed: all movement ceased, every man left his vehicle and lay flat on the sand 30 yards away. My motorcycle escorts opened fire with their machine-guns, but without success. We didn't know that the Hurricanes were armored on the underside. Their target was the flak platoon (antiaircraft platoon), which was eliminated before it could fire a shot.

On their second run up, the artillery platoon was hit and its vehicles badly damaged. As fast as they had come, the fighters turned away again. Everything had lasted only a few minutes.

The Hurricanes must have seen my armored reconnaissance vehicles. I figured we were in for a second attack. Again, I sent off a radio message.

"Have been attacked by Hurricanes, flak and artillery platoons largely out of action. Anticipate fresh attack, send Messerschmidts."

The British bases must have been close behind the front. After barely an hour, they were back again. This time, it was the turn of our armored vehicles. With dismay, I saw only a few yards away, how the Hurricanes fired rockets, which went straight through our armor. That was new to us.

The only one to remain in his vehicle, was my radio operator, who was sending off my messages. Next to the vehicle, stood my intelligence officer, who passed on to the operator what I shouted across to him.

Then a machine—I thought I recognized the Canadian emblem—approached for a low-flying attack on the armored radio station. At 20 yards, I could clearly see the pilot's face under his flight helmet. But instead of shooting, he signaled with his hand for the radio officer to clear off, and pulled his machine up into a great curve.

"Get the operator out of the vehicle," I shouted, "and take cover, the pair of you."

The machine had turned and now came at us out of the sun for the second time. This time, he fired his rockets and hit the radio car, fortunately, without doing too much damage.

This attitude of the pilot, whether he was Canadian or British, became for me, *the* example of fairness in this merciless war. I shall never forget the pilot's face or the gesture of his hand.

Except for two vehicles, which we had to abandon, all were in running order, though we had to take several in tow with our tracked motorcycles. But the British fighters were still circling over us; we had to anticipate a third attack. Suddenly, a squadron of Messerschmidts appeared high in the sky and, at once, engaged the British in an air battle. They moved off to the north, but not before we saw one British machine go down after being hit. So, at least a third attack had been prevented and we had had the satisfaction of one shot down.

We at once moved off again toward Foum Tataouine. We were now in the middle of the desert, which, in this part, was flat and provided easy going. By radio, I notified General Gause. And then we saw the little desert fort lying before us: a heap of stones piled on top of each other, not a tree or a bush. What an enervating existence for the garrison, to keep watch there for months or years.

We were met by machine-gun fire, which we very quickly silenced with our own MG24. Secured by our motorcycle escorts and two guns that were still intact, and under the immediate protection of armored cars, I drove into the fort. A French captain came toward us; his men had laid down their weapons and raised their hands.

"Why are you still here," I asked him, "now that the front has moved on to Tunisia?"

"We've been stationed here for over a year," he replied. "Our task is to keep the fort manned. I have no other orders."

I went with him into his bare office, where I saw a radio set. At a sign from me, it was put out of action by my intelligence officer.

"Regard your self and your men as prisoners," I told him. "Pack whatever you need; I shall have to take you with us."

Meantime, all the elements of my little combat group had appeared in the fort and searched it for weapons. I, at once, sent out patrols to the south and the southeast, which reported no contact with the enemy. I radioed to Gause.

"Foum Tataouine occupied, garrison taken prisoner, radio destroyed, reconnaissance far to the south, no contact with enemy. Am returning to Mareth position with combat group and several vehicles in tow."

We were still a good 50 kilometers from Mareth when it became dark. I decided to stay in the middle of the desert for the night. There was little danger; the British also suspended their movements during the night. The next day, we reached the Mareth lines unmolested, and were withdrawn behind them as reserves for further actions.

I used the opportunity to be briefed by General Gause. "Rommel's idea," said Gause, "is to use the freshly equipped 21st Panzer Division in collaboration with the newly arrived 10th Panzer Division of Colonel-General von Arnim, along with all available elements of the Afrika Korps, to disrupt American concentrations, prevent an advance against the coast, and thrust as deeply as possible into the American rear.

"Because of the Americans' complete lack of experience," said Gause, "Rommel considers this operation to be very promising. The Italians are to consolidate the Mareth position and hold it by every means, although a defensive position at and west of Gabes, would have been very much more favorable because of the salt lakes. But Mussolini and the Italian Commando Supremo insisted on the Mareth position.

Unfortunately, the collaboration with von Arnim didn't go very well; he likes to be his own boss," Gause concluded. "Thank goodness the heavy rains are still with us, as they make it almost impossible for the RAF to be used.

"Your battalion will reconnoiter west of Gabes to prevent our elements of the 5th Panzer Army, in the north, from being cut off.

"Rommel's health is not good but he wants to stick it out with his men and calculates that he still has a chance if his plan is approved."

We took hope again and made ourselves familiar with the terrain, which was so different from the desert. In the Atlas Mountains, we would be concerned with passes and steep mountain tops, in the plain with salt lakes, and, further north, with cultivated land.

"Rommel has just received a radio message from the Commando Supremo," Gause went on, "to the effect that, owing to his poor state of health, on reaching the Mareth position, he is to relinquish command of it to the Italian General Messe, who, up to now, has been commanding the Italian expeditionary corps in Russia. Rommel can determine the date of his relief.

"Rommel's plan seems to be aimed at two solutions: (1) either we receive, from Sicily, all the necessary materiel in tanks (including the superior Tiger), antitank weapons, ammunition, and massive air support, or (2) we try to thrust deep into the rear of the Americans, occupy the main passes, and hold up the British at the Mareth position, in order, by this means, to evacuate from Tunisia, the mass of battle-tried troops urgently needed in Europe. The second solution, unfortunately, would seem to be the most likely. Hold yourself ready for a thrust against the Americans."

While the Italians settled in to defend the Mareth position, the fully restored 21st Panzer Division moved against the Faid pass on 1 February 1943, to create a starting point for the northward attack behind the American lines. The surprised and inexperienced Americans lost the pass and 1,000 prisoners.

Then, in the middle of February, my old division set out from the Faid pass bridgehead, to the north, and came upon elements of the 2nd American Armored Division. In hard battles, tank against tank, the bulk of this American division was destroyed and a large number of Grant, Lee, and Sherman tanks left burning on the battlefield. In its pursuit, the 21st Division managed to gain further territory against the remaining American elements, now fighting grimly. The loss of about 150 tanks and 1,600 prisoners forced the Americans to surrender, also, the important town of Gafsa, which gave us our starting point against the north.

Combat groups of the Africa Army and the 5th Panzer Army, thrust on at once to the southwest, the west, and the north; large quantities of fuel were captured, and the Americans set fire to 30 aircraft on an advanced flying field.

My panzer reconnaissance battalion moved up, in order to advance north out of the Gafsa area and give the Americans no chance to rest.

From Gause, I heard that Rommel wanted to strike against Tébessa, hence, far into the enemy's rear. To the Commando Supremo, however, and also to von Arnim, this seemed too risky; they couldn't, and wouldn't, follow Rommel's plans. So orders were given merely to thrust against El Kef, far too close behind the Anglo-American front.

During the night of 18/19 February, I was given the task of taking the Kasserine pass in a surprise coup and of holding it open for the following units. With the motorcycle escorts in front, I moved off before dawn in the hope of catching the Americans unawares. They were on the alert, however, and straddled us with heavy artillery fire, which was directed by observers stationed on the heights on either side of the way through the pass. I couldn't get through. Neither could a rifle regiment that was sent in against the pass.

All the same, we took a few prisoners, who belonged to the 34th U.S. Division. We were surprised by the first-class equipment of the men, and, most of all, by the "daily ration" that everyone had on him. It was not just the bar of chocolate, the chewing gum, butter, and cigarettes, which, for us, were unaccustomed treats; we were fascinated by the printed slip that was enclosed with each package. On it was written: "You are the best paid and best equipped soldier in the world. We have given you the best weapons in the world. Whether you are also the best fighter is now for you to prove."

As we very soon discovered, the Americans had first-class tanks and antitank guns. Behind the front, large supply dumps could quickly replace any deficiency. The fact that they had no combat experience and were at a disadvantage against our "desert foxes," could not be held against them.

In one respect, they seemed to have the edge over their British allies: they were extraordinarily flexible; they adapted immediately to a changed situation and fought with great doggedness. I will never forget the sight of a few Tiger panzers, with their superior 88mm tank gun, knocking out one Sherman after the other, as they tried to advance through a pass to the east, and couldn't understand that they were hopelessly inferior to the Tigers. We admired the courage and élan with which the Americans executed their attacks, even though we sometimes felt sorry for them at having to pay for their first combat experience with such heavy losses. We discovered later, in Italy, and I personally in the battles in France in 1944, how quickly the Americans were able to evaluate their experience and, through flexible and unconventional conduct of a battle, convert it into results.

Our thrust to the north, begun so hopefully, came to a standstill, owing to the false start against El Kef on the one hand, and on the other, to inadequate supplies. In addition, after heavy downpours of rain, we made progress only with difficulty and, in the mountain valleys, we were straddled, time and again, by enemy artillery. We had to withdraw to the Kasserine pass, while in the north, the 5th Panzer Army started a relief attack, which failed to penetrate the Anglo-American resistance.

At the end of February, Rommel became commander in chief of "Army Group Africa," with the residual armies under General Messe in the south and under Colonel-General von Arnim in the north. The front was terribly long and could be manned at only a few points.

The materiel, especially that of the Americans, was overwhelming. Rommel would now have liked to give up the south of Tunisia and, with the remains of the Army

Group, form a strong bridgehead around the city of Tunis, with the Cape Bon Peninsula, in order to start evacuating from there, at least a part of the battle-tried Africa Army. The plan was rejected.

At the beginning of March, I heard from Gause that Rommel intended flying to "Fuehrer HQ" in order to save what there was to save. As I happened to be in reserve—my battalion had hardly any armored cars or ammunition left—I went to Rommel's command post, which was not far away.

"May I speak to Rommel and say good-bye to him?" I asked Gause.

"Of course, he will be glad to see the commander of his favorite battalion."

Rommel sat in his "Mammoth," as always, with his campaign maps before him. I hadn't seen him for some weeks and was shocked at how unwell he looked. He was visibly weak, suffering from tropical disease, and completely worn-out. Still, he had that unique sparkle in his eyes.

"Field Marshal, I have heard that you intend flying to HQ. From the state of things here, I don't think you will be coming back. As commander of *the* battalion, which was once the first to land in North Africa and has been allowed to fight every battle with you, may I, in the name of each individual member of my battalion, say good-bye to you, till we meet again, sometime, somewhere. We'll hold out here for as long as we can, always after the example you have given us."

Rommel stood up; he had tears in his eyes.

What must have been going on inside this man, who had always been hard on himself and had identified himself with his men and the theater of war? I had never mentioned these tears to anyone until, long after the war and my captivity, I met his wife, Lucie, and told her of her husband's prophecy and of his tears. Rommel's tears, the tears of a great man now cast down, moved me as much as anything I saw in the war.

Rommel went to a cupboard on the wall and came back with a large photograph, which showed him as a healthy and successful man. He signed his likeness with a dedication.

"Here, Luck, take this in gratitude and appreciation of your brave battalion. Keep well; I hope we shall see each other again at home. God be with you."

He turned around and I left him, deeply moved.

On 9 March, Rommel flew to Germany.

Now, everything happened very quickly.

Colonel-General von Arnim took command of Army Group Africa, supported by General Gause, *the* experienced general-staff officer in North Africa. While every day anticipating a major offensive by Montgomery against the Mareth position, we grappled with the Americans, who tried to break through from the Atlas Mountains to the coast. We had considerable losses.

On 23 March, Monty made a move and with a tank corps, bypassing Mareth, swept over the weak Italian positions. The Mareth line had to be given up; the bulk of the artillery could not be brought back. At Gabes, the remains of the Panzer-Army Africa tried, once again, to establish itself. My battalion had to cover the western flank. Our supply sections had already been transferred to the Cape Bon Peninsula.

Then, at the end of March, an order reached me to report at once, in person, to von Arnim. I had no idea what was wanted of me.

General Gause received me.

"Rommel has gotten nowhere with Hitler. We shall neither receive adequate supplies, nor does the Fuehrer want to know anything about a German Dunkirk. Rommel has been sent for treatment and forbidden to return to Africa as planned. Come, the commander in chief is expecting you."

What did von Arnim want from me? I didn't know him nor had I ever heard anything about him. A tall, slim man with sharp features awaited me.

"Here to report, Colonel-General," I presented myself.

"Good to meet you, Luck. I have the pleasure of presenting you in the name of the Duce with the *Medaglia d'Argento*, a decoration that corresponds roughly to our Knight's Cross." He pinned the order to my chest and handed me the certificate.

I was naturally pleased and undoubtedly had my friends of the Nizza Battalion to thank for the decoration. Associated with the order, there was even a small monthly pension and free first-class travel for two on all Italian railways for life.

But von Arnim had hardly sent for me because of the order. And then it came. "Luck, I have decided, in agreement with Rommel and Gause, that you will fly, at once, to Fuehrer HQ to lay before Hitler and explain a detailed plan for the evacuation of as many elements as possible of the Africa Army. For this, you will first fly to Rome and have the plan countersigned by Marshal Kesselring. You will then fly on to Berlin and report to Colonel-General Guderian (chief of the general staff of the army) and General Schmundt (head of army personnel), likewise, for countersigning. You then fly to Berchtesgaden, to Fuehrer HQ, and report to Keitel or Jodl, to be given an appointment with Hitler. Wherever you go, you will keep in contact with us through a 1,000 watt radio and a special code. General Seidemann (air chief for Africa, whom I knew well, and his wife "Seidefrau," from Berlin days) will let you have his Heinkel 111. Departure as soon as possible."

"I am honored by the task, Colonel-General," I replied, "but how should I, an insignificant frontline soldier, get anywhere with Hitler? Besides, I should like to be with my men in the final phase."

"We've thought of all that," said von Armin. "The army generals are extremely suspect to the Fuehrer; even Rommel is apparently to be left out in the cold. Even after the loss of Stalingrad, Hitler sticks to his 'victory or death, but no retreat.' That means we shall now lose about 130,000 men in North Africa, too, men with the best combat experience and of high morale. Hitler is more likely to listen, if at all, to an 'insignificant' major straight from the front, if you give him a clear idea of the situation and the feeling among the men. You will travel, and appear before him, in your dusty, faded uniform. That can't fail to have an effect. The plan you are taking was worked out some time ago and provides for the proportional evacuation of the most important officers, frontline soldiers, and technicians. General

Gause will discuss the details with you. I wish you, and us, complete success; report daily by radio." With a shake of the hand, I was dismissed.

Gause filled out the mission.

"You won't be returning to your battalion, but will go to the supply base in the Cape Bon Peninsula. There, I'll send you a Fieseler Stork, which will take you to the airfield the day after tomorrow, early enough for you to set off before dawn."

"Kesselring, Guderian, and Schmundt have been informed of your coming. I don't know whether you will be allowed to come back to Africa, but try. Speed is of the essence; every day lost makes evacuation more difficult. All the best, Luck." Gause handed me the "plan" in a large envelope and I was dismissed.

I had to stop and take a deep breath; this mission was altogether too unexpected and momentous. After all the years of frontline service, here was a task that went far beyond the level of a battalion commander.

It was not all that far to our supply base and I arrived there shortly before dark. The astonishment was suitably great when I had to tell my people that I would be flying to Germany on a "special mission." I at once notified Captain Bernhardt by radio. "I think I may be back in a week. Keep your courage up and see that as many men as possible get back to the Cape Bon Peninsula. Give my greetings to everyone."

Next day, I packed the essentials; my main baggage, including the picture of Rommel, I left behind in my command car.

In the afternoon, the Fieseler landed at our base. Its young pilot told me I had to be on the airfield at about 5:30 in the morning, so that the Heinkel could cross the Mediterranean before Spitfires made the airspace unsafe. Then, several officers appeared from the Nizza Battalion, which had been almost wiped out and had only one diminutive patrol fit for service that was still in action. They brought along a few bottles of Chianti and handed me letters and packets for their families in Italy, which I was to take with me. In the evening, we all squatted together under the palms. No sound of battle was to be heard; everything appeared so peaceful and unreal.

It was later than I would have wished; the pilot of the Fieseler had to wake me up—we were behind schedule. One last wave from the machine and we set off as dawn was breaking. The Heinkel was standing ready with engines running; the Fieseler taxied up to the entrance hatch. The pilot, apparently a very experienced sergeant, called out to me from the cockpit: "Hurry, Major, hurry, we're late, the Spitfires will soon be there."

I had to lie flat in the nose cone and as front gunner, man the 20mm cannon; there was no other way of transporting me.

"Are you familiar with the cannon, Major?" the pilot asked over the intercom.

"Listen, we had this gun in our scout cars when you were still wetting your pants," I replied.

"Okay, try it out, please, as soon as we're over the sea; we shall be flying very low," came the pilot's voice.

The day was dawning in the east as we lifted off with engines roaring. After a few minutes, we were over the sea, about 30 to 50 feet, I guessed, above the unruffled surface of the water. So I put in a magazine, fed it through, and pressed the trigger: nothing! I fed through again, again nothing.

"What kind of a stupid gun is this," I shouted to the pilot.

I tried again and again, and finally half dismantled the cannon. I fed through again, again nothing. The pilot was getting anxious.

"We need your gun in case British fighters attack from the front. Please keep trying, it's already light outside."

I was now fully occupied with the bloody gun and saw nothing, where or how high we were flying, or whether British fighters might appear out of the blue. Suddenly, the pilot drew the machine up.

"We're getting near Sicily," his voice came through, "soon be out of danger."

I hardly heard him; I was too busy with the cannon. And suddenly, it worked: a long burst of fire ripped through the skies.

"Hurray!" I cried, "it's working."

"Stop, stop," shouted the pilot, and already the first salvos of flak were whistling past us. The Italian air defenses took us for a Heinkel captured by the British. Luckily, their aim was not very good. My pilot fired recognition flares, the Italians stopped firing, and we were able to land.

"Thanks for the flight," I called to the sergeant. "Next time, I'll bring my own 2cm cannon."

That same day, I flew to Rome on a shuttle plane, was allotted a room in the famous Hotel Excelsior on the Via Veneto by the German liaison officer, and given an appointment with Kesselring for the following morning.

Rome seemed almost undisturbed. There was no blackout, as in Germany, there were hardly any military vehicles to be seen, and the famous Via Veneto was pulsating with life as in times of peace. In my faded tropical uniform, I felt out of place.

At the hotel, I gave the letters of my Italian friends to the porter, who at once congratulated me with great respect on the *Medaglia d'Argento*. After a bath, the first for so long, I decided to eat at Chez Alfredo. Alfredo was famous for his spaghetti and had received from the Italian royal family a set of golden cutlery with which he himself served the great personalities of the day. The walls of his little restaurant on the Piazza Colonna were covered with the photographs and dedications of famous politicians, actors, and writers; his Golden Visitor's Book offered a cross-section of the prominent from all the world.

When Alfredo saw me, he rushed across to me.

"*Comandante*, what an honor and pleasure, congratulations on the *Medaglia d'Argento*. I will serve you personally with the best spaghetti, which is still to be had here, in spite of the war."

From all the tables, people looked across to me as Alfredo drew his golden cutlery from his pocket to serve the spaghetti.

Then the climax; the lights went out, the head waiter brought a flaming *omelette surprise* to my table and Alfredo cried out it delight: "*Ecco maestoso.*" There was applause from all the tables. I had to get a grip on myself: that morning, I had still been on the last battlefield in North Africa, now a ceremony here that had nothing whatever to do with war and death.

I thanked Alfredo, "Wonderful, first-class, we could only dream of such things in North Africa. Now we'll cap the festive meal with a nice mocha."

Alfredo almost wept. "*Comandante*, there is a war on, we've had no coffee now for a long time. How sorry I am, this damned war!"

I put my hand in my pocket and took out a little packet of real coffee.

"Here, Don Alfredo, here's our mocha. It's for you, the chef, and a cup for me, Okay?"

Alfredo's eyes shone. Shortly after, he invited me into the holy of holies, to the chef in his kitchen. There, the three of us sat at the chef's table and enjoyed the mocha, an honor for me to sit with the chef in person.

I was not allowed to pay, but had to be entered in the Golden Visitor's Book, where my name now stood modestly beside that of so many prominent people. Relaxed and at peace, I strolled through the night up the Veneto, to enjoy a bed again after so long.

Next morning, a car from the liaison officer took me to Frascati, the wine center near Rome, where Kesselring had his HQ. There, time had stood quite still, not a trace of the war. It was already spring there and, surrounded by its vineyards, the romantic town nestled against a hill.

I was admitted at once to Kesselring; he was apparently fully informed. He was a charming man of medium height with warm and sympathetic eyes. We respected him as he was the only high commander to come to Africa.

"How was the flight," he asked. "Did Seidemann's Heinkel bring you safely over the pond?"

He had a good laugh when I told him the tale of the 20mm cannon.

"I haven't much hope of getting our plan through with Hitler, but we must try it, with the further signatures of Schmundt and Guderian. You can still fly to Berlin today, by courier plane. Every day counts. Good luck." And he shook my hand.

Still in my dusty, faded tropical uniform, I landed in Berlin, after sending off a report to von Arnim from Frascati.

What a contrast to Rome! The city presented a picture of destruction, many of the houses were now just ruins and the faces of the once busy Berliners were gray. One could see that they no longer believed in the "Final Victory" of Hitler and Goebbels, though no one dared say as much; the danger of denunciation was too great.

That same evening, I was admitted to General Schmundt. He, too, was well briefed. Responsible for the personnel side of the evacuation measures, he signed the plan without even reading it.

Next morning, I was with Colonel-General Guderian, the newly appointed chief of the general staff of the army. I had not seen him since the beginning of the war. He looked tired; only his eyes had their old sparkle.

"Luck, I'm glad to see one of the old hands of the panzer force again, alive and well. How many from the early days of our proud force have already gone! We've just lost Stalingrad. You know, perhaps, how many experienced officers and men have fallen there, or been taken prisoner.

"And now the same thing is looming in Africa. I can't even think about the seasoned members of the three divisions of the old Afrika Korps with their desert experience, or the new divisions sent into Tunisia.

"That is why I agreed at once to the evacuation plan, which had, of course, already been drawn up by Rommel, though we all had little hope that Hitler would agree to it. The idea of sending you to him, as an old trooper from the front, carries more weight, at any rate, than our opinion, which is regarded by Hitler as 'defeatist.' You can still go today, by the night train, and be in Berchtesgaden tomorrow morning."

"Colonel-General, one question before I leave: Why have you come back now, after Hitler had fired you? It's something we often ask ourselves."

"Listen," Guderian replied, "if I had refused, as I would have much preferred, someone else would be sitting in my chair, who might have known nothing of panzer tactics, or who might have been just a yes-man to Hitler's ideas. As it is, I can try to save what is to be saved and make some attempt to prevent the worst from happening. There is now, more than ever, the threat of an invasion by the Western Allies in Italy or southern France, or both. For that, I need an intact, experienced panzer force. Whatever I can do for all of you, I will do."

Guderian then made a surprising request.

"Luck, you have very good relations with Rommel, haven't you? As I've not come across him for some years, I would be very interested in a talk with him. If you should meet Rommel at Fuehrer HQ or anywhere else, please ask him whether he would agree to a meeting, preferably in Munich. No one must know of it. Hitler would at once suspect a conspiracy, with dire consequences for us. You've caught my meaning?"

"Of course, Colonel-General. I'll do what I can and let you know." With his winning smile, he dismissed me.

Once again, I sent off a radio message to von Arnim and told him I would be visiting HQ the next day.

Through a long night, I rolled south in a sleeping-car, undisturbed by air raids.

The first person I met in Berchtesgaden was Lieutenant-Colonel von Bonin, whom I had last seen on New Year's Eve 1942, when he accompanied Rommel to my command post in the desert.

"What are you doing here?" he greeted me. "I thought you were fighting your last battle in Tunisia." In confidence, I put him in the picture about my mission and asked through or via whom I could best get to make my plea to Hitler.

"My friend," he replied, "we're not on the battlefield here; here even Rommel has no say. Here, bureaucracy rules. That means you must first go to the officer-in-charge, Africa,' a certain Colonel X, who will then announce you to Colonel-General Jodl. He will get the okay from Field Marshal Keitel as to whether and when you will be allowed in to see the Fuehrer. Come, as a start, I'll take you to the first link in the chain of command. But from 1230 to 1400 hours there's the midday break, when no one at all can be seen. That's the way things are. In Africa, well over a hundred thousand men are bleeding and fighting for their lives, but here, the midday break must be observed, while the war comes to a stop!"

Colonel X received me in very friendly fashion. I stated my business and asked to be announced at once to Jodl.

"Listen, my friend, you can forget about the evacuation plan; the North African theater of war has already been virtually written off. We are still trying, of course, to send over as much materiel as possible, to continue the struggle, but we have no great hopes. Be glad that you are out of the mess; your mother will be thankful to see you again safe and sound."

I was shocked. It was as easy as that, apparently; the theater of war was simply "written off."

"Have you any idea," I replied somewhat sharply, "how things look down there, what we've been through, and that we are only losing the war because we have never received adequate supplies? Please arrange an appointment for me with Colonel-General Jodl for this afternoon."

It was fixed for three o'clock. Over a meal in the bare mess, Bonin gave me Rommel's address and telephone number. Whatever happened, I wanted to tell him of the outcome.

Then, with my large envelope, I was standing before Jodl. We knew he was an experienced staff officer, but we frontline troops didn't like him, as he was such a toady to Hitler. I explained my mission to him and why von Arnim had chosen me as intermediary.

"Things look very bad, Colonel-General," I began, "we're no longer equal to the pressure of the British and the Americans. The RAF, in particular, hinders almost all our movements, except when it's raining. The long front from Gabes to Tunis cannot anywhere near be covered by us. To prevent a disaster as many men as possible should be evacuated at once, to be available on fronts where the Western Allies are sure to land. For this purpose, I have an evacuation plan to deliver which has been carefully worked out by Rommel and von Arnim and countersigned by Kesselring, Guderian, and Schmundt."

With that, I handed him the envelope.

"I have been sent here," I went on, "as an insignificant field officer in the hope that this would make some impression on the Fuehrer." Jodl looked at me for a long time, without opening the envelope.

"Listen, Luck," he finally said, "there is absolutely no question of evacuating elements of the Africa Army, or of considering a 'German Dunkirk,' as you call it. The Fuehrer is not ready to think of retreat. We won't even let you see him personally. He would have a fit of rage and throw you out. Besides, we're glad to have the Fuehrer on the political tack for a few days, as he is just having a state visit by Antonescu of Romania." Without pausing, Jodl took my arm and led me to a huge campaign map that covered one whole wall.

"Here, you can see the front in Russia, when we were about to lose Stalingrad. What do you think about Stalingrad?"

"Colonel-General, we have so much trouble with our own theater of war, that we have no time to concern ourselves with Stalingrad. We merely ask ourselves whether it is necessary to abandon 200,000 battle-tried men to their fate. The word Stalingrad is, for us, a provocation, as we fear a similar fate, unless an attempt is made to save what is left to save."

Jodl was silent. After a short pause he gave me his hand.

"I can understand you all, but your 'mission' is of no avail. Inform von Arnim to that effect." When I left Jodl, I saw in his eyes a helpless sympathy for the Africa Army.

Deeply disappointed, I went to the radio office and sent off my message to von Arnim. "Not admitted to Fuehrer, plan rejected by Jodl, flying back to Rome and from there to Tunisia."

I reported my departure to Colonel X and met Bonin once more. "Please tell Rommel about the failure of my mission; I will try to fly back to Africa. If that proves impossible, I'll get in touch with Rommel," I told him.

There was nothing more to keep me in Germany; I wanted to be with my men. In Rome, I was told by the German liaison officer that strict orders were in force to allow no further personnel to fly to Africa; only supplies were to be flown to Tunis within the bounds of what was still possible. I didn't give up hope, however, of being able to get across; I stayed for the time being in Rome and was at the liaison office every day.

The daily news from the front was alarming. The Mareth position had been lost, but the remains of the Africa Army were still holding out at Gabes and the 5th Panzer Army west and southwest of Tunis. The Americans failed to push into the huge gap between the two armies, and thus separate them from each other. In the first half of April, it would still have been possible to move a large part of the troops to Sicily via the Cape Bon Peninsula and from north of Tunis. Earmarked for this were all the Junkers 52s ("Auntie Jus") that were flying in supplies and flying out empty, torpedo boats and the famous "Siebel ferries," large flat ferries that were driven by old aircraft engines. But, apart from the wounded, no one was allowed to leave Tunisia. One day in April, I met with General Gause in Rome—he had been sent to the Commando Supremo (I believe von Arnim wanted to save this seasoned general-staff officer for Rommel)—and General Bayerlein, who was very ill.

By the end of April, the front in the south was on the point of collapse; hardly any ammunition, fuel, or replacements were getting across. Suddenly, an order from Fuehrer HQ arrived in Rome: "A start is to be made at once with the evacuation of German and Italian troops from Tunisia; all available means of transport are to be employed."

And what followed was the very evacuation plan that I had delivered to Jodl weeks before. Junkers, torpedo boats, and Siebel ferries were brought into action. My battalion was still in the south with the Africa Army; it would have had no chance of getting through to the north to the Cape Bon Peninsula. I received a last radio message from Captain Bernhardt.

"Have no fuel or ammunition left, immobile awaiting decisive attack. We greet our commander and our families, Panzer Reconnaissance Battalion 3."

When the first officers and men arrived at the airfields for evacuation, American tanks were already there: "Come on boys, it's all over," they informed our troops. "Hands up!"

At HQ, they had hesitated for over two weeks, only to attempt a "German Dunkirk" after all. Thousands could have been saved if Jodl had authorized our plan at once.

On 6 May, after an all-out offensive by the Allies, the German-Italian remains of the proud Africa Army surrendered; more than 130,000 German soldiers went into captivity.

To be taken prisoner has been regarded, from time immemorial, as a "national" or personal disgrace. Although humane treatment could have been expected from the British and Americans, many tried to avoid capture. A few succeeded in adventurous ways. Some members of the paratroop division got to Sicily by tying themselves to the undercarriage of the few, overfilled Ju 52s.

Lieutenant von Mutius, from my battalion, turned up in Rome. "Since we had no reconnaissance vehicles or ammunition," he reported, "I was with our supply section in the Cape Bon Peninsula. When everything was coming to an end, I happened to discover a Siebel ferry in a bay, intact and well camouflaged. Technicians established that the ferry was ready to start. I asked the men, wandering around aimlessly in the area, who would like to come to Sicily with me. Nearly a hundred came forward, with whom I set off before dawn. Sailing only by my compass, we reached a port in Sicily without interference. There we were not allowed to land because we had no ship's papers. 'All right then,' I shouted to the Italians, 'we'll put to sea again.' We came ashore in an unguarded bay. Here we are, to rejoin our units."

Lieutenant von Wechmar, from my battalion, who, after the war, was a correspondent with the UP agency in Germany and is today our ambassador in London, years later, gave an account of his fate.

"During the final days, I was in action in the north. After the surrender, I cleared off with another officer and found an American jeep, in which we tried to get through to Morocco. We had gotten no further than Algeria, when we were discovered by the Amis and taken prisoner as we were trying to organize some fuel. Like almost all German prisoners, we were shipped to the USA, where I ended up in a POW camp in Trinidad, Colorado, and was well treated. Although, at the time, I much regretted falling into captivity, in retrospect, it may have saved my life."

Winfried von St. Paul, the nephew of a good friend of mine, was transferred to my battalion at the end of 1942, at my request, and saw action with the successful "Molinari" patrol. Long after the war, I met him again in Hamburg. He told me of the last days of my battalion.

"Once, when we were still operating in the south of Tunisia, our patrol just managed to escape the British, though they did capture our little workshop vehicle.

Next day, the vehicle turned up again. The crew reported that the British commander had said: 'We really can't leave you in the desert without spare parts or water. Here's some water, get back to your battalion.' " This was more evidence of fairness in this theater of war.

"When you flew to Germany," St. Paul told me, "Captain Bernhardt took command. At the beginning of May 1943, we were still fighting in the southern sector. The battalion still had 90 men in action, but no scout cars and only a little fuel when, on 9 May, we had to surrender. The British officer, who took us prisoner, went up to Bernhardt and said: 'It's an honor for us to capture you and Reconnaissance Battalion 3. Please keep your pistol. Is there anything we can do for you?'

" 'Please don't make us walk to Tunis,' replied Bernhardt, 'we're tired.' At that, British trucks were organized, which took us to the prison camp, past prisoners marching on foot, including a general.

"From Constantine," St. Paul went on, "we were taken by train to Casablanca, guarded by Americans with wooden truncheons. 'We aren't dogs,' we called out to them, 'put the truncheons away.' From then on, we were well treated and came into conversation with the guards. As we traveled west, we passed huge dumps of fuel and ammunition, as large as football fields. Our opinion was unanimous: With all this materiel, we never had a chance of winning the war. In the POW camp at Opelika, Alabama, in the States, we were treated really well, until we were discharged at the beginning of April 1946, unfortunately, to England, where it was another year before we were sent home."

All the accounts that I heard, some still in Rome, others long after the war, traced the sad end of a merciless, but always fair, war in North Africa.

While everyone in Rome was already speculating about whether and where the Allies would land in Italy, the African chapter had also ended for me; my thoughts went out to my brave men across the sea, for whom the war had ended for good.

14
Berlin and Paris, 1943–1944

Once again, my train rolled north, over the Apennines, the plain of the Po and the Alps. The countryside seemed so peaceful that I could hardly believe the Italians could be feeling the horrors of war in their own homeland. It was warm and summery; in passing, I saw people going about their work. Through the liaison officer in Rome, I received a movement order to Berlin via Munich.

In Munich, I not only wanted to see a few friends again, but to concern myself mainly with the meeting that Guderian had requested with Rommel.

I was allotted a room in the famous Four Seasons Hotel, which belonged to the brothers Walterspiel. I contacted Rommel by telephone at Semmering, where he was undergoing treatment.

I told him of the unsuccessful "mission" and the hopelessly delayed permission to evacuate. Rommel made no comment. His telephone may have been tapped.

In somewhat "coded" form, I conveyed Guderian's request, to which Rommel agreed at once. After referring back to Guderian, a day was arranged for a meeting at the Seasons. I asked Walterspiel to reserve a room and to keep this meeting of the prominent generals secret under all circumstances.

I welcomed Rommel on the day of the meeting and he questioned me closely about events during the last days before I was sent to Europe. He said that at the time he had fallen from favor with Hitler and that he was glad to be having an exchange of views with Guderian after such a long while. Shortly after, Guderian arrived; he greeted me briefly and the two men retired for their talk. I have never heard anything of its content.

Walterspiel, who felt honored by the distinguished visitors, had reserved a table for me somewhat apart from the hotel guests and he now dished me up a meal from his black-market store that could not have been ordered by an "ordinary" guest even for a large sum of money. As I was smoking a cigarette in the lounge while waiting for Rommel and Guderian, an elderly lady of good appearance came to my table. "You don't mind, do you?" she said, and, with that, took a silver box from her handbag, picked up my cigarette butt from an ashtray and put it in the box, in which I could see she already had several others.

"Please excuse me," she said in some embarrassment, "but the tobacco ration is so small that I roll my own from the remains of cigarettes. Now that coffee has been unobtainable for so long, cigarettes are all I have left to see me through the bad times. Do excuse me."

I was profoundly shocked. How hard it must have been for those at home to cope with rationing, air raids, and anxiety about their men at the front. When I gave the lady the rest of my pack of cigarettes, she smiled at me gratefully.

Rommel and Guderian came into the lounge separately. A quick handshake, "All the best to you, Luck," and the two men were gone.

After staying for a few days in Munich, I traveled on to Berlin, to the bombed one-time "capital of Europe."

Wenzel Luedecke, my orderly officer in Africa and the former assistant director with UFA, had offered me his penthouse near the Kurfurstendamm as a place to stay while I was in Berlin, and I gladly accepted. I reported officially to the replacement section, and picked up my faithful Mercedes cabriolet.

To see about my next posting, I had to call at the Personnel Office. I sent my name directly to General Schmundt, to whom I gave an account of the unsuccessful "mission."

What lay in store for me? The eastern front?

Schmundt cut short my reflections.

"Luck, you are assigned with immediate effect to the 'commander reserve' for one year. We've lost so many commanders that we are having to form a reserve for a possible new theater of war in Italy or France. I'll find you a job in which you can pass on your experience."

I was horrified. Not, for God's sake, a whole year of sitting around at home. I wanted to be back at the front.

Suddenly a thought struck me.

"General, you can't do this to me. Let me make you a suggestion. Instead of a year, only six months, and that in Paris, where the army has its school for panzer reconnaissance commanders. That's where I can best pass on my experience to future COs. What do you think of that?"

Schmundt couldn't help laughing.

"That's typical of you reconnaissance people, always flexible and ready with novel solutions. I agree."

A few days later, I was officially posted from August 1943 to March 1944 to the school in Paris, where I was to report to Colonel von Wechmar, a cousin of my predecessor.

Meanwhile, it was the end of May 1943. The warm spring made the troubled city of Berlin seem somewhat less implacable.

I installed myself in the penthouse. Each evening it had to be blacked out. The little suitcase always stood ready. It contained my most important papers as well as my stock of coffee and cigarettes, which I had organized at the supply depot in Tunis. As soon as the sirens wailed—and that happened almost every day—I hurried with the suitcase to the air raid shelter. In Berlin's sea of houses, I couldn't stay outside during air raids. The danger of being hit by debris or bomb fragments was too great. Besides, everyone had to comply with the directions of the air raid warden.

The Allies were now dropping more incendiary bombs, which immediately set off great area fires, or if there was a wind, the dreaded fire storms. Naturally, my penthouse was particularly vulnerable, but I accepted the risk.

I, too, now received food stamps, too many to go hungry, too few to eat one's fill. The food was better at the replacement section. The men, after all, had to be made fit for frontline service. In the Mercedes, I shuttled back and forth between the Kurfurstendamm and the barracks. Many of my friends were no longer to be found. Some had fled into the country, others, especially my Jewish and literary friends, had disappeared forever. Those who had not been able to escape abroad had probably been sent to concentration camps.

We frontline soldiers, but also the friends I asked, knew of the existence of the camps (in Berlin, nearby Sachsenhausen was the best known) and in connection with them we knew the term "protective custody." But we had no idea of what took place behind the barbed wire.

At the beginning of June, I was invited to a party given by a Prussian princess, whom I became acquainted with before the war through my friend von Papen. On account, probably, of my "exotic aura" of having come from Africa, but no doubt even more on account of my present of coffee, I was the favored guest. There I met Dagmar, the daughter of the proprietor of Europe's biggest tree nursery. She was celebrating her twenty-first birthday.

We clicked at once. I invited her for a meal the next day. There she told me right at the start ("so that you know where you are") that she was classified as "one-eighth Jewish" and enjoyed "Aryan rights." Her mother, one of the most elegant women of Berlin, was "one-quarter Jewish." It was macabre how bureaucratically the "Jewish question" was treated in Germany. I met Dagmar's parents, both cosmopolitans, who—like Dagmar—spoke fluent English and French.

We saw each other as often as we could. Dagmar slowly lost her aversion to all things military, which she regarded, along with Party functionaries, as the quintessence of the power of the Third Reich.

I thought of engagement, but also of my resolution not to form a close tie, in the interests of both, before the end of the war. I did promise, however, to bring her to Paris for the duration of my teaching job. I wanted to get her away from the confinement of Berlin and the danger of air raids, and to know that she was no longer exposed to what were often abusive remarks about her "one-eighth status."

At the end of June, I took some leave to visit friends in Hamburg and to see my mother and sister in Flensburg.

My friend, Boos, lived outside Hamburg, not far from Friedrichsruh, where

Bismarck lived in his retirement. During the night, before I was to go to Flensburg, Hamburg had its worst air raid of the war. Whole blocks collapsed. Losses among the civilian population were enormous. From Boos's garden, we could see Hamburg on fire. In the early hours of the morning, thousands of refugees arrived in the suburbs on foot, many of them with phosphorous burns. I can still see those poor people today; some had escaped with their bare lives. They were given shelter in emergency reception camps. Now I understood why all the wounded wanted to get back to the front as fast as possible; there they could play an active part in determining events, whereas the civilian population was condemned to passivity.

Flensburg, although a naval base, had so far been spared. Our large apartment had been requisitioned for refugees, except for two rooms. My sister had been called up and posted to the commander in Holland. My mother carried on a lively barter-trade with farmers we had known earlier. For valuable objets d'art, which my father had brought back from the Far East, she obtained butter and meat. In this way, she was able to supplement the meager ration from stamps. Being an older woman she was unable to make a contribution to the war effort and thus received no priority cards. Although it pained me, I nevertheless encouraged her to go on bartering, and at the same time promised to send her, from France, anything that might be useful to her.

I admired my mother, who bore with courage not only the death of my stepfather, but also the war service of her three children. We spent some happy hours together and I tried to comfort her. The coffee I had brought helped her along in the weeks that followed.

Back in Berlin the days and weeks went by. At the replacement section, I gave talks on my experiences in the different theaters of war to young soldiers who had just been called up. Dagmar's mother, who didn't have an Aryan identity card but was "tolerated" as the wife of a prominent man, had used a trip to friends in Switzerland to get away. To stay longer in Berlin had seemed to her too risky.

With Dagmar and a few friends, I celebrated my thirty-second birthday, for which Baron von Boeselager sent me some bottles of champagne and cognac from my "sunken hoard." Would it be my last? At all events, the last at home.

August 1943. Time to go, into a future that was becoming ever more uncertain. Parting from Dagmar was harder than I had expected. "I'll get you to Paris one way or another, you can count on that."

With a movement order for myself and the Mercedes, I turned my back on Berlin. My personal belongings from Luedecke's penthouse had been handed over to Dagmar, who stored them at the nursery outside Berlin. Two weeks later the penthouse was destroyed by an incendiary bomb.

After a stop at the Boeselagers' near Bonn, I arrived in Paris and reported to "Bubi" von Wechmar, the commander of the panzer reconnaissance school. Then on to local HQ, to the city commander, General von Boineburg, who, in Russia, had commanded the brigade of grenadiers in our 7th Panzer Division.

"I'm delighted to see you alive and well, my dear Luck. I expect you'd like an apartment near your school at the Invalides?"

"Yes, General, I would. I'd also be glad of a driving permit for my Mercedes, which gave such good service during my months in Russia."

I was allotted a wonderful penthouse in the Rue Bixio with a view over the whole of Paris. It belonged to a Swiss businessman who had gone home and put his apartment at the disposal of the military command—including a chamber maid, who lived in. For her it became a memorable time, as I was able to keep her supplied with foodstuffs that were no longer obtainable in Paris.

The first four-week course began. Between courses, there was a week's pause to assess the previous course. In one of these courses, my friend Franz von Papen turned up, who, till then, had been in action on the eastern front. In another, de Maizière, later a general in the Bundeswehr, and Major Waldow, later a commander in my panzer division.

I made contact with J. B. Morel and Clément Duhour, who were overjoyed to see me again, safe and sound. They had no doubts that the Western Allies would land somewhere in France.

"Hans, you won't hold out. You can't win this war, with two fronts and the overwhelming materiel. Once again, stay here when things come to an end. We'll see that you're not discovered."

"You know I can't do it," I replied. "We've been brought up differently and taken our oath. So I must, if need be, see it through to the bitter end."

After I had been in Paris for a few weeks, Clément came to my apartment in great agitation.

"Hans, the Gestapo have arrested J. B. We don't know where he is. I presume he belongs to the Resistance or that he'd made disparaging remarks about the Germans. You know, of course, that J. B. is a great patriot and was a serving officer in the French army."

I promised Clément to do whatever was possible.

It so happened that a very high Gestapo man lived in the same house as me in the Rue Bixio. We had met a few times in the elevator or on the street and had exchanged a few words with each other. He seemed to see in me the good type of frontline soldier and in some way to admire me.

I decided—albeit reluctantly—to ask for his help, and called on him in his apartment. I had mentioned J. B.'s name, I went on, "Listen, M. Morel fought against me in 1940. He was a brave opponent and is a staunch patriot. I don't believe he would have said anything disparaging about us Germans. He thinks too much of me for that. He may have said that after Stalingrad and North Africa this war is now taking a decisive turn. If so, that's an opinion I can only share. I would be grateful if you could get M. Morel released."

This was undoubtedly risky. What I had said would itself be regarded by the Nazis and the Gestapo as "defeatist."

Four days later, J. B. turned up in my apartment. He had tears in his eyes.

"Hans, I won't ever forget what you've done."

I conveyed my thanks to the Gestapo man with a bottle of cognac.

Meanwhile, I was trying to get Dagmar to Paris. I was told at HQ that this would be simple if she could show that she had a job with a French firm doing work for the German occupation. Near the Champs Elysées, I found a firm that was converting trucks to wood-burning (fuel had long since been scarce). They were glad to have Dagmar as an interpreter.

Through the military command, I obtained a residence and work permit for Dagmar and wrote to tell her, full of joy. But my letter crossed with bad news: the Gestapo had picked up her father. He was supposed to have made disparaging remarks about Hitler. I was appalled. This proud and conservative man would never be able to stand it. After my success with the Gestapo in the case of J. B., I had to try to get him out. I received permission from Wechmar, to whom I outlined the situation, to take four days' leave in Berlin between courses.

A week later the chance came. With the necessary movement order and a driver from the school, I drove nonstop the 1,000 kilometers and more from Paris to Berlin. I was equipped with a note from the city commander requesting all service stations of the SS and Gestapo to assist me as a frontline soldier.

The reunion with Dagmar was overshadowed by events. She loved her father dearly and being "one-eighth Jewish," moreover, she was certainly no supporter of the Third Reich. But she bore her fate with composure. Although she placed little hope in my "mission," she was grateful nonetheless that at least something was being done.

Next morning, we drove in my Mercedes to Sachsenhausen. My uniform (I was still in tropical dress), my decorations, and the note from Boineburg didn't fail to impress. The camp commandant himself came to the guard room. Dagmar was not allowed into the camp. So I took the big parcel of foodstuffs and was conducted to the visiting room. As we went, the commandant assured me, "We too on the home front are doing our great part for victory." It sounded like a sneer. I refrained from comment; I was, after all, trying to get Dagmar's father out of there.

And then he was brought in, a shadow of his former self, his eyes full of fear. What had those few weeks done to a healthy, upright man?

"How are you?" A superfluous question on my part. "Dagmar is in the guard room. She wasn't allowed in, but sends you a big hug."

What could I talk to Dagmar's father about? An SS man was sitting in the corner and could hear every word, and was probably meant to.

"I've brought you a parcel of food, coffee, and cigarettes, which your daughter has packed for you. I have an appointment tomorrow with Kaltenbrunner." (Kaltenbrunner was head of the Gestapo, at any rate, the second most powerful man after Himmler, the head of all SS units and organizations.)

"I have a letter of recommendation with me and will press for your immediate release."

I could see from his reaction that he had no great hope.

"Thank you for coming here specially from Paris. Give my love to my daughter. I wish you both all the best. May you be very happy."

He got to his feet, for the guard had indicated that our time was up. We shook hands.

"Chin up, I'll get you out of here."

A last wave, and with tired steps this upright German left the room.

Next morning, I went to SS head office and was admitted at once to Kaltenbrunner. By rank, he must have been a general.

"I'm delighted to be able to greet a highly decorated officer from the front. Like you on active service, we here on the home front are putting in a superhuman effort to achieve the final victory."

The usual blabber; I could hardly bear it any more. But, of course, I wanted something from the man, so I went along with him halfheartedly. I then spoke my request.

"I've been given just four days' leave. I drove to Berlin through the night and yesterday, visited my prospective father-in-law in Sachsenhausen. He is in a bad way. He doesn't even know why he has been arrested. Believe me, Obergruppen-fuehrer (or whatever his SS rank was), my father-in-law is a good German and a well-known personality in Berlin. I consider it out of the question that he had brought some kind of guilt upon himself. There must be a mistake."

Kaltenbrunner showed sympathy and sent for his adjutant.

"Fetch me the file on Herr ————."

After a short time the man came back. "All the files on inmates of Sachsenhausen have been transferred to Czechoslovakia. I would have to request it from there."

"I'm sorry, I will have to wait for the file; that could take a little while. But depend on it, I will see that your father-in-law is released. That's the least I can do for such a brave frontline officer."

I gave him my military post number and unit, and with a handshake was dismissed. Had I been successful? I didn't know. Could one trust Kaltenbrunner and the whole Gestapo apparatus? Had the "transfer" of files been just a trick to get rid of me?

Dagmar was highly skeptical.

"I don't trust these people. They're shameless and inhuman. Thank you for coming. I'm glad I can join you in Paris now. It will help to soften the blow. As it is, there's nothing I can do here for my father."

I had to go back to Paris. Dagmar would follow as soon as she had arranged things at home.

Dagmar in Paris: in normal times, the fullfillment of a dream; but the clouds in the sky were dark. I bought her a bicycle, so that she could be independent of public transport, which often didn't run. We enjoyed our days in the penthouse in the Rue Bixio. J. B. and Clément often came to see us, and we were often at Clément's, at the Cavalier. We spent one evening there with Max Schmeling and Vivianne Romance, a famous actress at the time who was a friend of Clément. Together with Dagmar, I bought perfume, silk stockings, and supplies, which I sent to my mother, so that she had something to barter.

The winter passed and with it my time in Paris. Dagmar and I decided to get engaged. We bought the ring at a well-known jeweler in the Place Vendôme and celebrated the engagement with J. B. Morel and Clément Duhour. It was overshadowed by the fate of Dagmar's parents. Dagmar had no news of her father. All inquiries at Sachsenhausen remained unanswered. She no longer had much hope of seeing him alive again. Contact with her mother was broken. Her mother had merely informed her that she was leaving Switzerland for America.

I too heard nothing more from Kaltenbrunner.

When I later inquired, through a friend at Fuehrer HQ whether anything stood in the way of permission to marry a girl who was one-eighth Jewish, I received the same sharp disappointment. The answer was that if Major von Luck had been a reserve officer, there would have been nothing against marriage to a one-eighth Jewess with Aryan rights. As an active officer, however, he cannot be given permission.

This showed a peculiar logic and interpretation of the "racial laws." From a racial point of view, did a reserve officer count for less than one on active service?

At the beginning of March, I was sent to Germany on a short course for regimental commanders. There I was told that I had been posted as a regimental commander to the Panzer Lehr Division, which was led by General Bayerlein, the experienced African campaigner.

I returned to Paris at the beginning of April, to wind up my household. Dagmar was to stay in Paris for as long as possible; I had notified the city commander of her presence. J. B. and Clément were going to look after her.

"If things get critical, I'll organize transport for you. If I can't, go to the city commander, so that you can travel to Germany in a supply vehicle."

That was our good-bye. Neither of us knew when or in what circumstances we would see each other again.

Bayerlein's division lay somewhere in Normandy or Brittany. I set out in my Mercedes and decided to go via Rommel's command post at La Roche Guyon, west of Paris, and pay my respects.

General Gause, his chief of staff and faithful general staff officer in Africa, received me.

"Good to see you again, safe and sound. I'm just initiating my successor, General Speidel. Congratulations on your posting to France, where we must reckon on a landing sooner or later."

When I asked whether I might see the Field Marshal, Gause's answer was immediate.

"By all means. Rommel is rather depressed because his arguments about how a landing should be met are cutting no ice with Hitler. He will be pleased to see you. Take a little walk with him. It will distract him."

Rommel received me with his familiar smile. He looked much better than I remembered from our last meeting.

"I'm glad I can greet you here on the western front. We've got something coming up in the weeks ahead. See that the regiment you are to take over is well motivated and aware of the seriousness of the situation."

We strolled through the beautiful park of the chateau as Rommel repeated the prophecy he had made in North Africa.

"I'm against any solution by force. I must convince Hitler that we can no longer win the war, but at most put off the end. As soon as the opportunity arises, I will try to make it clear to him personally, in writing if necessary, that the war will be finally lost if the Allies succeed in setting up a second front here in the West. Every opponent who sets foot on French soil must be thrown back into the sea in the first hours. That can only be done if our panzer divisions are stationed right by the coast, and if enough fighters are in the air which can be thrown against the powerful Allied air forces.

"But Goering has let us down once before in Africa, and at Stalingrad too he failed to keep his promise. I don't believe in the 'thousand fighters' which he means to send here.

"All the best to you, Luck, I'll be visiting your division quite often in the coming weeks. We must do our duty."

I took my leave of Rommel—deeply impressed and disturbed.

At the Panzer Lehr Division, I was received at once by General Bayerlein, who greeted me with some "bad" news.

"My dear Luck, I had marked you down as commander of the panzer regiment, but was told a few days ago to send you at once to the reorganized 21st Panzer Division. It seems your commander, Major-General Feuchtinger, has more pull at Fuehrer-HQ. I much regret that I won't be able to have an old African campaigner in my Division."

I was far from happy about this decision, but that was the way things were.

No one knew where the 21st Panzer Division lay, so it was back to La Roche Guyon, where I saw Gause again.

"The 21st is just back from its Hungarian expedition; it was sent there because of a suspected uprising in favor of the Russians. It's in the Rennes area, in Brittany, but has just received orders to move to the area around Caen, the capital of Normandy. Please report there to Feuchtinger."

It was early May 1944, when I found the division and reported my posting.

"A hearty welcome to you," Feuchtinger greeted me. "Colonel Maempel, commander of Panzer Grenadier Regiment 125, has had to go home for health reasons. I am giving you acting command of his regiment until the official appointment comes through."

This division, put together in Brittany in 1943, mainly from experienced units from the Russian theater of war and replacements from Germany, was in many respects an unorthodox panzer division.

General Edgar Feuchtinger, an artilleryman, had no combat experience, and none at all of panzer units. He had become known in Germany as the organizer of the military part of the so-called *Reichsparteitage*, the national Party rallies, and through that was very familiar with Hitler and his Party apparatus. He had apparently used this "connection" to get me into his division as Colonel Maempel's successor.

Owing to lack of sufficient supplies, the division had mainly French war materiel, which had been found after the French campaign of 1940. This was allowed to be used, with the approval of High Command West, in order to hasten its reestablishment. To that end a "Special HQ Paris" had been created, which was responsible for organization, etc. Here Major Becker, a reserve officer and the owner of a small factory in western Germany, played a decisive part. A highly gifted engineer, with excellent links with armaments industry, and a personal friend of Feuchtinger, he had a free hand to improvise and, with the French materiel, put some of his own designs into effect.

At the Hotchkiss works near Paris, Becker discovered a vast number of tank chassis, for which he organized guns and finished armor-plating in Germany in order to create an "assault-gun" battalion. In addition, he had rocket-launchers made to his design, which were demonstrated on the Normandy coast in May 1944 to Rommel and a few army commanders and filled even Hitler with enthusiasm when he was told of them. Because of his connections, Becker's battalion also received the latest radio equipment.

At first, we laughed at the monstrous looking assault-guns, but we soon came to know better. The assault-gun companies were trained to work closely with the grenadiers, and this was later to prove a decisive aid to our defense forces. Feuchtinger was naturally proud of Becker's achievement and was often at his "Special HQ" in Paris, therefore, so that he could follow up Becker's work. In addition, Feuchtinger was a live and let live person. He was fond of all the good things of life, for which Paris was a natural attraction. Knowing that he had no combat experience or knowledge of tank warfare, Feuchtinger had to delegate most things, that is, leave the execution of orders to us experienced commanders.

Such was the division with which I had to familiarize myself and of which I had to become a part. Panzer Grenadier Regiment 125, entrusted to my command, consisted mainly of various units that had been in action on the Russian front and young replacements from home: the regimental staff, I Battalion in armored half-track vehicles (SPWs), and II Battalion in trucks.

Feuchtinger put me in the picture concerning the general situation. "Our division is the only one near the coast behind the Atlantic Wall, which, here in Normandy, is not yet fully developed and manned by an inexperienced infantry division. The anticipated Allied landing is not expected in Normandy, but rather in the Pas de Calais, the shortest distance between England and the Continent. But Caen, as an important industrial city, is also a key point. That is why it was decided to move a Panzer division here by the Atlantic Wall. All the same, we have to reckon on airborne landings or large-scale commando operations, which would serve as a diversion from the actual landing.

"For that reason, Rommel considers it very important that the division should take up combat positions even in the hinterland.

"Your regiment, in accordance with the orders of Army Group B (Rommel), to which the division is directly attached, is stationed northeast of Caen, hence east of the River Orne; the other regiment, 192, north of Caen, west of the Orne. South of Caen are the panzer regiment, the artillery, and the division's other units. For your support, you have two companies of Becker's assault-gun battalion.

"Our division has *strict orders* not to intervene in the event of enemy landings until cleared by Army Group B. Rommel wants all units to make themselves familiar with the terrain—also by night—and regular combat exercises to be carried out. I hope, my dear Luck, that you will be happy with us and I wish you lots of luck."

In the course of May, Rommel appeared at the division several times, to acquaint himself with its state of training and the morale of the men. On one of his visits, he expressed himself almost prophetically.

"I know the British from France in 1940 and from North Africa. They will land at the very place where we least expect them. It might be here."

To make up for the inadequate fortifications on the coast, Rommel ordered stake-obstacles to be erected on the shore and in the hinterland, what was known as "Rommel's asparagus." In addition, mine fields were laid wherever airborne landings might be expected.

We were somewhat concerned that the civilian population could move about freely. We even had to leave passages open in the mine fields, so that the peasants could go about their business. Evacuation was not considered. Why should it be? We didn't know, after all, where a landing might take place. Through this, the Resistance, which was certainly active in Normandy, had the chance to let the British know our positions, where our tank and artillery parks were, and the location of the mine fields. And indeed we later found campaign maps on prisoners with precise indications of our positions.

The weeks went by. For a panzer division, which in the campaigns so far had been accustomed to a war of movement, the inactivity was wearisome and dangerous. Vigilance was easily relaxed, especially after the enjoyment of Calvados and cider, both typical drinks of the region. There was, in addition, the uncertainty as to whether the landing would take place at all in our sector.

I was on the move every day, in order to visit each unit in the regiment, get to know the officers and NCOs and present myself to the individual men to gain their confidence.

At conferences at divisional HQ, I met the other divisional commanders. All of them had combat experience and were highly decorated.

In May 1944, I went once again to Paris. Feuchtinger wanted me to visit "Special HQ Becker," to familiarize myself with the assault-guns and rocket-launchers that he had developed and to talk to Becker about close collaboration with our grenadiers.

I told Dagmar I was coming and she had a delightful surprise: Herbert von Karajan was conducting Beethoven's Fifth Symphony with the French Philharmonic. Since Dagmar was a close friend of Karajan's wife, she was able to acquire tickets right away. For a few hours, the music let me forget the war and thoughts of the future.

On 30 May, Rommel came to our division for the last time. Becker demonstrated his new rocket-launcher on the Normandy coast with live ammunition, which filled Rommel with enthusiasm.

At the closing conference, with all the commanders of our division, Rommel exhorted us again to be extremely vigilant, and he ended with the words, "You shouldn't count on the enemy coming in fine weather and by day."

It was put even more precisely by General Marcks, commander of the 84th Army Corps, to which we were attached, "From my knowledge of the British, they will go to church again on Sunday, 4 June, and come on the Monday."

The navy and our meteorologists calculated that the most favorable time for a landing would be 5 June, then not again until 28 June 1944.

In the first days of June, British aerial reconnaissance over the Normandy coast increased considerably. As the division heard from Rommel's HQ, there were about 130 Messerschmidt fighters available in France. Of a transfer to France of the "1,000 fighters" promised by Goering, there was, in what were now after all critical days, no sign. They were needed, as always, for the air defense of the Reich territory.

We didn't know at the time that Rommel, by his own wish, had been invited to a conference with Hitler and had left for Germany on 4 June. Nor did we know that General Feuchtinger and his first general-staff officer had gone to Paris to "Special HQ." During the possibly decisive night of 5 to 6 June, therefore, neither of them would be at his headquarters.

We only knew the fatal order not to commit ourselves to any kind of engagement without having been cleared for it by Army Group B (Rommel) or Supreme Commander West (von Rundstedt).

On 5 June 1944, the two panzer grenadier regiments lay in their established combat positions on either side of the River Orne, north of Caen. I gave II Battalion permission for No. 5 Company under Lieutenant Brandenburg to carry out an exercise during the coming night and to turn out for the purpose with blank cartridges. This was in accordance with the plan of training every company in turn for night action.

15
The Start of the Invasion, 6 June 1944

The evening of 5 June 1944 was unpleasant. Normandy was showing its bad side; during the day there had been rain and high winds.

I was sitting in a sparsely furnished house on the edge of the village of Bellengreville, a few kilometers west of Vimont, a small town east of Caen, the industrial center and port of the Normandy coast; before me were papers and maps to do with exercises I was preparing for my regiment. My adjutant, Lieutenant Helmut Liebeskind, was at the command post in the village. I was a major, thirty-two years old. I was to be promoted to lieutenant-colonel at the end of July, and after a further two months to colonel—rapid progress, it seemed to me.

The general weather conditions, worked out every day by naval meteorologists and passed on to us by division, gave the "all clear" for 5 and 6 June. So we did not anticipate any landings, for heavy seas, storms, and low lying clouds would make large-scale operations at sea and in the air impossible for our opponents.

That evening, I felt our lot was highly unsatisfactory: like most of my men, I was used to mobile actions, such as we had fought in the other theaters of war; this waiting for an invasion that was undoubtedly coming was enervating.

But, in spite of the inactivity, morale among the troops remained high, the more so since Normandy spoiled us with butter, cheese, "*crème fraîche*," and meat, as well as cider.

On that rainy evening, my adjutant and I were waiting for a report from No. II Battalion that the night exercise had ended. This battalion was in the area Troarn-Escoville, hence fairly near the coast, while No. I Battalion, equipped with armored personnel carriers and armored half-track vehicles, had taken up waiting positions further to the rear. I had given the more basic order that in the event of possible landings by Allied commando troops, the battalions and companies concerned were to attack immediately and independently; and to do so, moreover, without regard to the prohibition from the highest authority on engaging action except after clearance by High Command West. But in view of the weather report that we had been given, I had no thought of such an engagement that night.

About midnight, I heard the growing roar of aircraft, which passed over us. I wondered whether the attack was destined once again for traffic routes inland or for Germany herself. The machines appeared to be flying very low—because of the weather? I looked out the window and was wide awake; flares were hanging in the sky. At the same moment, my adjutant was on the telephone, "Major, paratroops are dropping. Gliders are landing in our section. I'm trying to make contact with No. II Battalion. I'll come along to you at once."

I gave orders without hesitation, "All units are to be put on alert immediately and the division informed. No. II Battalion is to go into action wherever necessary. Prisoners are to be taken if possible and brought to me."

I then went to the command post with my adjutant. The 5 Company of No. II Battalion, which had gone out with blank cartridges, was not back yet from the night exercise—a dangerous situation. First reports indicated that British paratroops had dropped over Troarn. The commander of No. II Battalion had already started a counterattack with uninvolved elements and had succeeded in penetrating as far as Troarn, to which elements of the 5th Company had already withdrawn under their own steam.

We telephoned the company commander, who was in a cellar. "Brandenburg, hold on. The battalion is already attacking and is bound to reach you in a few moments."

"Okay," he replied, "I have the first prisoner here, a British medical officer of the 6th Airborne Division."

"Send him along as soon as the position is clear."

In the meantime, my adjutant telephoned the division. General Feuchtinger and his general-staff officer had not come back yet. We gave the orderly officer, Lieutenant Messmer, a brief situation report and asked him to obtain clearance for us for a concentrated night attack the moment the divisional commander returned.

By now, we had a slightly better idea of and grip on the situation. Prisoners who had misjudged their jumps and fallen into our hands in the course of our limited counterattack were brought in to me. Before I had them escorted away to division, in accordance with orders, we learned during our "small talk" that the 6th Airborne Division was supposed to jump during the night in order to take the bridges over the Orne at Ranville intact and form a bridgehead east of the Orne for the landing by sea planned for the morning of 6 June.

Gradually we were becoming filled with anger. The clearance for an immediate night attack, so as to take advantage of the initial confusion among our opponents, had still not come, although our reports via division to the corps and to Army Group B (Rommel) must have long since been on hand. We made a thorough calculation of our chances of successfully pushing through to the coast and preventing the formation of a bridgehead, or at least making it more difficult.

I remember the British medical officer who was brought to me as the first prisoner. In his parachute equipment he looked like any other soldier. As a good Briton, he kept his composure, but seemed deeply disappointed, and unnerved, at being taken prisoner immediately on his first mission. Since he too would only give his name and number, I began, as always with a British prisoner, to make small talk. I spoke about my last visit to London in March 1939, about Picadilly Circus and my British friends. At that he thawed, and I learned more about British intentions and the task of the 6th Airborne Division.

The hours passed. We had set up a defensive front where we had been condemned to inactivity. The rest of the division, with the panzer regiment and Panzer Grenadier Regiment 192, was equally immobilized, though in the highest state of alert. My adjutant telephoned once more to division. Major Forster, IC and responsible for the reception of prisoners, came to the phone. He too was unable to alter the established orders. Army Group B merely informed us that it was a matter of a diversionary maneuver: the British had thrown out straw dummies on parachutes. At daybreak, I sent my adjutant to ask divisional command post to secure us immediate clearance for a counterattack. On his arrival, Liebeskind witnessed a heated telephone conversation which Feuchtinger was evidently having with the army: "General, I have just come back from Paris and I've seen a gigantic armada off the west coast of Cabourg, warships, supply ships, and landing craft. I want to attack at once with the entire division east of the Orne in order to push through to the coast." But clearance was strictly denied.

Hitler, who used to work far into the night, was still asleep that early morning.

At the command post, I paced up and down and clenched my fists at the indecision of the Supreme Command in the face of the obvious facts. If Rommel had been with us instead of in Germany, he would have disregarded all orders and taken action—of that we were convinced.

We felt completely fit physically and able to cope with the situation. I concealed my anger and remained calm and matter-of-fact. My experience in previous theaters of war had taught me that the more critical a situation, or the more alarming the reports, the more calmly every experienced leader should react.

The best way to calm an excited orderly officer, or a dispatch rider coming straight from an apparently desperate situation, is to sit him down, give him a cigarette and say, "Now tell me what has actually happened."

So the tragedy took its course. After only a few hours, the brave fighting units in the coastal fortifications could no longer withstand the enemy pressure, or else they were smashed by the Allied naval guns; while a German panzer division, ready to engage, lay motionless behind the front and powerful Allied bomber formations, thanks to complete air superiority, covered the coastal divisions and Caen with concentrated attacks. In the early hours of the morning, from the hills east of Caen, we saw the gigantic Allied armada, the fields littered with transport gliders and the numerous observation ballons over the landing fleet, with the help of which the heavy naval guns subjected us to precision fire.

The situation forced us to regroup. Strong combat units were formed on either side of the Orne, east and west. We continued to wait for clearance for a counter-attack. In view of this superiority, I thought, on seeing the landing fleet, there was no longer much chance of throwing the Allies back into the sea. Bringing up reserves was even now extremely difficult for us. The "second front" had been established. The enemy in the east pressing with superior strength, the ceaseless bombing of our most important industrial centers and railway communications—even the bravest and most experienced troops could no longer win this war. A successful invasion, I thought, was the beginning of the end.

What we didn't know at the time was some information which came into my hands at the beginning of May 1987. Werner Kortenhaus, a former tank commander in our division and the author of *Geschichte der 21. Panzer-Division* ("History of the 21st Panzer Division"), made available to me two letters that had been sent to him at the end of 1979 by General Speidel, formerly chief of staff of Army Group B (Rommel).

Extract from letter of 26 October 1979:

> I called Feuchtinger between 1.00 h. and 2.00 h. on 6.6.44, but couldn't get him. It was not until the morning of 6 June that my first general-staff officer got through to him. . . . Feuchtinger had a *general directive* to attack at once in the event of an *airborne* landing.

Extract from letter of 15 November 1979:

> The 21st Panzer Division had orders to go into action at once if the enemy made an airborne landing, and with the *whole* Division, in fact.

This general order, to attack at once in full strength, hence with my whole combat group during that very night of 5–6 June, in the event of an *airborne* landing, was known neither to me nor to my adjutant at the time, the later General Liebeskind of the Bundeswehr. Neither, apparently, did the other units in the division know of this order. Instead, we all adhered to the strict order not to carry out even the smallest operation until it had been cleared by Army Group B. The divisional staff must have known of the other order, as is clear from General Speidel's letters.

The question arises: If I had known of the order to take action in the event of airborne landings, I would on my own responsibility have launched an attack with the whole regiment, reinforced by the Becker assault-gun battalion, against the airborne landings east of the Orne. It is my firm opinion, and that of my adjutant at the time, that by exploiting the initial confusion among the enemy after their descent, we would have succeeded in pushing through to the coast and probably also in regaining possession of the two bridges over the Orne at Bénouville. Parallel operations would then have been started also by Regiment 192 and the panzer regiment.

This would not have been enough to prevent the invasion as a whole, but there would probably have been a delay in the seaborne landing, with great losses for the British.

An example of how imprecise issuing of orders can have an adverse effect on a large operation.

Further, highly interesting information came into my hands at the beginning of June 1987 through a former captain on the general staff, later General Wagemann of the Bundeswehr, who had given it to Lieutenant-Colonel H. D. Bechtold of the Bundeswehr, a student of the invasion, at the beginning of May 1987.

From May to July 1944, Wagemann had been posted to the divisional staff for training and during the night of 5–6 June, he was deputizing for the first general-staff officer, who was in Paris with Feuchtinger. Wagemann reported that late in the evening of 5 June 1944, the division's radio company had picked up a British clear-text radio message that indicated the loading of transport gliders. This report had been passed on. After the first reports of airborne landings, he had at once alerted the whole division and informed Feuchtinger in Paris between two and three o'clock in the morning of 6 June. Feuchtinger had then arrived at the command post with his general-staff officer between six and seven o'clock.

We were all surprised that Speidel in his call at two o'clock in the morning of 6 June, knowing of the "general directive," had not given the order "to attack *air*borne enemy forces at once with all available elements in my sector east of the Orne."

The fact that in the critical hours it was left to incompletely informed divisional commanders to cope with the situation seems to me, in retrospect, inexcusable.

On the night of 5/6 June, 1944, Lance-Corporal Hammel had been assigned to guard duty. He belonged to Panzer Reconnaissance Battalion 21 of our division, which was lying in reserve in positions near a village south of Caen.

As Hammel was later to relate: "The inactivity upset us greatly. We had always been in action as scouts and as the spearhead of the Division. Now we had been stationed there for weeks, waiting for something that might not affect us at all, the *landing*. On orders from Rommel we had to carry out exercises by night almost every day, so that in the event of airborne landings we would be familiar with the terrain as far as the coast. To occupy ourselves we had to set up "Rommel's asparagus' as a defense against gliders, and also prepare fortifications in the area behind the Atlantic Wall.

"Suddenly at midnight on 5 to 6 June all hell broke loose: from my post I could see flares in the sky, followed by a concentrated air raid on nearby Caen. 'Now the fun begins' was my first thought."

Lieutenant (as he then was) Rupprecht Grzimek of the reconnaissance battalion remembers it clearly. "During that same night of 5 to 6 June we were alerted that paratroops and gliders had landed in the sector of Panzer Grenadier Regiment 125 under Major von Luck. Together with the bombing of Caen this suggested more than a commando operation. We knew the order 'to attack *only* on orders from the highest authority.' In spite of that, within a very short time the battalion was ready for action. Our commander, Major Waldow, was on leave. He was due back on 8 June. At dawn a liaison officer whom we had sent to von Luck reported that not only had an airborne division landed east of the Orne, but the enemy had brought up a vast armada off the coast and was preparing a landing from the sea.

"Heavy naval guns now joined in the landing operations. The weak units on the coast were apparently already involved in fierce fighting. Soon after came the order: 'The Battalion is attached to von Luck's combat group and will move off at once in the direction of Troarn, about 12 kilometers east of Caen.' By making full use of cover we reached the area just west of Troarn in the early afternoon more or less without interference."

Lance-Corporal Hammel, later: ". . . As we moved forward to the northeast we saw toward midday on 6 June two Messerschmidt fighters flying north low over the Orne, the only German aircraft that day.

"East of Caen lay the first British paratroops to be killed. From their parachute-silk we cut ourselves scarves as protection against the dust. Our commander's deputy gave us the order to attack. We went into the attack practically from the march. Further west we could hear the sounds of battle. That, we heard, was where our armored group was supposed to attack. The enemy was apparently concentrating his naval fire against this, for him, dangerous thrust. His air force was also in action there. So we made good progress as far as the outskirts of Escoville, hence only a few kilometers from Ranville and the two bridges over the Orne."

In the early morning of 6 June the situation and issuing of orders in face of the airborne landings, the armada of warships, merchantmen and landing craft, and the incipient landing from the sea were more than confusing:

—Despite the supposed "general directive" we had not received permission to attack during the night.

—Feuchtinger, even in the early morning, did not receive clearance for his division to counterattack.

—The Commander in Chief West (von Rundstedt) was of the opinion, as was Hitler's High Command, that this was a diversionary maneuver. The real landing was expected in the Pas de Calais.

—Our corps commander, on the other hand, General Marcks, thought the landing was "genuine."

—Rommel, we heard, was en route to his HQ, without having met Hitler.

So the night and first hours of 6 June went by. *Too late, much too late!* was how it seemed to us. We were dismayed and angry that we had not been believed by the highest authority.

Finally General Marcks, whether authorized to do so or not, ordered our division to attack at once, with the whole division, *east* of the Orne and smash the units of the 6th Airborne Division that had landed there and cut their communications with the west. While the necessary orders were being issued and the division was forming itself for attack, the extent of the sea landings became evident. In the middle of our movements, which were constantly harassed by British planes, came a new order, this time from the 7th Army.

"The bulk of the 21st Panzer Division will attack the enemy forces that have landed *west* of the Orne; only elements of von Luck's combat group will attack the bridgehead east of the Orne." This involved time and further losses from air attacks.

The regrouping of the division took hours. Most of the units, from the area east of Caen and the Orne, had to squeeze through the eye of the needle at Caen and over the only bridges available in this sector. Caen was under virtually constant bombardment from the navy and the fighter-bombers of the RAF.

Feuchtinger informed me that an armored group, including my I Battalion in SPWs (*Schützenpanzerwagen*, armored personnel carriers), was to push through to the coast west of the Orne. His orders to me: "You will attack with your II Battalion, reinforced by Panzer Reconnaissance Battalion 21 and Assault-gun Battalion 200 (Major Becker) and a platoon of 8.8cm antitank guns, east of the Orne. Your task is to crush the 6th Airborne's bridgehead, recapture the two Orne bridges at Bénouville and establish contact with the coastal units. Elements of artillery will support you. Start of the attack: as soon as all elements have reached you."

The employment of the reconnaissance battalion worried me greatly. I had after all seen action in all the theaters of war as an "armored scout," always as the "spearhead" of the division. We were not equipped for direct attacking operations.

No. 4 Company of the panzer regiment arrived toward 1700 hours on 6 June, Major Becker's batteries not until the night of 7 June. So I had to start without them.

My II Battalion was engaged in heavy defensive fighting against the paratroops that had landed, who were obviously trying to extend their as yet very small bridgehead. I could free only limited elements of the battalion for the attack.

In the late afternoon, almost at the same time as the armored group west of the Orne, we set off. Our goal: to push through via Escoville-Hérouvillette to Ranville and the two Orne bridges. The reconnaissance battalion went straight into the attack from its march and, supported by the panzer company, penetrated to Escoville against their surprised opponents.

Then all hell broke loose. The heaviest naval guns, up to 38cm in calibre, artillery, and fighter-bombers plastered us without pause. Radio contacts were lost, wounded came back, and the men of the reconnaissance battalion were forced to take cover.

I had gone up with the attack and saw the disaster. I managed to run forward to the commander of the battalion and gave him fresh orders.

"To avoid further heavy losses, break off the attack at once and take up defensive positions on the southern edge of Escoville. Set up a line of defense there and prevent any further enemy advance. No. 4 Company of the panzer regiment, as well as Major Becker's assault-guns, when they get here, will support you. See that your men, and also the crews of the armored cars, dig themselves in."

I ran back to my regiment's radio station. My adjutant, Liebeskind, had to report the breaking-off of the attack to division. At the same time Feuchtinger sent word that the armored group had reached the coast through the gap between the landed elements of the British 3rd Infantry Division and the 3rd Canadian Infantry Division. Heavy fire from the navy, relays of attacks by fighter-bombers and, in the rear of the armored group, newly landed paratroops had forced them to withdraw, to avoid being encircled. My sister regiment, 192, had taken up a defensive position at about the same level as us.

Now the very thing Rommel had feared had happened: the enemy had not been attacked by our whole division and thrown back into the sea in the first hours of the landing.

The other two panzer divisions were lying in areas far to the rear. Of the "1,000 fighters" that Goering had promised nothing was to be seen.

Now, on the evening of 6 June, it seemed to have become clear even to Hitler that it must be a matter of a large-scale invasion. But, as Feuchtinger told us, Hitler and his High Command still reckoned on a further landing in the Pas de Calais. The panzer divisions and reserve units stationed there were not to be withdrawn, on express orders from Hitler.

At the same time it was also clear to the last man that the invasion had succeeded, that it could now be only a matter of days or weeks before the Allies would have landed sufficient forces to be able to mount an attack on Paris, and finally on the German Reich. If it were not for that damned air superiority!

Even by night "Christmas trees" hung in the sky bathing the whole area in bright light. The air attacks never stopped; the navy laid a barrage of fire on our positions and bombarded the city of Caen, which was a focal point in our lateral communications.

By day it was even worse: at any movement on the battlefield, even of an individual vehicle, the enemy reacted with concentrated fire from the navy or attacks by fighter-bombers. Either our radio communications were being intercepted or the navy had divided up the whole area into grid squares and had only to pass on the square number to launch a sudden concentration of fire.

Against such concentrations, and for the night, we all dug foxholes beside our vehicles, which provided some protection. All our supplies came from the Paris area and could be moved only by night.

During the night of 7 June I received orders to continue the attacks on Escoville also on the following days. "We must try to crush the bridgehead east of the Orne, which as yet is small," was the message from our divisional commander.

Then, in the morning, we saw on the rising ground north of Escoville up to a hundred gliders lying in the fields, a sign that further units of the 6th Airborne Division had landed.

Units of the panzer reconnaissance battalion were still dug in on the southern edge of Escoville. A combat patrol forced its way into the village and suffered heavy losses, but brought out thirteen prisoners. One of them talked, "We had the task of attacking southward through Escoville, to extend the bridgehead and reach our original objective. We are only waiting for reinforcements."

Back at my command post, I got into conversation with an NCO of the 6th Airborne Division. He was slightly wounded and was just being treated by our doctor. He thanked us for his fair treatment, but was somewhat embittered.

"I belong to B company under Major John Howard. We had the task of landing at midnight with six gliders by the two Orne bridges near Bénouville and taking the bridges intact. We had been trained for this operation for over a year. We landed right by the bridges. The enemy were taken completely by surprise. They didn't even have time to carry out the prepared demolitions. I think we were the very first to land on French soil. We were mighty proud, especially since we had only a few casualties.

"Major Howard had told us that after the operation had succeeded we would be flown back to England, to be held in readiness for another action.

"Then, yesterday evening, our Major received orders to attack the village of Escoville this morning. The little bridgehead had to be extended. A task for which, in my opinion, we were never intended. We forced our way into the village, but came under heavy fire from all sides, especially from your bloody 'eighty-eights.' I believe more than half our company have been killed, wounded, or taken prisoner. After the feeble resistance at the bridges we seem to have stumbled here on a strong, battle-tried opponent.

"Our Major was so proud of the *coup de main*. And now this disaster. All the same, we know our landing from the sea has been successful. You can't stop us any more from marching on Paris before long. You can't win this war any more."

One of the bridges is known today as "Pegasus Bridge," so called after the flying horse emblem of the British airborne forces.

Meanwhile reports were coming in from our right flank: my II Battalion was engaged in heavy defensive fighting, especially on the right flank near and north of Troarn. On no account must the enemy break through there on our unprotected, open flank. On 7 June its commander, Captain Kurzon, was killed. He was promoted posthumously to Major and awarded the Knight's Cross. Lieutenant Brandenburg, who with his No. 5 Company had been the first to make contact with the enemy during the night of the 6th, was also killed. Both were buried in ground to the rear and later reinterred.

These were heavy losses for us all. Division sent Major Kurz of the reserve that same day as the new commander of the battalion. He was an infantryman and had been in Russia; in that respect he was very suitable for the immediate task. Within a short while he had integrated himself and became one of my most reliable and successful leaders in the combat group.

On 8 June neither we nor the British attacked. On both sides the wounded had to be cared for and casualties replaced. To our surprise a few Messerschmidts suddenly appeared. They were at once involved in an air battle.

An RAF fighter was shot down over the British lines. The men all raised their arms in jubilation. Were the promised "1,000 fighters" about to turn up after all?

But a Messerschmidt was also shot down. The pilot was able to save himself by parachute and landed near the reconnaissance battalion. He was brought along to me. He swore and waved his arms about, "What are we supposed to do with a couple of fighters against this superiority? Where the hell are the 1,000 fighter planes?" We didn't know either.

In the afternoon Major Waldow reported back from leave. His men of the reconnaissance battalion were glad. He was very popular, especially as he stuck up for them and always tried to avoid unnecessary losses.

At the same time as Waldow came an order also came from division:

"Von Luck's combat group will assemble on the morning of 9 June for a decisive attack on Escoville, advance on Ranville, and take possession of the Orne bridges. Assigned to it for this purpose will be: Panzer Reconnaissance Battalion 21, No. 4 Company of Panzer Regiment 22, three batteries of Major Becker's Assault-gun Battalion 200, and one company of Antitank Battalion 220 with 8.8cm guns. The division's artillery will support the attack within the limits of its supply of ammunition."

Late that evening all the commanders, along with an artillery observer, gathered at my post.

"We assemble before dawn, before the enemy air force can intervene or the navy be effective. The motorcycle escorts of the reconnaissance battalion and the grenadiers of II Battalion not tied down by the enemy will lead, followed by I Battalion, and supported by the tanks of No. 4 Company, as well as Becker's SPWs. The 8.8cm antitank guns will take up positions on the hill south of Escoville, to ward off counterattacks by British tanks."

It would take a powerful and effective combat group to offset the impact of the naval guns and fighter-bombers.

We assembled an hour before dawn. I traveled with a little command group behind the reconnaissance battalion, so that I could make decisions on the spot.

During the night we had been plastered with heavy naval fire and bombs. Our preparations had evidently been spotted.

Lance-Corporal Hammel, who took part in the attack as a motorcycle escort, recalls, "With support from the tanks and assault-guns we soon forced our way into Escoville. The remaining civilian population had gathered by the church. We found a few children running around looking for their parents. We took them to the church.

"The British of the 6th Airborne Division put up fierce resistance. When it became light, heavy fire from the navy began to fall on the center of the village and its southern edge. We could make no progress. Then the news reached us that our beloved commander, Major Waldow, had been killed, only a day after coming back from his wife. This was a blow to us all. We couldn't even recover his body at first because of the barrage of fire. It was not until after dark that a patrol of volunteers, whom the British in fairness allowed to pass, was able to bring Major Waldow back and bury him further to the rear. Later the British transferred him to their military cemetery in Ranville, where he found his last rest among his former enemies."

Waldow's death greatly affected me personally. During the course in Paris I had often had talks with him from which I could infer his contempt for Hitler. As I heard later, he had belonged to the wide circle of "the men of 20 July 1944."

I had told Waldow of Rommel's prophecy. He too had set his hopes on Rommel. Waldow was an officer of the old Prussian school, highly decorated in Russia, modest and always considerate of the welfare of his men. His sister told me later, for example, that he had once been in a Russian village surrounded by partisans. The inhabitants had had nothing to eat for days. Waldow thereupon distributed his men's rations among the women and children. During the night a deputation of partisans suddenly appeared, "German, you have given our women and children food: *spacibo* (thank you). For that you may leave the village tonight with your men. We will not attack."

A sign of humanity on both sides.

Captain Brandt from the division's reserve of officers took over the reconnaissance battalion in place of Waldow.

For Werner Kortenhaus, too, at that time a tank commander in No. 4 Company, 9 June became a nightmare. "That day was for us one of the hardest actions ever. We assembled with about ten tanks under the trees of the avenue south of Escoville. We drove with closed ports, one tank after the other, to the right past the chateau into a large meadow, which was enclosed by hedges. There we intended switching to broad wedge formation for attack, the grenadiers behind and alongside us.

"Then everything happened very quickly: within a few minutes we had lost four tanks, knocked out by the naval guns. On my tank (a Mk IV with the short barrel) the turret jammed, so that I could only shoot into the hedges with my machine-gun. The fire became more intense, so that on orders from Major von Luck we had to withdraw, as did the grenadiers.

"The artillery fire continued unabated. Some 30 or 40 grenadiers must have been killed by it.

"On the evening of that 9 June we realized that we could no longer drive the British back into the sea.

"In 1960, when the ruins of the chateau were still standing, I went over the action again on the spot.

"Our attack could not have succeeded, for behind the hedge was a solid wall, which we could have broken through with our tanks only at the risk of disadjusting our guns. In front of the wall was a ditch—very convenient for the elements defending themselves there. And in the wall there were holes, made by artillery shells, through which the defenders could easily retreat.

"For us, therefore, it was an unfavorable sector for a tank attack."

From the reports of patrols it appeared that on 8 June the 51st Highland Division had been moved into the bridgehead to relieve the hard-pressed 6th Airborne. With that the likelihood of pushing back the bridgehead was further reduced. I knew the 51st Highland Division from North Africa; it had been regarded even then as an experienced elite unit.

To my surprise a combat patrol came back one day with a man on a DKW motorcycle. I looked at the machine. It was painted khaki and bore the sign of my

Reconnaissance Battalion 3 on its mudguard. This machine had been through its own little "safari." It had been captured by the British in North Africa, shipped to England and from there sent to Normandy, where my men recaptured it and returned it to me intact.

Meanwhile, during the nights of 7 and 8 June, the two panzer divisions, the Panzer Lehr Division and the 12th SS Panzer Division, having arrived at the invasion front after hard and costly marches from their concentration areas far to the east and south of Caen, had been thrown into counterattacks and defensive fighting west of Caen. But they, too, decimated and unnerved by the constant attacks of the RAF, were no longer able to make any impression on the bridgeheads west of Caen and were stuck.

1. A Stern and Tired Battalion Commander (sketched by a war correspondent, France, 1940)

2. Rommel Commands the 7th Panzer Division, France, 1940

3. Rommel Takes a Quick Breakfast on the Battlefield, France, 1940

4. A French Captain (*right*) Informs Rommel (*left*) that Marshal Pétain Has Asked for Armistice (*to left of Rommel stands von Luck*)

5. Typical Road in a Russian Rainstorm, 1941/42

6. Advance into Russia, 1941/42

7. General Guderian, Panzer Commander during the 1941 Advance to Moscow

8. Cossack Hetmen in the German Army, Russia, 1941/42

9. Rommel with Tactical Headquarters during Advance of Afrika Korps, North Africa, 1942/43

10. Rommel with Staff Officers and General Falley (*left*), North Africa, 1942/43

11. Field Marshal Kesselring Visiting Rommel (with Paratrooper General Ramcke, *left*, and General Bayerlein, *right*), North Africa, 1942/43

12. Rommel Visits von Luck's Armored Reconnaissance Group in the North African Desert, New Year's Eve, 1942 (*left to right*: staff officer von Bonin, Rommel, von Luck)

13. Rommel at the Kasserine Pass in Tunisia, after the Repulse of the Americans, North Africa, 1942/43

14. Rommel Inspecting Major Becker's SPW-Hotchkiss Battalion 200 just before D-Day, France, 1944

15. Normandy before "Operation Goodwood," 1944; The "Battle Group von Luck" Preparing a Further Counterattack

16
"Operation Goodwood," 18/19 July 1944

Hitler now seemed to grasp that this was the invasion and not a diversionary maneuver; but he would still not rule out a further operation in the Pas de Calais.

As Rommel told me on one of his visits to the front, he had begged Hitler orally and in writing to come to the front and form for himself an idea of the situation and the mood of the men. That seemed to us the least one might expect from an "army Fuehrer." Instead, he issued his orders from Obersalzberg. There we had to give credit to Churchill, who came to the invasion front, showed himself to his men, and gave them heart. According to one of Hitler's orders, no division might be sent into action without his personal order.

Not only Rommel but all of us were depressed that Hitler viewed the situation far too optimistically and "juggled" with divisions and army corps of which only decimated elements remained.

The morale of the men was still surprisingly good, although all realized that Allied success in the west meant the end. The employment of V1 and later V2 rockets, and the announcement of new "miracle-weapons," gave the men some hope of a turn for the better.

For 12 June, division issued another order to attack: the village of St. Honorine, lying on a commanding hill, was to be won back, to give us a view over the enemy battlefield and deny the British a view of our own positions. My combat group was to be further reinforced. A brigade of multiple rocket-launchers, "moaning minnies," with over 300 tubes 21cm and 30cm in caliber, was to support us. These launchers had a particular psychological effect: the projectiles flew over the battlefield with a loud, nerve-shattering whine and forced the surprised enemy to take cover immediately.

With the two motorcycle companies of the reconnaissance battalion and some grenadiers of I Battalion on foot, supported by the few operational tanks of No. 4 Company and Becker's assault-guns, we moved against St. Honorine shortly before dawn after heavy and concentrated fire by the rocket-launchers.

We took our opponents, elements of a Canadian division, by surprise and they gave up the village at once.

I went in close behind the motorcycles and saw the enemy lines for the first time. Hundreds of gliders were lying on the ground. We dug ourselves in at once on the northern edge of the village, to secure the hill for ourselves.

Then began the heaviest naval bombardment we had known so far. We could see the firing of the battleships, cruisers, and destroyers. The shells, of calibers up to 38cm, came whistling over like heavy trunks, to burst and rip vast craters in our lines. British fighter-bombers swooped down on us unhindered; a veritable inferno broke over our heads.

Then, taking advantage of the haze and dust of the explosions, the Canadians came back and after hand-to-hand fighting, with heavy losses on both sides, forced us to give up the village again.

What more could we set against this superiority in naval guns and fighter-bombers?

We now finally gave up hope of making any impression on the British bridgehead, let alone of eliminating it. We realized how important this bridgehead was on our unprotected right flank.

As Lance-Corporal Hammel was later to relate, "The barrage of fire on St. Honorine was the worst that we had experienced so far. We prayed. When we had pulled back to the village of Cuverville, a few kilometers further south, another heavy barrage of fire rained down on that village. Was there absolutely nowhere left here where one could get a breather and some sleep?"

One result at least came of our frequent attacks and patroling activities: the British began to mine themselves inside the lines they had reached. This was a sure sign that for the moment they had no intention of launching further attacks.

For a few weeks we had some peace in my sector. Patrols alone were deployed time and again, to put out feelers.

Only once more, on 15 June, with heavy artillery support, did we try to attack Escoville; for this was the key position in order to recapture the Orne bridges. But this attack too was in vain and brought heavy losses to both sides. Nor would the situation change for us all the time we were within range of the naval guns and the enemy had absolute control of the air.

The brave, hard-hit Panzer Reconnaissance Battalion 21 was pulled out on 16 June, but up to 29 June still had to ward off enemy attempts on the eastern edge of Caen to take possession of Caen and the Orne bridges there. On 30 June, the battalion was moved to the area south of Caen, to be restored to strength.

On a visit to my command post General Feuchtinger told me that the British and Americans had occupied firm, if sometimes small bases along the whole invasion front.

"There is no doubt that the Allies are bound to try, somewhere and sometime, to break out of the beachheads, if the invasion is not to have been in vain. Our weak point is our right flank, your sector, my dear Luck. South and east of you there are no reserves. The one advantage for you is that the terrain between the Orne and the overflowing Dives is so narrow that one division at most can attack out of the bridgehead. For that, however, we must be prepared, so you will be receiving further reinforcements and will set up a graduated defense in depth. The terrain is certainly suitable for a tank attack, but with its many villages, hedges, and bits of woodland it's even better 'tank-killing country.'

"Your task remains unchanged, to prevent any breakout or breakthrough from the bridgehead to the south or southeast."

June went by. July was particularly hot. We all suffered from the mosquitoes; some people had to receive medical treatment for their swollen eyes. The corn was high and ripe, but the peasants no longer dared to go into the fields for fear of being taken for an enemy and shot.

Almost every day II Battalion had to resist the attacks of strong assault groups and suffered heavy losses in the process.

One hot morning, when I was observing the front with Major Kurz, a sniper's shot went through my cap. A bit of luck.

At the beginning of July, the enemy suddenly attacked: "Operation Epsom" was started. (The British were fond of naming their operations after British race-courses.) The enemy tried to break through just west of the Orne, in the sector of Regiment 192. It was the 11th Armored Division under Major-General "Pip" Roberts, probably the youngest but most experienced tank commander. I knew Pip Roberts from North Africa, where he had led the tank brigade of the famous 7th Armored Division. His 11th Armored Division, on the other hand, was newly formed and inexperienced.

As almost always with the British, they carried out their tank attacks without accompanying infantry; as a result, they were unable to eliminate at once any little antitank nests that were lying well camouflaged in woodland or behind hedges. The main attack broke down under our defensive fire, although on the flank British and Canadian infantry were able to force their way into the western part of Caen. Our front still held.

As announced by Feuchtinger, my combat group was considerably strengthened at the beginning of July:

- —Tiger Battalion 503 was transferred to my sector. Because of its dreaded "eighty-eight" and its heavy armor, the Tiger was regarded as invulnerable and superior to all enemy tanks.

- —Major Becker, with all five companies of his Assault-gun Battalion 200, was attached to me and was to work closely with the grenadiers.

- —I was given the remaining battalion of our panzer regiment (the other battalion had been transferred to Germany to re-equip with the Panzer V "Panther").

- —A detachment of rocket-launchers was attached to me.

—A battalion of the Luftwaffe's Field Division No. 16 came under my command, to form a weak line in front of my positions.

—As Feuchtinger had told me, on and behind the hills at Bourgebus three antitank sections with 8.8cm guns were being brought into position. Added to these was the division's artillery.

—My two Battalions I/125 and II/125 were posted to the left and right behind the Luftwaffe's field units in so-called "block positions," from which they could either launch a counterattack or set up a defensive front. With them were Major Becker's companies.

We thus set up a graduated defense about 15 kilometers in depth, which would be able, sooner or later, to bring any enemy attack to a standstill.

Despite intensive aerial reconnaissance, the British failed to detect this echeloned defense in depth. As we discovered later, they reckoned on a depth of only 7 kilometers. From captured maps we found that the British had assumed there were at least two if not three German panzer divisions in the sector of their attack. This overestimate may have been the reason for their cautious advance later.

In spite of strong protests from the corps commander, an infantryman, the two panzer battalions were placed close behind the most forward positions. It would have been better to have held them further back in readiness for counterattacks. This decision was later to prove disastrous.

In the late afternoon of 14 July, I was summoned to the HQ of Obergruppenfuehrer "Sepp" Dietrich, our recently appointed corps commander. Sepp Dietrich knew me from the time I had asked him for advice about my problem of marriage to Dagmar. He had received the curious answer from Hitler's HQ for his part with sheer disbelief, and so had promised to make direct representations. Owing to the heavy fighting that set in, this remained unfortunately only an intention.

Also at the corps command post, where Sepp Dietrich greeted me, was Feuchtinger.

"Luck," said Dietrich, "in the six weeks since the landing you have led your combat group with distinction and prevented an early breakthrough by the British on our threatened eastern flank. Your commander has put you in for the Knight's Cross.

"I know also that tomorrow is your birthday and that your fiancée works in Paris. To give you a few days' rest, I have decided to send you instead of one of my staff officers on a special mission to Paris.

"You will leave tonight and return early on the 18th. I wish you happy days."

"Obergruppenfuehrer," I cried, "I can't accept this, tempting though it is. I can't leave my men on their own in this critical situation. I reckon the British will try their next breakout, or even breakthrough, in my sector. Thank you for the offer, but let me stay here, please."

"Luck," replied Sepp Dietrich, "according to our information there's little likelihood of a fresh attack for the next ten to fourteen days. After their costly 'Epsom' offensive, the British will first have to regroup and build up appropriate supplies, so it's all right to go."

I finally let myself be persuaded, after prompting also from Feuchtinger. The prospect of seeing Dagmar again was too enticing.

When I returned to my command post, I went to I Battalion and told its commander to take over leadership of the combat group during my absence.

My Mercedes was brought forward and loaded with the treasures of Normandy. Via the army telephone system I had myself switched into the local civilian network in Paris and told Dagmar and the *femme de chambre* of my coming.

It was with mixed feelings that I left my command post. For security reasons, and to keep an eye on the air, I took a driver with me. Before me lay three days in Paris!

After I had completed my "mission" and paid a short visit to our "Special HQ Paris," I was free for Dagmar and my friends. Dagmar and I were more in love than ever, even though the fool regulations and racial laws prevented us from marrying. We promised to wait for each other until after the war and then marry.

The foodstuffs I had brought with me, a total of about 50 kilograms, caused great delight all around, but especially the two kilos of coffee, for it was no longer obtainable in Paris. "We live here on ersatz," said J.B. "We've borrowed that wretched word from you."

Despite the pleasure of our reunion, I was uneasy. I telephoned division every day. "All quiet here, pretty normal, no noticeable change in the situation," I was told each time. I talked over again with Dagmar and my friends what was to be done if Paris should be threatened. Dagmar wanted to stay to the last possible moment, so as to be near me.

In the evening of 17 July we all sat together again over a bottle of champagne. On 18 July, I set off while it was still dark, in order to reach my command post before dawn, before the Spitfires and Hurricanes arrived. The journey took longer than expected, because of the nightly supply traffic. It was not until just before nine that I was on the hills east of my combat sector. Only a few kilometers now separated me from my command post. I stopped and we searched the sky for fighters. It was very hazy over the area of operations. Everything seemed to be in order.

Shortly after nine, I arrived at my command post and was looking forward to a Normandy breakfast, after which I intended changing from my uniform of the day into combat attire.

The commander of I Battalion greeted me briefly. I sensed that something was not right, for all the men at the command post seemed nervous.

Then came the report that almost took my breath away.

"Since five o'clock this morning the British have been bombing our sector, especially the area of I Battalion, endlessly with thousands of bombers. This bombing was followed by a creeping barrage from the artillery. The firing stopped barely half an hour ago."

"How are things with your I Battalion, have you any news?" was my first question.

"Not yet, we've no radio contact," came the answer.

"How about the Tigers and the panzer battalion of our regiment?"

Answer: "No radio contact. I don't know how things look there."

"And II Battalion? Major Becker's assault-guns? Have you told division?" My questions became more and more pressing, but it was clear that nothing had been done.

This was of course the renewed attempt at a breakout. Yet nothing, nothing at all, had been done! My deputy appeared to be in shock. He seemed absolutely helpless. I ordered him to be at my disposal. After a few days I instructed my adjutant to go in person to Army Personnel and demand that the commander be relieved. This was granted at once.

I had become the richer by experience: I had witnessed anew how officers and NCOs, who in peacetime had been outstanding instructors, popular with their superiors and comrades, lost their nerve in an emergency and were unable to cope with reality. General Pip Roberts, as he told me later, had undergone the same experience. For the same reasons as mine with the battalion commander, he had been forced to have the commanders of a brigade and a regiment relieved. The experience had shown, moreover, that the relief had to be made at once, if the unit was not to be affected and demoralized.

So there I was at my command post. No one knew what had happened, although it was obvious that the enemy was mounting a decisive attack.

I dismissed all thought of a good breakfast and my combat clothes. I ran to a radio Panzer IV that the panzer regiment had put at my disposal, offered the driver a cigarette and said, "Let's go! Take the main road to Caen."

To my adjutant I shouted, "I'll call you as we go along. Make contact with division at once, even if you have to go there in person. Tell them what's happened and ask for reserves so that we can stop the British. Send an officer to the tanks."

Slowly and without interference I approached the village of Cagny, which lay exactly in the middle of my sector and was not occupied by us. The eastern part as far as the church was undamaged; the western part had been flattened. When I came to the western edge of the village, I saw to my dismay about 25 to 30 British tanks, which had already passed southward over the main road to Caen, which ran from east to west.

A glance then to the north, to where my I Battalion ought to be, or had been, in combat positions. The whole area was dotted with British tanks, which were slowly rolling south, against no opposition.

"My God," I thought, "the bombing and artillery barrage destroyed the battalion."

It was quite clear: the British, with a bombing of unprecedented extent, were trying to break through our positions on the narrowest of fronts. How could I plug this gap? Perhaps with an attack by the superior Tiger Mark VIs?

So, back to the command post, to try to organize countermeasures.

As I was driving past the church of Cagny, which lay in the undamaged part of the village, I saw to my surprise a Luftwaffe battery with its four 8.8cm antiaircraft guns, all pointing to the sky.

"What are they doing here?" went through my mind. "I didn't see them on my way here." Under a tree I called a halt, "bailed out," and ran to the battery.

A young captain came up to me. "Major," he said, "can you tell me what's going on here?"

"My God, what are you doing here? Have you any idea what's happening over there to the left of you?"

He answered calmly, "I belong to an air-defense ring to protect the factories and city of Caen against air raids. At the moment I'm waiting for the next raid."

"Man," I replied as calmly as I could, "you've already been bypassed by enemy tanks. North of here it's absolutely swarming with tanks. You will move into position at once with your four guns on the northern edge of Cagny and attack the advancing tanks. Don't worry about tanks that are already going south. Hit the enemy from the flank. In that way you'll force the advance to a halt."

His reply came just as calmly, "Major, my concern is enemy planes, fighting tanks is your job. I'm Luftwaffe."

He was about to turn away. At that I went up to him, drew my pistol (which we had to carry for trips to Paris), leveled it at him and said, "Either you're a dead man or you can earn yourself a medal."

The young captain realized that I was in earnest. "I bow to force. What must I do?"

I took him by the hand and undercover of the hedges and trees ran with him to the northern edge of the village.

"Here, place your four guns in this apple orchard. The corn over there is so high that you will be well protected and just have a field of fire across it. Shoot every tank you see. I'll see if I can send you a platoon of grenadiers to guard you against surprise attacks. Should the situation become critical for you, destroy your guns and withdraw to the south. I hope our Tiger battalion will soon be able to mount a counterattack from the right flank. With them and with you we should be able to beat back the enemy attack, especially as it's not accompanied by infantry as far as I can tell. Listen, I'll be back in half an hour. All clear?"

He still seemed to be undecided, but finally nodded. "Okay, Major."

Back at my command post I realized the full extent of the preparatory carpet bombing.

My orderly officer reported that the Tiger battalion had been thoroughly saturated by the heaviest American bombers. He himself had seen some of the 62-ton colossi upside down; craters 30 feet across had made the whole terrain almost impassable; there could be no question of using the Tigers in the next few hours. The fate of the Panzer IV Battalion had been much the same.

Major Becker, who was now at my command post, had made contact with his batteries.

"One battery has been completely knocked out by bombs," he reported. "Two batteries on the left flank are intact and will support the grenadiers of I Battalion, who have gone into action against the British infantry. The other two batteries will be going into action at any minute on the right flank, where Major Kurz, without first waiting for orders, has set up a defensive front with his II Battalion."

Captain Liebeskind, my adjutant, came back from division. To stop the gap on my *left* flank there were no reserves, was the message from Feuchtinger. However, I was to be sent the reconnaissance battalion to secure my weak *right* flank; Captain Brandt would be reporting to me. My orders were: To prevent without fail any attempt by the enemy to break through to the east on the open right flank.

Captain Brandt reported that same morning. "Major, I am again under your command, lying with the reconnaissance battalion about 7 kilometers east of Troarn. Since 6 July we have been lying in reserve south of Caen and have to some extent been replenished with men and materiel. We could see the terrible air attacks early this morning. Has your combat group been badly hit?"

I put Brandt briefly in the picture. "On my left wing there's a yawning gap to Caen and Regiment 192, which I can't fill. But three antitank sections with 8.8cm cannons are in place on the hills of Bourgebus. They should in fact be able to stop any tank advance, so long as the British don't employ infantry. But there's also a very dangerous gap between my command post here and Major Kurz's II Battalion. If the British were to push through it, the way to the southeast would be open to them. This gap is where I'm putting you. Keep contact on your right with Kurz and on your left with me. One of Major Becker's batteries with their 7.5cm antitank guns (long) will be under your orders to combat enemy tanks. Send a liaison officer to me here. Good luck to you, Brandt, we've got to survive the day."

From official reports, messages from my units, and the statements of prisoners, a gloomy picture of the situation emerged. Accounts that I have been able to see since the war have confirmed the situation at the time.

Montgomery had decided to launch a general attack out of the little bridgehead and thrust into the French hinterland in the direction of Falaise. With matchless logistics and in the greatest secrecy the following were assembled for the purpose:

—one tank corps, with the 11th Armored Division, the Guards Armored Division, and the 7th Armored Division, well known to me from North Africa;

—to protect each flank, one Canadian infantry division (on the right) and one British infantry division (on the left);

—over 1,000 guns of every caliber, plus naval artillery;

—the 6th Airborne Division and the 51st Highland Division, who were to remain in the bridgehead to protect it;

—to prepare the attack, the biggest aerial armada so far assembled in the war, made up of about 2,500 British and American bombers. Over a width of about 4 kilometers and a depth of about 7, the strips of attack were to be so saturated that virtually no one would be able to survive the bombardment;

—the air attack was to be followed by a creeping barrage from the 1,000 guns,
   plus the naval artillery, behind which the first waves of tanks were to advance
   in quick succession;

—the initial goal: the hills at Bourgebus, about 15 kilometers from the starting
   line.

"No one will survive this inferno. We need only march in with our tanks to open
the way to Paris." That was the unanimous opinion of the Allies engaged in the
attack. "How very wrong we were was soon to appear," was what I heard after the
war from many commanders in the British tank corps.

Since all the units had to squeeze through cleared passages in the mine fields,
one division followed the other, to advance after the breakout on a wide front toward
the hilly terrain near Bourgebus.

My one hope was that the 8.8cm battery at Cagny and the two 7.5cm assault-
gun companies would delay the enemy long enough for reserves to be brought up.
These were the 1st SS Panzer Division and the 12th SS Panzer Division of "Hitler-
jugend." Both had recently been taken out of the front to be restored to strength
in the Falaise and Lisieux area, where they now were.

Late in the morning of 18 July, reports came in from two of Becker's batteries,
which were in action with I Battalion on the left flank: "Individual companies of I
Battalion have taken up the fight against the following infantry. We gave support
as far as possible.

"A second wave of British tanks had turned west after the disaster at Cagny and
was advancing toward the Bourgebus hills. We gradually had to disengage, therefore,
to avoid being encircled."

Major Becker was at my command post. I called him over.

"Listen, Becker, I need your batteries more urgently than ever, since for the
moment the two panzer battalions are out of action owing to the bombardment.
All the batteries, especially those isolated on the left flank, must operate on their
own responsibility, cover the grenadiers for as long as possible and above all attack
the advancing British tanks from the flank. We must bring the tank thrust to a
halt."

Major Bill Close, British, who led one of the tank companies of the regiment in
the 11th Armored Division that had veered west, is today a good friend of mine.
As he was to tell me later, "We had warned the Guards Armored Division coming
after us about Cagny. In spite of that they pushed on and within seconds lost about
20 tanks at Cagny. We could see how the front regiment tried to avoid the fire
from Cagny. In so doing several tanks were again knocked out, this time from
woodland in the east. The attack came to a standstill. We were glad we had been
able to turn off to the west and so escape the fire of your damned 'eighty-eights.'
We pushed forward to the south across the Paris-Caen road. We saw fires burning
here and there in Caen, lying on our right, and in front of us, about 5 kilometers
to the south, the Bourgebus hills, our first objective, which we should have reached
early that morning.

"Unhindered we moved forward in wide formation, my company in the lead.

"Suddenly, when we had got to about 1,000 meters from the villages on the hills, we came under concentrated fire from 'eighty-eights.' Within seconds about 15 of our tanks were stationary and on fire. All attempts to turn aside to left or right failed. By late afternoon I had only a few tanks left that were still intact. The other company fared no better. We had to break off our advance and withdraw. Shortly after came the order from Brigade to suspend hostilities for the day. New orders followed next day."

After the arrival of the reconnaissance battalion I felt I had stabilized my right flank to some extent. I had still not had time to change, let alone have something to eat. For the next few hours everything hung on the flak battery at Cagny. I got into my tank again and rolled cautiously into the village. By the church I stopped the tank and ran to the four guns, where an almost indescribable sight met my eyes:

—The 8.8cm cannons were firing one salvo after the other. One could see the shots flying through the corn like torpedoes. The men on the guns were proud of their first engagement as an antitank unit. All four guns were intact and had not been attacked.

—In the extensive cornfields to the north of the village stood at least 40 British tanks, on fire or shot up. I saw how the tanks that had already crossed the main road were slowly rolling back.

—Becker's assault-guns had also joined in the battle. From the right flank they shot up any tank that tried to bypass the village.

The young captain came up to me. I congratulated him. "A platoon from my staff company will be here in a few minutes to protect you from surprise attacks. I repeat my orders of this morning: you will hold your position for as long as you can and oppose the enemy tank attack. As soon as the situation becomes critical, destroy your guns and retreat with the grenadiers to my command post."

With that I left this battery, which had played such a decisive part on that 18 July.

Back at my command post I made contact with Feuchtinger. I described the situation as it appeared to me at about midday on 18 July, and ended, "General, I believe that the whole British attack has come to a standstill, thanks to the engagement of all elements of my combat group, and thanks not least to a Luftwaffe 8.8cm battery that I found by chance at Cagny and put to use in the ground fighting. I see a great danger, however, on my right wing. If the British were to move up their infantry things would look pretty bad for my rather thin defensive front. For the moment it's all right still, but reserves ought to arrive in the course of the afternoon."

"Congratulations, Luck, on this successful defense. I can give you good news: the 1st SS Panzer Division has orders to move up to us at once from Falaise and strengthen our defense, especially on the Bourgebus hills. The 12th SS Panzer

Division also has orders to support us on our right, hence your flank, and prevent a breakthrough to the southeast.

"The 1st SS will arrive today in the late afternoon, the 12th SS not before midday tomorrow. We *must* hold till then."

In the late afternoon Feuchtinger came through again, "The first elements of the 1st SS have arrived. Together with them we have knocked out a lot of tanks. With your tally the British have probably lost at least 200 tanks. I am reassured that you can hold out on the right flank. Convey my appreciation to Kurz (commander of II Battalion)."

In the afternoon I finally changed and at once felt better. The Tiger battalion sent word that about ten Tigers were again operational, and that they would be mounting an attack on the enemy's left flank.

Lieutenant (as he then was) Freiherr von Rosen, commander of a Panzer VI (Tiger) company, has given the following account: "The bombardment early in the morning of 18 July was the worst we had ever experienced in the war. Although we were in foxholes under our tanks, we had a lot of casualties. Some of the 62-ton machines lay upside down in bomb craters 30 feet across; they had been spun through the air like playing cards. Two of my men committed suicide; they weren't up to the psychological effect. Of my 14 Tigers not one was operational. All had been covered in dust and earth, the guns disadjusted, the cooling systems of the engines out of action. Yet by early afternoon a few of my Tigers were ready for battle. I was to use them to attack westward in the flank of the British tank attack."

From captured maps and operational plans we knew that the guards were supposed to attack in a southeasterly direction, the 7th Armored Division in the center southward, and the leading 11th Armored Division to the southwest.

While the guards—it was their very first engagement—felt their way forward cautiously and were beaten back time and again with heavy losses in tanks, the 7th Armored Division had not as yet put in an appearance. It was not until the late afternoon of 18 July that it was able to pass through the small number of gaps in the mine field.

The British offensive, for 18 July, had come to a halt. The gain in territory was not as yet very great; of a breakout or a breakthrough there could be no question. We were certain, however, that the British would be preparing themselves for the next day. The question remained whether, with our depleted forces, we would again be able to stop the attack.

The morning of 19 July remained surprisingly quiet. In the course of individual tank thrusts a number of British tanks were again knocked out. But then, in the early afternoon, Monty took the field with all three tank divisions, supported by infantry and artillery, which had been brought up in the meantime.

While the guards division operated very cautiously for lack of experience, we discovered to our surprise that the 7th Armored Division was doing the same. It was going through the same experience that we had been through: it was *over-*experienced and for that reason operated with extreme caution. We managed to fight off all attacks on the right wing and in so doing inflicted heavy losses on the two British divisions. For that we had to thank the skillful engagement of my II Battalion under Major Kurz, as well as the panzer reconnaissance battalion and Becker's assault-guns.

A liaison officer came to me from the reconnaissance battalion. "Major, I have to report that by our own counterattacks we have forced the enemy to retreat again and again. For a while there was a British field dressing station behind our lines.

"An hour ago a British tank appeared with a white flag and brought back some of our wounded. We thanked them at once."

That was true fairness!

From division and from Becker's two batteries now operating alone on my left flank we heard that the 11th Armored Division, with grenadiers and supported by tanks and heavy artillery, had mounted an attack about four o'clock against two villages on the northern edge of the Bourgebus hills, which were defended by elements of the 1st Panzer Division.

Shortly after came the following report from one of the assault-gun batteries: "Both villages have been taken by the enemy, but further attack halted. Our two batteries have arrived fighting—sometimes parallel to the British—without loss on the hills."

Now things became critical; but the British attack was not continued and again came to a halt. It was astonishing that the attack in my sector should be so hesitant. The shock from our 8.8cm antitank guns, the few Tigers, and Becker's assault-guns seemed to have struck deep among the British. With only about 400 grenadiers left we had to hold the long front in the east. That was too few to withstand a vigorous attack.

Finally, about five o'clock, the first elements of the 12th SS Panzer Division arrived. A general-staff officer made contact with me, "The division has been through a costly march. We were shot up time and again by British fighters and forced into cover. The bulk of the division will be here in the course of the night. How do things look with you?"

I put him in the picture and learned that my combat group was to be relieved by this division. Shortly after came the order from my own division: "In the course of the night von Luck's combat group will disengage from the enemy and hand over to the 12th SS Division. You will take up a defensive position on either side of Troarn on the east bank of the flooded Dives. Rauch's combat group will also be relieved and stationed east of the Dives."

The relief went through without difficulty. I hoped to be able to give the thoroughly overtired and battle-weary men a little rest. By the late evening of 19 July it was possible to see what the British had managed or failed to do: The little bridgehead had been extended by about 9 kilometers; Caen had now been fully occupied. But the breakthrough in the direction of Falaise had not been made. Monty was to maintain later that more was not supposed to have been achieved, that "Operation Goodwood" had had as its objective the tying down of as many German panzer divisions as possible to make it easier for the Americans to break out as planned further west.

Others besides me have had doubts about this version of events and for the following reasons: (1) captured Canadians told us that shortly before the attack Monty had called out to them: "To Falaise, boys, we're going to march on Paris"; (2) anyone who knew Monty and his ambition, and had analyzed his operations in North Africa, would have taken it for granted that he would not have been content with a mere "tying down of German panzer divisions" and an "extension of the bridgehead."

Be that as it may, "Operation Goodwood" cost the British about 450 tanks. It was a masterpiece of preparation and logistics. And yet we were able to prevent the enemy from making a breakthrough.

Only now did we hear that on the day before "Operation Goodwood"—the start of the offensive—our own Field Marshal Erwin Rommel had been severely wounded in a fighter-bomber attack on his individual car. We could hardly take it in; to us Rommel had always seemed invulnerable.

Nevertheless, the deep defensive front set up by Rommel had held against Montgomery's attack. As late as 15 and 17 July he had checked this defense in the area of our corps. It is probably true to say that with this Rommel had denied his constant adversary the way to Paris, his last military success.

During the night of 19/20 July, torrents of rain set in, which made our relief more difficult. I shall never forget on our night march to the north the stink of the dead cows lying in the fields. On 20 July, moreover, there was a further heavy thunderstorm, which turned the battlefield into a swamp. The British air force had to stay on the ground.

Late in the evening of 20 July we learned—first through leaflets dropped by the British, then also from our own radio station—of the attempt on Hitler's life. The older ones among us had mixed feelings; the younger were angry, "It's a stab in the back to us here at the front."

My own thoughts went back inevitably to my talks with Rommel in North Africa in 1943 and in France in 1944. "An attempt on Hitler's life would create a 'stab-in-the-back' legend. As soon as a second front has been established and the end is in sight, we must force him to abdicate, to avoid further losses and to concentrate on the war in the east."

Next day a war correspondent appeared at my command post. "Major, what do you say here at the front about the assassination attempt on the Fuehrer?"

My answer was prompt. "Listen, we've been engaged in heavy defensive fighting here for weeks; we haven't had time to give it a thought. Come back when the situation has calmed down a bit."

An offhand, risky answer, but what was the use?

Worth noting is a piece of information that came to me only recently, from a reliable source. When our corps commander, Oberstgruppenfuehrer Sepp Dietrich, of Army Group B, was told of the attempt on Hitler's life, his first question was, "Who was it, the SS or the Army?"

Although the RAF launched endless attacks and the guards division, with strong patrols, tried to find a gap to the east, the days that followed seemed to us almost like a holiday. Owing to the heavy downpours of rain the flooded River Dives had become even more impassable. For me the important thing was to recreate I Battalion, which had been almost wiped out by the bombing on 18 July.

At the division's field replacement section a new battalion, built up from remaining cadres and well-trained replacements from home, with factory-fresh SPWs (armored personnel carriers), was brought to operational level in only a few days. We marveled at the logistics by which, time and again, replacements, ammunition, and vehicles were brought up to the front.

After only a week in our defensive "resting" position the division was pulled out, to be restored to strength. We all hoped for a few days' peace to lick our wounds.

But signs of the next British offensive, which they called "Bluecoat," began to appear and put an end to the respite. After only two days the division was transferred to the area south of Villers Bocage on the important road No. 175 south of Bayeux. Together with the brave 21st Panzer Reconnaissance Battalion we managed to hold the front.

The men were tired, our losses heavy. We had been in action now for eight weeks without a break, longer, therefore, than any other division. But in spite of that morale was high. The men fought until they dropped. Then, however, on 25 July, after a four-hour aerial bombardment, the Americans managed to break through at the Panzer Lehr Division. We pulled back our front a little and now held a line from Avranches-St. Lô to south of Caen.

Then, on 31 July, came news that General George S. Patton, probably the most flexible of the Allied tank commanders, had broken through at Avranches, near the famous Mont St. Michel. With that the way to the French interior, to Paris and Reich territory, seemed to be open. Hitler reacted at once: He threw General Eberbach on Avranches with a hastily assembled panzer group, in order to cut Patton's lines of communication.

Once again it was the people at Bletchley Park, who were cracking our codes, and the U.S. air force that nipped our attack in the bud. Worse still, however, was the fact that all our divisions engaged in the west were now threatened with encirclement, since Patton would obviously be able to continue his eastward thrust unchecked.

Then everything happened very quickly. We had to fall back; for our decimated, exhausted divisions would not have been able to withstand another big push.

17
Retreat to Germany, August–November 1944

It took a further two weeks—of delaying actions and continual evading movements to the southeast—before we reached the area of Falaise, south of Caen. With that the whole Contentin Peninsula, with its important harbor of Cherbourg, was finally lost.

Montgomery, meanwhile, had also emerged from the bridgehead enlarged by "Operation Goodwood" and with the 4th Canadian Division and a Polish tank division was pressing forward into the area northeast of Falaise. Monty's attack from the northwest and Patton's thrust from the southwest threatened to envelop almost the whole of the German Normandy front in one vast pocket.

On 17 August both the Canadian division and the Polish tank division pushed through and split our division in two: Rauch's combat group, with Regiment 192, Reconnaissance Battalion 21, and the last eight tanks, fell into the pocket that was forming; my combat group and divisional HQ remained just outside.

From now on Allied bombers swooped down without a break on our retreating divisions. The excellent American artillery covered all roads and routes with heavy fire day and night.

Worse off were the infantry divisions, which, with their horse-drawn units, struggled east on foot and blocked all the roads. Appalling scenes took place: the tanks, armored elements, and motorized supply units ruthlessly forced their way through to the east. On and beside every road and track leading east shot-up vehicles had broken down; the cadavers of horses lay around. Even ambulances, packed with wounded, stood burning by the side of the road. Valiant officers tried to bring a little order into the chaos, but usually without success.

With my combat group I received orders to set up a defensive block fronting to the west, to prevent any further advance by the Polish and Canadian divisions. From the heights west of Vimoutiers, where Rommel had been severely wounded on 17 July, I had a wide view into the great valley. There, enemy planes were swooping down uninterruptedly on anything that moved. I could see the mushroom clouds of exploding bombs, burning vehicles, and the wounded, who were picked up by retreating transports. The scenes that had to be enacted in the pocket were indescribable, and we could do nothing to help.

"Man, horse, and truck by the Lord were struck." This saying, from a poem on the battles of the Crusaders in Palestine in about 1213, had come to my mind twice before: in December 1941 by Moscow and in 1943 in North Africa.

The jaws of the pocket had not yet quite closed: further south, near the little village of Chambois on the River Dives, there was still a gap, as yet unfilled by the Americans and Montgomery's two divisions. This was probably because, on the one hand, we had managed time and again to hold up the Polish tank division, and on the other, because Patton no longer seemed to be interested in exploiting his advantage, but in pushing on fast to the Seine east of Paris. A certain animosity on Patton's part toward Monty helped us after all to rescue sizable elements from the pocket, though without their materiel.

Colonel Rauch and Major Brandt, commander of the panzer reconnaissance battalion, were to report later under what adventurous circumstances they had managed to extricate themselves from the encirclement. Together with the remnants of some SS panzer divisions, which forced a breach in the closing pocket, and held open the way to the east, Rauch's combat group was able to ford the River Dives by night under heavy artillery fire.

Corporal Korfluer, commander of one of the last Panzer IVs of No. 4 Company, has given the following account. "On 19 August came the order 'Every man for himself.' With a second Panzer IV we set out on the way to the east. At the sight of naked, half-burned tank-men we promised ourselves that we would not let ourselves be finished off in the pocket. It was a hellish journey. In bypassing a horse-drawn column we skidded so badly that we had to abandon our tanks. We continued on foot. During the night we slipped past the enemy, some of whom looked at us in bewilderment.

"In the morning we were through and—for the moment—saved."

Lieutenant Hoeller, of No. 8 heavy Company of Regiment 192, took part in the breakout. "We received orders to abandon our positions during the night of 19/20 August and break through in the direction of Trun. There was still a gap of 5 kilometers, in which only a few enemy patrols had been detected. For our battle-weary unit the withdrawal by night was almost superhuman.

"The closer we got to the breakout point the more ghastly was the scene that met our eyes. The roads were blocked by two or three shot-up, burnt-out vehicles standing alongside each other, ammunition was exploding, tanks were burning, and horses lay struggling on their backs until they were eventually released. In the fields far and wide was the same chaos. The enemy artillery fired into the turmoil from all sides; everything was pressing east. We had to pass through St. Lambert.

There, a small operations staff had been set up; Panther and Tiger tanks of the SS divisions took the lead.

"While the enemy fired nonstop into the village with antitank guns and artillery, we forced our way through regardless. Shot-up tanks and vehicles were pushed aside; many dead and wounded from previous breakouts lay by the side of the road. As far as room was available we took the wounded with us, or at least cared for them.

"We jumped out of our armored personnel carriers to cover SS tanks that a number of enemy antitank guns had neutralized.

"Two generals, whose infantry divisions had been wiped out, just shook their heads over our reckless attempt to break out. They marched with us.

"During the night we made a brief stop, so that the men could rest and the wounded be attended. Through the vigorous thrust of the SS tanks the enemy sustained such heavy losses that they were unable to close the pocket even on the following day, 21 August. While the tanks held the gap open, more and more groups, some quite small, filtered through the hole to the east. We set a course by compass and marched off; we had escaped the inferno once again."

In the afternoon of 21 August it was all over; the pocket was closed. How, if at all, could the men recover from this blood-letting and terrible experience?

Precise figures for the chaos in the Falaise pocket are hardly possible. According to estimates, there were between 90,000 and 100,000 men in the pocket before the last gap was closed on 21 August. Despite urgent requests, Hitler had neglected to pull back our divisions in sufficient time. It is known that about 10,000 men were killed and that between 40,000 and 50,000 were able to break out. Some 40,000 men in the pocket were taken prisoner, including several GHQs and the remains of 15 divisions, mainly infantry. The fact that such a large number of men were able to escape from the pocket, and at once reassemble to offer resistance, showed their high level of training.

The danger was not yet over.

I eventually got through to the divisional commander, who told me, "The situation is completely out of hand. All that is known for certain is that General Patton had already reached Chartres, southwest of Paris, on 18 August, and the Seine near Fontainebleau on 21 August. According to unconfirmed reports he has been able to form two small bridgeheads there over the Seine.

"From Chartres," General Feuchtinger went on, "Patton has turned north with part of his army and is advancing on the Rouen area. No one seems able to stop him. We are now threatened with a new pocket south and west of the Seine, and all the bridges across it appear to have been destroyed.

"I am authorized to bring Rauch's combat group and the panzer reconnaissance battalion, which lost almost all its materiel in the pocket, over the Seine at once and to move it to an area northeast of Paris, where it can be restored to strength. Divisional HQ will move even further east, probably to the region west of the Vosges, to establish a defensive position there and a reception line for the units withdrawing from southern France.

"You, Luck," continued Feuchtinger, "will take over all elements of the division that are still operational; these are to assemble northeast of Rouen. I no longer have any tanks, but you will get the last two patrols of the reconnaissance battalion.

"If Montgomery now pushes forward vigorously, I don't give much for your chances of still being able to cross the Seine. In the first place, you will withdraw gradually in the direction of the Seine, where remaining elements of the engineer battalion will wait for you with the last pontoons.

"From now on you are on your own. I can't tell you where you will get fuel, ammunition, and food. Help yourself. As to the route of your march to the east and its destination, where the division is to assemble, you will receive further orders before I move out.

"All the best, Luck. Bring me back lots of men from our division."

On that decisive 21 August, my units were disposed for defense. On 22 August I disengaged from the enemy. Montgomery, thank goodness, did not vigorously follow. Quite the contrary, he operated very cautiously, without risking anything. That gave us a bit of leeway. The Allied air force could no longer intervene so specifically, for it was too difficult to tell friend from foe.

On 23 August, we felt our way forward in the direction of Rouen, still unmolested by Montgomery's divisions. I was concerned about Feuchtinger's report that on the same day Patton was advancing on Rouen practically parallel to us. Who would get there first, and how would we cross the Seine fast enough? Patton, however, according to our own reconnaissance, was not yet in evidence. Instead, we were joined by elements of an SS panzer division. We agreed to cross the river, with the help of the engineers, at one of the loops in the Seine west of Rouen.

Not until after the war did I learn that Montgomery had drawn a new line of demarcation between the British and the Americans, which ran past Mantes on the Seine, west of Paris, far to the northeast via Amiens-Lille as far as Ghent in Belgium. This meant that Patton had to recall his elements advancing on Rouen and use them elsewhere.

We were concerned at the time only with Monty, and he, for whatever reasons, was moving forward very hesitantly.

When we reached the Seine, we covered ourselves to the south with the SS tanks, but all the makeshift Seine crossings were hopelessly overcrowded. Infantry supply units and parties of stragglers were competing there, sometimes with the use of force, for the few ferries.

When we had chosen our crossing point we let no one else through. We intended to save our fighting vehicles and our men. While the engineers were constructing a pontoon ferry, every possibility was considered and tried for getting over the 400-meter wide river. Captain Krieger, my adjutant at the time, told me a few days later that he and his men had taken doors off their hinges in the neighboring villages and made them buoyant with empty fuel cans. Each of these mini-ferries was able to convey about eight men. Our collaboration with the SS tank people went well. I assured them that they would be carried over on our pontoon ferry last of all. We kept calm; the men waited quietly in the woods near our crossing point, until they were called. There was none of the hectic atmosphere of Rouen, to which the bulk of the troops had withdrawn in order to cross by a railway bridge that had remained intact.

My HQ company had a VW amphibious car, which till then I had never used. I asked if it was serviceable. "It should float," came the answer, "as far as we can tell."

Despite all the preceding hardships and the tense situation, I decided to cross in this car, as the last of my combat group.

By 26 August, all elements of the group were over and issued with orders for assembling.

During the night of 28/29 August we camouflaged the car with tree branches, to avoid being spotted and sunk by Allied fighters. In the morning I took the wheel, beside me my adjutant Liebeskind and behind us the driver and an observer.

We soon found a flat spot and I drove cautiously into the river. "Watch out for leaks!" It floated. I let myself be carried downstream by the current. Liebeskind looked for a spot where we could land. Carefully I nudged the car to the right to approach the opposite bank.

"Fighters to the left!" cried our observer. I at once switched off the engine and let the "bush" drift downstream. The fighters seemed to take us for what we had intended by our camouflage, a bush. Liebeskind looked desperately for somewhere to land. But we were thwarted everywhere by steep banks and heavy undergrowth.

Finally, after a river trip of almost 15 kilometers, we found a flat spot where we were able to drive ashore comfortably and unseen. An hour later we were with my combat group, which by then had almost given us up for lost.

I made contact for the last time with our divisional commander, who briefed me on the situation and our task.

"Luck, I'm glad you have managed to bring virtually the whole of your combat group safely over the Seine. The situation at the moment is completely out of hand. I was summoned to corps, but they had to leave their command post in haste because the Americans were coming. No one knows where our own units are, let alone those of the enemy. I received a clear order two days ago according to which divisional HQ, the hardhit units of Rauch's combat group and all supply elements are to be moved at once to the region of Molsheim, west of Strasbourg, to be restored to strength. The division is to form a prepared position as far west as possible for elements of the weak 1st and 19th Armies withdrawing from southern France via Belfort.

"On 15 August, strong American elements landed in southern France; these are now pressing forward to the north.

"As soon as you've got your group together and organized, you will march east, in order to reach the area west of Strasbourg as quickly as possible. Watch out that you don't fall into the hands of the Americans, who are now advancing over the Seine along a wide front. Where and how you will be able to organize fuel, ammunition, and food, I don't know. You will have to help yourself. All the best."

We had only a little ammunition left, so we couldn't be drawn into any battles.

It was a long way to the Strasbourg area; I figured a week at least, assuming we made good progress.

To avoid being taken unawares by the Americans pressing north, I issued the following orders:

—The two patrols of the panzer reconnaissance battalion were to reconnoiter south of my planned line of march and report every contact with the enemy by radio.

—Every 100 kilometers an officer with a radio set was to be posted at the most important road crossings, to report enemy movements.

—A supply party with the last three trucks and two SPWs (armored half-track vehicles) with radio were to search constantly for supply depots, which were bound to be located near large towns.

—The bulk of my combat group were to march east at wide intervals, in part along minor roads. I laid down our destination each day.

We then set off, first swinging well north of Rouen and then east, passing well north of Paris. For the first two days we made only slow progress. We were marching parallel to the front and across the American line of advance. On the third day fuel became short. The supply party had been told to organize fuel without fail, but if possible also ammunition. In fact, the trucks turned up that evening, loaded with what was wanted; they even brought some food. We were all grateful to these men, who had after all managed to find a depot somewhere or other. The report from the officer responsible made us laugh, but also swear.

"When we found the depot," he told us angrily, "and demanded fuel for our combat group, we received the typical, impudent reply: 'We can issue nothing without written authority.' When I asked, 'And what will you do if the Americans get here tomorrow, which is highly likely?' the answer was: 'Then in accordance with orders we would blow the depot up.' That made my men so angry that they advanced threateningly on the storekeeper. I had to restrain them.

"Calmly but unmistakably I gave the bureaucratic gentleman my answer, 'If I don't have fuel, ammunition, and food within half an hour I can no longer be responsible for anything. So get on with it, get your stuff out.' "

While our supply problem, thanks to my excellent search party, would be safe until we arrived in the prescribed concentration area, no danger, thank goodness, emerged on my right, southern flank.

The Americans seemed to have no idea that a combat group was marching east in front of them, across their line of advance. Even the air force failed to show up. Only once did one of our two patrols report: "Contact with American patrol, which turned away, however, apparently without seeing us."

Via Compiègne, where four years earlier Hitler had signed the armistice with France, we marched past Verdun in the direction of Metz. We were out of the actual battle area and made more frequent stops, to give the weary drivers a little rest and to assemble our units. Supply was now less of a problem, though the threat of force had to sometimes be used.

While still some way from Metz, we turned southeast in the direction of Nancy, and on via Baccarat. On 9 September, after an eleven-day march, we reached the prescribed area west of Strasbourg. We were all dead tired.

We had been in action without a break for over three months. We needed rest and, urgently, replacements of men and materiel. The strength of my grenadier companies was down to 50 men.

Our assembly area lay between the Vosges and Strasbourg, between the Maginot Line and the Western Wall. I let the men find billets in the surrounding villages and went in search of the divisional command post.

The autumn sun still had some warmth. The Rhine valley lay peacefully below me as I ascended the winding road to the Vosges Highway. For more than four years the war here had been suspended. I met one of the division's supply vehicles. The driver thought divisional HQ must be somewhere on the western fringe of the Vosges. I had been unable to make contact by radio.

Suddenly a jeep with an army pennant drew up beside me. I saluted and found myself standing in front of General Hasso von Manteuffel, a "colleague" from the 7th Panzer Division, who in Russia in 1941 had commanded a grenadier regiment.

"Luck, how nice to see you again after so long," he greeted me. "What are you doing here?"

I put him briefly in the picture and asked if he knew where our divisional HQ might be and what the situation was in general.

"The situation, my dear Luck, is bloody awful. I too only got here yesterday from Belgium, to take command of the 5th Panzer Army."

The picture Manteuffel gave me was not encouraging. "Before I left Belgium, Montgomery had taken the offensive with his Army group and, against weak resistance, had reached Brussels on the 3rd September and Antwerp on the 4th.

"Far more dangerous, however, was the thrust of the Americans, General Patton, with his 3rd U.S. Army. It was Patton who managed to make the decisive breakthrough at Avranches and who then, without regard for his open southern flank, pushed vigorously to the east. I would almost call him the American Rommel. He has a high standing with Eisenhower, and in the U.S. he is feted as a hero. Statements from prisoners confirm this time and again.

"By the end of August the Americans were being forced to pause; their supply lines from Cherbourg and several ports in Normandy were becoming too long. Since the beginning of September, however, the Americans have taken the offensive again: the First U.S. Army reached Mons on 2 September and took 30,000 prisoners. Patton, without regard for his right flank, has pressed forward the furthest; he's reached Verdun and is now advancing on Metz and Nancy, hence on the Moselle.

"The 6th U.S. Army Group, including the 1st French Army, is approaching from southern France and is supposed to join up with Patton. The remains of our retreating armies from the Mediterranean and the Atlantic coast are, it is true, still holding a wedge that extends as far as Dijon, but for how much longer?

"The worst of it is," Manteuffel went on, "Hitler is juggling with divisions that are divisions no more. And now," ironically, and with a shake of his head, "Hitler wants to launch a tank attack from the Dijon area to the north, in order, as he likes to put it, 'to seize Patton in the flank, cut his lines of communication, and destroy him.' What a misjudgment of the situation and the possibilities open to us."

I was deeply disturbed.

"What do you think should be done?" I asked Manteuffel.

"Conduct a mobile defense here on the western slopes of the Vosges and to the west of Saarbruecken, in order to make the Western Wall defensible again, and to occupy it. That would offer a chance of delaying the enemy for a longer period of time. Here in the west we need time, to enable us to prepare for the Russian offensive.

"But that, my dear Luck, is likely to remain an illusion. I wish you all the best; come through the last battle in one piece." A handshake and he was gone.

I was not to see Manteuffel again until long after the war.

I eventually found divisional HQ. Feuchtinger was pleased that I had brought him back the combat group intact. I told him of my meeting with Manteuffel.

"I'm glad to hear a little about the general situation," he said. "Our division belongs to Manteuffel's 5th Panzer Army, but I haven't met him yet."

"First of all, something pleasant." Feuchtinger beckoned to his adjutant. "In the name of the Fuehrer I have the honor and great pleasure to bestow on you the Knight's Cross of the Iron Cross."

Ceremonially he took the order from its black case and hung it around my neck; and, as if to order, someone was there with a camera. I had to "pose" with Feuchtinger.

"The decoration has been here since August, but then, of course, you were still on the 'long march.' I had recommended you long ago for exceptional bravery and for your personal commitment in Normandy, especially in the defense against Monty's 'Operation Goodwood' on July 18."

Someone was on hand with a glass of champagne. We drank, not to Final Victory, but to our all getting home safely after the war.

I was naturally proud of the decoration.

"General, I can and will accept this order only on behalf of all my people. Without them I could never have succeeded in achieving what you are honoring me for."

We had to pass on to the order of the day.

"Give your men a little rest," Feuchtinger began. "Materiel and a Luftwaffe replacement battalion have arrived. Just imagine, among them are fully trained pilots and boys of 16 and 17. How are we supposed to stop the Allies now with their inexhaustible materiel, when we're sent mere cannon-fodder as replacements?

"You already know from Manteuffel that our task is to set up a defensive barrier, so that the remains of the two armies withdrawing from the west and south can be brought into the gap between us and the Swiss border.

"Yesterday, with a heavy heart, I had to send Colonel Rauch with his patched-up regiment into the Epinal area, to guard the Moselle crossings. According to reports in our hands, elements of Patton's forces are advancing south from Nancy and the 2nd French Armored Division from the west on Dijon; we simply have to stop them.

"You too must anticipate going into action in the next few days." With that I was dismissed.

Molsheim is a small town in the Rhine valley west of Strasbourg. There and in the surrounding villages my combat group was to be given a chance to recover. The local people spoke French and German. Like all Alsace-Lorrainians they had changed nationality more than once during the wars between France and Germany. At the moment, Hitler laid claim to Alsace-Lorraine. In a few weeks, it looked as though it would again be French territory.

The villages, where the houses resembled those of the Black Forest in style, provided billets for my men. Most of them were sleeping in beds again for the first time in months. As for me and my staff, we were quartered in a little inn. My adjutant and the other officers were seated at the bar with a glass of Traminer, the famous wine of the area. A great cheer went up when I came in. I had forgotten that I still had the Knight's Cross around my neck. "Congratulations, it was about time, Lieutenant-Colonel."

I gave a deprecatory wave. "It's meant for all the men of our regiment. I'll wear it with pride—for them." That was all I could say.

"I just want to try to call Berlin, then I'll tell you something about the situation and our task."

After only 15 minutes my intelligence officer was back. "We have the connection to Berlin."

Dagmar was on the line. "Thank God, you're alive. I haven't been able to sleep. I tried to get news through friends at the Personnel Office. No one could tell me anything. 'The situation is too confused,' was all they said. How are you?"

"I'm fine, as far as it goes. I'm just terribly tired. I too have been worrying about you every day and wondering whether you got out of Paris safely. How did it go?"

"As arranged. Two days before the Allies marched in, a truck appeared from H.Q., Paris, and took me and my bicycle to Berlin. Saying good-bye to our friends in Paris was hard. They again offered to hide me in the south of France until the war was over. They all send their greetings."

Just as I was going to tell Dagmar about the Knight's Cross, the connection was broken. At least each of us knew that the other was alive and well.

I sent for all the commanders and briefed them on the situation, as it had been described to me by Manteuffel and Feuchtinger.

"In the next two or three days every unit, in collaboration with the division's supply posts, should receive replacements of men and materiel. See to it that our experienced corporals and lance-corporals take the young men in hand and fit them in quickly. We must anticipate action at short notice."

Then we all had a drink together, a closely knit team that had survived the past months.

It suddenly dawned on us that only a few kilometers now separated us from the

"Reich," and that Hitler required us to fight "till the Final Victory" or "go under," as his Propaganda Minister Goebbels proclaimed every day.

"Lieutenant-Colonel, do you believe the rumors that Hitler is trying to make a separate peace with the Western Allies, in order to have his back free for the fight against the Russians?" It was one of the questions that were also being discussed by the men.

"No," was my reply. "Like me you probably listen to the British radio now and then, on the sly. Churchill and the Americans are out to destroy Hitler and his regime. There's no room there for a separate peace."

I was able to speak fairly freely; we were all levelheaded enough to distinguish between facts and pipe dreams. No one would think us defeatist for that.

"I believe Manteuffel's idea is the only solution, that is, to man the Western Wall again, if it's not already too late for that. As far as I know all the weapons and communication systems were dismantled in 1940 and reinstalled in the Atlantic Wall. If that is so, we might be able to use the Western Wall as shelter from bombs and artillery fire, but not for defense.

"I'm alarmed about the situation on the eastern front, where the Russians will undoubtedly be mounting their last great offensive, which will carry them far into German territory. The reports of atrocities to our wives and daughters make one fear the worst."

We were very thoughtful as we sat for another hour over our glasses of Traminer. Each of us was thinking of our own situation and the weeks and months that lay ahead of us.

After two days any hope of rest was over.

Division ordered my II Battalion to join Rauch's combat group at once and take up positions at the Moselle crossings in the Epinal area. Major Kurz had received only a few replacements and little materiel.

"See that the young newcomers are taken in hand by veterans and quickly acclimatized to combat conditions," I said as we went along. "I'm expecting to be sent into action again myself in the next few days. I'll try to get Major Liehr some new SPWs for his I Armored Battalion. I'm sorry, Kurz, we can only try to set our longer war experience against our opponents' superiority in men and materiel."

Kurz was an experienced commander, who in the battles of the past months had more than once shown circumspection and personal bravery.

It was indeed not long before I too was involved. I was summoned to division.

"Luck, Colonel Rauch is sick and has to go home. You will take over his combat group at once; it will now be known as the 'Combat group of the 21st Panzer Division.'

"Hitler is sticking to his intention of attacking from the area west of Epinal, northward deep in Patton's flank. Madness, if one considers the physical state of the two sides.

"Three newly created panzer brigades have arrived, a new conception of High Command. They are certainly equipped with the latest war materiel, such as the Panther, and they have experienced commanders. But they don't know each other.

The units have never practiced combat maneuvers. After our heavy losses, why don't they give us this new materiel?

"Your task is to hold the Moselle crossings north of Epinal with your front to the west, while a panzer brigade west of Epinal thrusts north, supported by the remains of the infantry divisions. But watch out!

"After French units of the 2nd Armored Division and elements of the 1st French Army coming up from the south have met and taken Dijon, they will be threatening to push eastward, to encircle the remains of the infantry and the Panzer brigade. That will depend on how the French fight. Take over the division's combat group with your staff this very evening. Further orders will follow."

On the morning of 12 September, I received orders to support the panzer brigade's attack, which was to thrust north in front of me with its panzer group west of Epinal and against the 2nd French Armored Division with its Mk. IV group. I was to support the panther group.

So began the "Debacle of Epinal."

Perhaps, remembering 1940, we underestimated the French: in the 2nd French Armored Division, which—supported by massive air attacks and the excellent American artillery—was equipped with the best materiel and brilliantly led, moreover, by General Charles Leclerc, we were up against an opponent that had not only been the first to march into Paris, but now saw the chance to play an active part in liberating France from the "hated Nazis."

As we were told by prisoners, civilians had informed the French Colonel Langlade that my combat group was on the way from Epinal to the west. Langlade decided to attack the Panther group in the north early on 13 September and separate it from the southern group before I could come to its relief with my combat group.

The plan succeeded. Only four remaining Panthers were able to fight their way through and meet up with me. Owing to fierce air and artillery attacks by the Americans, the Panzer IV group operating further south was unable to stop the French division.

On that 13 September, the two panzer groups lost 34 Panthers and 26 Panzer IVs. Our infantry in the area was destroyed. To prevent a complete debacle, I launched an attack with my combat group, though without tanks, in the late afternoon. At first we made good progress, but then, owing to strong resistance, I was forced to call off the engagement.

On 14 September, my combat group was able to join up with the Panzer IV group. Together with the remaining 17 tanks we once again mounted an attack. With only 240 grenadiers and hardly any artillery of our own, we were able to gain a little ground, but were then brought to a standstill by the massive American artillery.

As a result, Corps HQ gave orders that rearward positions west of Epinal were to be occupied during the night; for we were to be "spared," so that we would be available for the attack on Patton's flank that Hitler was still planning.

It proved impossible to free our 16th Infantry Division from the encirclement. Only 500 men reached our lines, 7,000 men died or were taken prisoner.

After the 2nd French Armored Division and elements of the 1st French Army coming from the south had again joined forces, they crossed the Moselle south of us on 14 September. On 15 September Nancy fell into the hands of the Americans. On 16 September there were virtually no German forces left west of the Moselle.

Hitler's senseless, unrealistic plan of seizing Patton's army in the flank and destroying it had become illusory, as had been foreseen by Manteuffel and all of us.

Three rivers flow from the Vosges to the northwest practically parallel to each other: the Moselle, the Mortagne, and the Meurthe. We clung to all three in turn, until we were either bypassed or our weak defensive barrier was broken through. Lunéville on the Meurthe, southeast of Nancy, was an important junction. If, after Nancy, the enemy managed to capture Lunéville too, the way to the north past the Vosges to Saarbruecken and Reich territory would lie open to him.

In the second half of September fierce fighting broke out around Lunéville. American units penetrated into the town. In bitter counterattacks elements of two out of the total of three new panzer brigades regained part of the town. Tough hand-to-hand fighting from house to house led to heavy casualties on both sides.

The combat group of the 21st Panzer Division under my command had the task of blocking the crossings over the Mortagne south of Lunéville with one battalion and then, with the main body, also advancing on Lunéville from the south.

Despite its replacements through the Luftwaffe battalion, the strength of the battalion of Regiment 192 that was carrying the attack against Lunéville was down to only 100 grenadiers, while my II Battalion under Major Kurz had just 140 men left with which to defend the long stretch of river. While Feuchtinger was conducting the battle for Lunéville, my interest concerned my II Battalion.

We were again confronted by the 2nd French Armored Division. On the Moselle, Major Kurz had still been able to take a bridgehead from this division and gain a considerable success. Now we were exposed to the onslaught of the whole division, which was supported once more by heavy and concentrated fire from the American artillery. A first attack by a reinforced French armored group was successfully beaten off with the help of our artillery and some 8.8cm antitank guns. With an even stronger attack, however, the French, in a skillful operation, managed to cross the Mortagne during the night of 18/19 September and form a bridgehead.

The enemy now threatened to roll up our weak front on the Mortagne from the south. Under this impression Army Group G authorized the withdrawal of the combat group of the 21st Panzer Division behind the Meurthe, over which our engineers constructed a pontoon bridge that very night.

The battle for Lunéville was still raging while we were already being forced to abandon the second river defense. Thank goodness the enemy had to pause again, to bring up supplies. Even so, the French sounded out the ground with patrols as far as the Meurthe, where they were at once repulsed by us. After hard fighting, Lunéville was lost.

At the beginning of October, I was summoned with my commanders to the divisional command post.

General Feuchtinger awarded Major Willi Kurz the Knight's Cross and Major

Liehr of I Battalion the German Cross in Gold. Both received their decorations for their personal commitment during the fighting in Normandy.

On 25 October 1944, I was again sent for by Feuchtinger, this time with the commander of my HQ Company, Lieutenant Karl Sommer, and a man from his company, Lance-Corporal Maurer.

For their unprecedented commitment during the defensive fighting at Epinal, Lunéville, and Chatel, Lieutenant Sommer was formally awarded the German Cross in Gold and Maurer the Knight's Cross. It was rare for a lance-corporal to receive the Knight's Cross. So in this case a war correspondent and a film team recorded the event.

The deed for which Maurer received his great honor was not only remarkable but showed also the high level of training and the high morale of our men.

During one of our disengaging movements I had placed my HQ Company on high ground to cover the withdrawal of my combat group long enough to enable us to reach our next position. Without the support of artillery or antitank weapons, but depending only on their own heavy machine-guns, Sommer, from his commanding position, had forced the enemy to take cover again and again and had thereby procured us the necessary time to set up a new defense.

Lance-Corporal Maurer, with his machine-gun and an ammunition bearer, had been engaged on the left wing of his company, to secure its left flank. His task: to hold up the enemy and only withdraw in the event of heavy pressure. In looking for a suitable spot Maurer had strayed too far to the left and virtually lost touch with his company. But he had found an ideal position on a commanding hill and knew what he had to do.

Suddenly he saw in the valley below him an enemy column marching south. "They're planning to go around us and attack in the flank," was his first thought. The enemy had apparently assumed there was no one left on the hills, for vehicle by vehicle the column moved past him below.

When the enemy had come close enough, Maurer opened fire on the column, which at once stopped. The men jumped out of their vehicles and took cover. Maurer saw the wounded collapse. With the help of his ammunition bearer he fired one belt after the other from his MG. The first trucks caught fire; the confusion was complete. Then came the first reactions: antitank guns and light artillery were brought into position and opened fire.

Maurer laughed. "There's no way they can hit us from that angle; come on, let's have the next belt."

The shots did in fact whistle over his head. The enemy then formed up for an attack on the hill.

"You've just had the last belt of cartridges, pal. We've got to get out of here," shouted his ammunition bearer. "Come on, back to the company."

But Lieutenant Sommer had already moved off and from the start had not noticed Maurer's absence.

"Okay, then we'll just march east. We're bound to find the company, or von Luck's combat group, somewhere or other."

As the two set off on foot, they could still hear the enemy's guns and in the distance the shouts of the attacking infantry.

When Maurer had found his company and was brought to me by Lieutenant Sommer, he wondered more than anything why such a fuss was being made of him. "It was my job, wasn't it?" was his surprised comment.

Never had a recommendation for a Knight's Cross been complied with so quickly as with Maurer. He was at once held up in propaganda as a "shining example" to all young men, who were being sent to the front in ever greater numbers.

In November, Sommer was unfortunately taken prisoner.

October went by. The Allies' supply problem seemed to have been solved. General Patton was on the move to the northeast in the direction of Saarbruecken. We now stood with our backs to the Vosges behind the River Meurthe. Opposite us was still the 2nd French Armored Division.

Among those serving in its ranks was a successful entrepreneur called Michel Dufresne. Though neither of us could have known it at the time, when the French private and the German colonel were facing each other in anonymous hostility, we would later become friends.

In normal times Michel Dufresne lived in a beautiful old chateau in Normandy, which his wife Elisabeth, scion of an ancient aristocratic family, had brought with her into their marriage. The Chateau Vimer lay only a few kilometers outside Vimoutiers, an idyllic little town which in 1944 had gained a sad fame: in July, in its outskirts, Field Marshal Erwin Rommel had been severely wounded in a fighter attack. In August bitter fighting had taken place in the town and its vicinity between the Germans breaking out of the Falaise pocket and the Allies trying to close it. I myself had set up a defensive front with my combat group north of the town, to prevent any further advance by the British.

While Elisabeth Dufresne had converted her chateau into a military hospital— the roof bore a huge Red Cross and she took in wounded without regard to person—her husband Michel served in the 2nd French Armored Division. All this may have been one of the reasons why after the war Michel became an enthusiastic amateur historian, concerning himself with the fighting in Normandy and especially with the fighting around the Falaise pocket. Besides studying archive material and obtaining interviews with prominent commanders on both sides, as well as many well-known historians, Michel looked me up in Hamburg and we became good friends.

"At that time," he told me later, "I was the driver of a jeep for a platoon commander in the 4th Engineer Company of the 2nd French Armored Division under General Leclerc. On 30 October our division attacked, to force a crossing of the River Meurthe. This attack was apparently badly prepared and was repulsed. Then in the night before 31 October we crept up to the Germans and cleared away their mines. After good artillery preparation we accompanied our tanks and were able to cross the Meurthe northwest of Baccarat. In a little village we took a few prisoners, boys of sixteen, one of whom I kept the whole day in my jeep. We knew from prisoners that the German 21st Panzer Division lay opposite us."

I could remember the fighting around Baccarat well, and also that we had been able to beat off an attack by the French.

Unfortunately, Feuchtinger turned this defensive success of ours into a victory report: "With the combined fire of the artillery and our few antitank guns we were able in a very short time to destroy more than 40 enemy tanks."

It was humanly understandable that in such a desperate situation as ours attempts would be made through such reports to gain a little glory with the higher commands and give one's own people heart. But as the responsible commander of the combat group, I cannot confirm the defensive success in this form.

Michel Dufresne naturally wanted to know later how things had seemed to us. When I told him of Feuchtinger's report, he said, "We had several dead and wounded in our patrol. In the attacks of 30 and 31 October the division lost about a dozen tanks and 40 men. This is confirmed by the *Fonds Historique, Archives-Musée* in Paris, and by General Cholley, who found Feuchtinger's statement 'somewhat fanciful.' "

During the following days, we managed to hold the western outlets of the Vosges. Then the order reached us to move to the area west of Strasbourg on 12 November, to be rested there for 14 days.

On 9 November heavy falls of snow set in. The roads were soon iced over and passable only with difficulty. We were afraid that the enemy would push us into the Vosges, where we would have had enormous problems in getting over the icy, winding roads. But the enemy, too, slowed his advance. He was now aiming northeast in the direction of Strasbourg. An infantry division brought in from Slovakia relieved us. We were pulled out and very pleased at the prospect of a few days' rest, of replacements of men and materiel.

Instead of that, in the evening of 11 November the division was sent north, to stop Patton's advance on the River Nied, between Metz and Saarbruecken. After a few days of heavy defensive fighting we were outflanked on the left and in the evening of 18 November pulled out.

We started to feel like the fire brigade, which has to go wherever there's a fire to put out. But it was burning everywhere.

The very next day we were sent north, to occupy the approaches to the Western Wall at Saarlautern (Saarlouis). As we crossed the French-German border, it came home to all of us that from now on we would be fighting on our own native soil.

At the beginning of November my adjutant, Liebeskind, became very ill and had to be admitted to hospital. He didn't come back until 22 December. His duties were taken over by Captain Krieger, who on Liebeskind's return had to be given special leave: his only son was killed in an air raid on Solingen. The French chapter was closed.

18
Fighting the Americans, December 1944

As yet we were in the approaches to the once proud "impregnable" Western Wall. A quick inspection of the fortifications confirmed our fears. Since the end of the French campaign in 1940, the bunkers and defense installations had come to resemble the castle in *Sleeping Beauty*. Armaments and communication systems had been dismantled and reinstalled in the Atlantic Wall. In the approaches to the bunkers a wild growth had sprung up which certainly made the hideous concrete blocks look more peaceful, with trees, bushes, and flowers, but it reduced the field of fire to nil. I at once sent a party to the Western Wall to find out whether it would be at all usable.

My orderly officer came back with this report. "Lieutenant-Colonel, we first had to round up the responsible 'caretaker' from the local theater, to get the bunkers unlocked. It would take weeks to put the installations into a defensible state, to say nothing of arming them with heavy guns and antitank weapons and mine fields. The 'caretaker' hasn't even got a plan of the installations and doesn't know whether one exists. We can forget about any effective defense from the system of bunkers."

On the western bank of the Saar lay the little town of Wallerfangen, its houses clustered around a manor house. It suddenly occurred to me that the manor house of Wallerfangen was the seat of the von Papen family. I drove there at once and met the two sisters of my friend Franz von Papen. Both told me in no uncertain terms that they wanted to stay there whatever might happen. I tried to persuade them to leave the manor house, since there would be heavy fighting and no one would be able to have any regard for them or the house. With heavy hearts they eventually agreed. Not long afterward Wallerfangen became a heap of ruins.

We set up our positions between the bunkers, which could now serve only as shelter from heavy artillery and air attacks. Then, on 19 November, the Americans began their attack on the Saar crossings between Saarlautern and the "Orscholtz block" east of Metz. We were concerned with the 10th U.S. Armored Division and the 90th U.S. Infantry Division, which attacked our line Saarlautern-Orscholtz along a wide front. Their goal seemed clear to us: to push through, over the Saar to the northeast, past Kaiserslautern, to the Rhine.

My combat group was split up: while Major Kurz with II Battalion defended in Saarlautern and became involved in tough house-to-house fighting with black Americans, who climbed the houses with knives in their mouths, I had to send Major Liehr with I Battalion to Merzig, to help the 25th Panzer Grenadier Division, which was engaged in heavy defensive fighting there. Again, the excellent American artillery helped to force small breaches.

Between 23 November and 11 December, fierce fighting raged in the whole area of Saarlautern, Dillingen, and Merzig, where on 29 November the enemy managed to open a deep breach to the east at Saarlautern (Saarlouis). Owing to its heavy losses, our division now consisted solely of my combat group. We were pulled out in the middle of December and sent far to the east, past Saarbruecken, to the area between Pirmasens and Wissembourg, to be restored to strength, as reserve for Army Group G.

For the 3rd U.S. Army the way to the Rhine lay open. It thrust north of Saarbruecken toward Kaiserslautern.

The next danger now looming came from the U.S. army group that was advancing northward from the south and southwest; from the Nancy-Baccarat area, past the slopes of the Vosges, it was trying to penetrate the Rhine valley between Kaiserslautern and Colmar, with the goal of taking Strasbourg and crossing the Rhine.

Yet we were granted a short respite. We had now been in action for more than six months without a break. Our losses had been high. All the same, our young replacements—thanks to our veterans—had been successfully integrated time and again. Here at the front the young men had quickly shed their illusions about marching with Hitler into a "Thousand-Year Reich." They had soon grasped the difference between propaganda and reality.

We lay with the combat group between the now useless installations of the Western Wall at Zweibruecken on the Saar and Pirmasens. On New Year's Eve we all got together. We didn't know how things would go, but we understood nevertheless that the war was no longer to be won. We only knew that we had to do our duty.

Meanwhile, something had been happening: on 16 December 1944, Hitler had started the Ardennes offensive. We had heard about it marginally and had heard Goebbels's strident voice on the radio: "The Wehrmacht has launched its great offensive. We will destroy the enemy and cut all his lines of communication. Paris is our goal."

Our comment on this news had been unanimous: How did Hitler think he could ever succeed in getting through the snowed-in Ardennes, over the icy, winding roads, with battered or inexperienced divisions and under the complete air superiority of the Allies?

What we didn't yet know on that New Year's Eve was that the unexpected offensive on our part had at first been successful, but then, on 28 December, had come to nothing.

The turn of the year had just been celebrated; we had drunk to a New Year full of question marks with a modest glass of punch, when a message reached us that the division was to prepare to move out that very night. I was summoned to Feuchtinger at his command post. He was very grave, wished me a happy New Year, and gave me the following briefing.

"On 28 December, I was called to Army Group G, where I met all the Army, corps, and divisional commanders. From there we went to Field Marshal von Rundstedt, who told us that Hitler wished to speak to us all that afternoon at his HQ in Bad Nauheim. There we also met Field Marshal Keitel, Colonel-General Jodl, Himmler, and Bormann.

"The presence of the highest Army and Party leaders pointed to an important communication from Hitler. He began as usual with a long speech and emphasized that we were waging an ideological war, the loss of which would destroy the German people. 'I haven't the slightest intention of losing the war. Think of Frederick the Great and his Seven Year War.'

"Hitler then came to speak of the Ardennes offensive, in which 'not all the objectives had been achieved' (a highly optimistic view, it seemed to me), but which had had an 'incidental' consequence, namely, the weakening of the American front opposite us, where 'Operation North Wind' was to begin. He estimated the strength of the Americans on our front as down to only four or five divisions, which he proposed to 'destroy' with eight offensive German divisions, in order to follow up with further blows. Hitler then ended his address by saying, and these were his words: 'It must be our absolute goal to settle the matter here in the west offensively; that must be our fanatical goal.'

" 'Operation North Wind' began on New Year's Eve," Feuchtinger went on, "our division is the Army group's reserve. Hitler's plan is to break through the Maginot Line south of Pirmasens with an armored group and advance south along the western fringe of the Vosges, in order to make contact with the 19th Army's bridgehead at Colmar. Five divisions of Volksgrenadiers are to push through the (snowed-in) Vosges from the west into the Rhine valley and join forces with a bridgehead west of the Rhine. Although we've received replacements and now have 74 Panthers and Panzer IVs again," Feuchtinger concluded, "two things are being overlooked: we have no air superiority and nothing equivalent to set against the massive U.S. artillery. Our men are spent and the replacements have no experience. In accordance with orders, we shall assemble in readiness today, 1 January 1944, just north of the Maginot Line. God be with you!"

Major Spreu, who had now been given command of Regiment 192, and I looked at each other. Although nothing was said, it seemed to both of us that Hitler had decided to fight to the last man and to be prepared if necessary to have the German people conquer or go under.

What happened was inevitable: the Americans had made very good preparations for an attack on their right flank and established themselves in the Maginot Line. The division of our forces into two assault groups, especially with the inexperienced infantry group, was unable to produce the desired result.

Nevertheless, as we learned from prisoners and intercepted messages, Eisenhower, under the impact of the Ardennes offensive and "Operation North Wind," begun on New Year's Eve, had ordered the attack on the Western Wall in northern Alsace to be abandoned for the time being. According to reports, Eisenhower and de Gaulle had agreed, on 3 January, to withdraw to the Maginot Line in lower Alsace, retaining weak forces for the defense of Strasbourg.

"Operation North Wind" made no progress. In the snowed-in Vosges and to the west of them the two assault groups came to a standstill.

A new plan was conceived. Our division and the 25th Panzer Grenadier Division, swinging east from the area south of Wissembourg, were to break through the Maginot Line and trap the enemy in the Haguenau depression.

The two divisions were moved east and received orders to prepare themselves for this attack. One last dramatic battle lay before us.

As I was leaving the divisional command post, an orderly officer of the staff took me to one side.

"Lieutenant-Colonel," he said, "I feel obliged to inform you, in your own interest and in that of your people, that court-martial proceedings are likely to be started against our divisional commander. Ten days ago General Feuchtinger was ordered to High Command West to provide information as to why on the night of 5 to 6 June 1944 he was not at his command post but in Paris.

"Feuchtinger was not at his command post but in Germany. I had to fetch him from there on 24 December and take him to HQ West.

"I feel obliged to inform you of this, as the commander of our combat group, so that you will know why our brave division has such a bad reputation with the higher commands."

I was speechless. On Christmas Eve, while we had been putting up a desperate fight in the Western Wall at Saarlautern, our divisional commander had been at home.

Certainly, we knew of Feuchtinger's fondness for *la dolce vita*. We knew of his contacts from prewar days with high functionaries of the Nazi regime and disapproved of them. We also had been unable to understand why, during the decisive hours of the invasion, he had been in Paris, and not, moreover, only at the "special HQ."

We commanders had always maintained our loyalty to Feuchtinger whenever our friends in other panzer divisions had sneered at his style of leadership and his way of life. Now even I felt this to be the last straw.

Although I too hold to the saying *de mortuis nil nisi bene* ("of the dead say nothing but good"), when I think of our brave men, who fought so brilliantly, and of the thousands of dead, wounded, and missing of those six months, I cannot help reproaching Feuchtinger with having done us all poor service.

At the end of January 1945, when the bitter fighting was over, General Feuchtinger said good-bye to us, his commanders. Impassively we received his thanks for what we had done.

In March, Feuchtinger was condemned by a court-martial. The sentence, however, was mitigated on "orders from above" and under the pressure of events was not carried out. I only heard of the court-martial proceedings against Feuchtinger long after my return from captivity.

After his release from American captivity, he had eked out a living at various jobs and died at the end of the 1950s, shortly before new proceedings were to be brought against him.

THE BATTLE FOR HATTEN-RITTERSHOFFEN

At the beginning of January 1945 the Vosges were deep in snow. In the lowlands between Wissembourg-Haguenau and the Rhine the snow was a foot deep. It was bitterly cold; the roads were icy. The civilian population was apprehensive, fearing that the war would once again ravage their villages. In many farmhouses there was no running water; the pipes were frozen.

Wissembourg is a small town in northern Alsace on the border with the Palatinate. On the slopes of this area, around Landau-Ahrweiler and Bergzabern, the good Palatine wine was grown. To the east the Rhine was not far away, on the other side of which lay Baden-Baden in the Black Forest.

Between the eastern slopes of the Vosges and the Rhine a wide lowland stretched south as far as Strasbourg.

Our concentration area lay north of Wissembourg, where we arrived during the night of 5 to 6 January after a difficult march over icy roads.

It was planned that the 25th Panzer Grenadier Division which had been unable to break the Maginot Line west of the Vosges, was likewise to assemble behind us during the following night.

Our task was to push southward through the Maginot Line with two combat groups hard by the eastern foothills of the Vosges, close all outlets from the Vosges, and cut the enemy's communications with Strasbourg.

I asked for maps with the exact location of bunkers and other fortifications. There were none. Not even the upper echelons had maps. To reassure us, we were told that the Maginot Line was barely manned and constituted no obstacle.

"Blind," we set off south on 6 January. Even before we had reached the first bunkers, we came up against fierce resistance and once again the concentrated fire of the American artillery. By the afternoon the two combat groups had indeed driven the enemy back, but we had still not come across the bunkers of the Maginot Line.

We continued the attack during the night of 6 and 7 January. Thick mist lay over the Rhine valley, visibility was down to a hundred yards. Suddenly we could make out the first bunker, which received us with heavy fire. Our leading men and the accompanying SPW landed in thick mine fields; the artillery stepped up its barrage of fire. There was no doubt about it: the enemy intended to hold his position on the Maginot Line under all circumstances and keep his lines open to Strasbourg and the Rhine. Our division, which was now reduced to the fighting strength of a grenadier regiment, would not suffice to force a passage.

From the prisoners we took in the approaches to the Maginot Line we knew who our opponents were: the experienced 79th U.S. Infantry Division, part of the 14th U.S. Armored Division and elements of the 42nd U.S. Infantry Division, as well as strong artillery. These were to be our concern for the next 14 days.

Army group seemed to have realized that the Americans were far stronger than expected.

On 8 January, Captain Herr, accompanied by grenadiers and army engineers, once again moved south. This assault party, with 12 Panthers, managed to force one bunker into surrender, shoot up three Shermans, and take many prisoners. He lost one Panther through mines. Then such heavy artillery fire descended on the bunker that Herr lost 20 grenadiers and engineers, who had been sitting on his tanks. He had to withdraw.

Army group issued fresh orders: "Two days ago, south of the Haguenau forest, we managed to form a bridgehead over the Rhine north of Strasbourg. From this bridgehead a westward thrust is to be made to cut the communications of the enemy north of the Haguenau forest. The 25th Panzer Grenadier Division will move west on 9 January along the northern edge of the forest, break through the Maginot Line, and advance down the eastern slopes of the Vosges. The 21st Panzer Division will assemble on its right and after the first breakthroughs will likewise move west at once."

On 8 January, 20 assault-guns arrived from Germany; Captain Herr still had 11 tanks available. On the same day the 25th Panzer Grenadier Division assembled in two combat groups, our division just north of it with my regiment in contact with the 25th Panzer Grenadier Division.

It was bitterly cold and snowing. Only rarely did the moon shine through. Then one could see the dark monsters looming up out of the snow. We knew that we had to cut through barbed-wire entanglements and clear mines. For this only a few engineers were available and young replacements, soldiers of 16 and 17.

During the night of 8 and 9 January the first assault party of the 25th Panzer Grenadier Division worked its way up to the first bunker. Without a sound the youngsters crept forward and began to cut a passage through the barbed wire. Whenever the moon came out all movement froze. Toward four in the morning a path had been cleared; it was only another hundred yards to the bunker. On all fours the assault party worked its way forward. Then they were there. The Americans seemed to be asleep. The barrel of a gun poked menacingly from its embrasure. The men crept around the bunker. The armored door was closed. An NCO beat against it with the butt of his gun and it slowly opened.

The American crew had been taken completely by surprise and were quickly overcome. The noise alerted other bunkers and the intermediate positions. Heavy fighting broke out at once. The American artillery laid down a barrage of fire on the bunker.

Then a combat group of the 25th Panzer Grenadier Division, supported by assault-guns, moved up to attack through the gap. Heavy artillery fire prevented a rapid advance. The group turned left and forced its way from the north into the little village of Hatten.

At the same time an armored group from my division also moved up, with the intention of pushing past Hatten. Several tanks drove over mines. The attack made no progress. One of my battalions also entered Hatten from the north and relieved the elements of the 25th Panzer Grenadier Division that were there. The southern part of the village was fiercely defended by American infantry, who mounted a counterattack, but this was repulsed.

By the evening of 9 January only a small breach had been achieved. Army group and corps pressed for a continuation of the attack. The breakthrough in the Maginot Line was to be extended, in order to push through to the west.

During the night of 9 and 10 January, my combat group, with Regiment 125, moved up to the bunker, to the right of me our sister Regiment 192.

The division had been supplied with a further artillery regiment, so we were somewhat better supported.

The armored group of the 25th Panzer Grenadier Division had tried in vain to force its way also into the neighboring village of Rittershoffen; our division now prepared to take Rittershoffen on 10 January.

Reserve Major Willy Spreu commanded Regiment 192 in place of the sick Colonel Rauch. His attack on the Maginot Line north of Hatten had also come to a standstill on 9 January in front of the bunkers, his companies heavily reduced. As last reserve he still had his engineer platoon, consisting of one sergeant, one NCO, and 20 mostly inexperienced men. That evening Major Spreu positioned his antitank guns and heavy weapons opposite a bunker that was standing out clearly.

As Major Spreu reported later, "At first light I moved up with the platoon of engineers, while my heavy weapons fired nonstop at the gun-ports in the bunker. We charged through the snow and within a few minutes were at the bunker. The engineers threw hand grenades into the ports, while others cut through the barbed wire and cleared mines. When we ran around to the rear entrance, the door opened and a white flag appeared with five officers and a garrison of 117 men. Four of the officers had suffered severe eye injuries from the firing at the ports. They were treated at once by the regimental doctor; the others were sent to the rear. The bunker turned out to be a heavily armed stronghold in an extensive system of fortifications, so I at once made it my command post."

Next day, in the attack on the hills north of Rittershoffen, Major Spreu was severely wounded and taken to the hospital. On 24 February, for his "personal bravery," he was awarded the Knight's Cross.

On 10 January, I moved up with my regiment for the attack on Rittershoffen. That night I succeeded in forcing my way into the village, but there too, just as at Hatten, the enemy held out in the houses and at once mounted a counterattack with tanks and infantry. This hit my II Battalion in particular, which had established itself in the center near the church.

In these two villages of Hatten and Rittershoffen there now developed one of the hardest and most costly battles that had ever raged on the western front.

The Americans strained every sinew to regain the Maginot Line, to avoid being cut off in the Strasbourg area. In Rittershoffen we were only 20 yards apart. Sometimes we would be in the first floor of a house while the Americans were in the cellar—and vice versa.

This bitter house-to-house fighting raged for nearly two weeks. Both sides used their artillery nonstop, also flamethrowers. The Americans set fire to almost all the houses with incendiary shells. We took prisoners from the 827th U.S. Armored Battalion, which consisted almost entirely of blacks. They told us their instructions were to shoot up or set on fire any house in which Germans—they said "Nazis"—were to be found. I had to leave my own cellar in a hurry when an incendiary shell burst in front of my look-out and we were in danger of suffocation. I moved into another cellar quite close to the command post of Major Kurz, who with his II Battalion was having to bear the brunt of the attacks.

Prisoners from the 14th U.S. Armored Division cursed, "God-damn it, this is the bloodiest battle we've ever fought, worse than the legendary battle of Anzio in Italy."

Even now the civilian population remained in the two villages. Women, children, and old people, packed in like sardines, sat in the cellars of the houses. Electricity had been cut off, the supply of food was short, and there was no water for the pipes were frozen. We tried to help as much as we could. By day any movement was fatal; our supplies could be brought up only by night in armored vehicles. In this we were helped by a hollow, which concealed us from the enemy, whose flares threw the area into brilliant light.

As early as the second day my regimental doctor came to me and angrily said, "I have up to 50 wounded lying in a cellar who are in urgent need of medical treatment. I have no morphine left and hardly any dressings. In another cellar there are more than 40 dead, who can't be buried here. I'm also doing what I can for the civilians."

On many nights I was at least able to send a few wounded civilians and men of my unit to the rear, past Hatten, and have ammunition brought up. My orderly officer, Dr. Mueller-Temme, had to get the ammunition boxes forward to the grenadiers, since all the other men of my staff were in action, to compensate to some extent for the losses in the two battalions.

But neither the Americans, who now had elements of an armored division and two infantry divisions fighting in Rittershoffen, nor we would give way. Our battle in the two villages, as we heard later, was constantly being mentioned in army communiqués. After a few days I discovered that there were also elements of the 25th Panzer Grenadier Division in Rittershoffen, who had got stuck there, while the bulk of them were fighting in Hatten. In both places we had elements of the 79th U.S. Infantry Division encircled for a time, but they fought their way out again with heavy losses. After eight days we had news that a parachute battalion was coming to Rittershoffen as reinforcements.

The place became a phantom village after only a few days. Almost all the buildings, including the church, which was defended by Major Kurz's men, were in ruins. Many of the houses were on fire and lit up the scene at night. The dead lay about the streets, among them many civilians. We couldn't recover their bodies, since the enemy here was often no more than 15 or 20 yards away. The cows bellowed in their stalls unattended; the cadavers of animals stank and infected the air.

After eight days we still didn't know whether we were continuing to fight there for reasons of prestige, or whether there was a tactical significance to our holding the positions.

It seemed to me that we and our brave adversaries were no longer thinking of anything but survival. Contact with division had been lost after only a few days. Through our death-defying SPW crews of I Battalion, who every night ensured the removal of wounded and the provision of supplies, we heard that things looked much the same in Hatten as with us. There too a battalion of the 79th Infantry Division had been encircled at the beginning and had only freed itself after days of fighting. There too the northern and western parts were in our hands. The rest of the village was being defended tenaciously by the Americans.

We heard that on 10 January a strong assault party of the 25th Grenadier Division had managed to crack a stronghold near Hatten and take 300 prisoners. With that the Maginot Line had been broken through over a length of 10 kilometers. In Hatten and Rittershoffen, and to the north of them, we were hopelessly bogged down. Artillery duels on a colossal scale took place every day, heavier than we had ever experienced in Normandy.

What oppressed us most was the fate of the innocent civilians. Over 100 dead, most of them children and old people, were later counted.

On 14 January the Americans tried to recapture Rittershoffen and, in Hatten, free two battalions of the 79th U.S. Infantry Division that were trapped there. Thanks to the courageous performance of my combat group and elements of the 25th Panzer Grenadier Division, the attack was successfully beaten off with heavy losses for the enemy. We heard from prisoners that from 14 January command in the "Battle of Hatten-Rittershoffen" had been taken over by the 14th U.S. Armored Division. Attached to it in Rittershoffen were one battalion of the 79th Infantry Division, which for a time had been surrounded by us, and elements of the 42nd U.S. Rainbow Division.

As the chronicle of the 14th U.S. Armored Division was later to record: "It was a brutal, bloody and slow business, worse than anything we had experienced."

On the following day, the Americans tried again, and again came to grief. On the two sides more than 10,000 shells were fired every day.

On 17 January it snowed again heavily; visibility was down to a hundred yards. At dawn the Americans attacked Rittershoffen and Hatten with 45 tanks and infantry. They were supported by very heavy artillery fire. In the half-light, a strong assault party forced its way unexpectedly into Rittershoffen and took prisoner members of the regimental and battalion staffs of Panzer Grenadier Division, as well as some resting elements.

Shortly after, a messenger rushed into my cellar, "Lieutenant-Colonel, the Amis have captured almost all our staff officers and a lot of men. I just managed to get away. Can you help?"

Thank goodness some elements of the parachute battalion and our own reconnaissance battalion were available and I was able to send them into a counterattack at once. They managed to free most of our men and take more than 80 prisoners.

On 18 January, beginning at 1400 hours, the enemy again laid down a heavy artillery barrage on both villages and at 1700 hours, as it grew dark, moved in to attack Rittershoffen from the north and south. He thereby came up against the paratroops and my II Battalion. After heavy losses he was thrown back, our artillery having given us effective support.

During the night an orderly from division arrived to see me. "Lieutenant-Colonel, I am instructed by the divisional commander to brief you on the intentions of Army Group G.

"On 19 January an attack will be launched south of the Haguenau forest with a tank corps and the paratroop division from the extended bridgehead over the Rhine. Our division was to have been detailed for this. It was appreciated that for the moment a disengagement is impossible. The two burnt-out divisions engaged in Hatten-Rittershoffen are to simulate further attacking intentions, through increased activity by assault parties and the heavy use of artillery, in order to tie down the enemy forces employed there. The goal is to push past Haguenau to the west and then surround the enemy forces standing north of the River Moder.

"It will interest you to know," the young officer continued with amusement, "that Himmler has been entrusted with the high command of Rhine-sector south. Hitler himself, moreover, has ordered the new attack south of the Haguenau forest. Nothing more can now go wrong, Lieutenant-Colonel."

We had become so bold and full of gallows humor in the meantime that such remarks, which were punishable by demotion or even the death penalty, were now permissible.

"Very well," I dismissed the young lieutenant, "let us then rely on Himmler and his 'war experience.' "

In spite of heavy artillery fire, the fighting for our two villages, up to 90 percent destroyed, subsided in the next two days. Only in Hatten did the paratroops, supported by a few tanks, once again attack the brave 79th U.S. Infantry Division. The Americans defended themselves with guns, pistols, bazookas, and knives house by house, so that the attack had to be broken off.

In the evening of 19 January advance parties of the 47th Volksgrenadier Division arrived; they had been brought up by train from Germany and were to relieve us. During the night the heavily reduced elements of the 25th Panzer Grenadier Division were relieved, to be restored to strength further to the rear. The remainder of this brave division were pulled out during the night of 20 and 21 January.

On the morning of that cold winter day, the 21st, a suspicious calm lay over and around Rittershoffen. I asked Major Kurz to find out, by means of an assault party, what the enemy was up to.

I myself glanced as usual from my cellar window across to the ruined houses on the other side of the street, where we had often seen individual Americans flitting back and forth.

Everything was quiet; even the enemy guns were silent. Then Major Kurz came running the hundred yards to my command post.

"Lieutenant-Colonel, the Amis have gone; they've evacuated the place during the night, under cover of their artillery."

Kurz looked at me from his red-rimmed eyes. I pressed his hand.

"So that's it, Kurz. Thanks for all you and your men have done."

Unshaven, with our "U-boat" beards, we stood facing each other. We couldn't grasp that the murderous battle was over.

"There are no winners and no losers here. So what was it all for?"

Slowly the exhausted men came out of their cellars; a few civilians appeared. They had tears in their eyes.

"Is it all over now? Can we bury our dead?"

"We are so sorry for you and your lovely village. This damn war! For you it's now at an end."

Thoughtfully Kurz and I walked with slow steps to the church, only a part of which was still undamaged. Through a gaping hole in the wall we went in. I stood facing the altar, which lay in ruins, and looked up at the organ. It seemed to be unharmed. A few more of our men came in.

"Come," I called to a lance-corporal, "we'll climb up to the organ."

On arriving above, I asked the man to tread the bellows. I sat down at the organ and—it was hardly believable—it worked.

On the spur of the moment I began to play Bach's chorale *Nun danket alle Gott*. It resounded through the ruins to the outside. More and more of my men climbed into the battered church, followed by old women and children, who knelt on the ground and quietly prayed. My men were not ashamed of their tears.

What had happened? What had made the Americans abandon the two villages and relinquish the chance of retaking the Maginot Line still, in spite of everything?

After a few days we knew. Captured officers stated that the 7th U.S. Army, which was responsible for the sector, had reported to their Army group that the divisions engaged in Hatten-Rittershoffen had become so reduced that they could no longer hold their positions. The U.S. Army group had thereupon ordered the villages of Hatten and Rittershoffen, along with the Maginot Line in the area north of the Haguenau forest, to be abandoned. Prepared positions were to be taken up on the River Moder, which flowed east from the Vosges through Haguenau.

The 39th Panzer Corps and the 14th SS Panzer Corps, following the paratroop division, had moved west out of the bridgehead over the Rhine and had reached Haguenau. With that the Americans were threatened with encirclement north of the Haguenau forest. On 21 January, strong combat detachments were already pushing west out of Rittershoffen. During the morning of the 22nd we were relieved by the Volksgrenadier Division and reached the River Moder west of Haguenau. The brave 25th Panzer Grenadier Division, struggling south over icy roads through the snow-covered Haguenau forest, also reached the Moder. Our grenadier companies were down to 20 or 30 men. All the same, success was within our grasp: the Americans could be cut off from Strasbourg.

Then, with no previous warning, orders reached us to pull out, on 25 January, and assemble in the area of the little town of Kandel, west of the Rhine on the hills by Karlsruhe, to be restored to strength. The 25th Panzer Grenadier Division had already been pulled out on 24 January and moved to the area north of Kandel.

We were naturally pleased to have a few days rest after the heavy fighting at Rittershoffen, but couldn't understand why we had been withdrawn so close to reaching our goal.

We were to learn the reason sooner than we would have wished. At Kandel we found brand new material, as well as a replacement battalion. Welcome though that was to us, we often didn't know who would drive the new tanks, SPWs, and assault-guns, or man their guns. Our casualties in trained drivers, gunners, and commanders had been too great. So by day and by night people from the replacement battalion were given a makeshift training.

On 30 January all commanders were summoned to the divisional command post. I had the good old Mercedes brought to me, which in the past months had been used as a courier vehicle.

On our arrival we were greeted for the last time by General Feuchtinger. "Gentlemen, you know that I am being posted to the commander reserves. Until the arrival of a new commander, Colonel Zollenkopf from the commander reserves, whom I now introduce to you, will take over the division.

"In addition, I have the pleasure of announcing the promotion of Lieutenant-Colonel von Luck to Colonel, and I hereby present him with the second star. At thirty-three von Luck is one of the youngest colonels."

My pleasure was somewhat muted. In this last phase of the war, promotions and decorations had become irrelevant. All that mattered now was to bring as many men as possible, for whom one was responsible, safely through the last weeks and to survive.

"On the eastern front," Feuchtinger went on, "the news is alarming: on 14 January the Russians, with three army groups, started what is probably their last great offensive and after a few days reached the Oder in Silesia. In the center they are storming through Poland toward the frontier of the Reich and in the next few days will already be threatening Frankfurt-an-der-Oder and the old fortress of Kuestrin. With that Berlin will be in immediate danger. Our battle-weary divisions are unable to offer much more resistance to the onslaught of the far superior and freshly equipped Russian armies. For that reason Hitler personally has ordered the immediate transfer, by express transports, of the 25th Panzer Grenadier Division and our own 21st to the area west of Kuestrin, to prevent any advance on Berlin. The transports will have absolute priority; a transport officer has been assigned from division and will be responsible for rapid entraining.

"I regret," Feuchtinger concluded, "that our brave men are having to drink this cup to its bitter dregs. I wish that each one of you and your people may survive this last battle too, and I hope that all are aware that a further advance by the Russians into our homeland must be prevented."

It sounded to us rather too pathetic, but what was the use? We knew that from now on it was up to us, as frontline soldiers, whether commanders or tank gunners, to bear the responsibility and make the decisions. After seven and a half months of unbroken action we had, from now on, to defend our own homeland.

Thoughtfully I went back to my car. Suddenly it occurred to me that on no account were the Russians to have the Mercedes, nor if possible were the British or the Americans. I had an idea: the car must go to Dagmar, who was at Nauen, west of Berlin, at a branch of the nursery. I at once got in touch with the transport officer.

When I had given him a brief history of the Mercedes cabriolet, he proved cooperative. "I'll have the train make a short stop at a ramp southwest of Berlin," he suggested. "There you can easily off-load the car. We'll probably need a whole night for the journey around the south of Berlin, because of the danger of air raids and a huge increase in traffic. You can board the train again at the army station of Zossen, Colonel, southeast of Berlin."

Since the transport officer would be traveling in my compartment, nothing ought to go wrong.

I then went to the nearest telephone and called Dagmar.

"Wonderful to hear you again. How are you?" I asked. "Are you more or less safe at Nauen?"

"Where are you? Are you all right?" she asked in return. "I'm safe here from the air raids. Every night I can see the long fingers of the searchlights and hear the drone of the bombers and the explosions. You know, all of us here have gradually got used to this 'war on the home front.' But there are endless rumors that the Russians will soon be advancing on Berlin. Do you know anything definite?"

"The rumors sound right. At any rate we are being transferred to the eastern front with other panzer divisions. Where, I can't and mustn't tell you."

"Now listen carefully," I went on. "On the 4th or 5th of February I shall turn up at your place with the Mercedes. You will then drive me back to our troop train in the car and take it home with you. I'll tell you everything else then. Please stay at home for those two days so that nothing goes wrong. All right?"

"Yes, of course. It'll be wonderful to see you again, if only briefly. I'll wait for you here."

So it was arranged. Before the start of my conference, I sat down with Liebeskind and together we drew up a "movement order" for Dagmar.

> From the Combat Group of the 21st Panzer Division to all military, civilian, and Party officials:
>
> Fraeulein Dagmar S_____ is authorized to convey the Mercedes car WH_____ by the quickest route to Flensburg and deliver it there to the garrison commander, who is to hold the car until the arrival of the Special Combat Group of the 21st Panzer Division.

All officials are requested to let the vehicle pass without hindrance and give
Fraeulein Dagmar S————————— every assistance necessary.

For the Combat Group,
Signed, Colonel von Luck, Combat Group Commander.
(with various seals and signatures)

As Dagmar told me later, after my return from Russia, the "movement order"
had not failed in its effect. "Special Combat Group," the various seals, and the
signature of a colonel and frontline soldier were so impressive that none of the
officials or supply depots worried about how a 23-year-old woman came to be sitting
at the wheel.

"I often had to laugh to myself," Dagmar said, "at how officiously they all fussed
about me. The fact that Admiral Doenitz, as Hitler's appointed head of government,
had moved his headquarters to Flensburg at the end of April seemed to everyone
to underline the importance of my 'mission' for the combat group."

Thanks to her good contacts at GHQ in Berlin, Dagmar was able to leave Nauen
in good time before the "Battle of Berlin" and within a few days reach my mother
in Flensburg safe and sound. Unfortunately, the "faithful Mercedes" suffered the
same fate as my 1,000 bottles from France and the cut-glass from Baccarat: the
British occupation discovered the car and confiscated it as war booty.

I very much hope that this worthy vehicle is enjoying retirement today as an
"old-timer" somewhere in England or Scotland.

In a little café in Kandel I sat with my battalion and company commanders. I
told them of the meeting with Feuchtinger and Colonel Zollenkopf, the new,
temporary divisional commander.

"We are being transferred to the eastern front."

Everyone drew a deep breath.

"That's the last thing we expected, out of the frying pan into the fire," was the
general verdict.

"How much longer is the war going to last? Now even old men and boys of 14
and 15 are being called up into the Volkssturm. The last reserves?"

I had my work cut out explaining to them all that we had to prevent any further
advance by the Russians and save the civilian population from terrible sufferings.

"We can only hope that the Western Allies will push east as far as possible. We
entrain between the 3rd and 5th of February. Use the time to rest and train the
replacements."

We went on sitting together for a long time. Over a cup of *muckefuk*, as the
coffee substitute was called, we thought back to the battle of Normandy, to the
terrible events in the Falaise pocket and, of course, to the bitter house-to-house
fighting in Rittershoffen.

I knew from division that our losses in dead, wounded, and missing since 6 June
1944 amounted to about 16,000. An awful number, when one remembered that
we had started the defensive battles on 6 June with a divisional strength of at least
15,000 men.

We also asked ourselves where the Russians, despite their huge losses, kept getting these masses of men and material from, and how they were able to solve the enormous problem of transport. I only heard in captivity that under the Lease-Lend agreement concluded with President Roosevelt, Stalin had received, among other things, 100,000 Studebaker trucks, without which the Russian army could never have carried out its offensive so quickly, if at all.

The mood among my men, mainly the veterans, was by no means as bad as it might have been in view of the state of affairs. In the first place they were all keen to stay with the "old gang," which for them meant protection and security. They took pleasure in a made bed, in a telephone conversation with their families. They were ready once again to face the enemy in the east. For them news of atrocities meant motivation.

One of Hitler's basic orders arrived—in private he was now known only as *Gröfaz* (*Grösster Feldherr aller Zeiten*, that is, "the greatest general of all time")—according to which every Wehrmacht unit from the regiment up had to appoint an NFO, "National Socialist Leadership Officer" (*Nationalsozialistische Führungs-Offizier*), whose job was to keep a political eye on the unit and its command. So, *politruks* for us too. That showed us how suspicious of the Wehrmacht Hitler had become since 20 July. I nominated our chaplain as NFO. A joke, when one considered what the church thought of Hitler. In this way defeatism was to be prevented and the "will to Final Victory" strengthened.

I knew that in this last phase I would not see my people again as a body and be able to speak to them. So I gave orders for my panzer grenadier regiment to assemble en masse in a large clearing in a forest near Kandel.

There they stood, men with tired, gray faces. They had been through all the battles together since 6 June 1944, and survived. Standing there also were young, baby-faced recruits. As yet these boys had no idea of what was to come.

It was hard for me to find the right words, but I had to speak to them, to let them know that I would not leave them in the lurch, to give them confidence and to remind them that comradeship and a feeling of solidarity were more important than anything else.

"After many months, and today perhaps for the last time, I should like to speak to you all. I will not use many words. All who have fought with me since 6 June 1944, and the youngsters from home who will be experiencing for the first time the meaning of war and the fight for survival, should know that I will remain your commander to the end and share every hardship with you.

"To all of you who have stuck it out with me during the last months, my thanks for your efforts. You were magnificent!

"In the next few days we are to be transferred to the eastern front; there, on the Oder at the old fortress of Kuestrin, we are to prevent the capital, Berlin, which has been so badly hit by bombs, from falling into the hands of the Russians.

"It will be our last battle.

"Forget all the slogans, about a 'Thousand-Year Reich' and the 'Final Victory that must be ours.'

"From now on we are fighting solely for survival, for our homeland, our wives, mothers, and children, whom we want to save from a fate none of us can imagine.

"That must be worth fighting for in the coming weeks and months. May God help you and protect you!"

Between 3 and 5 February 1945, the division was loaded onto a number of troop trains, which rolled eastward across one of the last undamaged railway bridges over the Rhine. Although frequent stops had to be made, because air raids threatened or junctions had been destroyed and had to be repaired, we marveled at the outstanding organization of the transport authorities. The closer we got to Berlin, the longer the stops became. The inhabitants, insofar as we came into contact with them, often had an air of hopelessness. Sometimes remarks were dropped such as, "Why don't you pack it in. There's no point any more," or "Every day you prolong the war makes the sacrifice greater."

The Party functionaries, who greeted us at some of the stations, displayed an "unbroken will to Final Victory"—but were quick to seek safety whenever the enemy came near them.

As arranged, the train stopped southwest of Berlin. I off-loaded the Mercedes and drove to Nauen to the nursery. Dagmar was out looking for me.

"My God, I can't believe I'm seeing you again. What are you up to?" she greeted me.

"We've no time, Dagmar, a cup of decent coffee from my little supply, then we must be off, to catch up with the train again."

On our drive around the south of Berlin, I explained my plan to her.

"Here's a movement order with which you will leave Nauen as soon as the situation gets critical. You've got your contacts at GHQ. They will tell you there whether and when it would be wise to leave Berlin. You've enough reserves of fuel in the trunk to reach Flensburg. Drive to my mother's and wait there for the end. Try and hide the car somewhere. If I come through safely, at least we'll have a vehicle and be mobile in the first weeks after the catastrophe.

"Have you any news from Sachsenhausen about your father?"

"No, of course not. I didn't expect any. Phone calls are pointless. They don't put me through to anyone, or else they 'have no information.' I've not much hope of seeing my father again alive. I must live with that now, in the next weeks and months."

We were at Zossen. The train wasn't in yet, so we had a little time to ourselves. An hour later I was back in my compartment. One last wave and Dagmar had gone.

19
The Eastern Front: The Last Battle

Our transports rolled on to the east around the south of Berlin. Thanks to a wonderful effort by the German Railway, the newly restored division was conveyed to its destination in only 48 hours. On the "Eastern Line," which linked Berlin with Koenigsberg in Prussia, and on which as a young cadet officer I had traveled so often to Dresden or Berlin, we stopped suddenly on an open stretch. We must have been about 50 kilometers east of Berlin and 20 west of the fortress of Kuestrin.

An improvised ramp enabled the train to be unloaded. The divisional staff had already arrived and I was at once summoned to Colonel Zollenkopf.

"Our task is to launch an attack, immediately and without waiting for further transports, from the southeast against the Russian bridgehead in the southwestern outskirts of Kuestrin and establish contact with the encircled garrison of about 8,000 men. Our friends of the 25th Panzer Grenadier Division have already been in action since 31 January. They've managed to prevent any extension of the individual bridgeheads, but they have not been able to clear a way to Kuestrin.

"You will move into the attack with your regiment, reinforced by some tanks and artillery, as soon as your regiment has been detrained. The other elements of the division will be sent in to reinforce you from the detraining.

"Hitler personally has ordered this attack and wants the Russians thrown back over the Oder. We are up against the First White Russian Front of Marshal Zhukov, which has stormed through Poland in only 14 days and has almost annihilated the weak German forces.

"You will get the details from my general-staff officer. All the best!"

There I learned that our division, after its restoration in Alsace, now had available to it again more than 30 Panzer IV and Jagdpanzer IV tanks, as well as 30 Panthers. My Regiment 125 was back to 75 percent of its full strength, and our artillery to

90 percent. This was welcomed, even if the quality of the crews and young officers, insofar as they were replacements, came nowhere near the fighting strength and experience with which we started on 6 June 1944.

Kuestrin was a fortress with twelve-foot-thick walls and casemates that dated from Napoleonic times, all of which had been laid out to face east. The Russians, however, from small bridgeheads north and south of the town, were trying to roll up the fortifications from the rear. Kuestrin was an important road and rail junction: from the west "Reich Highway 1" and the Eastern Line, from Berlin to Koenigsberg in Prussia, crossed the railway lines from Frankfurt-an-der-Oder to Stettin on the Baltic, and the rail link from Breslau in Silesia to Stettin and Koenigsberg in Prussia. The 30-kilometer-wide Oder valley was bounded in the west by a range of hills that offered itself for defense, to bar access to Berlin.

The attack scheduled for 6 February was delayed because the road to Berlin was hopelessly choked with fleeing civilians, and it was only through vigorous action by our military police that gaps were kept open to allow us through to the south.

On 7 February we set off before dawn and came up against stiff resistance, but with assault parties we were able to inflict heavy losses on the enemy and gain a little territory. On the following day we again made only slow progress. Meanwhile the last elements of the division had been detrained and were holding themselves ready for a decisive attack on 9 February.

The 25th Panzer Grenadier Division to the north of us was to attack a further bridgehead. We had been promised that we would receive support from the famous fighter-bomber squadron of our most highly decorated soldier, Colonel Rudel. His "specialty" was to use his JU 87 dive-bombers, equipped with antitank weapons, to swoop down on Russian armored units and destroy their tanks with direct hits.

At first the battle on 9 February raged back and forth. Then Rudel's fighter-bombers appeared and dived on the Russian tanks, antitank guns, and artillery positions. After so long it was a great feeling again for us old hands no longer to be exposed without hope to the enemy air force. Much more important, however, was the effect on the morale of our youngsters, who were seeing action for the first time.

At midday some assault parties managed to penetrate the suburbs of Kuestrin from the southwest, take the bridges there and, together with the following combat groups, clear a 2-kilometer-wide corridor into the fortress.

That same night a supply convoy, which had been standing ready, rolled in to the occupying forces. Another bridgehead further north was eliminated by our friends of the 25th.

We were glad to have been able to help the gallant garrison of Kuestrin and bring them urgently needed supplies. Hitler had declared Frankfurt-an-der-Oder and Kuestrin to be "fortresses." In his language that meant "fighting or dying to the last man."

After this success, combat activity, from midday on 9 February, diminished appreciably. The Russians made no further attempt to regain their lost bridgeheads.

Our monitoring service intercepted messages which indicated that Marshal Zhukov had supply problems.

Since 12 January, when Marshal Zhukov had massed on the Vistula, his army group had gained 350 kilometers of terrain. Transport space for the overland route seemed to be inadequate. Rolling stock on the railways had first to be converted from the Russian broad gauge to the narrow European gauge. In addition, Zhukov had an exposed right wing. There was a large gap to the Second White Russian Front under the command of Marshal Rokossovsky. After 9 February we lay west of the Oder, organized for defense. Access to Kuestrin was kept open.

To gain some protection from enemy artillery and air attacks, I had set up my command post in the cellar of a farmhouse. We couldn't believe our eyes when we saw hundreds of bottles of French perfume, cognac, and champagne piled up in the cellar, besides dozens of silk stockings, bales of material, and elegant shoes. This was the outcome of the barter deals common throughout Germany, by which the towns supplied themselves with butter, meat, and milk, to augment their meager food rations.

Outside, our artillery could be heard now and then, and sporadic gunfire; not, we hoped, the quiet before the storm. It was already growing dark when the door opened and Dagmar appeared. I was flabbergasted.

"What! Are you mad? How on earth did you get here? How did you find me?" My adjutant and some orderly officers stood about incredulously.

"You know about my contacts at GHQ in Berlin. They told me there where your command post was.

"I first took a train, early this morning, right across Berlin," she went on. "Then I got on my bike and cycled east on Highway 1, until I was picked up by a truck. My bicycle is outside."

"Listen, you simply can't turn up here on the battlefield; there's shooting going on everywhere still, and you might have run into a Russian counterattack.

"I'm very worried. Happy though I always am to see you, Dagmar, this venture of yours is highly risky."

Without a word she handed me a letter. It was a document from the Sachsenhausen concentration camp, which ran as follows:

> This is to inform you that your father, Herr S_____, has died of cardiac insufficiency. The urn may be collected by previous arrangement with the camp administration.
>
> With German greetings, Heil Hitler!
>
> Signed . . .

I was profoundly shocked and didn't know what to say.

"I had an idea this would happen," Dagmar forestalled me. "I knew from a reliable source that the whole camp was to be moved, before the Russians took

Berlin, perhaps, and discovered the camp. So all the weak and the sick were liquidated. A crazy " 'Final Solution,' don't you think." ⌐

"Dagmar, listen. You must get away from here again as quickly as possible. The balloon may burst at any time. I am so sorry about it all. And I had been so hopeful after my talk with Kaltenbrunner. It's outrageous that we should be fighting here for survival and for our families, while at the same time good patriots are being killed in cold blood."

I asked an orderly officer to find out whether there was a truck of any kind going in the Berlin direction, to get supplies. We were in luck. Within half an hour Dagmar and her bicycle would at any rate be out of the danger zone.

Suddenly the door of our cellar room opened and a colonel appeared in peacetime uniform with a Distinguished Service Cross on his chest. Was this a madhouse? First Dagmar and now this apparition. We all stared at the colonel with his highly polished riding boots.

"What brings you here?" was my first astonished question. "Have you lost your way?"

"Herr Reichsminister von Ribbentrop and Reichsjugendfuehrer Axmann would like to speak to you."

"Am I supposed to go to Berlin, or what's going on here?" I asked in return.

"No, the two gentlemen are waiting for you outside in the car."

"Then perhaps they would be kind enough to step in. I'm not leaving my command post."

The two then appeared.

"Heil Hitler, Colonel. The Fuehrer has sent us here to learn something of the situation at Kuestrin. Is there any danger that the Russians will march on Berlin?"

"Herr von Ribbentrop"—I avoided addressing him as Minister, as I didn't like him; he was always known to us at the front as "champagne salesman"—"to find that out it would be best for the two of us to go to my grenadiers and tanks, which are in positions on the west bank of the Oder. That's where one can form the best impression of the situation."

Von Ribbentrop at once declined. "That will not be necessary, if you tell me how you assess the situation."

At that his eye fell on Dagmar, who had been following our dialogue with amusement.

"My apologies, I didn't know that army auxiliaries were in service so far forward. Is it not too dangerous for you, madam?"

Without answering his question, Dagmar handed the Minister the letter from Sachsenhausen.

"Please read this letter, Herr von Ribbentrop. It's because of it that I have come here from Berlin to my fiancé, Colonel von Luck."

Ribbentrop paled on reading the letter and seemed rather irritated.

"Well, yes I am naturally sorry about that, my apologies," and he turned to me. "I have the impression that the situation here before Kuestrin has been cleared up through the efforts of two experienced panzer divisions, and I shall pass this welcome news to the Fuehrer. Heil Hitler!"

The two gentlemen abruptly left my cellar.

We all shook our heads and started to laugh out loud.

"My God, what have we come to, that a foreign minister should appear at the front so that he can reassure himself and Hitler!"

20

The 21st Panzer Division as "Fire Brigade": The Beginning of the End

It gradually grew dark. On both sides the artillery and machine-gun fire intensified, the usual "good-night greetings."

I was glad to put Dagmar and her bicycle onto a truck going to Berlin. We waved to each other one last time, and never suspected for how long.

Shortly after came an "urgent" order to pull out at once and transfer our position to our friends of the 25th Panzer Grenadier Division. Our division was to be moved that same night, via the highway and rail to the south, to the area of Sagan. While Marshal Zhukov was at a standstill on the Oder at Kuestrin and Frankfurt, Marshal Koniev, with the "Ukrainian Front," Army Group South, had launched an attack in the Silesian area, across the Oder to the west, and had overrun the weak defensive forces.

Our command was trying to guess the direction of this thrust: to the west, toward Dresden-Leipzig on the Elbe? Or to the south, into the important industrial area of Moravia round Ostrava in Czechoslovakia? I very soon realized that the Russian command had learned a great deal about its job since I had left Russia at the beginning of 1942: the preparation of their offensives and their strategic planning were well thought out, and supplies well organized.

While we were on the move from the early morning of 10 February, Lieutenant-General Werner Marcks arrived as our new divisional commander. I knew him slightly from North Africa, where he had received the Knight's Cross for bravery, dropped out because of a serious tropical disease until the beginning of 1944, and had then, as commander of the 1st Panzer Division in Russia, been decorated with the "oak leaves." Thereafter he had again fallen seriously ill. I was not altogether happy at the thought of now having to work with Marcks. He was regarded as ambitious, a hard man, and ruthless in carrying out orders.

In that he resembled the commander in chief of Army Group Center, Field Marshal Schoerner, in whose area we now entered. Schoerner, like Rommel, had been decorated in the First World War with the "Pour le merite," on the Italian front. It was said that he envied Rommel his fame and popularity. He seemed to want to give himself a high profile through exceptional severity and success. Schoerner was notorious for the operations of the so-called "flying drumhead courts-martial." On Hitler's orders any incipient defeatism, desertion, failure to carry out orders or malingering were to be nipped in the bud by the imposition of death sentences as a deterrent, against which there was no appeal. On the contrary, specially selected judge advocates, who were accompanied by a firing squad, could pronounce death sentences and have them carried out immediately, without informing, let alone hearing, the man's commanding officer.

A few weeks later I too was to be confronted with one of these "flying drumhead courts-martial."

I had sent one of my best sergeants, the highly decorated leader of an antitank platoon, to our workshop in the rear, with a couple of drivers, to bring forward some armored tractors that were being repaired. I had told him to put the screws on as we needed the vehicles urgently. He passed word to me through a messenger that he would be arriving with the vehicles the following morning. What happened then was told me the next day by one of the drivers. In tears, hardly able to control his voice, he said, "We were sitting together in the evening, after we had made sure that the last vehicles would be finished during the night, in a little inn, eating our day's ration and talking about the future, our homes and all the other things that soldiers talk about. Suddenly the door was pushed open and in rushed a staff officer with some military policemen. 'I am Chief Judge Advocate under the direct orders of Field Marshal Schoerner. Why are you sitting about here while up at the front brave soldiers are risking their lives?'

"My platoon leader replied: 'I was ordered by my regimental commander, Colonel von Luck, to bring some armored vehicles that are being repaired here up to the front as quickly as possible. Work will be going on through the night. We'll be able to go back to the front tomorrow morning.' "

"The judge advocate: 'Where is your movement order?'

"Answer: 'I had it from the commander by word of mouth.'

"Advocate: 'We know about that, that's what they all say when they want to dodge things. In the name of the Fuehrer and by the authority of the commander in chief Army Group Center, Field Marshal Schoerner, I sentence you to death by shooting on account of proven desertion.'

" 'But you can't do that,' shouted our platoon leader, 'I've been at the front right through the war. Here, look at my medals.'

"Advocate: 'But now, when it matters and everyone is needed up at the front, you soon decided you'd like to dodge things after all, didn't you? The sentence is to be carried out.'

"Then the military police took our platoon leader and shot him in the garden behind the inn."

The man could hardly go on.

"We then had to bury him under the supervision of the MPs." Deserters were not allowed to have a cross on their graves.

"After that the advocate disappeared as fast as he had come."

Although we were in the middle of an action, I got in touch with divisional HQ, seething with rage, and reported the unbelievable occurrence. I demanded the name of the judge advocate, so that I could prefer a charge against him.

"That will hardly be possible," one of the officers replied. "Our divisional commander, General Marcks, is in full and complete agreement with Schoerner's measures."

I was appalled. So we had come to this.

"For God's sake, one of my best platoon leaders has been shot without further ado and nothing is supposed to happen? I shall make a written report and insist that the judge advocate be found."

Military events and the bitter end made it impossible for any amends to be made for a flagrant injustice. My men of the workshop company were at least able to tend the grave properly and put up a cross with name and unit. I informed the parents that their son had unfortunately met a soldier's death "in the performance of his duty."

Certainly, there were signs of dissolution, especially where the Russians had overrun our defensive positions and stragglers then tried to escape captivity or get back to their units. The psychological pressure was immense, especially on the old men who had been called up to the Volkssturm, and on the boys of 14 and 15, who were supposed to stop the enemy in close combat with antitank grenades. None had any experience; all had only one desire, to save their lives.

Wherever we, and other divisions that were still intact, came upon stragglers, we incorporated them into our own units and gave them fresh support. We too condemned all forms of desertion, which undermined the morale of our men. But anyone who saw the civilian population fleeing in panic, who heard of the maltreatment and raping of women, or who listened to the stragglers, whose divisions had lain for hours under a barrage and then been overrun by the Russians, had to judge differently, more humanely. At any rate, this war was no longer to be won with flying drumhead courts-martial. The endless slogans and proclamations emanating from Hitler's HQ in the Chancellery bunker in Berlin sounded to us here at the front like sheer mockery.

On 12 February the motorized elements of the division rolled along the Berlin-Breslau highway in the direction of Sagan in Lower Silesia. Owing to fuel shortage we had to organize a shuttle service. The armored elements came by rail.

In the morning of that day the Russians launched an attack along a wide front and threatened to cross the highway. Weak elements of the "Brandenburg" panzer division had to yield to the pressure. In the morning of 13 February I moved into the counterattack with a combat group. We were able to free the highway, but were bypassed in the flank. With further elements of the division that had arrived in the meantime, and with a combat group of the 17th Panzer Division, which was hastily brought up, we managed to hold the enemy for the short term. In the days that followed the Russians made constant attempts to outflank us; our own division was split up into a number of small combat groups.

On 17 February, the Russians succeeded in making a breakthrough, which cut off elements of our division and threatened to destroy them. In this critical situation it was shown yet again what a high value the concepts of comradeship and independent action always have.

Major Hannes Grimminger, a battalion commander in our sister Regiment 192, spotted our desperate situation and didn't hesitate for a second. He attached to his own unit the reconnaissance battalion under Major Brandt, which was then just available, as well as a number of our tanks, and at once launched a relieving attack. The Russians were taken completely by surprise and withdrew after suffering losses. The encircled elements were freed.

In March Grimminger was given command of Regiment 192 and was wounded again. During a short stay in a military hospital at home he received the Oak Leaves to the Knight's Cross, on 11 March; on 21 March he married and after his return to the front fell on 16 April, married less than a month. His men buried him in the park of the manor house at Drebkau; our divisional chaplain, Tarnow, delivered the funeral oration. After the war Grimminger was transferred to the forest cemetery at Halbe, where 20,000 graves recall the last, hopeless battle.

In spite of the utmost efforts, and the ever-present sight of the desperate refugees, the area round Sagan was no longer tenable. The risk of encirclement for the few intact panzer divisions was too great.

So Schoerner's Army group ordered a withdrawal over the Neisse. One or two bridgeheads were to be kept open to enable rear guards, stragglers, and civilians to pass to the west.

The Neisse flows from the mountains of the former Sudetenland, via Goerlitz, due north and into the Oder south of Frankfurt. The Neisse-Oder line constituted the last natural barrier before Dresden, the Elbe, and Berlin.

On 20 February the tired and battle-weary men crossed the Neisse north of Goerlitz and at once began to dig in.

From Goerlitz via Guben to the confluence of the Neisse with the Oder, the remnants of a few reliable panzer divisions and stragglers from infantry divisions that had been wiped out were used to set up a new defensive line, in the center of which were the shrunken elements of our own division.

Marshal Koniev at once moved up to the eastern bank of the Neisse; but then he stopped and the only further development was strong patrol activity and battles for our few bridgeheads. As with Marshal Zhukov at Frankfurt and Kuestrin, Koniev appeared to have supply problems.

The Neisse-Oder line would be held like this until the middle of April.

At divisional HQ I received a rough outline of the situation:

—While the Oder-Neisse line was being consolidated, all areas of Silesia east of the Oder were already in Russian hands. The fortress of Breslau was encircled (it was able to hold out to the end of the war). The important Upper Silesian industrial area east of Gleiwitz was also already in Russian hands.

—From Goerlitz our front ran east, passing north of Lauban and south of Breslau, and then turned south at Oppeln down to the mountains of the High Tatra. This line was only weakly held and would be unlikely to withstand a vigorous attack on the Czech industrial area at Ostrava in Moravia. This, it seemed, was the very thing that Marshal Koniev was planning.

On 15 March 1945, the First Ukrainian Front started an offensive from the area of Upper Silesia southwest of Gleiwitz, which forced our Army group to pull back our front to the former German frontier in the mountains bordering Czechoslovakia, connecting up in the west with the Neisse position at Goerlitz.

THE BATTLE OF LAUBAN

At the end of February, Hitler decided to fight through to the fortress of Breslau by means of a major attack from the Lauban area. This operation, I heard later, was to be the prelude to a "spring offensive" that he was planning.

While we gave "Operation Lauban," as we called it among ourselves, a certain chance, the freeing of the fortress of Breslau was to us pure utopia and the idea of a "spring offensive" sheer madness.

Hitler and the High Command of the Wehrmacht were still juggling with divisions that no longer existed or, despite the latest material and the intake of replacements, lacked the fighting strength to be capable of stopping a far superior enemy effectively. So I was horrified after the battle of Lauban to be given a "stomach and ear battalion" as replacements. This was made up in part of patients with severe stomach trouble, who had been gathered up from military hospitals and from back home, and who were accompanied by a special "diet" catering company. It was becoming increasingly clear that the last reserves were now being mobilized, to wage the "Total War" to "Final Victory" proclaimed by Goebbels.

For the battle of Lauban two tanks corps were placed in readiness, one to the east and one to the west of Lauban, completely unnoticed by the enemy and even by the Volksgrenadiers stationed there, without doubt a fine bit of work by Schoerner and his staff. During the night of 1 and 2 of March 1945 we attacked. I and my combat group were attached, by Schoerner personally, to the left-hand tank corps.

The Russians were utterly surprised by this massive attack, supported by 8.8cm antitank units. In heavy fighting, which lasted until 9 March, Lauban and the important railway line were freed and the Russians driven back far to the north, losing in the process more than 80 T34 tanks and 48 undamaged guns. My own combat group alone managed to knock out about 25 tanks; the rest were dealt with by the 17th Panzer Division. With this the main objective was achieved; but all plans to free Breslau remained illusory, in view of the great superiority of the Russians.

The battle of Lauban was, and remained, the last major German offensive operation of the war, and as such was naturally exploited by Goebbels's propaganda.

For all of us, a terribly depressing experience was to stay forever in our minds. In the villages we recovered, we ourselves saw for the first time how the Russians had rampaged in the past weeks. Never in my life shall I forget the sight of the maltreated, violated women who came to meet us, screaming or completely apathetic. Neither old women nor girls, who were still children, were spared; the houses were plundered, old men were shot.

Faced with these sights we asked ourselves: Was this the revenge for the millions of Russians, including civilians, who had died in the last four years, or been carried off to Germany? Or had instincts been liberated here, as in all the German territories conquered by the enemy, which were uncontrollable? We did not know.

These fearful atrocities had a very depressing effect on all of us, especially on the men who came from the eastern regions. On the other hand, they reinforced our determination to fight all the more grimly now for every square yard and help the civilian population as much as possible in their flight to the west.

After the success at Lauban, I was released by Schoerner in the middle of March and went back with my staff and the remainder of the tanks to our division, which was lying north of Goerlitz in the Neisse position.

There I was confronted with an incident in which my II battalion commander had been involved.

THE STORY OF MAJOR WILLI KURZ

While Koniev made strong thrusts in the Goerlitz area, in an attempt to divert attention from his planned major offensive over the Neisse, elements of my division were constantly engaged in counterattacks, in which my II Battalion under Major Willi Kurz was also involved. On one of these operations Kurz was wounded. This hit me particularly hard, for Kurz, since the invasion days of June 1944, had been a highly decorated commander admired by all and with whom I had bonds of true friendship.

When I visited him in May 1986 in Massassauga, Toronto, I heard for the first time of his odyssey. Here is his story.

"After various meanderings in ambulances and hospital trains, I ended up, with some other wounded, in the military hospital of Leitmeritz in the Sudetenland. On 8 May 1945, after the Czech uprising, we were loaded onto trains again. Meanwhile Krieger (my adjutant for a time—Author) had also arrived among us, wounded. We traveled in the direction of the famous spa of Karlsbad, which was a meeting place of the Russian and American 'spheres of influence.'

"We hoped to be taken in by the Americans. But American officers, who were apparently sticking precisely to the demarcation line agreed with the Russians, forced us to go to Karlsbad in the Russian zone. The Americans seemed to be unaware of the fate to which we were now consigned.

"In Karlsbad there was complete chaos. Three hospital trains were standing in

the station with an ammunition train between them. Suddenly fire broke out in
one of the carriages of a hospital train, right by the ammunition train. Those of us
who could still stand were able to put out the fire, thank goodness; the Russians
just looked on. It was boiling hot and there were no more bandages. Next to me
lay a sixteen-year-old boy with legs amputated; his dressings had not been changed
for fourteen days. The boy was enduring his pain with the last of his strength in
the hope that he might yet end up under American 'protection.'

"Our nurses slept between us at night, with huge bandages round their heads to
disguise them as wounded soldiers.

"We all stuck close together, though the Russians constantly tried to take away
our boots, watches, and other belongings. We received no food from the Russians.
The walking cases begged something to eat every day from the civilian population.
Suddenly we hit on the great idea: one of our doctors explained to the Russian
commandant that an epidemic had broken out in two of the trains. What was to
be done? The Russians got into a panic and sent all three trains to the Americans.

"Thank goodness the commandant in charge appreciated our white lie; nevertheless, he declared our three trains to be an 'open hospital.' A precarious situation
for us, for armed Czech 'half-soldiers' were drifting about everywhere, looking for
a late revenge for the occupation of their country by Hitler. But all went well. After
a few days a column of American trucks arrived and took us to a military hospital
in Franzenbad, right on the frontier with Germany. There at last the severely
wounded received treatment. I myself was transported after a fortnight to Eger,
near Franzenbad, and arrived in an overcrowded POW camp, in which 30,000 men
were gathered together in the open air.

"After a few days the loudspeaker suddenly announced: "Major Willi Kurz to
report to the gate!' A jeep from the Military Police appeared. 'Come on, Major,'
they said, somewhat brusquely. 'We've got to take you for interrogation. Get in!'
I had a very uneasy feeling.

"Standing in front of the command building was a young officer. 'Come in!' he
said. I still wore all my medals and insignia of rank. On stepping into the large
room I saw American officers lined up on either side to form a long aisle, down
which I was led to a huge table, at which sat a general and a row of senior officers.
A court-martial, I thought, but what for? As I arrived at the table, the general and
his officers stood up.

" 'Are you Major Willi Kurz of the 21st Panzer Division?'

" 'Yes, I am.' I still didn't know what was going on.

" 'Did you belong to Regiment 125 under Colonel von Luck and were you in
action at Rittershoffen, in Alsace?'

" 'Yes, that is so. They were probably the hardest fourteen days I went through
on any front.' Were they going to punish me now for Rittershoffen?

" 'I am the commanding officer of the 79th U.S. Infantry Division, which fought
against you in Rittershoffen; these here are my staff and behind you my officers
have formed an aisle in your honor. In the name of all my officers and men, and

myself, I should like to show our regard and appreciation for the brave conduct of your men. We owe you our respect.'

"I was speechless and struggled to hold back my tears: after the heavy fighting in Rittershoffen and the last difficult months and my wound, now suddenly this great gesture by our enemy. I finally pulled myself together and replied.

" 'May I also express our respect for you, General, and your division. We admired your courage and the doggedness with which you defended the villages of Hatten and Rittershoffen, although three of your battalions were encircled at times for days on end. We were particularly impressed by the way you finally managed to disengage, by night, without our noticing. When you had gone, we were all of the opinion that in Rittershoffen there had been no victor and no vanquished. In the morning after your withdrawal, my commander, Colonel von Luck, played a chorale on the undamaged organ of the ruined church, at which our men and the sorely tried civilians were moved to tears.'

" 'In the next few days,' the General resumed, 'I should like you to talk over with me and my officers how *you* on the German side conducted the engagement at Rittershoffen, what your problems were, and your tactics. I believe we can learn something from you.'

"I was surprised," Willi Kurz ended his account, "with what interest the Americans followed all I had to say, also about the front in Russia. I sat with them for several days and, as one of the wounded, was soon released."

It was not until the beginning of 1988 that I received an account of "the Cross of Lorraine," *A Combat History of the 79th Infantry Division*. This mentions that "when the war in Europe was over, a United Press dispatch, quoted in the *New York Times*, reported 'the Major Kurz Story.' "

In 1960, Kurz went to Canada for his firm as a timber salesman, then for a few years to Brazil and back again to Canada, which became his second home.

After our conversation in his pleasant house in Massassauga near Toronto, I saw him for the last time in 1987, a few months before he died, unfortunately, from a heart attack.

Back in March 1945 I was glad that Major Kurz and Captain Krieger had received their "homers", although I greatly missed them with all their experience.

21
The End

At the beginning of April it became increasingly clear that Marshal Koniev would attack frontally over the Neisse, and not toward the southwest.

Schoerner, therefore, on his own account, ordered our 21st Panzer Division and the Fuehrer-escort division to move to the area of Spremberg Cottbus, that is, about a hundred kilometers south of Berlin on the edge of the lake-studded Spree Forest, west of the Neisse.

During the night of 12 and 13 April our division rolled north in express troop trains. Owing to the great air superiority of the Russians we could only travel by night. Early on 15 April the first 21 trains arrived in the new combat area; 6 others were on their way. Hitler subsequently authorized this displacement and declared the two divisions to be Army reserves.

From our monitoring service we knew that Zhukov's First White Russian Front had seven armies on the Oder at Kuestrin and two armies at Frankfurt-an-der-Oder, and that Koniev's First Ukrainian Front had six armies opposite our Neisse position. The relative strength of the Russian and German forces was assumed to be as follows: infantry, 6:1; artillery, 10:1; tanks, 20:1, air force, 30:1, whereby the German divisions no longer had their former strength and fighting power.

We were not even familiar with the new terrain when, on 16 April, the great Russian offensive began: from five o'clock in the morning the Russians opened massive fire from over 40,000 guns on our defensive positions, simultaneously in the Kuestrin area and on the Neisse. Supported by fighter-bombers and bombers, the Russian tank armies moved forward and in the first onslaught broke through our positions.

After that everything happened very quickly.

In an immediate counterattack a dangerous gap opened up between ourselves and the Fuehrer-escort division. Strong armored units thrust right into this gap, so that our division was forced away to the north and into a pocket that was forming, which contained the bulk of the 9th Army under General Busse.

The weight of the attack split our division into several parts. The artillery group lay in the north, no longer far from the outer districts of Berlin. It broke through to Berlin independently a few days later and escaped from the pocket. Our sister Regiment 192 fought in individual combat groups. I had no further contact with them to the bitter end. My own combat group, reinforced by the last tanks under Major von Gottberg, was at once involved in heavy defensive fighting on the right wing, at the very point where the Russian tank armies were now thrusting into the gap between us and the Fuehrer-escort division.

We still had contact with divisional HQ, but clear orders were no longer forthcoming; they had probably lost control. To avoid being taken in the rear and destroyed, I ordered the right wing to bend back with its front to the south. On the evening of 16 April, my defensive front was holding; during the night there was some slackening of combat activity.

Late in the evening, my intelligence officer handed me the telephone receiver, "The divisional commander is on the line."

"Von Luck here." I could say no more, for all I could hear in the receiver was shouting. "Who's there? I can't understand you, please don't bellow so."

The shouting continued. I heard something about "court-martial."

"I still don't know who is on the line; speak more quietly."

Gottberg, my adjutant, and the orderly officers were already laughing.

"General Marcks here," came a somewhat quieter voice. "Who permitted you to draw back your front?"

"The Russians and the situation on my right wing 'permitted' this adjustment of the front. Please come up here and satisfy yourself personally about the situation. You can't judge the matter from your command post."

We commanders knew very well that it was now up to us alone to make decisions and save the lives of our men. Without further comment Marcks hung up.

To find out something about the general situation, of which we knew nothing from division, I decided to go to HQ early the next morning.

The divisional command post was in a sort of manor house. On entering I saw the general-staff officer sitting at a table in the hall.

"Good morning, I should like to speak to the commanding officer." Dirty and unshaven I was quite out of place in the elegant surroundings.

"The CO is still asleep," I was told. "Can I help you, Colonel?"

"No," I replied, "after the shouting on the phone last night I must insist on speaking to the CO. I haven't much time, so wake him up."

No doubt woken by our loud conversation, our divisional commander appeared on the landing of the first floor—in a nightshirt. I saw him sway slightly. The general-staff officer made an unmistakable gesture, "a few cognacs." It rather shook me that this highly decorated officer was no longer up to the situation psychologically.

"General, I should like to know something personally about the situation of our division and about the situation in general. Also, I should like to ask you to come to the front with me, so that you can obtain a picture in person of how things look among our people."

"The situation is completely obscure," he replied, "so I must remain here at my command post. As for you, Colonel von Luck, I warn you. You have to fight where you are put. I will not tolerate unauthorized actions."

"General, take note that in the last phase of this war I will make *those* decisions that I believe to be right."

With that I left what was to me a spectral scene.

Far too late, Hitler authorized the withdrawal of the units fighting on the Oder, which were already outflanked on both sides.

The "Halbe pocket" formed the highway triangle, Berlin-Dresden and Berlin-Frankfurt, about 80 kilometers southeast of Berlin. By the evening of 19 April 1945, the bulk of the 9th Army, including unfortunately, the remains of the 21st Division, which had been forced away to the north, were almost surrounded.

After Krieger had been wounded, Liebeskind was with me again as adjutant. When the fighting had died down that evening, we were sitting, exhausted, in the command post when out of the radio came the bombastic voice of Goebbels. From the Fuehrer's bunker in the center of Berlin we heard, "On the eve of the birthday of our beloved Fuehrer, I call to the German people and our brave soldiers, 'Trust the good star, believe in God and follow our Fuehrer in the hour of need.' "

With a reference to the death of Roosevelt, Goebbels then recalled "the power of fate" and drew parallels between Hitler and Frederick the Great.

Rumors were going around in those days, deliberately it seems, that the Western Allies had fallen out with the Soviet Union.

One of Hitler's statements was broadcast, which he was supposed to have made over the radio " . . . I take responsibility for everything," and " . . . if the German people cannot achieve victory, then they have no right to survive."

This was a bit much. There were cries here and there of, "Turn the thing off!" and "What good does it do *us*, our families and ruined cities if Hitler takes responsibility for everything, which no one man can do anyway."

We here outside, before the gates of Berlin, knew that now only a miracle could save us from death or captivity.

On 20 April about 360 Russian tanks and double that number of trucks were reported to be on the move behind our backs, northward in the direction of Berlin. From the south, tanks probed my right flank. In the next few days the Russian attack struck us head on and forced me to pull back the front again.

Hitler seemed to have no intention of giving up. We received the announcement that the newly created "Armee Wenck" was now no longer to prevent the advance of the Americans on Berlin, but was to fight to free Berlin and, with our 9th Army under General Busse, which was breaking out of the pocket, stop the Russians. Over a hundred kilometers separated us from Wenck, who was supposed to advance on Berlin from the area of Magdeburg on the Elbe.

As the division's rear guard, we withdrew slowly to the north and on 25 April arrived in the area of Halbe, the town that was to achieve sad fame as the "Halbe pocket."

Unexpectedly, I was put directly under General Busse and given the following orders:

"You will attack in the coming night at 2000 hours with your combat group and all available armored vehicles, which will be brought to you, westward across the Dresden-Berlin highway, in the rear of the First Ukrainian Front advancing on Berlin, with the aim of reaching the Luckenwalde area on the Berlin-Leipzig highway. The point of breakthrough is to be kept open, to enable those elements of the 9th Army following on foot to reach the west. All vehicles not earmarked for fighting are to be destroyed, fuel to be transferred into fighting vehicles. The civilian population is not to be informed; thousands of refugees would hinder the operation."

By 1900 hours a few more tanks had indeed arrived at my command post, mainly the fast little "harriers" (*Hetzer*). Naturally, our preparations could not remain hidden. At nightfall hundreds of civilians gathered in the village with primitive carts and emergency bundles of belongings. I took no steps to send the pitiable women and children back. I could not and would not do so, though I had the gravest misgivings that they might become involved in fighting.

At 2000 hours on 25 April I moved off with the combat group. Thank goodness we had maps. Our first objective was Baruth, on the important Dresden-Berlin railway line. We had to go through a huge wooded area, ill-suited to an advance, along forest tracks and firebreaks, and by night at that.

At first we made good progress. On the nearby Dresden-Berlin highway Russian supply vehicles rolled north now and then. We at once closed the road, to the south and the north. At every stop hundreds of civilians, who were following us on foot, moved up and kept still until we moved on. At about midnight we approached the village of Baruth, with the important railway line and behind it the road running parallel. As we emerged cautiously from the wood, we suddenly came under heavy fire from antitank guns, mixed with machine-gun fire. Although we were operating far in the rear of the Russians advancing on Berlin, Marshal Koniev had apparently seen to it that his long, open right flank was secured. A violent tank duel broke out. We spotted "Stalin" tanks, which were superior to ours, especially as they were dug in and thus hard to get at.

I decided to regroup, bypass the town to the north, and then take it with my grenadiers while it was still dark. I sent off a message to the 9th Army to the effect that we had come up against stiff resistance, but hoped to crack it and then break through further to the west.

It was clear to me that things would be easier for us if the central point of Baruth was taken. We couldn't let ourselves in for a fight of any duration. We had only one allotment of ammunition and just enough fuel to get us to the Elbe. Every hour we were held up here meant a strengthening of the Russian defense, which in such situations was very flexible.

I asked the Army, therefore, for permission to move on at once. This was refused: "You will wait until further elements are able to break out of the pocket."

At that moment a Panther V rolled toward me in the dark. From the turret an

SS officer jumped down and came up to me—my friend and army classmate Ruediger Pipkorn.

"My God, Ruediger, what are you doing here, and how come in SS uniform?"

"Luck! What a way to meet after all these years! As a general-staff officer I was transferred, without option, from the army to the SS and now command the 35th Police Division. I too had orders to break through, south of you, but was forced aside. I have a few Panthers with me: what's up here?"

I put Pipkorn in the picture, also about the 9th Army's order to wait there.

"That's utter nonsense," said Pipkorn. "The Russians have already closed up again behind us. We ourselves are now surrounded. What do you propose?"

"My plan is to attack Baruth from the north and eliminate the Russian defense before they send reinforcements at daybreak. I suggest that you, Ruediger, provide cover here with your Panthers and advance as soon as I am in the town."

"Good idea, Luck, we'll do that and then nothing but forward to the west. I'll just see how things look on the outskirts of Baruth."

"For God's sake, stay here, or steal forward on foot. There are Stalin tanks dug in, with nothing but the turret showing; they're dangerous."

Pipkorn didn't listen to me, but climbed back onto his tank and drove out of the woods. A few moments later I heard heavy tank fire and Pipkorn's tank came rolling back to me, into cover: beside the gun lay the body of my friend Ruediger, who had to die now, so shortly before the end.

Meanwhile we had regrouped, in order to attack Baruth from the north. I took over the SS tanks. As we moved into the attack, we came under heavy fire, this time also from Russian artillery. Shells burst among the trees; fragments now hit the hundreds of civilians too, who ran about wildly, screaming, some of them wounded. I had to get through here; there was no alternative.

For several hours we carried on a gun battle, but all attempts to swing further north came to nothing. The Russians had brought up considerable reinforcements. Then it had come to this: we were out of ammunition; we hadn't been allowed to take ammunition vehicles with us. Fuel was getting short. I had now to come to a decision. Shortly before dawn, I called the unit commanders together.

"Listen, we have already been cut off in the rear. We are virtually out of ammunition; fuel is getting short. I hereby release every one of you from my command. Any remaining fuel is to be transferred from the SPWs to the tanks. Try to get through to the west by night in small groups, with grenadiers sitting on the tanks. Our regimental doctor is staying here with the wounded, including the civilians. I personally, with my adjutant, an orderly officer, and a runner, will go back into the pocket, to report to Army command and assist with operations. My thanks to you all. May God protect you!"

I could see in each of them how hard the moment was for them, but also that my decision was understood. I had no wish to be regarded as a coward or a deserter; that much I owed myself. While the unit commanders said good-bye to each other, we grasped our machine-pistols and set off on foot along the route back into the pocket.

As I heard many years later, a few small groups did in fact succeed in reaching the Elbe and falling into American hands. The bulk of my officers and men ended up in captivity. As for the women and children, I have never been able to discover anything about their fate.

After marching east for a few kilometers through the woods, our little group—it was 26 April—decided not to march by day, but keep under cover. We intended to go on that night. We had practically nothing to drink or eat; in the confusion of the last hours we had simply forgotten about it. In the distance we could hear the bark of machine-guns, in the east the rumble of vehicles. On crossing a broad forest track we saw about a hundred yards away a stationary column of Russian trucks. The Russians were talking to each other in the dark; they were probably making a halt. Like shadows we flitted across the track; we had not been seen. In fact we ought soon to be back at the highway, the last obstacle. Meanwhile it was growing light; we had to look for cover. We found a hiding place under a thick clump of bushes. Suddenly we heard Russian sounds. To our dismay we saw a line of Russian soldiers combing through the wood and heading straight for our hiding place. "We must get away from here," we whispered to each other.

"Over there, about 80 yards away, there's thick undergrowth. We must try to run there and disappear into the bushes."

The Russian skirmish line came menacingly closer.

"Go!" I whispered. With a bound we ran out and reached the undergrowth. The Russians had seen us. Giving their shouts of *"Davai, davai!"* ("Hurry, hurry!), they ran after us. Some fired on the move, but without hitting us. To our dismay once again the undergrowth was only a few yards deep; behind it we were suddenly confronted with a lake. The end, all over. There was no more escape.

"Weapons in the lake!" I shouted to the others.

Surrounded by Russian soldiers, with their guns at the ready, and with no chance of getting away, we slowly raised our hands on that morning of 27 April 1945.

22
Capture and Deportation

So this was it: after more than four and a half years of war on almost every front, the end where I would have least wanted—the Russian front. Since the Allied landing in Normandy, we had all known that the end was coming. We hoped, however, that if we *were* to be captured it would be by the Western Allies, among whom we could take for granted respect for the Geneva Conventions. Goebbels's propaganda about "subhumans" and rumors of atrocities by Russian soldiers now made us fear the worst, along with what we knew of what the SS had done in the USSR.

What does a soldier feel when he is taken prisoner? First of all, that for him the war, and the danger of being wounded or even killed, is over.

He then asks himself some worrisome questions: Where will he be going? How will they treat him? Will they torture him or even shoot him? He tries to master his rising fear and show courage, and he is concerned at first to suppress any thoughts about the implications of the lost war, or about his personal fate in the coming months or even years.

At this decisive moment in my military life all that mattered to me personally was to show no fear, and hence weakness, but to maintain in this heavy hour my bearing and self-respect, a bearing which we had so often admired in the past years among Allied prisoners.

So there we stood with our hands up: from all sides the Russians came at us with their tommy guns at the ready. I saw to my dismay that they were Mongolians, whose slit eyes revealed hatred, curiosity, and greed. As they tried to snatch away my watch and Knight's Cross, a young officer suddenly intervened.

"Stop, don't touch him. He's a *geroi* (hero), a man to respect."

I looked at him and just said, *"Spasivo* (thank you),"* surprised at this unexpected reaction.

This correct young Russian officer took us at once to the nearest regimental command post, where he handed us over to a colonel of the tank corps. My adjutant and dispatch rider were separated from me, and I was taken to a farmhouse. The colonel was agreeably impressed that with my slight knowledge of Russian I was able to answer his questions.

"I see that you are like me a *polkovnik*, a colonel. What unit do you belong to? Where have you been fighting in the past weeks?"

It turned out before long that it had been his tank regiment on which we had inflicted such heavy losses at Lauban. This burly man, who made such a brutal first impression, slapped his thigh and laughed.

"You see," he cried, "that's poetic justice: you shot up my tanks and forced us to retreat; now in recompense I have you as my prisoner."

He fetched two glasses and in Russian style filled them to the brim with vodka, so that together we would drain them with one swallow.

When I asked where my adjutant and dispatch rider had been taken, I received what was for me a very surprising answer.

"They are both with my people of the same rank," he said. "You know, in the Russian army we have four categories: generals and colonels, the staff officers, field officers and lieutenants, and other ranks. So don't you worry about it."

There were also, incidentally, corresponding differences in their food rations.

It passed through my mind that this division was hardly compatible with the idea of Communism. These social differences were quite unknown in the German army.

In the middle of our conversation, we suddenly heard a wild burst of firing. The colonel jumped up and said, "Give me your word that you will not leave this room till I come back. I rely on you." And he rushed out.

I looked through the window and saw that elements of my own tank reconnaissance section of our division were advancing from the wood opposite, another attempt to breakout, so it seemed to me. I saw the Russian colonel draw his pistol and run toward his tanks. He drove them forward with threats from his pistol and loud cries, with the result that the attempted breakout was foiled. He came back cursing, "These sons of whores are still afraid of you."

In the night that followed I remained with the colonel, guarded by a tired soldier, to whom I passed on one of the *papyrossi* cigarettes the colonel had given me.

My thoughts took shape. The conduct of the young lieutenant and the colonel scarcely fitted into the image of the Russians that we had formed for ourselves. Certainly, the atrocities of the masses that had invaded Germany were indisputable and exceeded all that could be imagined, but then what had been inflicted on the Russians in huge losses, also among the civilian population, in the treatment of Russian prisoners in Germany and in the devastation of the areas conquered by us had with reason given rise to immense hatred, which had been further inflamed by Russian propaganda and was now venting itself. In personal encounters, however, as in my own case, it appeared that soldiers all over the world have one thing in common: they have chosen their profession or been called upon to defend their homeland. They respect their opponents, who are doing no more than they themselves, namely, their duty.

Wars are begun by politicians. They are the true militarists.

The conduct of the Russian officers gave some hope for the time that lay ahead. In spite of all the misfortunes that all of us were to endure in the following years, I was still to meet, time and again, officers and many ordinary soldiers who behaved like the colonel, especially as the effects of the propaganda began to subside with the ending of the war.

The next morning, the Russian colonel came to tell me, without vodka thank goodness, that he now had to send me to a collecting camp. He gave me his hand in farewell and passed me over to one of his men.

We set out on a three-day march. New prisoners constantly joined our ever growing column. We were guarded by Russian soldiers of a special unit assigned to the task. At night we were usually quartered in deserted villages, close together so that we could be guarded better. On the second day we marched through wooded country that seemed to me ideal for escape. We were only about 30 kilometers from the Elbe, where we supposed the British and the Americans to be. Unfortunately, on that day, because of my rank and knowledge of Russian, I was appointed German commandant of the prisoners and now had always to march at the head of the column with the Russian commander.

Once or twice I managed to distract our guards, so that about a dozen prisoners succeeded in escaping into the woods and, we hoped, in reaching the Elbe. I did not know, unfortunately, that the number of prisoners to be delivered had been precisely determined. When it turned out at our next stop that a few were missing, the guards threatened to shoot me if further prisoners were to escape. But what was worse, they fetched civilians at random from the nearby villages to make up the number. These now had to share our fate. I told the column about this, so that no further attempts at escape would be made.

The physical condition of some of the prisoners began to cause concern. I eventually persuaded the Russian commander to requisition two horse-drawn carts, on which the weakest were allowed to continue the march.

After a few days, we reached Hoyerswerda, near Dresden; this was the site of one of the collecting camps, which was very overcrowded with about 10,000 prisoners. Again I was appointed commandant and had the task of maintaining contact with the Russian commander and maintaining discipline and order in the camp, which in view of the wretched state of the prisoners was not easy. Many tried to resist my instructions with remarks such as, "No more orders, we're all equal now. Officers no longer have any say." While the bulk of the frontline soldiers behaved in exemplary fashion, ugly scenes arose with others who had taken part in the war, not in the front but in service behind the lines. It was harder for these men to come to terms with the new conditions.

Here too the preeminent problem was the everyday one, not the fate that lay before us.

Provisioning was catastrophic. It consisted essentially of a thin soup, cooked from unhusked oats or fish meal, which was normally used for pig swill. In addition there were 300 grams of bread.

I often had to go with a Russian officer to nearby depots and villages to procure rations for the following days. On one of these journeys I saw some sacks of raw coffee standing in the corner of a warehouse. I suggested to the Russian officer that we should take some of these green beans along as well, to which he raised no objection. So I had several sacks of Colombia coffee loaded up and brought back to the camp. When we arrived there the Russian officer wanted to try the beans himself. When they failed to soften after lengthily boiling in water, he said, "You Germans no *kultura*, you eat funny hard beans." In this way I secured the beans for ourselves and told the German camp cook to brew a cup of pure coffee for the whole camp on the following Sunday. The pleasure of the inmates can be imagined.

After a few days, we discovered that transports had begun to be assembled for our removal to Russia. The Russian camp doctor, a good-natured, elderly man for whom everything revolved around alcohol, told me that only healthy prisoners fit for work would be taken to Russia. There were four categories, of which Category 4 meant "unfit for work."

All the prisoners now had to present themselves to the Russian camp doctor and his assistants for examination, and all those classified as Category 4 were sent home. In the course of this I managed to get a few very young men, who had been thrown into the "final battle" at the age of fifteen, even with antitank weapons, as well as some people of my own unit into Category 4 by using a simple trick. I made them run around the block four times and do some knee bends before they had to report for examination. Then, when the doctor listened to them, he found a rapid or irregular heartbeat and graded them in Category 4. From the stock of one of the medical stores I managed to scrounge a bottle of pure ether, which the doctor received from me for "looking after us."

We naturally tried to give those who were being released some sign of life for our relations at home. Since written communications were not allowed and contraventions were liable to severe penalties, the only chance was for those who were going home to learn the addresses by heart. My sign of life never arrived, so neither my mother nor Dagmar nor my friends knew whether I was still alive.

Almost every day transports left for the east and the camp began to empty. Last to be assembled was a transport of officers, of which I too formed a part.

Up to 60 men were loaded into barred cattle trucks. To the right and left two-tiered wooden bunks had been fitted, so that not everyone could sleep at the same time. In the middle of the compartment was a hole for calls of nature. Little slits provided some illumination, but one could not see out of them. The doors were closed tight and were only opened a crack three times a day, for our watery soup to be passed in. We were left entirely to ourselves. The guards, mostly unfriendly and unapproachable, stood by the truck with tommy guns at the ready the moment the train came to a halt. Even under these conditions they were obviously still afraid of escape attempts. In fact only one single person managed to get away, through the toilet hole during a stop. Whether he ever reached home I would venture to doubt. Control over the vast empire was too perfect and the danger of denunciation too great.

Days and weeks went by. Even the destination of our journey was kept from us. We went on, further and further to the east. At one of the stops, when we heard the word "Brest-Litovsk," we knew that we had arrived at the frontier between Poland and Russia. Here we changed into Russian 18 ton wagons each loaded with 48 men. Here again many diseased were sorted out and left behind.

Suddenly we heard German voices. "*Kameraden*, we're on our way home. We were taken prisoner at Stalingrad and come from a camp in Siberia. Throw out slips of paper with your addresses. We'll tell your families." Before we could do so, the guards had chased our friendly helpers away.

And on went the journey. We were in fact still unaware of the extent of what was in store for us. The situation was too new. We tried to organize ourselves as well as we could. Many tried to keep fit with exercises, while others lay apathetically on their bunks. Because of my rank on the one hand, but especially because of my knowledge of Russian, I was appointed leader. To relieve the monotony, at least for a while, each of us related something of his life. One of our number was my later friend Harald (Hally) Momm, a well-known German equestrian and Derby-winner. Because of his "defeatist" remarks about Hitler, he had been demoted from colonel to lieutenant and transferred to the notorious "Dirlewanger Brigade." He told of his encounters with prominent people from Hitler's entourage.

The longer the journey lasted—we had been traveling for more than four weeks—the more accustomed we became, of necessity, to the ever-repeated daily routine. It was inevitable that discussions arose about why the war was bound to be lost. Some, mainly the older ones among us, saw Hitler as the guilty party, who by his assault on Poland, and encouraged by his blitzkriegs in Poland and France, thought he had first to conquer Russia, so that he could then dictate his terms to Britain. The incapacity of the German generals, for not having put him in his place, was condemned. It was felt that Hitler had shamelessly exploited our "loyalty to the oath."

Others, mostly younger ones, could not or would not grasp that National Socialism was played out. They saw the loss of the war more in our materiel inferiority and even put some of the blame on the German generals, who had failed to support Hitler's ideas and had even stabbed him in the back with the assassination attempt of 20 July 1944. The longer their captivity lasted, the more they too came to recognize the fatal consequences for Germany of the so-called "Third Reich."

No one, however, disputed that the German soldier had fought bravely and had tried, even in a hopeless situation, to defend his home and family. This consciousness determined the behavior of the so-called ordinary frontline soldier even in captivity in the years that followed and earned the respect of the Russian guards and officers.

Already on the transport we had our first deaths from malnutrition or resignation. We had to witness the bodies being thrown out of the truck by the guards the next time the train stopped. No one will ever find their graves.

Day after day we traveled through endless steppes and it was only during the short stops for the issue of food that we could tell from the position of the sun that we were traveling in a southeasterly direction, hence not toward Siberia. Suddenly— after nearly five weeks of travel, during which we had never left the truck—came a longer stop. According to those who knew the area, who had fought there, we must have been in the vicinity of the Crimea or the Sea of Azov. Parade for delousing!

Truck by truck we were taken to a delousing station. The Russians had a mortal fear of epidemics, so not only the prisoners but even the Russian soldiers were shorn to the scalp and the houses were periodically disinfected and whitewashed on the outside. The delousing was certainly an unpleasant procedure, but a welcome break in the monotonous journey. Our clothing, and the few possessions that remained to us after all the frisking, went into a separate room, while we had to go naked through the delousing. It was like a gift from heaven to be able finally to soap oneself. At the end of the procedure we had to search out our clothes from a huge pile of rags.

During the whole procedure, our trucks and the delousing buildings were surrounded by Russian soldiers with tommy-guns, and we could see from their faces that they were obviously still afraid of us. That was for us—and probably still is today—a remarkable fact. More than a thousand emaciated prisoners of war, for whom any attempt at escape would have amounted to suicide, still seemed to the Russians to be a potential danger. Fear—especially of the Germans— is deep-rooted among the Russians and runs through all social classes, as I was to find confirmed indeed time and again in the following years of captivity. Every attempt to relieve them of this fear was to no avail.

Back to the truck. The journey continued. The short break had done us good. It was October; the temperature slowly rose. Clearly, we had already come a long way south. We were tormented by thirst, but the water ration remained as small as it had ever been. We were climbing; the air became thinner. We appeared to be crossing the Elbrus mountains. Behind them lay the Caucasus. Finally, after exactly 35 days of travel by rail in a closed truck, we were at our destination, a small town on the southern slopes of the Elbrus.

Our journey lasted from 15 September until the end of October, 35 endless days. Only twice did we leave our wagons, in Rostawi for delousing and in Kutaisi for climbing coal-transport wagons, each with 100 standing men, in order to reach Tkibuli, the "local town," as it was called.

23
In the Coal Mines of the Caucasus Mountains

The mountains of the Caucasus, which means "snow-covered," separate the north Caucasus from the south-Caucasian tropical lowlands. The Elbrus, at 5,629 meters (18,481 feet), is the highest peak. Along its southern edge runs the ancient military and trade route to Persia and Turkey. To the south, the valley, 1,300 kilometers long, is closed by the mountains that rise toward Turkey and Persia; Ararat is the highest peak. The southern Caucasians (Georgians, Armenians, and Azerbaidjanis) were regarded even in antiquity as freedom-loving peoples. Prometheus is supposed to have been chained to a rock here and Jason to have searched for the Golden Fleece.

By the fourth century A.D. Christianity had become the state religion; in about A.D. 800 Islam began to spread. Under David II in the twelfth century, the kingdom of Georgia experienced its highest flowering; he made Tiflis (Tbilisi) the capital city. His successor, Queen Tamara, is still revered today. Later, Georgia was occupied by the Mongolians. Under pressure from the Turks and Persians, the kingdom collapsed in the fifteenth century. Protection was sought in the north. The Russians all too gladly concluded a "treaty of friendship" with the Georgians. Catherine II could realize Russia's old dream of opening a way to India. In 1801 Alexander—treaty of friendship or not—incorporated Georgia into the Russian Empire. Russian became the official language.

An uprising of the Caucasian peoples was suppressed with much bloodshed in 1860. Many withdrew into the inhospitable mountains. After the October Revolution in 1917, the Caucasus was bolshevised, again after heavy fighting, and incorporated into the Union of Soviet Socialist Republics. Today I cannot help thinking of the comparison with Afghanistan, where a freedom-loving people want to spare themselves a similar fate.

Because of its tropical climate, the southern Caucasus was regarded even in tsarist times as a favorite spa or holiday resort, which it still is today. Pushkin, Lermontov, and Tolstoy all lived there at one time or another and described the paradise and the freedom struggles of the Caucasian peoples. Alexander Dumas dedicates his book *Caucasian Journey* to these peoples.

The atmosphere is very oriental. In contrast to Russian women, who all look the same in their padded jackets, and who frequently do heavy men's work, the thoroughbred girls of the Caucasus, often very beautiful, take great delight in pretty clothes. Many of the men, we noticed, had a long nail on the little finger of the left hand, a sign that they did no physical work, we were told.

All tropical fruits grow in the lowlands and most Russian tea is also grown in this region. The slopes of the Elbrus mountains are the source of highly prized timber. The delicious wild strawberries are not even picked. After the opera houses of Moscow and Leningrad, that of Tiflis takes third place.

In spite of all its troubles, the Caucasus enjoyed an economic boom at the beginning of the twentieth century through the opening up of the oil deposits on the Caspian Sea and the great coal and mineral mines in the area of Tkibuli. This prosperity more or less disappeared under the Bolshevik regime.

During the First World War, the Georgians made one last attempt to win back their independence. They placed their territory under Germany as a protectorate. With the help of Germany's ally Turkey, the German General von Kress managed to gain the sympathy of the Georgians, which we prisoners of war came to feel even 30 years later.

In 1918, after Germany had lost the war, the British took over the "Georgian Protectorate," mainly to prevent Russia from extending her sphere of influence too far to the south, thereby threatening the dominion of India. They even forced Russia, weakened by the disorders of the Revolution, to recognize the independence of Georgia, Armenia, and Azerbaidjan.

It was not until 1921 that the Russians marched into the southern Caucasus again and this time stayed for good. The tragedy of history would have it that it was a Georgian, Joseph Stalin, who made it possible for the Caucasian peoples to be finally incorporated into the Russian Empire. Stalin was at the time People's Commissar for National Questions in Moscow and thus shared responsibility for the fate of his own people.

Even in 1947 there were Georgians working with us in the coal mines who in 1936 had tried for the last time to shake off Russian rule. Today the KGB, through an ingenious system of spies and informers, knows how to suppress all opposition. So our few attempts at escape, which were supported by Georgians, also came to naught.

Of the beauty of Georgia we Germans, about 1,500 emaciated officers in closed trucks, saw nothing as our train rolled slowly through Kutaisi, a provincial city in the valley, and then climbed the mountains to reach Tkibuli at a height of 1,500 meters—the destination of our 35-day journey.

This little town exists from the mining of the vast deposits of bituminous coal.

Around it camps had been set up in which Russian convicts and prisoners of war were quartered as work force.

Our camp 518, later 7518, consisted of six camps, with the main camp 518/I and camp 518/II in Tkibuli. Besides the German camp 518, which consisted of Tkibuli and one near Kutaisi, there was another camp in our area for Hungarians and a further camp for Japanese prisoners. In addition to these one of the notorious *saklutchoni* camps, which is as much as to say "the enclosed," was in the area. Here criminals and political opponents lived under the severest conditions, without knowing whether they would ever regain their freedom.

The most astonishing thing to us were the camps containing Russian soldiers, who had marched into Germany with the Russian army and were now supposed to "forget" in two years in camps all that they had seen of "Western decadence" in "capitalist Germany." In return for having helped to achieve victory, these men were now locked up for two years before they were allowed to go home, "all Russian soldiers who had become prisoners were punished by staying in special camps."

In main camp 518/I there were 1,500 of us officers and some 2,000 rank and file soldiers, who received us with curiosity and suspicion and shouts of "It's all up now with giving orders," and "Now show us if you're as good at being *plennis* (the Russian word for prisoners) as you were at being officers." This did not sound very encouraging. Our common fate and the will to get the better of the situation permitted us in the course of time to grow together into a community.

The camp was about as primitive as one can imagine a camp in Russia to be. It was surrounded by a high fence. At each corner stood a watchtower, from which searchlights at night cast a bright glare over the neighborhood; there heavily armed Russian guards performed their watch.

Three wooden barracks with some 40 to 60 men per room provided quarters for us 3,500 prisoners of war. Two-tiered wooden bunks with thin straw mattresses, a table, and a few chairs were the only furniture. A simple iron stove for the cold winter months in the high mountains nevertheless did give us good service. Further parts of the camp were a kitchen barrack, a room for drying our clothes, a delousing barrack, and a latrine with wooden beams, where about 60 men could relieve themselves, semi-exposed to the elements. Additionally there was a hospital barrack and a kind of dining room used for all kinds of performance.

Outside the camp compound was a barrack for the guards and a further barrack for the Russian commanders and the camp administration.

The very next morning we were greeted with, "My name is Jupp Link." He was the German camp commandant, a wiry young man of 25 who was responsible for order in the camp and for liaison with the Russian commandant.

He said that everyone there had to work, even the colonels. Moscow was far away; the Geneva Conventions were unknown here. Those who were unsuitable for outside work had to do camp work.

Jupp Link, a German noncommission officer, as commandant? Was he to be trusted? What part did he play with the Russians? As was very soon to appear, we all had a lot for which to thank him.

Born as a so-called "Danubian-Swabian" German in the former Austro-Hungarian Empire, modern Yugoslavia, he spoke Serbo-Croatian, Hungarian, and Russian fluently and was suitable therefore as a go-between with the Russians. Here again the typical Russian tactic appeared, namely, of keeping themselves in the background and letting others solve the problems.

Jupp Link had come to Tkibuli some months before us and had helped to construct the six 518 camps.

The men in the upper main camp 518/I, about 2,000 of them, had been going to work ever since their arrival as "pit brigades" or as brigades for outside duty. Specialists were sorted out and employed in the camp as mechanics, radio experts, cobblers, tailors, etc., or were sent down the mine as mechanics. Since the Russians lacked qualified craftsmen, and since those there were did their work in a slovenly way, our specialists had to work in place of the Russians.

I remember an amusing story which the German watchmaker told. One day a Russian guard turned up in his workshop with an alarm clock that he had brought back from Germany with the request, "This clock too big. You make me two watches from it for wrist." When the watchmaker tried to tell him that this was impossible, he grew angry and threatened him, saying, "You sabotage. You Nazi swine." It took help from Jupp Link to calm him down.

In the days that followed, Jupp Link enlightened us about the "work structure."

"All prisoners are 'hired' by the state mining authority, which is responsible for all work in the locality. For this a certain sum per head and hour of work has to be paid to the camp commandant. From these receipts the Russian commandant has to defray all the expenses of the camp, for provisions, clothing, and the maintenance of the accommodation. Every prisoner has a wage sheet kept for him. From the balance left over each is supposed to receive monthly pocket money; the remainder of the money is credited to him until such time as he may be released."

That was the theory. In practice things were rather different.

Considerable sums were "privately diverted" by the Russian commandant for himself and one or two familiars. I know of no case in which anyone received pocket money or a look at his account. The best example was our fellow prisoner Oehlschlaeger, a Communist of long standing who had been in a German concentration camp to begin with and had then got into the notorious "Dirlewanger Brigade" on "probationary frontline service."

Although this was known to the Russians, he worked for years on end as a welder down the mine, and the only privilege he received was a double portion of watery soup per day.

In 1949, when the first prisoners were released and Oehlschlaeger was assigned to a transport home, he tried to get the camp administration to pay him the credit balance for which he had worked. He was told that the transport officer had his money; rubles could not be taken into Germany, so his money would be exchanged at the frontier with East Germany. He never saw a kopeck of it and, disappointed as he was, had himself discharged, not in his old homeland in East Germany, but in the West.

"I'm fed up with all that I have seen and been through," he wrote on a postcard that reached us. "This isn't the Communism for which I went to a concentration camp." Some fellow prisoners, however, received a small sum credited to them.

The next morning we all had to fall in on the parade ground to be detailed for work. The Russian commandant, an army officer, accompanied by the NKVD officer (now the KGB), appeared with Jupp Link. In a loud voice and with much gesticulation the commandant told us that we now had to atone for Hitler's misdeeds and work off all that we had done to the Russian people.

He then gave the order, "Everyone to the doctor now, the strongest down the mine, others for road building, everyone is to work, *davai* (hurry up)!"

The Russian camp doctor was Dr. Hollaender, who was assisted by his wife. Both were Jews and for understandable reasons not well disposed toward us. Not only had they to make the sick fit for work again as soon as possible, but they were also responsible for the delousing and disinfection of the barracks. Dr. Hollaender's standard remark was, "If not clean, you wipe with caps, must all be solid white." We understood his Yiddish, and also that he was not to be trifled with.

After the examination the detailing began. For those of us who had to go down the mine the simplest clothing was issued. Shifts were formed, one for the morning, the afternoon, and the night. We were away from the camp for twelve hours altogether: eight hours down the mine and a further four hours taken up by the march out and back. If we came back tired and with clothes wet through, the thin soup was quickly slurped up and then it was on the bunks to sleep.

To my great surprise one day I was appointed German camp commandant. Jupp Link became inspector of work. The Russian commandant even insisted that I wear my insignia of rank and my Knight's Cross as "signs of my dignity." I received a *propusk*, an exit permit, which entitled me to leave the camp, alone and without supervision, up to ten o'clock at night. Among my duties I had also to maintain contact, in collaboration with Jupp Link, with the over-*natchalnik*, the head of the coal mines and the most powerful man in the town. It was with him and his officials that the work norms had to be negotiated. Here too, for the most part, the Russian camp administration kept out of things.

When this great man heard that I had fought in Russia in 1941 as a German colonel, he asked me one day, "Where were you in action? With what division?"

"In the middle sector, with the 7th Panzer Division, via Smolensk and Vyazma to Klin and Yakhroma, north of Moscow."

"Tell me about Yakhroma," he went on, "exactly when were you there?"

I was surprised by his interest but told him, "In December 1941 I advanced with my tank reconnaissance section via Klin to the Moscow-Volga canal and was able to cross it, the first unit to do so, at Yakhroma, about 30 to 40 kilometers north of Moscow. I can well remember how we went into a little Russian inn to get warm. On the table stood the steaming samovar and an almost untouched breakfast, which we ate up with a good appetite."

I was interrupted by his roar of laughter.

"That was *my* breakfast. I was a colonel in the reserve and during your surprise attack I had to leave Yakhroma and my breakfast rather abruptly. So small is the world, *polkovnik*, now you are here as a prisoner of war, and I am the boss of this town, in which I found myself at the end of the war. If you have any requests, I'll try to help you, although your camp commandant is responsible for you and I have merely engaged you for work."

After this meeting, our ways were to cross more often.

My activity as German camp commandant was only of short duration. The Russian camp commandants were replaced. The six camps in the Tkibuli area were in the province of Colonel Laroche, who came from a Huguenot family that had fled to Russia. With him, however, we had practically no dealings.

Our camp 518 came under Guard Captain Samcharadse, a Georgian. His deputy was a Russian colonel (this too is possible in the Russian army). Both were army officers and were watched over by the NKVD, to which the notorious "Black Nena" also belonged, a *politruk* who came from Armenia.

I was summoned to Samcharadse and asked to specify by name all those in the camp who had been SS officers, members of police units or units that had been employed in partisan warfare. In return he offered me special rations and other privileges. Beside him stood a NKVD officer, who watched me with mistrust.

My answer was confined to the words: "I don't know of anyone in the camp who was a member of these military units."

Naturally, there were several fellow prisoners whom I knew had been in the SS or the police, and several others of whom I suspected as much. But I took the point of view—and still do today—that every German prisoner of war was to be respected as such. If he had incurred any guilt he should, after his eventual release, be brought before a German court. In no event, however, was he to be handed over to the Russians.

Since I declined to name any names, even after being given time for reflection, I was replaced as commandant. Jupp Link was given the post once more. At the same time I had to remove all my insignia and orders. Now we were all equal, and that was good.

The state of the barracks was wretched. Apart from periodic disinfection, delousing, and the whitewashing of the rooms, nothing was done. We suffered terribly from thousands of bugs, which nested in wooden bunks or dropped down from the ceiling at night. We got hold of some old tin cans from the mine and filled them with scrounged petrol, to prevent the bugs from climbing up. Every few weeks we took the bunks outside to burn them off with blowlamps, likewise scrounged, and destroy the hatching bugs. In all the years it remained a hopeless struggle.

We suffered most from the rations. The 300 grams of bread per day, which officially was allowed to contain up to 30 percent water, drove some people to throw their portions angrily against the barrack wall, where the bread then stayed, stuck. The thin soup contained nothing nourishing apart from some millet flour or maize. Bread and watery soup formed the basis of our diet. Sometimes we received all kinds of fish. Fellow prisoner Winand told me that he used to boil down the fish heads to get a soup and that he grilled the bones for another meal.

There was hardly any fat, no seasoning, no vitamins. As a result, the mortality rate from malnutrition rose rapidly. While the familiar diseases of civilization were virtually absent, almost all the prisoners had retention of fluid in the legs. If this reached the heart, here too death was certain. Further causes of death were the frequently occurring cases of twisting of the intestine, through lack of fat. The medical team was helpless.

Our German doctors pointed out to the Russian commandants time and again that more workers would perish if the diet was not improved. But since the rations were fixed by Moscow, there was nothing to be done. On the contrary, we were cursed all the more because our "imperialist war" had made the food situation in Russia so bad.

A further disease of frequent occurrence was the infectious paratyphoid fever. Since it usually ended in death, the Russians were very anxious about the danger of infection and for this reason set up a closely guarded isolation ward.

One night Graf Hohenlohe, a young lieutenant, appeared by my bunk. He had been in the isolation ward with paratyphoid and in his delirium had walked out of the hospital barrack. The guard had obviously been asleep. We at once alerted the Russian doctor, as we were terribly afraid of infection. Hohenlohe died two days later.

None of us will forget the sight of the dead from the sick wards being piled onto old carts each morning and drawn out of the camp by emaciated prisoners of war, then to be hurriedly interred. We were not allowed to bury them and furnish their graves with crosses and names. Despite the fact that it was forbidden, we wrote their names on scraps of paper, but these were then taken away from us again during the regular searches. So we arranged that each person would make a mental note of one or two names, so that if he should go home relatives could be informed.

In the first two years, especially in the severe winters in the Elbrus mountains, about 50 percent of the prisoners of war died.

To be fair, it should be said that even the Russians, in the years 1945 and 1946, were not much better off than we as far as food was concerned. Many of them, however, had the chance of procuring something at the little market, where peasant women from the vicinity sold maize, eggs, and millet cakes.

After two years, we who had been spared by diseases and had not yet abandoned hope of going home had become acclimatized. Hunger indeed remained, but so astonishingly did our strength.

There was a German dentist in the camp, who was supervised by Dr. Hollaender. His only equipment was a hand-driven drill. There were also no anesthetics, so when necessary diseased teeth were extracted without any.

Worst of all were the military guards, who examined us for gold crowns and when they found any, broke them off with a pair of pincers without our being able to resist, so as to sell them later and thus supplement their miserable pay. For me personally, the result was that when I returned home I had to have my lower jaw chiseled out, as it was full of pus and the roots of the teeth had rotted.

One other peculiarity struck us. Moscow had ordained that officers, in addition to the bread ration and the watery soup, which were the same for everyone, were to receive twenty grams of butter and a little sugar every day. Via Jupp Link we requested the Russian commandant to treat us exactly like the rest of the men. With a reference to the Moscow regulations, this was rejected out of hand. Jupp Link collected 400 signatures from among the officers and finally succeeded in getting the special rations distributed equally to the whole camp, in the way we were accustomed to in the armed forces.

I was replaced, then, as German commandant and assigned to work in the pits. In the circumstances I felt fit and was glad in some ways not to be in an exposed position anymore, caught between two sides as it were, where it was a question of helping my many fellow prisoners and at the same time of keeping the Russian camp administration happy. I can understand better today how difficult the task must have been for young Jupp Link and how grateful we should all be for his efforts.

The main pit, in which I worked, had what was for European miners an incredible seam, which in parts was up to 15 meters thick. Rich bituminous coal, gleaming bright, was mined on a kind of chamber system. We worked alongside Russians and Georgians, who proved to be good mates and often shared their last bit of bread with us.

The authorities had forgotten to take away my *propusk*, so I could leave the camp at any time. The guards, who meanwhile knew me well, often asked me to get them something from the market and for this pressed their kopecks trustingly into my hand.

As in every enterprise in Russia, a "norm" was fixed for the extraction of coal, which everyone had to fulfill each day. Although we were in poor physical shape, our mine workers in the early days worked at fulfilling the quota with German thoroughness and application. One day one of the brigades exceeded the norm. The Russians pounced on them at once.

"Are you mad," they cried. "As soon as the norm is exceeded even once, it is immediately raised for everyone the next day, and in spite of that we don't get one kopeck or one gram of bread extra. Fulfill the norm and that's it."

It was a lesson to us.

On the other hand, I have seen some Russians, usually *saklutchonis*, in protest against their bad treatment, not fulfill the norm, or down tools for a while. To this the reaction of the management was as simple as it was effective: for "transport reasons" there would be no bread for a few days, and the norm was soon fulfilled again.

In the pits hard coal was mined to a depth of up to 15 meters. Safety measures in the pits were virtually unknown. On the one hand the management, centrally controlled from Moscow, could not get the necessary articles such as protective helmets, etc., diverted to the Caucasus, and on the other it was for them merely a matter of criminals and prisoners of war, among whom one more or less was not of great consequence. In place of protective helmets we wore primitive caps. The mined areas were scantily supported. I am still astonished today at how few serious accidents occurred.

In the cold winter months we had to see to the heating of our barracks ourselves. The Russian commandant was in fact liable for this too, but since there was enough coal in the pits, he spared himself the expense. The mine administration strictly forbade the taking out of coal, but after every shift the mine workers had fair-sized lumps of the rich mineral under their arms, which they carted back to the camp. There it was distributed equally between all the rooms. Thus the right hand did not know what the left was doing.

At the start of 1946—after only a few months down the mine—I was suddenly taken out and transferred to a road construction brigade. I do not know to this day whom I had to thank for this "transfer," Jupp Link or the over-*natchalnik*, my "breakfast colonel" from Yakhroma.

Another chapter of my captivity began.

24
Kultura and Corruption: The Russian Mentality

The terrible, never-ending hunger remained. So too did the exhortations of the Russian guards and overseers. Their inevitable *"Davai! Davai!"* was our daily accompaniment. We, the "survivors," slowly found our own rhythm and began to adapt ourselves to the Russian mentality. Not only the mine workers but even the outdoor detachments were soon regarded as *the* specialists, honest and industrious and not as corrupt as our Russian "colleagues." If we were shouted at, we shouted back. To our surprise we were then implored, "Please go on working or we shall be in trouble."

Anyone who imagined that working on Russian roads meant repairing macadam surfaces or laying out new roads with earth-moving equipment, as would be done in the West, would have been very much mistaken. We had rather to pave and make fit for traffic a mud road that led to the wooden houses of the *natchalniks*, which lay somewhat apart. For this, Studebaker trucks, which the Americans had supplied by the thousand, brought us rough, unhewn stones. Kneeling on the ground, we set these in the mud. Sometimes I saw the over-*natchalnik*, my "breakfast colonel" from Yakhroma, drive past in his state limousine. One day he recognized me, stopped, and spoke to me. "What are you doing here? Why have you been set to work as a mere laborer and not as a 'specialist'? I shall speak to your commandant."

He obviously did so, for a few days later I was summoned to Samcharadse. "From tomorrow on you will be working as leader of a concrete brigade. Pick yourself a few specialists in the camp. An escort will take you to your new work place."

Jupp Link helped me to find a few of the strongest men who were left. The only "specialist" among them was a bricklayer. The others were physicists, farmers, and clerks, who were too weak for mine work.

Next morning the escort came and took us to a building site above the mine, where a Russian brigade was already at work.

"Clear off, you sons of whores," the Russian manager shouted at this brigade. "You've stolen most of the cement and sold it. The *Nemetzkis*, the Germans, will show you how to work."

What was there for us to do? We had to dig out a hole roughly four meters by four to a depth of eight meters and then shore it up with balks of wood and line it with concrete. It was supposed to form a cuff for the filling in of an exhausted section of the mine. By way of equipment we had balks of wood, gravel, and a few sacks of cement, as well as shovels, an iron plate for mixing, and the famous, notorious *nasilkas*. *Nasilkas* are simple hand-barrows with two grips at each end. These are used throughout Russia for carrying materials.

With the help of a simple diagram that had come from Moscow, the Russian overseer then told us what was to be done, and then once more came the "*Davai,* get going!" And "Dig hole deeper, shore up hole and line with concrete. Mixture should be one to seven. I'll come back in a few hours. Heaven help you if you steal cement." He then abandoned me and my men to our fate.

He had hardly turned his back on us before the first Russians and Georgians came along. "Comrade, you sell us cement," they begged. "House falling down. We give you bread and rubles."

So that was how it was with corruption!

Since many of the necessities of life, then as now, are not available and cannot be bought by the ordinary citizen, for everything had to go through state organizations, they have to be "fiddled." Thus corruption is a matter of course, almost "legal."

So I allocated my men according to their strength and told our Russian sentry in unmistakable terms to guard our materials. "If one single sack of cement is missing, you'll be for it," was my terse comment.

After little more than a week we had dug out the pit, lined it, and begun the backbreaking work of mixing the gravel and cement by hand with our shovels and carrying it on the *nasilkas* to the pit. Then the over-*natchalnik* appeared.

"I must say, the Germans are all specialists and good workers. I am very pleased. The norm is fulfilled and no material sold." And turning to me: "You're a good concreter, *polkovnik*. So I have a special job for you. Can you build me a stone staircase onto my house and a fountain? All the materials will be there."

"That's okay," I replied, "but you must ask the camp commandant and pay us every day with bread and kopecks."

Next day he was there again. In the meantime he had "arranged" everything. I do not know how much he had to pay Samcharadse.

To carry out this commission I chose the bricklayer again, the physicist, who was still very weak physically, and a farmer from my home district. The *natchalnik* took us personally from the camp.

"No escort for you. Here's a *chleb*, a loaf of bread, for each of you."

"And where are the kopecks?" I asked.

"*Saftra*, money comes tomorrow."

"No, now, or we won't even start."

At that we received our money, with which we at once bought some vegetables and a Georgian maize flat cake at the local market.

After a week the fountain was finished, though without any water, as the pressure was too low.

"It doesn't matter," said the *natchalnik*, "the fountain is very nice as it is."

Next, we set about building him his spiral staircase out of concrete slabs. Each day we received our bread and kopecks before the start of work.

Word had gotten around about our "skills." Other under-*natchalniks* and functionaries appeared to see for themselves. One of them spoke to me.

"Wonderful. You soon finished here. Will you build my house? All materials there and well guarded."

Again I gave the same answer. "Ask the camp commandant and then a loaf and a ruble each for the four of us every morning."

He too apparently came to an agreement with Samcharadse, for when we had finished the first job, he took us to another hill, on which his house was supposed to be built. We found a lot of materials there, which had all been fiddled together during the past months, as the man told us with pride. But there was only a little cement. Four Russian convicts had already been working there and had just laid the foundations and raised a bit of walling.

"The sons of whores have been working here for two weeks already. Come and see what they've done."

He gave the finished piece of wall a kick and it fell over at once. Instead of working with the correct mixture of cement, they had sold as much of the cement as they dared and mixed it in a ratio of only one to twenty.

I looked at everything; naturally I had no idea of house building, but said to the man in a convincing tone: "Good, I'll build your house. You pick the four of us up each morning. Don't forget the bread and the ruble for each of us. Now tell me, where are your plans? How is the house supposed to look?"

"I no plans, I need two rooms with windows and entrance. You can make everything all right. And tomorrow cement will be here again, and then at night a guard will always watch over everything. Here, your bread and rubles."

What was to be done with my three weak comrades?

The weakest, our physicist, had only to hold up a piece of string with a stone as plumb line. The farmer and the bricklayer had to stir the mixture and bring along the bricks and mortar on a *nasilka*. To "save face" with the Russians, I had to do the bricklaying, with professional advice from the bricklayer. I soon got the hang of how to work correctly with mortar and cement. Once again the villagers tried to buy cement from us. But we remained firm and made it a point of honor to build our employer a solid house.

On the second day the man was already in raptures: "Good house this will be, can kick it and nothing falls over."

We built the two rooms at our own discretion, the windows facing the Elbrus mountains, and also a doorway. We put up the walls in little more than a week.

"We are only specialists in masonry. For the wooden roof you'll have to find others." We wanted to give the other prisoners too a chance to earn something extra.

When we had finished our work, I said to the *natchalnik*, "Listen, if you will pay us something extra, you can have something special from us, something no one else has in the whole Caucasus. All you have to provide is a bit more cement and some chalk."

He agreed at once, and we painted the red brickwork with white stripes.

"That is the most beautiful house I have ever seen. You give me monopoly of this. I want to be the only one in the town to have this marvelous thing."

In return for the payment of further rubles, I gave him my promise.

On the next day, our last, a stream of inquisitive people came up the hill to admire the marvel. A lot of functionaries now asked for the same decoration for their houses, but I kept the promise I had given.

After a few weeks, my "building master" took me and, full of pride, showed me the completed house and its bedroom suite, consisting of two beds, a wardrobe, and a table. It had been allocated to him from Moscow and was to remain the only one to reach the area in three years. A fresh stream of marveling people from the little town made the pilgrimage past the house on Sunday, this time to admire the bedroom through the window.

This was a further impression of conditions in the great Russian empire, together with its corruption.

During the period in which I was still building the fountain and the spiral staircase, I saw the SIS state limousine of the over-*natchalnik* leave his property almost every morning to drive his two children to school. On the return journey the chauffeur then bought milk, butter, cigarettes, flour, and sugar in the special shop for functionaries and *natchalniks*. To my dismay, I saw one day that the milk was fed to the pigs. I was equally dismayed at the sight of sacks of flour and sugar being unloaded in front of his house, at the same time the inhabitants were lining up at the state shops for a piece of bread or the rare sugar and flour rations.

I still had my *propusk* (exit permit), which I often used so that I could come back to the camp on my own after work. In doing so I often had conversations along the way with Russians and Georgians, and many confided in me, the stranger. They were discontented, but powerless in face of a system which they could not change by their own efforts. I enjoyed talking in particular with an old gentleman who had been a professor in what used to be Petersburg and was now exiled here for life. He lived out his days in humble circumstances and earned his keep as a letter-writer for the many illiterates.

With regard to our camp life, too, a certain amount had happened in the meantime. By order of Moscow, something was now supposed to be done about *kultura*. First, with vigorous support from Jupp Link, a library was set up, in which there were only Russian books and newspapers. Much more important for us was permission to start a camp orchestra and a theater group, and the fact that we were allowed to pursue sports. In our camp, with about 3,500 prisoners, there were musicians, music arrangers, stage designers, producers, actors, writers, and others ready at once to put plans into action. To our astonishment we were supplied with all the instruments necessary to form a complete orchestra. As an offshoot, there was a jazz band. The technicians and lighting experts, by order of Samcharadse, had to scrounge everything required for decor from the mine or on outdoor work. Props were made by our stage designers and painters from stolen materials.

Thus, in the course of time, the operetta *Der Fischerjunge von Capri* ("The Fisherboy of Capri") came into being, composed by Walter Struve and "Koebes" Witthaus, who also made the arrangement for the orchestra, and text by Helmut Wehrenfennig. The whole score of the operetta *Die Czardasfuerstin* ("The Csardas Princess") was written down from memory by E. Kalman, the composer of the operetta. Professional singers were on hand, among them the tenor Reini Bartel. The women's parts were played by young amateurs, who before long were already acting like pros. The rehearsals alone evoked memories and longings in all of us.

In the winter of 1946/47, the first performance was attended by Samcharadse with his officers and NKVD minders, the over-*natchalnik* and the functionaries of the district, the dignitaries, so to speak. The production was a great success. When the over-*natchalnik* asked about the origin of the floodlights, cables, etc., Samcharadse replied: "The prisoners found them." At that a benign and understanding smile spread across the face of the over-*natchalnik*.

In time the theater and orchestra group acquired such fame that members of the opera in Tiflis, who came to our performances, asked whether the "prisoners' ensemble" might not be allowed to appear in their own opera house. We felt very honored, but unfortunately this went beyond what was practicable for the Russians. What would the consequences have been if prisoners had given a guest performance in a state opera house? Instead, our ensemble was sent to other camps including those of the Hungarians and the Japanese, and everywhere its success was assured.

The jazz band, of course, was particularly popular. Willi Glaubrecht, the drummer, is still alive today. Since any kind of jazz was forbidden in the Third Reich as "alien" and decadent, and since listening to Western transmitters was punished by concentration camp, interest in this music was particularly great. But no one was familiar with it.

As a Glenn Miller fan, I had found my way in Paris, during the time of our occupation, to a Negro band in a secret place, in a cellar, and there I had soaked up Glenn Miller's "In the Mood." So I sang the melody note for note to our arranger. He wrote it down and arranged it so the band could play "In the Mood."

Georg Vieweger was the reciter of the cultural group. Cabaret evenings were organized with Karl-Heinz Engels, and they were always monitored by our Russian *politruk*, Black Nena. She belonged to the NKVD and was responsible for *kultura*; she was ill-natured and by no means well disposed toward us. On one occasion the band had rehearsed and put on its program, which had always to be presented first to Black Nena for approval, the march "Open Fire."

"*Niet*", was her reaction. "All you want to do is fire, nix *Krieg*."

Next day the title "Fire in the Camp" was presented to her.

"That is good, we Russians like camp-fire," came the approval.

It was the same march, only the title had been changed.

The Russians have a special relationship with *kultura*, as they call it. On the one hand they are very musical and allow their creative people special rights, provided they stay true to the party line. On the other, they have realized that music and other cultural delights motivate people and make them forget for the time being how bitter reality appears to them.

At the same time as the introduction of "cultural life" for the prisoners, the Antifa was also set up in the camp, an anti-Fascist group that was attached to the German camp commandant and watched over and "re-educated" by Black Nena. It was joined by a few long-standing German Communists and also by some opportunists who hoped for alleviations and privileges through their membership. With the rest of us, the Antifa held no interest. The names of some of its particularly zealous supporters were remembered, and many of them were well and truly beaten up when we were released.

Besides the official activity of our orchestra and theater group, all the rooms had evening lectures by fellow-prisoners, among them doctors and scientists, who read papers on selected subjects or spoke of their experiences.

A particularly active member of the theater group proved to be Boris von Karzov. Born in Yaroslav in 1894, the son of a well-to-do family, he had even attended the tsarist cadet school in St. Petersburg, modern Leningrad, before he had to flee with his two brothers after the October Revolution. His brothers had chosen Paris and Madrid as their places of exile; Boris on the other hand went to Germany. He first attended a drama school, although the theater in the difficult years after the First World War was a waste of time. So he switched to industry, married and had a daughter, Tamara. She lives today in north Germany and has since told me much about her father and placed letters and photographs at my disposal which have provided a nice contribution to what I experienced in common with her father in our Camp 518.

Karzov spoke five languages fluently and for that reason was enrolled in the army at the start of the Second World War as an "interpreter special-commander." I have a press photograph before me which shows Karzov with German and Russian officers when the "demarcation line" was drawn, after the Polish campaign in 1939, which was to partition Poland anew and bring so much suffering once more to the tormented Polish people—this time from both sides.

In the course of the Russian campaign, when the famous "Vlassov Army" was formed from captured and "liberated" officers and men, Karzov was employed as interpreter with a Cossack unit. Photographs show him with Cossack officers in their distinctive uniforms on horseback.

These were units that stood no chance in the murderous battle with tanks. It was obvious that Karzov's activity and his Russian origin were bound to be highly suspect to the Russians. Both were to prove fatal for him later.

In our camp Karzov remained unmolested at first. The authorities profited from his knowledge of languages and allowed him to take part in the theater group.

I will never forget the sessions when he read aloud the works of Pushkin and

Dostoyevski. Even the Russian officers and NKVD functionaries frankly admitted, "Karzov speaks a wonderful Russian, such as we no longer know today. Our language has become simpler."

At the request of many, Karzov translated Pushkin's *Eugen Onegin*, and in doing so tried to retain the melodiousness of the Russian language even in German.

Karzov was very popular with everyone. We had some fine evenings together when Karzov told us stories of old Russia and gave us an understanding of Russian culture, music, and mentality. In contrast to the former SS and police officers, who were constantly being interrogated, Karzov to our surprise was left in comparative peace.

Then suddenly, one summer night in 1948, Karzov was removed from the camp. We had forebodings of something terrible.

His daughter Tamara has since confirmed to me what we came to know at the time through secret channels: Karzov had been transferred to a special camp near Smolensk, where he became quite seriously ill. As a result, he entered a military hospital near Roslavl, south of Smolensk. According to a report by a German doctor, after his release from the hospital Karzov had been thrown into prison and attempts had been made to extract "confessions" from him. Since nothing could be proved against him, he was taken to all the places where he had fought during the war in Russia and put on public display there. When he was released from prison in an extremely weak state, the same doctor again restored him to health.

According to the information of the Red Cross after the war, Karzov is supposed to have died in July 1949 in Smolensk. Thus the treatment, which he had bravely resisted for as long as he could, had probably in the last analysis meant his end after all.

Karzov's fate resembled that of the many who perished in punishment camps, former members of the SS and police, and the German soldiers who had fought against partisans.

After the first hard years in the camp there were now a few signs of improvement. From the radio sets taken out of Germany by the Russians and passed on to him for repair, our radio mechanic had succeeded in removing enough parts that in the course of time he was able to construct a transmitter and receiver of his own, without rendering the Russian radios unusable. Other camps, too, had apparently hit on the same idea.

Naturally, only a few people could be let in on the secret of the existence of this set, which enabled us to listen to the West on shortwave and thus keep ourselves informed about the situation at home and in the rest of the world.

To prevent our set from being discovered, we packed it in a plastic cover and lowered it by day into the latrine. No one would look there, we hoped. Then at night we brought it out. Until the day of our release the Russians were unable to solve the mystery of why we were always so well informed.

Probably the hardest psychological burden for us during the first years was the lack of any contact with our families at home. No one knew of the other, whether they were even still alive.

Then—probably through pressure from the Western powers—we were allowed at last to write a postcard once a month, which was permitted to contain 25 words, including the address. It was not much, but it was at least a sign of life which one could send and receive. Then, later, we were allowed to write a card with an unlimited number of words. This condition brought forth true artists in minute writing and competitions were held to see who could get the most words on a card. From the spring of 1948, we were then allowed one letter every three months. This chicanery too, for that was how we saw it, had to do with the Russian mentality.

The postal system is marked by the slackness and disinterest of the officials. But the vast distances in the great empire, this side and beyond the Ural mountains, as well as the ponderous system, also make normal communications almost impossible. In addition, the Russians have no feeling for time and space. These are for them abstract concepts. How often in answer to our question about when we would finally be allowed to go home we were told, "What do you want? Russia is a big place. You can find bread, work, and women here. Why don't you want to stay here? Your wives at home have long since found other men." With our different way of thinking what was there to say to this attitude to life?

The Russians with their fatalism put up with these conditions, the more so since they do not know how things are elsewhere or how much we in the West depend upon our means of communication. I have known of Russian workers who have been taken from their beds at night somewhere in north Russia, put in a truck, and brought here to the Caucasus to work. To our question about what their wives had to say about it and what they would now live on with their children, the usual answer was, "*Nitchevo*, wife will work and perhaps get a man too, who will feed her and the children. I must see to it that I get by here."

Following on the "liberalization" through the *kultura* program and the activity of the Antifa group, a community had gradually formed which could offer resistance to the bad treatment and the food, which was as wretched as ever. Our activity as "German specialists" had made us indispensable in many fields, which we exploited wherever possible for our own ends. Nevertheless, the treatment was often cruel.

Time and again individuals would be taken away at night for interrogation, either to prove them guilty of atrocities during the war or to extort from them statements about members of the SS and police who were in the camp.

Thus Ernst Urban, with whom I often spent the evening sitting by the camp fence, was taken away one night to the NKVD. He was accused of atrocities which one was supposed to know about. His name, place of birth, and other details were held up to him as proof that they knew all about him. When he protested his innocence, he was placed between two red-hot stoves and a bucket of cold water was poured over him. Black Nena thought that this would force him to confess. It was not until he was able to make the Russians see that on the basis of his date of birth he had not yet been twelve years old at the time of the atrocities that it became apparent that there must have been a confusion over names. We heard of many similar cases time and again. The Russians tried again and again to blackmail us anew through psycho-terror.

But to return to corruption. I met with a classic case through my "concrete brigade." One evening the deputy of the Russian camp commandant came to see me and said, "You tomorrow not to work, have special job for you. Find yourself twelve men who don't work in the mine. Escort will fetch you."

I suspected that some deal was being done here and scented a chance for us. So I said, "If it's a special job, you'll have to pay, otherwise I'll write to Moscow about your schemes."

The Russians knew only too well that a few people had previously managed to smuggle cards or letters out of the camp and send them by normal mail to Stalin personally or to the Supreme Soviet. They contained complaints or merely a simple inquiry about when we would finally be released in accordance with the Geneva Conventions. As we learned through our "secret channels," a few cards had arrived and had subsequently been delivered back to the camp commandant endorsed with directions. To that extent our threat to write to Moscow was taken extremely seriously.

"If work good, you get reward," was the answer of the deputy Russian camp commandant.

So next morning we were collected by one of the guards. It was still winter. Snow lay in the mountains. We marched off without knowing where we were going. The snow reached up to our chests. In single file we started to climb, for five hours each of us taking it in turns to open up a way through the deep snow. Suddenly we heard a shout from our escort, "*Stoy*, stop!"

The guard pointed to a stack of wood covered with snow and intimated that we were to take it down to the valley.

"Have you got the money with you?" I asked him. "Otherwise nothing's going to happen here."

To my surprise he pulled out a bundle of ruble notes from his pocket. Our warning had obviously been effective.

We cleared the snow off the stack of wood. The timber was in lengths of about five meters. It was valuable mahogany. Each of us tucked a length of wood under his arm and we slithered in our tracks down to the valley. This time it took only two hours.

It had become clear to me in the meantime that an illicit sale of valuable timber was involved here, on a considerable scale. There was no doubt that the commandant had received a handsome sum for assigning prisoners to the job, and the guard too would certainly have received his share.

Somewhat apart from the entrance to the town two trucks were waiting, on to which we had to load the lengths of timber. We then drove to the railway station. Here a single truck was standing, on to which we loaded the wood, but only after we had received our rubles from the guard.

At the same time the guard warned us, "You seen nothing, and say nothing."

We marched dead tired back into the camp, where a special portion of soup was waiting for us. Once again we were warned by the Russian officer to remain absolutely silent.

Through our German truckdriver, Fred Sbosny, who often had to drive to Kutaisi and Tiflis, we heard the continuation of this story.

A highly placed functionary in Tiflis had commissioned the "transaction." First the state forest officer had to be bribed, who was responsible for the cutting and extraction of the valuable timber. He accounted for the absence of a stack of wood as "sabotage," the way of putting it in cases of corruption, if these are ever exposed. Besides us, the guard and the truckdriver had to have their palms greased. Then there was the station master to be considered, who had provided an empty truck. One must know also that there was a customs and guard house at the town boundary of Tkibuli, where every train with coal had to stop and be registered. So the "customs post" had received its share too. So far all the bribe money was paid by the camp commandant, who had previously received abundant rubles for the purpose.

At Kutaisi, the provincial capital, the truck was hooked on to a train for Tiflis, unregistered of course, for which gesture the stationmaster had received his due. A further payment then became due on arrival in Tiflis, where the "client" was finally able to take possession of his goods. There he sold off the wood at vast prices to high, well-to-do functionaries, who had furniture made from it by joiners who had been "detailed" for this from state firms. The functionaries have plenty of money, but they can buy nothing with it except on the black market.

Normally all building projects and the fulfillment of norm schedules are checked by commissions that appear irregularly in all concerns. But they too have no objection to little presents, and then report "sabotage" to their superior authority, if they discover shortcomings or that allocated material is missing. But if the case is so blatant that it can no longer be glossed over with "sabotage," a culprit has quickly to be found. What happens then is that some innocent little overseer disappears to Siberia for five to fifteen years.

Such unfortunately was the experience of a sympathetic Russian engineer who had now become the superintendent of our concrete brigade for an important project. Somewhere in the Ukraine he had been designated the "culprit" in a so-called "economic crime" and exiled for five years to Siberia, north of Vladivostok. Without ever being able to get in touch with his family, he had to work in the Siberian forests. After that, for probation and so that he could get used to normal conditions again, he was sent to the Caucasus for two years.

I quickly became friends with this poor man, whose first probationary job was the supervision of a proposed foundry. The foundry was supposed to be built below our camp at the edge of the town Tkibuli, and our brigade was supposed to lay the foundations.

On our first day on the job the Russian engineer showed me a working drawing sent from Moscow, which served as the standard plan for all similar projects.

"Take a look at the plan," he said. "I can't understand it all; I'm not sufficiently trained for that. Can you tell from it how the foundations are to be laid?"

I felt sorry for him, but nothing surprised me any more. I consulted our only specialist, therefore, the bricklayer. The site of the building had been fixed by the mine administration, which was also to have control over the foundry. So we started by marking out the limits of the foundations in length and breadth and gathered from the plan that they were to be laid three meters deep and of reinforced concrete.

On the basis of painful experience I strongly urged the engineer to take care of the materials, since he was the one who would otherwise be in trouble. Then we began to dig with picks and shovels, until we struck groundwater after just over one meter. So we took a break, to consider what to do.

I went to our guard and said, "Give me your machine-gun for a moment. Here's a few rubles. Go and buy some maize cakes for us all over there in the market, for you too and for the engineer."

He handed over his gun without hesitation and was happy at the prospect of extra food.

"There's groundwater here already," I told our helpless engineer.

"You must go on digging. The plan from Moscow must be carried out," was his convincing answer.

So we went on digging. When we were finally up to our ankles in water, I called a halt to the work.

"We can't go on like this. How shall we ever get down to a depth of three metres?"

I had seen from the plan that heavy traveling cranes were to be installed later, for which the three-meter foundations were indeed necessary. The engineer promised to get us rubber boots and pumps if only we would go on working. We said nothing further to this amusing idea.

But the next day pumps really did arrive. And we got the promised rubber boots. But after two more days we were already 16 inches deep in water. I refused to go on.

"Do you want to pump away all the rivers of the Elbrus?" I asked the engineer, now really annoyed. "It's pointless. We won't work under water."

"I speak to *natchalnik*, we see tomorrow."

The decision was as simple as it was senseless.

"*Natchalnik* understand problem. Stop digging. Lay reinforced concrete, even if only 1.30 meters deep."

It was obvious to us that with these weak foundations the whole building would collapse, if it ever got finished and came into operation. So we mixed the concrete in the correct ratio of one to seven, tied down the steel rods, and ended our part with an inadequate foundation.

And that was how it remained. In the months that followed nothing further was done at the building site. When I left the camp at the end of 1948, I could still see our steel rods sticking up in the air. The rest of the materials, already delivered, were rusting away, if they had not been stolen in the meantime. I have no idea how the mine administration explained all this to Moscow or what became of the poor engineer.

With this project my activity as leader of the concrete brigade came to an end. I received a new job.

But back to our camp. All of us who had the chance to earn ourselves some extra money or bread on the outdoor detachments tried to see that our weaker fellow-prisoners, who stayed behind in the camp and had no such opportunity, received something through purchases in the market. Our guards, whose poor pay and meager diet were insufficient to satisfy their appetite, also received something from us as a gift, or else they bartered tobacco with us for food. We did in fact receive a small tobacco ration every day, but this was only *machorka*, the stringy bits of leaves that are left over from the making of *papyrossi*. *Machorka* can only be smoked if one twists oneself a little cone of newspaper, fills it with chopped-up *machorka*, twists the cone to at the top and then lights it.

All over Russia *machorka* is the "tobacco of the poor." Russian newspapers are designed for smoking in this form; they contain no size, and the saying goes that *Pravda* is the most widely smoked cigarette in the world.

Matches too are scarce in Russia. Only once in four years, in my experience, did an allocation of matches from Moscow arrive in the little town of Tkibuli. And the ration disappeared very quickly into one of the functionaries' shops. So we fell back on our ancestors' way of making fire; lighters were made from flints and fuses.

Signs of humanity were not lacking in the camp. There was in the first place Natella, the "angel of Tkibuli and Camp 518." She came from an old, Georgian, princely family and helped the German *maladois*, the sick, wherever she could. At the risk of her life she procured medical supplies that were intended by rights for the Russians. Then there was Dr. Kamdelaki, a woman doctor in the camp hospital and responsible for all six camps. She too came from an old, princely family and was thus no friend of the Russians, who had occupied her country and robbed her of liberty.

Others were Nastasia (I have changed her name, since she is probably still alive and I would not want to cause her trouble) and her friend Sina. Nastasia was a great-granddaughter of Lenin's. The two young women were engineers and had been exiled to the Caucasus for fifteen years.

It is thanks to Nastasia that there are a few photographs of the camp and of our cultural group, which she took at risk of her life and which Jupp Link, with whom she had become friendly, was able to smuggle out of the camp under the cockade on his cap. Jupp Link, who today lives near Munich, has spoken to me about these girls, who liked us Germans, and about the sad parting when he left the camp, the last to go, and Nastasia begged him to take her with him.

What may have become of all these women who helped to preserve in us the faith and hope of human kindness?

The time passed and we had learned to come to terms with the wretched conditions. It had become clear to us that apart from the hard work in the mine and in the outdoor detachments, and apart from the cultural activity, something had to be done to keep us physically fit. Jupp Link managed to procure some balls for us and I organized handball teams. Handball was at that time a very popular field game (as against the modern indoor handball) in my north German homeland. We played this game on every free day, to the wonderment of the Russians and cheered on by enthusiastic spectators.

Next, a football team was set up and matches arranged with the other camps.

Even Russia's national game, chess, soon enjoyed great popularity. To begin with we carved ourselves chess men in a primitive way. The Russians were so enthusiastic that they gave us chess sets, and guards played chess matches secretly, since it was forbidden to them, against our best players.

All this may sound like a fun time. But it was not that by a long way. The decisive impulse for it was, rather, the will to survive, which gave us the strength even in these circumstances not to give up. Some of our fellow-prisoners often criticized our activity and maintained that by it we would be supplying the Russians with evidence that we were still strong enough for even harder work.

In the winter of 1947/48 I received my last assignment in Camp 518/I. I became the brigadier of a "coal-seeking detachment." Above our camp, on the slopes of the Elbrus mountains, the Russians had begun to look for new coal deposits with the help of drilling machines supplied from Sweden.

A Russian detachment had already come upon a rich seam at a depth of about 800 meters, and a great effort was now being mounted, in three shifts, to trace the seam and mine it.

My brigade was to take over a day shift. It was distributed over six boring sites and given precise instructions by the Russian brigadier. Although spring was close at hand, much snow still lay in the mountains and it was bitter cold. Each morning— accompanied by our escort—we climbed up through the snow into the mountains, where we relieved the night shift, who would be sitting freezing around a fire.

My job consisted of visiting the individual boring sites during the course of the shift and solving whatever problems arose. By rights our guard was supposed to check the individual boring sites and see that work was going on everywhere. But he usually preferred to seek out the best place by the fire, lean his machine-gun against a tree, and go to sleep. If I spoke to him about this, his reply was: "*Polkovnik*, you good brigadier, you have *propusk* and can see everywhere if work good. I freezing, stay rather by fire."

In spite of the backbreaking work to be done with the heavy boring machines, and in spite of our often inadequate clothing, we experienced a little bit of freedom up there in the mountains, with a view over the little town and our camp. It was inevitable that we had our fun. Once we hid the guard's machine-gun, for instance, while he was asleep.

"*Kamerad*, give my gun back. Not say I sleeping, or I in glass-house. Here, have some *machorka* to smoke."

Spring came, the snow melted under the hot southern sun, and the first flowers came out. The work became more bearable, and we even savored the unique beauty of the south Caucasian landscape. Sweet-tasting wild strawberries, wild pears, and all sorts of herbs, which the guard showed us, were a welcome source of extra vitamins, which we had gone without for three long years. And whenever possible we provided some also for our sick in the camp.

Gradually I extended my "beat." The bore gangs were working reliably. While they did so, I gathered strawberries and wild pears for them in a homemade basket.

One spring day, not long before the German Easter, I set off quite early in order to climb a ridge, to see what lay beyond it. Lying in the valley I saw an enchanted little village. It was irresistible. I climbed down to it and came to a forgotten world.

The village, inhabited only by Georgian peasants, had no street leading out of it. Only mules and donkeys could pick a way out of there and serve as means of transport into the normal world, which ended with the little town of Tkibuli.

Everyone ran together to gape at me, the stranger. I asked for the village elder. An old man came toward me. Skeptically and timidly he asked me in a mixture of Georgian and Russian who I was and what I wanted.

"I am a German *plenni*, a prisoner of war. I am working over there in the mountains and have been living for several years in a camp in Tkibuli."

His face lit up. Excited, he called out to me and to the other villagers, "I know Germans from the war. They and the Turks freed our country from the bad Russians. I never forget good Germans."

Clearly, time had stood still for him in the First World War, when Georgia had been a German protectorate.

"German good. Come, you our guest."

I was taken into a simple but clean house. His whole family gathered there and other villagers thronged the entrance inquisitively.

As in all the houses, in the middle stood the place for the fire and for eating, made of hard clay; on three sides lay hides for sleeping, for the family; and in a corner there was a space for the chickens and goats. I felt at home there after my years in the barrack and on our wooden bunks.

Over the fire long iron chains hung down from the roof.

"You now eat Georgian with friends. Come, sit down."

With crossed legs we squatted around the fire, and the farmer's wife hung iron cauldrons on the chains. One cauldron she filled with water for the tea, in another the maize mash was prepared, and in a third was the goat-meat with every possible herb.

When everything appeared to be ready, the wife approached us. Only the men had taken a place with me. The women stood modestly in a corner. The wife passed us a bowl of water, in which we washed our hands. Then the cauldrons were unhooked, the tea was brewed, and I was invited to start eating.

There were no forks and no spoon, only the cauldrons with the hot foods. How was I supposed to eat? So as not to show these friendly people my uncertainty, let alone offend them, I said, "Many thanks, farmer, but with us in Germany the head of the house always begins the meal, symbolizing the fact that the food is fit to eat. So will you please begin?"

He was impressed. With one hand he took a handful of maize mash from the hot cauldron, shaped the mash neatly into a flat pancake, and with this pancake of mash helped himself to meat from the other cauldron. Skillfully he wrapped it all up into a roll and began to eat. I had come to know a similar way of eating previously among the Bedouins in Africa. So I copied him, and although my hands seemed to be on fire, as a hungry prisoner I enjoyed the delicious food and the strong tea.

Then the wife brought out an earthenware jar with a homemade brandy, whole ingredients of which I was unable to identify. Toasts now followed, of the sort customary also in the Arabian countries.

"I drink to great friendship with good Germans, who are friends of us Georgians.

You will convey our greetings to your great Kaiser Wilhelm. I know from the war that he is good, just man. We no more Kaiser, or our beloved Tamara. They come back and we shall be free."

I did not enlighten the good man that Wilhelm II was long since dead and that we already had the Second World War behind us. I said, "I wish that your lovely country and the proud Georgians may one day be free. I greet the friendly farmers of this village and drink to the health of the Empress Tamara."

The women wept and the men embraced me.

The atmosphere seemed to me suitable for buying a few eggs cheaply for Easter and for the sick back at the camp. When I asked about this, the farmer referred me to his wife, "Wife responsible for goats, chicken, and flour. You bargain with her."

I saw at once the sparkle in her eyes at being able to bargain now, like all orientals, with a buyer. Her first price was far above that of the market in Tkibuli. So I offered less than the market price. She duly gave way a little, at which all the women started to chatter together.

Unfortunately I had no time to continue this game for long, much as I too enjoyed it.

"Listen, I haven't much time. I am saving you the long way through the mountains in order to sell your eggs in the market in Tkibuli. So you really must offer them to me more cheaply."

"I like to walk through the mountains and hear the news in the market. So will you buy now at my price?"

I gave up, with the argument that the eggs would get broken on my way through the mountains or be taken away from me by the Russian guard. With many friendly words and embraces we said good-bye. Happy people, for whom time had stood still.

Shortly before Easter I visited the village again. I had brought with me a carved knife, made by our men in the mine, as a present for the village elder in thanks for his hospitality. This time he persuaded his wife to let me have a few eggs as a gift. I thanked them in the name of everyone in the camp.

So we had Easter eggs on our table after all.

After the discovery of the rich new seam, the Russian mine administration had started to build a new pithead in the valley. Now that the results of the coal-seeking detachments were so positive, the project was pursued at full blast.

The work was being done, once again, in a slipshod way and without great expertise according to plans supplied from Moscow. The building site and the first part of a tunnel that was to be driven into the mountain looked catastrophic. The construction managers seemed unable even to understand the plans. Materials were stolen. The Russian work force kept strictly to their norms, which were set comparatively low.

Then one day, a German mining engineer, who until then had been working down the shaft, was sent for and given superintendence over the whole project— much to our astonishment.

"You are now responsible for everything. The Russian workers will be subordinate to you. You take from your camp all the specialists you can use and you will receive all the materials that you request."

So ran the clear direction of the over-*natchalnik*, who had obviously arranged matters with the Russian camp commandant.

The further construction and development of the tunnel, the laying of the rails for the underground railway, all the electrical fittings, the building of a machine house and the barracks scheduled for the administration and for the Russian personnel now came under the German engineer.

At first he was hesitant in asserting himself and was up against some of the functionaries, but then in command, he convinced everyone that work there would be done professionally and well. He demanded a lot from the Russian construction managers and workers, but his expertise and fairness soon made him popular. I visited him one day on the building site and was surprised at the almost European appearance of the place and the zeal with which the work was being done. Some trucks arrived while I was there with gravel that had been taken from the Caspian Sea. Our engineer tested the gravel in his laboratory, primitive as yet, and refused to accept it.

"This gravel contains oil and is therefore unsuitable for cementing the tunnel lining. I need clean gravel."

The mine administration at once ordered the delivery of clean gravel, and a few days later it actually arrived.

By the time of my transfer to another camp at the end of 1948, the new pithead had grown extensively and the administration as well as the mining personnel had already moved into their barracks.

So we no longer wondered why the Russians ignored the Geneva Conventions and tried by every means to retain us as prisoners of war. It was again apparent that with a state-directed system, an army of millions of Russian convicts and conscripted workers and the lack of any incentive to work, and of the most elementary consumer goods, no production was to be achieved of the sort that is taken for granted in the West as the basis of a liberal—in Russian eyes, capitalist—economy.

In Camp 518 meanwhile, more and more prisoners were managing to obtain extra "earnings," so as to improve the wretched, unbalanced, and meager camp diet.

The mine workers, who had no contact with the outside world, began a lively trade in coal, which they sold to freezing Russian families, having previously paid the guard a small commission. Or they used the mine workshops to make artistically carved knives and other useful articles which could not otherwise be bought anywhere by the local inhabitants.

Our German truckdriver, Fred Sbosny, with whom I once drove to Tiflis to buy things for our theater group, tried to maintain his Studebaker truck in good condition. As he told me, whenever a spare part was needed, he always received the same instructions from the Russian commandant, "You get from mine. Guards in vehicle park must not notice." This meant that he often had to go on a "scrounging trip" by night, at great risk and by bribing the guards.

Spare parts for the Studebakers, over 100,000 of them, which the Americans had supplied under the terms of a "Lend-lease" agreement in the last years of the war, were not available, or were sold "under the counter." Thus, in the course of the years, three trucks became two, and two became one, until even this last gave up the ghost.

Under the terms of the same treaty the Americans, mistaking the conditions, had supplied vast quantities of pajamas. For the Georgians, who loved everything colorful, these were a very welcome gift, and so one still saw them after 1948 running about the town in their pajamas, even during the day.

The Russian officers and the NKVD people undoubtedly knew that the camp was slowly beginning to change, and they were realistic enough to put a higher value on our achievements.

The summer of 1948 was marked by two events, each of which impressed me in its own way.

One day I was detailed for technical working reasons to go for a week to the Hungarian camp, which was one of our group of camps. When I arrived three Hungarians had just been locked up for complaining about the working conditions. The whole camp at once went on hunger strike, sent a delegation to the Russian commandant, and demanded their release. As this was refused, the hunger strike went on, and I found myself compelled to join it.

Hunger strikes, unusual cases of death, and suicides are for the Russians an alarm signal. A commission at once appeared from Moscow to look into it. The three were released and the hunger strike was called off.

What impressed me was the unanimity with which the whole camp had joined in the strike. The Hungarians hated the Russians, who had occupied their country as well.

I profited from the strike by learning to knit from a Hungarian shepherd. After I got back to our own camp, mine workers made me some knitting needles, others brought me fourteen-ply insulating yarn from stolen electric cable, and I began to knit stockings. Since we and the Russian soldiers knew only of foot-cloths, which provided no warmth in winter, my stockings were a "hit." In the course of time I became so proficient at knitting that I produced several pairs a week, which were bought, and often ordered in advance, by fellow prisoners and the soldiers who guarded us.

The second impressive event involved our camp. Late one afternoon after work the Russian commandant came to see me.

"*Polkovnik*, get hold of another three strong men and come to the guardroom in ten minutes."

Another deal seemed to be in the offing.

The four of us duly appeared at the guardroom, where the commandant handed us over to a Georgian, whom he treated with great respect and who seemed to us to be a prominent man in the town. An escort was provided for us and we marched down into the town. When I asked what there was for us to do, the man looked at us sadly. "You will see what has happened. You help me."

We came to a quarter of the town where the *natchalniks* and functionaries had their wooden houses, which stood out from the usual ones. We went into the house and saw before us, standing on the living-room table, an open coffin in which lay a very pretty young girl, his daughter. Standing around the coffin were a number of women, who in accordance with oriental custom were tearing their hair and singing laments. In some consternation we stood still and asked the good man what in heaven's name we four had to do there.

"You bear coffin ceremoniously to the churchyard. I bury daughter there. You also Christians with respect for dead."

We knew that the former churchyard lay at the other end of the town.

"*Gospodin*, we will do everything with dignity. But it is a long way, so take a stool so that we can set the coffin down when it gets too heavy."

At that we shouldered the open coffin in which the young girl lay, in a white dress and adorned with flowers, and marched off, followed by the father with the stool. Behind him came the family, and behind them all the friends and strangers. The procession grew longer and longer. On either side of our long way to the churchyard stood many of the inhabitants of the little mining town.

As soon as we gave the sign, the father came up with the stool. Hardly had we set the coffin down, than female mourners came running up to the coffin to touch the girl once more. Finally we arrived at the churchyard. The dilapidated church, which served as a food store, the overturned tombstones and the rank weeds gave the place a sad impression and offered no atmosphere of peace. The father and his sons had already dug the grave, so we set the coffin down beside it.

The place meanwhile had filled with people. After a last farewell, the coffin was closed, and we lowered it slowly into the ground. I had arranged with my three companions that after the lowering of the coffin we would remain standing by the grave and say the Lord's Prayer. As we did so, and then in addition threw three spadefuls of earth into the grave, the assembled people looked at us in amazement, but seemed to be so overwhelmed by this gesture that some of the mourners crossed themselves and began loudly to weep.

Then, together with the father, we started to fill in the grave. As we did so I could not help asking him what his beautiful daughter had died of so young.

His answer was unexpected, "The silly cow, I always told her she shouldn't make love to her boyfriend in the open air. Now she's had pneumonia and kicked the bucket because of it."

We were somewhat taken aback. The four of us then marched with the father back to his house, where the table had been laid in the meantime with what was by Georgian standards a sumptuous funeral feast. We were overwhelmed by the meal, for years an unaccustomed one for us. There were maize cakes, eggs, fruit, meat, goat's cheese, home-baked bread, and in addition, Georgian wine and brandy. When our escort arrived to collect us at about eleven o'clock, he too was invited to eat and drink, an offer he did not refuse.

We then took our leave. The family thanked us again for the beautiful funeral.

Swaying slightly we appeared at the guardhouse, where the night sentry greeted us with a great hello and envious remarks.

With a somewhat guilty conscience we told our fellow prisoners about this "Russian-style" funeral.

25

Punishment Camp: Hunger Strike and the KGB

Late autumn, 1948. Winter was advancing slowly over the land. We still had hope of being home for Christmas. The opposite occurred.

Without warning, as always, a selection was suddenly made. All staff officers, former members of the Waffen-SS and the police, and those who were considered such by the KGB, as well as prisoners who had fought against partisans, had to ready themselves for a transfer to a special camp. We were very depressed.

Leave-taking from those who remained behind, with whom we had endured so much in common for more than three years, was hard for us. We were just able to give them our home addresses for memorization before the Russian commandant appeared on the scene.

"I can't do anything. Orders from Moscow. You good workers, mine management and many people will miss you."

"You too soon *domoi*, go home."

Although there was little comfort in his words, they were well meant. The Russian soul showed through for once.

We found ourselves once again in closed trucks with new guards who were not to be trifled with. They behaved as though they were dealing with dangerous criminals.

In the afternoon the train rumbled down to the valley, out of the mountains in which so many of our comrades had been buried or thrown into makeshift graves. We went past the little wooden house that had once let our "wood transport" through. Higher up, where I had worked with the coal-seeking detachment, we could see the first snow.

Our thoughts went back to the other prisoners. As we heard later, all prisoners of the main Camp 7518/I were sent at the end of September to a camp in the outskirts of Kutaisi. It was said that this camp had been used before as camp for the "Wehrmachtshelferinnen" (girls serving in the Army as assistant workers). The camp was quite near an Opel factory dismounted in East Germany and now slowly rusting.

Winand told me later that, with some exceptions, they were released during October 1949. He himself left the Caucasus on 12 October and reached his home in Cologne on 28 October.

Fellow prisoner Koellreuter managed to visit Ktibuli as a tourist in 1978. He reports that our Camp 7518/I does not exist anymore. So all signs of our passion faded away.

We rumbled east through the Caucasian lowlands and were detrained unexpectedly in the neighborhood of Tbilisi (Tiflis), the capital of Georgia.

The collecting camp to which we were taken was already partially occupied by selected prisoners from other camps. They too had no idea what was to become of us.

We were "greeted" by the camp commandant, "You here well treated, Moscow very correct. Staff officers not work."

I was again employed as interpreter, but my *propusk* from Tkibuli was unfortunately not valid here. We staff officers took no great pleasure in not being allowed to work, although the decision was correct and in accordance with the Geneva Convention.

There was no radio anymore, no chance of earning a little extra or of making contact with the local population. We sat about the camp in idleness and were dependent on the rumors of the outside brigades.

It is hardly believable, but we thought back to our camp in the mountains with a certain nostalgia. The work had been hard, and mortal for many, but it had been a distraction. We who in the course of the years had come through physically and mentally had been able in work to forget something of our hard fate.

Treatment in the camp at Tiflis was correct, but we were degraded from prisoners of war to convicts. Once again I was required to denounce police and SS officers. When I refused, I had to spend a day in the standing box. With only a little piece of bread and a bowl of watery soup to eat I had to stand for 24 hours. There was an air hole in the ceiling, but otherwise only concrete around me. I don't know how many days one could bear it.

My inactivity in the camp gave me the chance to draw up an interim balance.

In the three and a half years I had gathered a good many experiences. I had learned to do work which I had known before only from hearsay. I had learned that the will to survive and training to survive were decisive in overcoming a fate such as mine. Equally important was to keep alive the hope of returning home one day. I had learned also that a clear, intelligible attitude and language impressed the Russians. They despised opportunists, let alone informers.

I remember a conversation with an NKVD functionary in which he said, "We use traitors of course, but we don't like treason."

The picture I had been able to form over the years was fundamentally different from that which Hitler and his Propaganda Minister Goebbels had tried to give us, namely, of the Russians as subhumans who had no right to exist.

I think the period of the war in Russia, but especially my years in captivity, had helped me to understand a good part of the Russian mentality. I don't mean the power centers in Moscow, but the Russian population.

Like children the Russians could be cruel, but ready at the next moment to share with another their last crust of bread. I liked these people, who despite permanent oppression had never given up their identity or lost their love of their country. In the evening we often heard, wafting over to us from the Russian camps and villages, melancholy songs, sung in harmony, which seemed to express the destiny of these people.

But there were other experiences which made our blood boil and reminded us of medieval methods of torture.

Gold crowns were broken off our teeth; we had to carry the dead out of the camp on hand-barrows and bury them unceremoniously; and we had to undergo periodic "frisking," in which we were deprived of our last possessions. All this seemed to us cruel and unfeeling. Even photographs of our families were taken from us and torn up before our eyes. Our pleas to spare us the photographs at least were met with derisive hoots and the words, "Lovely woman, we had in Germany. Your wife long ago has other man."

And we could no longer bear to hear the inevitable *davai*, the word with which our overseers drove us on, any more than the word *saftra*, tomorrow, which was the answer to every question about returning home. To us it seemed like mockery.

At work our relations with the Russians who labored alongside us as convicts were much better. Perhaps it was the common fate that bound us together, to which they, however, were more easily reconciled than we. At the time there were about 3 million Russian prisoners, distributed all over Russia. In the towns and villages there was hardly a family that didn't have one of its members working in a punishment camp. But was not the whole of Russia one vast prison camp?

Despite the monotonous daily round the weeks went by. Previously, mail from home had still been a bright spot. Here even that no longer applied at first, for it would take weeks for our new address to reach home.

We couldn't understand why the Russians had lumped us staff officers in with members of the police and the Waffen SS, whom they designated as "war criminals." Were we perhaps potential *revanchists*? This term is still part of the Russian vocabulary even today.

Hally Momm complained in particular, "I opposed Hitler and because of that was demoted and put 'on probation' in the notorious 'Dirlewanger Brigade.' So why have I been sent here?"

Slowly the rumor gained ground that our stay at the collecting camp was to end and that we were to be transferred to a punishment camp. A Russian officer told us, "You are going to a punishment camp and will be sentenced there."

Was it malice or the truth? He proved to be right. From the end of 1948 to the beginning of 1949 transports were assembled which left Tiflis for an unknown destination. We too were on one of them. Again a truck, again closed doors, and once again unfriendly guards. Hope gave way more and more to apathy. We trundled north, back over the Elbrus mountains, and ended up in the region of Kiev, the capital of the Ukraine.

On the long railway journey we discussed what had become of Lenin's worker and peasant state: a state capitalism of the worst kind, the apparatus of power ossified and only maintained by an ingenious system of supervision. What had come into being was a state of functionaries, in which on the "toady principle," treading on those below and cringing to those above, everyone tried to work his way up out of the mass. I didn't come across any officer or functionary who treated his people humanely. The less Marx's ideas and Lenin's program could be realized, the more the system had to be maintained by force and supervision. Any relaxation would in the long term lead automatically to collapse. Great disappointment was evident in those of our fellow prisoners who in Germany had been enrolled members of the Communist party, who had had to endure much suffering for their ideology. Their faith had been shaken.

A few days before our removal to Kiev, I had a further unusual experience. On my way to get food a young man suddenly stopped in front of me.

"Colonel! My God, you here! Don't you recognize me?"

It was the orderly officer on the staff of my 1st Battalion of the Panzer Grenadier Regiment 125, which on 18 July 1944, had been in the thick of a hail of bombs during "Operation Goodwood" and had been completely wiped out. At the time I had tried in vain to make contact with this battalion and was afraid even then that casualties would have been heavy.

"Good heavens, where have you come from? I didn't think you were still alive. Tell me what happened to you."

We arranged to meet that evening and he told me his story.

"As we were well dug in and kept our heads, our losses were not all that heavy. Then, after putting up fierce resistance, we were all taken prisoner by the British. For some unknown reason we were handed over to the Americans. I ended up eventually in the USA, more precisely in the Middle West. Our treatment was first class. I was even able to continue my geological studies and take my exam before a Swiss commission. We didn't have to work, it was on a voluntary basis. I did work and earned so much money that I was able to buy all the books for my studies and have suits made at the tailor's."

"Then how in the world did you get here?" I wanted to know.

"In 1948 we were released," he went on. "I was allowed to take all my things with me, which I packed up in several boxes. The boxes were then shipped by the Americans. When I arrived in Germany I produced my discharge certificate and was asked by an American officer where I wanted to be discharged to. I told him I wanted to go to my mother in Dresden. 'For God's sake,' he replied, 'that's in the Russian zone. You'll have problems. Stay here in our zone.' Relying on my discharge certificate, I stuck to my decision. 'All right, I wish you luck. I hope you won't regret it.'

"I never got to my mother's. As soon as I had crossed the demarcation line between the Americans and the Russians, I showed my discharge certificate and asked for permission to go to my mother, but my request was to land me in trouble.

" 'Certificate from Americans no good here,' was the Russian reaction. 'You German officer and *revanchist*, go to Russian camp.'

"Next day I found myself, along with a lot of others who had made the same mistake, in a train for transportation here," he said, ending the account of his unfortunate journey.

My young orderly officer at least had the good fortune to be able to work as a geologist outside the camp at Tiflis, although not under as good conditions as with the Americans.

In the Tiflis camp I had another, rather amusing experience. At the end of 1948 a few POWs arrived there who had previously been in a camp in Romania on the Black Sea. One of these men, also deeply disappointed, told us his story.

"I belonged to a brigade that was supposed to repair some slightly damaged houses in what was once a spa. Russian occupation officers were then going to move into them. At the house on which I was working a Russian lieutenant-colonel turned up every day with a little wooden chest and his day's ration of dried salted fish.

" 'When house finished? I sleep in car, want to move in here.'

" 'In a few days. There's no water supply yet in the bathroom,' I said, each day giving the same answer.

"One day his patience came to an end.

"He turned up again, but this time with the words, 'I now stay here. I no need water in bathroom, I wash outside at well' (which didn't exist).

"He set down his little wooden chest, took his salted fish and said, 'You no *kultura*, no well, no water in house. Where I can wash salt from fish?'

"I showed him the lavatory. 'This is the only place where the water is already running.'

"I went back to my work. Suddenly I heard a terrible cursing and shouting from the lavatory.

" 'Fish gone, damned *kultura* here. You find me fish.'

"I tried to tell him how pointless it was to look for his fish, but he grabbed me by the hand and rushed with me from one story to the other.

"Eventually he gave up and went to get himself another fish."

Who can blame this man for his disappointment? Even a lieutenant-colonel was not necessarily familiar with this kind of *kultura*, but rather with a draw-well somewhere in Russia.

So now to Kiev.

Weather conditions were far worse than in the south-Caucasian lowlands. We were freezing in the new camp, which was also far worse equipped than the previous camps. We tried, however, to make ourselves at home. It was still not clear to us why staff officers even here were lumped together with "war criminals." But our common fate united us and we got on well together. Although it was not official,

I was called in as interpreter for the camp commandant's interrogations and addresses. The commandant and guards were recruited solely from the NKVD, which had its own units parallel to those of the Russian army.

I made friends with the Russian woman interpreter, the camp doctor. From her I learned something about the regulations from Moscow with regard to foodstuffs and other matters. According to these we were entitled every day to butter, sugar, and more bread than we were receiving. So, hardened as we had gradually become, I demanded in the name of the camp the fulfillment of these regulations. But the complaint was rejected.

Remembering how successful the Hungarians had been, I suggested a hunger strike. Long discussions arose. Many were hesitant and fearful. But the argument that things couldn't get any worse but only better, and that we had nothing to lose anymore, was conclusive.

So one morning we refused to accept our miserable meal. After two days of the hunger strike, the commandant realized that we were in earnest, whereupon he became "active."

"You stop, sons of whores, or I shoot some."

This again caused a few of us to waver, as to whether the action was now right or not. The rest of us encouraged them to keep their word and go on.

When the commandant saw that his threats were having no effect, he tried the friendly approach.

"Good, tomorrow you get butter and bedclothes, if you stop."

To which we replied, "As soon as our conditions are met we will end the strike."

Next day nothing happened. Nor could it. As the interpreter confided to me, there were no supplies of either butter or bedclothes. So where was the commandant supposed to get them from?

"All right," we decided, "the strike goes on."

After another five days, a commission appeared from Moscow. Hunger strikes were an alarm signal. There might also have been concern about their former Allies, for news from Kiev reached the West faster than from the mountains of the Caucasus. So I was hauled out of bed in the night and summoned before the Russian commission as the German interpreter for the German delegation. As interpreter on the "other side" was the woman doctor. An NKVD officer, a man in his mid-thirties, sat opposite us with some civilians, doubtless also from the secret service. His facial expression was less threatening than that to which we had become accustomed.

"Why a hunger strike?" he asked in a calm voice. "Why not talk to the commandant, then everything will be settled."

"But it wasn't," I replied through the interpreter. "That's why we're striking. We drew the commandant's attention to the regulations, but received only a negative response and were abused into the bargain.

"We know the Geneva Convention," I went on. "We know the instructions from Moscow about how prisoners of war are to be treated. We know that letters which we have sent to Moscow have been received and noted. We know also that negotiations have been conducted between the governments of the USSR, the USA, Britain, France, and China to the effect that German prisoners should be released in accordance with the Convention.

"We are in a position to get reports through to Western governments which state the real nature of the situation, especially in this camp. Don't ask how we shall manage this, but we shall. It won't be very nice for Mr. Stalin to have to hear from his Allies what conditions are like here.

"We merely demand that the regulations be followed, neither more nor less."

The reaction was astonishing. After a brief consultation with his companions, the NKVD officer gave us his answer.

"Your conditions will be met. Owing to the poor state of food supplies and transport not everything has worked as it should. We are not inhuman, so you can end the strike."

All right, he had saved his face, and we agreed to end the strike as soon as our conditions were met. After two days we did in fact receive bedclothes and the stipulated food rations. What is more, we saw with relief that the commandant was not angry with us.

Much to my surprise, the NKVD officer expressed a wish to speak to me alone in the presence of the interpreter.

"*Polkovnik*," he said, "a question: how many convinced Communists do you think there are in this and the other German POW camps?"

Was it a catch question? It was hard to answer, and it also seemed to me dangerous to give my own views. So I said, "About ten percent, I should think."

"Oh, no; at most six to seven percent," he replied. "And *Polkovnik*, how many do you think there are in East Germany?"

"Since you have been in East Germany now for nearly five years, it might be some eight to ten percent."

"At most three to four percent. And what about West Germany?"

Surprised by his figures, I suggested, "Less, about two to three percent."

To which he gave an even more astonishing reply, "Nil! You see, we are realists in Moscow. And because we are, we see no chance of being able to convince the German people of communism." His conclusion, "Neither the Italian nor the French Communists can be numbered among us. They are first and foremost Italians and Frenchmen. Britain is on the other side of the Channel, the Americans are far away. But we do have to reckon with *you*."

And then his words held doubt and fear again, "One day you will want to have an army again, with which you will invade us again. There lies our whole interest in keeping Germany 'neutral.' With a neutral Germany danger for us is banished. We can convince Europe of our desire, but also of our intention, never again to allow a war on our territory. That's how things look, *Polkovnik*."

This was one of the most interesting and instructive conversations I had as a *plenni*. The view was in keeping with that of ordinary soldiers, Russian convicts, and civilians, who had already said to me previously, "Although it will be hard for us, we shall one day forget what has happened. But you will go back to your country.

Then you will build up a new army and march into Russia, destroy our villages and kill or carry off our people."

How can this fear ever be removed from the people or from the "realists" in Moscow? All the noisy reactions to the rebuilding of the *Bundeswehr*, the federal army, and to the alliance with the American superpower are to be seen against this background.

26
Release

The weeks and months went by.

Hope of returning home dwindled more and more. It was especially depressing for us to hear that men had begun to be released from the "normal" camps.

We, the "convicts" were clearly not among them. All the same, after our successful hunger strike, we were in no mood to give up hope. The outcome of the strike had been like a tonic to us. Since then we had no longer been sent to work; our day was made up of getting food and discussing the rumors that were going around.

In the late autumn of 1949 the Russian winter was descending on the land and snow began to cover the broad expanse of the Ukraine. Then came the Russian interpreter's announcement that releases were imminent in our camp, too, albeit only up to 85 percent. The euphoria triggered off by the prospect of going home was unimaginable, but it gave way yet again to doubt. We had been fed too often with empty promises, with the monotonous *saftra domoi* ("tomorrow home").

Then at the end of October the first commission appeared from Moscow. The first prisoners were fetched for interrogation—as usual by night. "What did they ask you? Who questioned you? What was your impression?" No one knew the results of the interrogations. KGB people were impenetrable; they gave no sign of either benevolence or disfavor.

Who would be among the 15 percent who were supposed to remain behind?

The uncertainty, the hope, and anxiety remained. The commission disappeared again. It had interrogated only a proportion of the prisoners. What would be done with the others? Nothing happened. Our nerves were stretched to a breaking point. A deep depression settled over us all.

Then, after a few days, NKVD officers appeared in our barracks. They had lists from which they read out names. Those concerned had to pack their things and assemble in the courtyard. As always, by night. No one could sleep from excitement. When the rest of us crowded into the courtyard to see what was happening, we were brusquely pushed back. Worst off were those who had in fact been interrogated but then not called. We didn't know how to console them.

Once more we heard the loud *"Davai!"* From the windows we saw the small column move off and leave the camp. Where were they going?

Next morning I met the interpreter.

"What's happening?" I asked. "Are the others going home?"

"I think so," she said. "The train pulled out with the doors unlocked. That should mean *domoi.*"

"And the rest, those who were questioned but not called, what will happen to them?"

"I did tell you," she said, "fifteen percent." Even the interpreter could only guess, so hermetical were the workings of the NKVD.

"Was that the lot?" I questioned her further. "The commission has gone away, after all."

"The next commission will come," she said by way of consolation. "Then they will talk to everyone and decide who shall go home."

Shortly after, I came across a familiar face, a fellow prisoner from our old Camp 518/I. He was very downcast.

"After all the years of privation," he said, "and the heavy work in the mines, I was suddenly accused of having fought against the partisans and was told that I had to go as punishment to a special camp. I have never fought against the partisans and was in action in Russia for only a short time. But I can't prove anything. They must be mixing me up with someone else. I was brought here by a guard."

We were terribly sorry for him. What a price for an individual to pay, and an innocent man at that.

"How do things look in the old camp," I asked him, "what are our friends doing?"

"We were transferred to Camp II at the very beginning of 1949. After a short time releases were made. I hope that in the meantime everyone has gone home."

A new commission arrived from Moscow.

The same procedure took place once more: interrogations by night, selection and transportation. Then came a third commission. The camp was beginning to empty. Although we, the residue, were waiting full of hope for the next commission, we tried to console and raise the spirits of the fifteen percent who had been picked out to stay behind. Finally—after the arrival of the fourth commission—it was my turn and I had the memorable experience of my interrogation.

We who were called to pack our few belongings had first to go to the clothing room, where we were given new Russian winter clothing: padded jackets and trousers, as well as fresh foot-cloths, or foot-wrappings, which replaced socks.

The stockings that I had knitted for myself, of which I was so proud and which I wanted to show my mother, were taken from me. "Nix *kultura,*" said the Russians.

I did manage, however, to keep my Knight's Cross, which I had been able to hide from the Russians throughout those years. For a pair of my homemade stockings the German camp carpenter made me a little wooden chest, with a hollow space chiseled in one of its sides to take the Knight's Cross, which was then glued over.

The irony of fate: my first lodgings in Hamburg were burgled shortly after I had moved in and the Knight's Cross, among other things, was stolen.

Our train rumbled west across snow-covered fields, fields that five years earlier had seen the last stages of the struggle with Russia. Beneath them now lay the fallen, in hundreds of thousands.

At Brest-Litovsk, the boundary between Poland and Russia, drawn anew in 1939, came to the first stop of any duration. Again we changed from Russian into European wagons.

Suddenly Russian officers appeared in the trucks with lists. Our joy gave way to renewed fear. And indeed, ten of our fellow prisoners were taken off the train and led away. What a cruel fate!

Was the torment of uncertainty to have no end even now? We realized again that true freedom would be reached only after the border to West Germany had been crossed.

At every further stop we cowered in the corners of the truck, always in the hope that we wouldn't be discovered. We were now traveling through Polish territory toward East Germany, but we were still in Russian custody.

One day we stopped on an open stretch of the line. Nearby we could see a village. Some peasants came up to our train across the snow-covered fields.

"Where from? You German prisoners?"

We nodded, but were afraid they might be NKVD people in disguise.

"You're lucky, comrades, you're going home. We from Brest, once Poland, now Russia. We find new homeland, once Germany, but now given to us by Russians as home. Things bad for us; we must give Russians everything, our cows, grain, butter. Because of that we have to go hungry. Don't be angry with us, we didn't rob you of your homeland."

After nearly five years we were now confronted with reality. German territory taken from us Germans and handed over to the Poles, from whom their land in the east had been taken in exchange. What a political game of chess!

At the end of December we reached the border between Poland and East Germany. At last we were on home ground, albeit the so-called "Eastern Zone" occupied and controlled by the Russians. We were taken over by east-German guards, who were very unfriendly and declined to enter into any conversation. Yet we felt safer here.

We had completely forgotten that in the meantime Christmas, the festival of peace, had been celebrated and a new year begun. We stopped suddenly on an open stretch.

"Get out! Everybody stand by the trucks!" came the order.

What was happening now? Our nerves could stand no further strain. The tension was hardly bearable. Perhaps the East Germans had been told to keep us in their zone?

"We will now march in line to the border with West Germany. There each man will be called out by name. He must then cross the border without any further stop." We heard the words with relief.

One by one we took the path to freedom, for which we had yearned so long; cautiously at first, but then everyone ran as fast as he could past the open barrier. In the bare wintry branches of the trees we could see dozens of Russian fur caps. Realizing what had taken place there, we tore off our own caps and with a loud cry hurled them likewise up into the trees.

Free! After nearly five years, free at last!

Helpers and nurses of the German Red Cross took charge of us. A few men had to be supported; their legs gave way when the tension finally eased. We were taken to the Friedland camp, which still exists today, where the extensive but necessary formalities then began.

But before that everyone was allowed to have a bath. What a treat after all the years!

Then came the registering and questioning, about where one wanted to be discharged to, but also dispassionate interrogation by British officers, with questions about the camp in Russia, the food, treatment, and much else.

Then, finally, we were given the chance to telephone our families free of charge. The scenes that took place were unimaginable. No one was ashamed of his tears.

I wanted to be discharged to my mother's in Flensburg on the border with Denmark and was given a ticket, as well as my "discharge pay" of DM 300.00, to which every prisoner of war was entitled. Winand and his fellow prisoners were accompanied by Captain Samcharadse, the commandant of Camp 7518/I, until they reached the Russian border at Brest-Litovsk. There for the last time all prisoners were gone through. We were scolded and they took our last little properties. "Samcharadse's last action" they called it.

I decided to stop off in Hamburg on the way to Flensburg, to see some old friends again.

On 5 January 1950, the official day of my discharge, I arrived in Hamburg early in the morning. Waiting for me on the platform was my old friend Boos. He hardly recognized me in my padded clothes, but then we fell into each other's arms.

"Come on, old man," he said, "we'll go straight home. My wife is waiting there with a breakfast 'fit for a king.' Do you remember how we used to enjoy such a breakfast when you brought back all those delicacies from the front, things which we here at home no longer knew except by name?"

At his lovely country house my padded clothes were first taken from me. At last I could be human again!

"We'll burn these things right away," said my friend. "On the one hand so that you'll forget your captivity quickly, and on the other hand so that no bugs or lice will be brought into the house. Here are some of my things."

After a generous bath we sat in front of a blazing fire and ate and drank whatever the kitchen and cellar had to offer. For me it was like a dream.

To crown it all my friend opened a bottle of champagne, Veuve Cliquot Rosé 1937.

"Do you remember? You once brought me a case of twelve bottles of this from France. We drank one bottle on New Year's Eve 1944 to your good health and to peace in 1945. Ten bottles we bartered for food at the British officers' mess. But we didn't dare touch the last bottle, because we thought that if we did you would never come back. Now the moment has come to empty it to your safe return and to our reunion."

"You really do have some good friends still," I thought, deeply touched.

Next day I traveled on to my mother and sister. They and my brother, who had served on a minesweeper in the navy but had been given an early discharge, were standing at the station with flowers. What a reunion!

When we got home, I found many of the old things that I had grown to love no longer there. In order to survive, my mother had bartered many of our valuable pieces from China and Japan for food. Only the Japanese tea service had not been touched, for reasons similar to those of my friend with the bottle of champagne.

It was a question now of building a new life. When I went to Hamburg later, to look for a job, the friends just mentioned invited me to stay with them for the time being. On my arrival, my friend came up to me and ceremonially handed me a present. It was the champagne cork, set with a silver band, on which was engraved "5 January 1950."

27

A New Start

DAGMAR

My fresh start on "Day Zero" began with a body-blow. On reaching Flensburg I at once phoned Dagmar in Berlin. She was to come in a few days' time for a long weekend; her work at the TV station allowed her no more. I looked forward to our meeting, after exactly five years, in great agitation.

From the few cards of greeting to Russia I knew that she had become a successful reporter, much in demand; but also that she had maintained her commitment to me throughout and had planned our first meeting with care. In her apartment in Berlin a room was kept for me, and for me alone.

Now, on the cold station platform, we faced each other somewhat shyly.

"You look well," I began, to get over the moment I had thought about day and night in the camp. "You look even more attractive, but a bit on edge and run down."

"You look well too, much better than I expected after the long years in Russia."

"Well, I kept myself physically fit; I never gave up hope of coming home and lived for this moment of seeing you again."

Then we were sitting together over a cup of coffee. My mother and sister had left us alone.

Dagmar told me about herself, of the successful journey to Flensburg with "my" Mercedes, her job with the British as an interpreter, and her start with North German Radio, until the switch to TV. Dagmar had carved out a remarkable career for herself, from sheltered, well brought-up girl of "good" family to sought-after reporter.

"I've already made inquiries," she went on, "about possible openings for you in TV, radio, or the press. Unfortunately with no luck; there are too many pros lining up for any jobs that are open."

Dagmar then spoke of her many interesting colleagues, of the prominent people she had interviewed, and of the pleasure she took in her work.

Suddenly, and painfully, it dawned on me that I had stood still, like all my fellow prisoners, in the state I had been in at the beginning of 1945, with no chance of further development. We were worlds apart, and a bridge seemed scarcely possible. Dagmar too appeared to feel this.

"We'll have to think it all over," she said. "Everything is so different from how I imagined it would be through the years. Come to Berlin as soon as you can. You will see how I live and work, and get to know my friends and colleagues."

As I took Dagmar to the train I knew it was all over. In spite of the shock, I was glad we had not married. Many of my friends were facing the wreckage of broken marriages, which had not stood the strain of the five years of separation.

After a few days my friend Boos phoned from Hamburg.

"Come and see us. I've been thinking about what you should do."

In Hamburg I told Boos of the situation in which Dagmar and I found ourselves.

"Luck, I know Dagmar well. She was often here during her time at the radio. The two of you have grown apart. No one is to blame. But there's nothing to be done about it. Dagmar is sure to be suffering just as much as you and looking for a fresh start. But you won't find it together."

I went to Berlin all the same. Her apartment was enchanting, very Bohemian. "My" room was a museum: on the walls were pictures of our time together in Paris, everywhere there were things we had bought together. Her friends, almost all journalists and TV people, came and went. Everything was hectic, professional, and to some extent superficial. "Nice to see you. Dagmar has told us about you. Was it bad?" No real interest. When Dagmar took me to one of the many parties I stood around and felt I did not belong.

Dagmar had to go to the studio early in the morning and she came home late in the evening. Boos was right: we were worlds apart.

On the third day I decided to leave.

"Dagmar, let's remain friends. We can't take up again where we left off five years ago in quite different circumstances. Your apartment, 'my' room, everything seems like a commemoration, it recalls the past, but it's no longer alive."

So we parted.

In this too 5 January 1950 drew a line under my previous life. It really was "Day Zero."

I only saw Dagmar once more, a few years later. Suddenly there she was at my door.

"There's a man outside who wants to marry me. I like him. Will you have a look at him, talk to him? If you think he's suitable for me, I'll marry him. If not, I won't."

I had to laugh. The end of a romance born in the war was taking on an element of tragicomedy.

I thought the man was a decent sort: a successful businessman with a house in Ronco on Lake Maggiore, and a Porsche.

"I think he's all right, Dagmar. I hope you'll be happy with him."

Two years later I saw an item in a newspaper: Tragically, the well-known TV journalist, Dagmar S., has been killed in a car accident.

NIGHT RECEPTIONIST

Back in Hamburg I was sitting with Boos.

"My wife and I have been wondering what you ought to do as a start, until the discrimination against former officers has died down and you can find something suitable.

"You would hardly want to begin your new life as a traveling salesman, the only job for which you would need no training. But with your knowledge of human nature and your languages you ought to be of interest to one of the international hotels in Hamburg. Why don't you try them?"

The idea appealed to me and I applied to one of the largest hotels.

"Madame," as the proprietress was respectfully known, listened to me with close attention.

"You can make a start with me. The post of night receptionist has just become vacant. With your name and your languages you are just the sort of person I'm looking for. Perhaps I can launch you on a career as hotelier."

Beaming with joy I told Boos and thanked him for his advice. Until I had found a room in Hamburg, I would be able to stay with him.

"Good evening, Mr Y. Your room has been reserved for you as usual. We hope you will have a pleasant stay in Hamburg."

I stood behind the reception desk of the hotel, half of which was still requisitioned by the British occupation forces.

It was almost midnight on that cold day in February 1950. After 38 years, Day Zero had begun for me. As I write these lines a further 38 years have elapsed. The second period of my life has been no less interesting than the first, merely less dangerous. At its center stands my "African adventure," with many pleasant, but also unpleasant experiences.

I had to get used to civilian life. When the last guests had arrived and the night prowlers were back, the quiet, silent hours began. The night porter was a decent, older colleague who had survived the war in Hamburg and told me about the air raids, the shelters, and the hunt for extra food. He asked me, very warily, how it had been at the front and in captivity. My replies were brief; I wanted to put that time behind me.

I had to get used to the new rhythm: while most people were asleep, I was standing at the reception desk. When they went to work, I tried to sleep, before going to work again. Every night I looked at the guest list to see if I could find an old friend among the hotel's patrons.

Then came a little episode that was to change my whole attitude for the future.

Early one morning a guest from Finland was leaving. He had to pay his bill with me. As I wished him a good journey, he pushed a ten-mark note across the counter.

"That's for you. Thank you for the excellent service."

I was staggered. Never in my life had I received a tip. The situation was very painful.

"That's not necessary, thank you very much. I hope you have felt at home here." And I gave him back his money.

The Finn looked at me in disbelief, shook his head, and picked up the money. He had hardly left the hotel when the night porter rushed over to me.

"Are you mad? We live off the tips. Why do you think we're so badly paid? Every hotel management knows we get tips." Then, a bit more calmly, "I can understand you well enough. It's not easy for you to adapt. But you must. Every job has its rules."

An important lesson for me: it was now essential to think commercially. From then on I accepted tips, without a guilty conscience. Before long they doubled my pay.

I took increasing pleasure in talking to the guests, who came from all over the world. Back from a stroll in the town or along the Reeperbahn, they were often in the mood for a chat.

I had still not come across any of my former friends; my little address book was in the hands of the Russians.

Then, standing before me suddenly was Jürgen Graf Rittberg, orderly officer in our reconnaissance battalion and severely wounded in France in 1940. He had married into an old family in Düsseldorf which owned an automobile dealership. He offered me a job with his father-in-law as a salesman, but I declined politely. We saw each other frequently in the years that followed, until Jürgen was killed in a car accident.

I still dreamed of a job abroad; the urge to travel would not let me go.

Meanwhile I was in touch also with Hally Momm, the show-jumper and a fellow prisoner. He came to Hamburg every year for the horse show. Then Helmut Liebeskind, my adjutant since the invasion on 6 June 1944, turned up. Our delight was immense; we hadn't seen each other since we had been captured in April 1945.

Over a glass of wine he told me he had been approached by the Bundeswehr, just then in the process of being organized, to join it as a general-staff officer.

"What would you advise? Should I give up my good job?"

"That's something you'll have to decide for yourself, Liebeskind," I replied. "You are still young and could have a great career, even if you were not as well paid as at present."

His idealism won. A few years ago he retired as a lieutenant-general, after a distinguished career with many foreign postings.

Finally, a meeting came about for which I had always hoped: indirectly, through a number of people, I was brought in touch with the proprietor of an export firm which for generations had had close contacts with Japan, China, and Hong Kong.

"I intend to set up a new firm in Angola, West Africa, where competition as yet is not very strong. To do so I shall be going to Africa for a year and I'm looking for someone to represent me here. You have been recommended to me. Does the idea appeal to you?"

"It certainly does," I replied, "but I'm no businessman."

"The mechanics can be learned. Good management and reliability are innate. And that's what I need in a colleague who can run my newly founded firm while I'm away. My staff would show you the ropes. So, what about it?"

I agreed on the spur of the moment, especially since I was given the prospect of taking my turn in going to Angola for a year or two.

"Madame" quite understood my decision when I handed in my notice for the hotel job.

At evening classes in commercial law, bookkeeping, and Portuguese, I made myself familiar with the new subject matter; my young colleagues were a great help to me.

With my new boss I visited all our customers in Germany and elsewhere in Europe, and after a few months, I took him to the cargo boat that was to start him on his long journey to a new country, which later would also become my own second home.

I had found a new vocation, to which I am committed still today. The past became a memory; I devoted myself wholly and utterly to my new work.

There was, however, one more occasion when I was confronted by my former profession. I was summoned to an anonymous office in Bonn which for the time being was responsible for organizing the new Bundeswehr.

I was asked whether I would be interested in making my experience available by joining up again.

"You are still young, you've served in the Reichswehr and the Wehrmacht, with the tank force, and you've fought in almost all theaters of war. Your experience would be of great value to the future Bundeswehr."

My answer came very promptly.

"I have struggled to build a new profession for myself, which I enjoy and which takes me abroad a lot. To give that up I should have to have some guarantee from you that I would serve either in the tank force or as a military attaché. Can you guarantee that?"

The reply was not encouraging. "We might have a place for you in either capacity, but," I was given to understand, "we can give no guarantee. Ranks of colonel and above need approval from the political parties."

"Then I must decline with thanks. I have no wish to find myself back as a parade-ground commander all of a sudden, just because my face doesn't fit somewhere. Without any guarantee I would not give up my present position. I am grateful to you all the same for having thought of me."

Similar decisions were made by many of my friends who had built up good positions for themselves in industry or commerce. For me this was the end of the matter.

BACK INTO THE PAST

Then, in the 1960s, when I had just completed my first spell in Angola, I received a call from the British military attaché in Bonn.

"We have been told by your Ministry of Defense that you took part on the German side in Operation Goodwood, as commander of a combat group of the 21st Panzer Division.

"The Staff College at Camberley would like to invite you to their next 'battlefield tour' in Normandy, to give an account of your activity during the operation, which for Montgomery was a costly one. Would you be prepared to come, naturally with all expenses paid?"

The prospect of seeing Normandy again and the scenes of our heavy defensive fighting appealed to me. I agreed.

The terrain near Caen, east of the Orne, looked just as I remembered it from more than twenty years earlier. It was June, the corn was ripe, the villages had been rebuilt and the farmers were going about their business as they had been doing before D-Day. Caen, completely destroyed, had risen from the ruins, thanks to sensitive architects, more lovely than ever. The French with whom I came into conversation had by no means forgotten what had been done to their tormented land by both sides, but they had forgiven it, and to me, the former *sale Boche*, they were friendly. "*C'était la guerre*, Monsieur; you did your duty, although it was for an evil regime."

The CO and the staff officers of the college greeted me as their "fair and courageous opponent" and introduced me to the other guest speakers.

I met General "Pip" Roberts, probably the youngest and most flexible of the British tank commanders. I had known of him from North Africa and was aware that during Operation Goodwood he had been in charge of the leading 11th Armoured Division, which had had to bear the brunt of the battle and suffer the heaviest losses. Bill Close, one of his tank company commanders; David Stileman, of the grenadiers in his division; and other former participants in this fierce engagement greeted me like an old friend. I was overwhelmed by the kindness with which I was accepted and by the fairness with which it was acknowledged that Goodwood had been only a hard-won partial success, and that the action by our combat group had amounted to a successful defense, which we owed to our greater war experience and to Rommel's order to defend in great depth.

With the exception of one or two years when I was living in Africa, I was a regular guest of the Staff College until 1979.

Parallel to "presentation Goodwood" in all those years was a "presentation Overlord," which was concerned with the landing of the 6th Airborne Division, including the capture of the two Orne bridges by a company under Major John Howard. I was interested in this *coup de main* operation during the night of 5/6 June 1944. On a free day I joined the Overlord team and listened in fascination to the "John Howard story." Afterward I went up to him.

"I am Colonel Hans von Luck, commander of the combat group of the 21st Panzer Division, which was not allowed to attack during the night on which you, however, arrived in Escoville on your mission. I am pleased to make your acquaintance in person."

"Oh, Hans, I am so glad to meet you," he replied. "We must get together. There's so much I should like to know from you."

In a little bar of the seaside resort of Cabourg we then sat together that evening with other paratroopers who had descended on my combat area during the night in question. That was the start of my friendship with John Howard, which has lasted to the present day and has grown ever deeper. What madness to fight to the knife and then become good friends!

In 1979 the British Ministry of Defense made the film *Goodwood*, so that this important battle, and the personal experiences of those who took part in it, would be preserved for posterity. It became a fascinating film: original photographic material from both sides was accompanied by commentaries from the veterans, and the point of the battle and its outcome were explained by historians.

Since then the Goodwood film has been sold to almost all European general-staff colleges and tank divisions as training material for young officers and NCOs.

A few years later, again on the recommendation of John Howard, I was approached by the Swedish Military College and general staff.

"Would you be prepared to go around Normandy with us and talk to our officers about Operation Goodwood?"

I was astonished. Why should a traditionally neutral country be interested in the history of the Second World War?

"We are well aware," I was told by the sympathetic commandant of the Military College, "that in the event of a military conflict between the great powers no one would respect our neutrality. We should like to learn, and practice, how we as a numerically inferior country could succeed in preventing a landing on our coasts. Or, if that is not possible, how we could prevent an enemy who has landed from invading our country. For this purpose Operation Goodwood seems to us a very good example."

For about eight years now, always near 6 June, I have been the guest of the friendly Swedes.

1984—THE FORTIETH ANNIVERSARY OF D-DAY

The 6th June 1944 came around for the fortieth time. Great remembrance celebrations took place, attended by the British royal family, several crowned heads, the president of the United States, and representatives of all the countries that took part in the invasion on the Allied side.

John Howard's *coup de main* at the Orne bridges had been most spectacular. It was no wonder that the great TV companies of all countries looked here in particular for people to interview. It was John Howard again who referred them to me, if they wanted to know something about "the other side of the hill."

At the end of 1983 I had already been sought out in Hamburg by Professor Stephen Ambrose, a well-known historian in the U.S., who had been asked to write "the story of Pegasus bridge" in time for the anniversary. The interview lasted five hours, without my suspecting that it was being recorded. After going over the tape, Steve telephoned me.

"Hans, what you have been through is unbelievable, not to mention your relationship with Rommel and your experiences in Russia. You must write your memoirs. I'll see to it that they are read everywhere in the world."

That was the moment this book was born.

At the invitation of Steve Ambrose I was in Normandy at the end of May 1984, to speak to a group of Americans he had organized about the invasion, Rommel, and the Russians.

"Are you taking part in the celebrations on 6 June? After all, you played a decisive role at the time."

"On no account," I replied. "It's a day of remembrance for the Allies; it's their victory over Hitler Germany. I would have no business to be there."

The reaction to reports on German TV, in the press, and in radio broadcasts, in which I told of our action during the night of the invasion, was overwhelming. Letters and telephone calls from members of my former units came flooding in.

"I heard you on the radio. . . . Read your article with the photograph."

"You were on TV—are you my former commander, Hans von Luck?"

"I didn't know you were still alive. I thought you had disappeared in Russia, and then, all at once, there you were on TV!"

All of them asked if they could see me, meet me, or hear from me.

The past had caught up with me.

Thank goodness sufficient time had gone by since the events. I could see things in perspective, without too much emotion. All the same, the meetings, in Hamburg or elsewhere in Germany, showed me that even after so many years a friendship once established, and sufferings endured in common, created a feeling of solidarity that had nothing to do with the war tales of old veterans.

Then Fritz Winand called me from Cologne.

"How marvellous! I saw you on TV. Do you remember? We were together in the camp in the Caucasus, you the Colonel and I the young soldier, both of us suffering the same fate as prisoners, in the mines or on the building sites. Did you know that since 1945 there has been a Camp 518 Association, which has kept several hundred former members of the camp in touch, from 1950 onward, in Cologne, Berlin, and Munich? We meet regularly—in Cologne in two weeks. Couldn't you come?"

Naturally I had to go. We former prisoners of war had endured more than the battles in Russia, Africa, and France, and we had mastered our fate together.

Sitting in a room were some forty elderly gentlemen, who sprang to their feet as I came in.

"Our Colonel, von Luck! What a pleasure! To think that you're still alive and with us now!" Many had tears in their eyes, and it was no different with me.

I had to relate what had happened to us in the punishment camp in Kiev. I told of the hunger strike and of the interrogation before my release. Then I wanted to

hear what had become of the many people I had known and with whom I had
worked.

Fritz Winand, the enterprising initiator of the meeting, told me that our Camp
518 Association was probably the only one of its kind. In 1965, 426 members had
met regularly and 375 were still doing so in 1984.

I asked about Jupp Link, our German camp commandant.

"Jupp is living in a farmhouse near Munich. He is severely disabled but mentally
as lively as ever. We can give him a call."

"Jupp Link here," came the familiar voice, "who's calling?"

"This is Hans von Luck. Do you remember, Jupp? I am here in Cologne with a
lot of our friends from the hard times. It's a great pleasure to be in touch with you
again after more than thirty-five years."

"Colonel . . . Hans von Luck . . . my God!" His voice faltered. "How wonderful
to speak to you. Are you well? Do you ever come to Munich? You must pay me a
visit. I live very peacefully here in the country."

"Of course, Jupp. I'll come. I'll let you know."

I went from table to table. What had become of the *plennis* who in those days,
in their coarse denims and padded jackets, had all looked alike? I was interested in
the theater and music group, with whom I had spent so many pleasant hours.

At one table I was detained.

"Do you remember us? I'm Glaubrecht, the one-time drummer. Next to me here
is 'Köbes' Witthaus and Walter Struve, the arranger for our orchestra and band.
Do you remember how you hummed Glenn Miller's 'In the Mood' to us note for
note, and how we played it at the beginning of every performance?"

Helmut Wehrenfennig came to the table. He had written the librettos for our
operettas.

"On my return I went to the university and became head of a training college.
Besides that I've been writing poems and novels, which have been published by an
Austrian publisher."

"What became of the others, Karl-Heinz Engels, for instance, who as actor and
director helped to set up the theater group?"

"Engels," I was told, "was not released until 30 April 1950. Why so late, he
himself has no idea. He remained true to his profession: he became administrative
director of the municipal theaters in Dortmund and then one of the directors of the
Recklinghausen Ruhr Festival. He's been retired since 1985.

"Reinhold 'Heini' Bartel, our tenor, studied singing and was engaged by various
theaters, including the well-known opera house at Wiesbaden. He subsequently
became assistant professor of singing at Mainz University."

Bartel wrote to me somewhat later: "I was so pleased to hear of you. On the radio
I once had to sing the song 'Ninou, lach' mir einmal zu.' I only wish our Jewish
doctor, Dr. Fuchsmann, could have heard it. He once sang the song to me; he was
very fond of Jan Kiepura, its interpreter."

At the next table sat Drews, our camp cook, the most important person of all.

"I still remember quite clearly how Major Samcharadse told me to give the theater and music group a double helping of gruel. As he explained to me, 'For *Kultura* we do anything.' "

"I'm Fred Sbosny, the driver of the camp Studebaker. Do you remember how we once drove to Tbilisi together?"

"Of course!" Everything came back to me. "I know too how nervous you were when you had to steal tires, on orders from Samcharadse, from the mine depot. The guards might well have killed you. A lot of our 'special' jobs really were dangerous and quite an adventure."

Back to Fritz Winand's table, the energetic organizer of the meeting of our camp association. On his return he had completed his training and is today a municipal inspector in Cologne, responsible for the care of the mentally and physically handicapped.

"Meeting my fellow sufferers of that time," he said, "has left its mark. I cannot and will not suppress or forget those years in the Gulag; they became for many a turning point in their lives. It is quite clear to me that it was only the feeling of solidarity, and the comradeship without regard to rank or social origin, that enabled so many to survive."

In Cologne we asked ourselves a question: would we like to see Tkibuli again? Opinions varied, from "Never again!" to "Yes, why not, if the Russians would let us in?"

A business graduate, Eberhard Koellreuter, was at the time one of the very young prisoners; today he is professionally employed in the Munich area. He took the initiative and in 1978, 1982, and, most recently, in 1985, he traveled to the Caucasus quite officially with groups of German tourists. He organized the last trip himself. With his permission I pass on his account of it.

" . . . in 1985 I made up a party of sixty-seven people who wanted to see the beautiful state of Georgia on the edge of Asia. Apart from me, no one had anything to do with wartime captivity. My application to Intourist to include Tkibuli in our itinerary was rejected: 'For that, responsibility lies with the veteran's association.' Why is still a mystery to me today.

"On 6 September 1985, our party arrived in the Caucasus. I asked the young and friendly Georgian woman who had been allotted to us as guide whether we might go via Tkibuli. 'I happen to have heard of the place,' I said by way of explanation. 'Yes, of course, the town is on our way to Lake Ox-eye, high in the Elbrus mountains. There we shall be visiting the famous cathedral of Nikorzminda, built under Bagrat III, A.D. 1010 to 1014.'

"I was very excited; no one in the group had to know why I was so interested in this God-forsaken hole. On 7 September, after a horrible breakfast, we traveled north into the mountains in a dilapidated bus. The road was full of potholes, as it always had been.

"On either side of the road were vast tea plantations (Georgia is the third largest tea-producer in the world), then virgin land again, lying under the peaceful glow of the warm autumn sun. Parallel to the road ran the single-line railway, along which we had been transported to our camp, cooped up in freight cars.

"After two hours of jolting we arrived in the outskirts of Tkibuli. Passing the custom-house, we came to the dreary railway station, where we had once been unloaded and had had to drag ourselves to the camp laboriously on foot. I asked the guide whether we might stop for a moment, 'a call of nature, you understand.' From a point of concealment I took a few photographs. (May the Russian law forgive me! Taking photographs is strictly forbidden.) From here the town, set against hills and mountains, looked as untroubled as a health resort. When I thought of the many hundreds of our comrades who lay somewhere up there in unmarked graves, tears came to my eyes. I was not ashamed of them.

"As we drew nearer, the little town appeared as it really was and how I remembered it: plain wooden houses, neglected streets, a place built only for prisoners, who brought out the precious coal. We stopped in the middle of it. I spoke to some Georgians, asked about our camp and the coal mines. They looked at me in amazement, a *plenni* who was visiting the scene of his tribulation? 'Your camp has been pulled down long ago,' they replied. 'Other camps still exist for Russians.' Although most of them had not been alive at the time, or living there, they all showed much sympathy.

"We went on up, past the electricity works, which we had once built and which now looked pretty run down. Along a winding road we climbed the mountain to the Nakerala Pass. There, in 1949, I had been on my last building site: accomodation for mine workers. The houses looked neglected; what must they be like inside? The view back to Tkibuli was of matchless beauty; up there nothing recalled the suffering of that time.

"I took endless photographs, the view to the north stretched across to Lake Ox-eye and on to the untouched mountain world of the Elbrus range. Then we were at our destination. The beautiful old cathedral appeared to be undamaged, a show-place, perhaps, for the few tourists who strayed this far? We were at once surrounded by mountain peasants, to whom we distributed T-shirts and other little gifts. The friendly pope came up to us, posed for my Polaroid camera with evident pleasure and tucked the picture proudly into his cowl.

"When the peasants realized that we came from 'Ferge,' the Federal Republic, we were submerged in a torrent of words.

" 'We've heard from our parents how a lot of Germans had to work here as prisoners of war and that some of them starved to death. We like you Germans; we too are freedom-loving people. There must never be war again.'

"On the way back we passed once more through Tkibuli, that place of horror. Time has spread its cloak of oblivion. And it is well that it has. . . . "

So ended Eberhard Koellreuter's account.

What he, as an individual, managed to do should one day be made possible for everyone, in order to extend a hand to the people there and to the whole of Russia.

At the beginning of July 1987, my way took me to Munich. I would visit Jupp Link.

I called Ernst Urban in Munich, who was to arrange the meeting. In the camp I had often sat with Urban in the evening and heard his story, of how he had been placed between two glowing ovens and dowsed with cold water, in order to force a "confession" from him. Urban was afraid that the reunion with Jupp Link might be too much for Link. His wife said, "Come all the same, but treat him gently."

Through the lovely countryside, basking in the warm July sun, our way led us to the village in which Jupp lived, in the foothills of the Alps. We stopped in front of one of the typical Bavarian farmhouses.

"There's Jupp, he's looking out for us," cried Urban.

Leaning on his stick, Jupp hobbled up to me. He had tears in his eyes. And so had I, at this reunion after forty years.

Jupp fell on my neck.

'That I should live to see this! Our Colonel von Luck here at my place, well and apparently the same as ever. Come, Colonel, you are most welcome. This is my wife, the mainstay of my life."

"My husband has told me so much about you; I am so pleased for his sake. He didn't know whether you were still alive until we saw you on TV. I'll make you a Bavarian snack. Till then, sit here on the bench with my husband. He loves this place with its view of the mountains."

We three "old *plennis*" sat together. Jupp had put his arm around me and he spoke of the days and years in the Caucasus. I hadn't known till then that he had taken photographs in the camp, secretly and at the risk of his life, and that he had managed to smuggle the negatives out of the camp with the help of Georgian women. Today these photographs are valuable, because of their rarity.

It was so peaceful there on the bench that we forgot the hard times and were simply glad to still be alive.

After the expertly prepared snack, I had unfortunately to continue my journey. I promised Jupp I would come again, whenever my way took me to Munich.

"God preserve you, my dear Jupp. I shall never forget what you did for us all as a young man and as the German camp commandant."

A last wave and, sadly, Urban and I drove away.

I have no regret that the past, in multifarious form, has caught up with me again. The bridge to my earlier life has been built. I can cross it without heartache.

My second life, with its many fresh and strange adventures, has taken on new meaning.

Epilogue

To forget is good—but hard.
To forgive is better.
Best of all is reconciliation.

In *1952* I had a surprise visit from Erich Beck, my companion in many theaters of war, who used to regard himself as my "constant shadow."

"I got your address from your mother and took advantage of a business trip to look you up at last."

Our delight was immense. We had known nothing more of each other after my flight from North Africa in April 1943.

We sat together and talked: I of the heavy fighting up to the bitter end and of the hardships of Russian captivity. Erich Beck for his part was full of praise for the humane treatment he had received from the Americans, who let him go home early.

"The Amis showed by their attitude that they wanted to forget and be reconciled. 'After all,' they implied, 'you were only doing your duty.' "

We saw each other frequently in the years that followed. Beck's diary and notes have been a great help to me in writing this book. Colonel and corporal turned into friends. In late 1988 Erich Beck died. Unfortunately I had not the time to attend his funeral. I lost a true friend.

In *1956* I had business in Paris. I enjoyed renewing my acquaintance with this unique city. Much had changed, but the little *quartiers* remained.

I wanted—was determined—to find J. B. Morel again, my friend from the hard days of the war. The Russians had my little address book and he was not in the telephone directory (he had a private number). I couldn't even remember the name of the street where he lived, but I knew what the house looked like and that it was in Neuilly, near the Bois de Boulogne. I went there on the off chance, and in the Rue du Dobropol suddenly found myself in front of the familiar house in which J. B. had had his little apartment. The concierge would help me; the concierges of Paris were all-seeing and all-knowing.

She was sitting in her cubbyhole talking to an elegant lady.

"Excuse me, Madame, does Monsieur Morel still live here?"

"I am Madame Morel," said the lady. "Can I help you?"

"Madame, you don't know me, but I am Hans von Luck, a good friend of your husband's from the war years."

"Hans, *mon Dieu*, you're alive!" Both women suddenly had tears in their eyes. "I know all about you, J. B. has told me so much. Come in, my husband will be home any minute.

"My name is Mary. We married a few years ago and for the time being have kept the little bachelor apartment."

The apartment was unchanged, a few more feminine touches, perhaps. How often had I sat there and talked about the wretched war.

Mary was running around excitedly.

"Hide in the sleeping alcove. We'll give J. B. a surprise."

Suddenly, there he was.

"*Bonjour, chérie*, have you had a good day?" Then he turned around and saw me standing before him. His coat and briefcase fell to the floor, tears sprang to his eyes.

"*Non, Hans, ce n'est pas vrai, Mon Dieu*, it really is you."

We rushed together and fell in each other's arms. I too had tears in my eyes.

"Mary, put something on, we're going to celebrate. I'll give Clément a ring; he's got to come along."

We all sat together in a little restaurant that belonged to a friend of J. B.'s.

"Pierre, you won't believe it, I've found my friend Baron Hans von Luck again. Bring us a bottle of champagne and cook up something special for us."

There was so much to tell and to ask about.

At the end of the war J. B. had left no stone unturned in his efforts to find me: he tried the French embassy in Moscow, the German embassy in Paris, and even the Russian KGB.

"All I could discover was that you had fallen into the hands of the Russians. But no one could tell me where you were or even whether you were still alive."

Clément Duhour turned up with a bottle of very old champagne, Veuve Cliquot Rosé. He, meanwhile, had become an eminent film producer, his liaison with Vivianne Romance long since ended.

"How is Dagmar? After her flight from Paris in 1944 we heard nothing more of her."

I told my friends how and why things had come to an end between us and the dreadful circumstances in which she had lost her life. We sat together far into the night and promised each other never again to allow contact between us to be broken.

Two officers, who had once confronted each other as enemies, had become friends in the best sense of the word.

Everything divisive was forgotten and forgiven.

In *1967* I received a phone call from a director of Pathé films in France.

"The ORTF is planning to make a documentary film in North Africa called *The War Without Hate*, using newsreel material on the desert war from 1941 to 1943. In making it, an eyewitness from each of the four countries that took part in the war, Britain, France, Italy, and Germany, is to be present as commentator. The project is under the auspices of the French minister of defense, Messmer (who at the time was one of the defenders of the desert fort of Bir Hacheim). We shall be flying with the team in a government plane to Alexandria, and from there go to Tobruk and deeper into the desert. If you would like to take part, Monsieur von Luck, I'll come and see you with an ORTF editor to discuss all the details."

I agreed at once, for the job appealed to me.

We arrived in Egypt about four weeks before the outbreak of the Six Day War. The country was highly unsettled. For security reasons we were not allowed to go to Tobruk. So we made the film somewhere in the desert.

The outcome was a conciliatory, objective film, which has been shown with great success in many countries of Europe and overseas.

From the end of the *1960s to 1979* I was, as already mentioned, a guest of the British Staff College, Camberley, which organized a "battlefield tour" in Normandy each year, so that young general-staff officers could hear on the spot comments on the most important battles in Normandy by former participants in the war.

There is virtually no senior British officer today who as a student did not hear my talks in Normandy. Among them is the Duke of Kent.

Opponents have turned into friends, who together, and without emotion, try to draw lessons from the events of that time.

Since *June 1980* I have been a guest each year of the Swedish military academy, which for the reasons given is interested in the German defensive operations during the invasion.

Finally, in *November 1983*, I was visited by Steve Ambrose, today my good friend, to be interviewed for his book *Pegasus Bridge*, which was to reconstruct, for the fortieth anniversary of the invasion, the *coup de main* by which Major John Howard had been able on that occasion to take the important bridges over the Orne.

In *May 1984* I gave a talk in Normandy to a group of Americans, who were being guided around the battlefields by Steve Ambrose.

"Will you be coming to the celebrations on 6 June?" he asked me.

"No," I replied, "that is a day of remembrance for the Western Allies. As a former combatant I would have no business to be there.

"In all the efforts at reconciliation, one should on such a day respect the feelings and memories of others."

At the end of *May 1984* things were very hectic at the little Café Gondrée, which stands right by the Pegasus bridges and was probably the first house to be liberated by the Allies. Steve Ambrose, the American historian, John Howard, the British liberator, and I, the German colonel and "man from the other side," sat in front of the café in the sun. We were served by Madame Gondrée and her daughters. For me the moment was symbolic: opponents of forty years earlier sat together as friends, to sign Steve's book for the hundreds of visitors who had come from all over the world for the approaching 6 June.

The Cafe Gondrée had presented me with a problem from the start. Madame hated the Germans. Her husband, a member of the Resistance, had died shortly after the end of the war. Since then John Howard, the liberator, had been regarded by Madame Gondrée and her daughters as the *patron* of the house.

Both the Staff College and the Swedes always took lunch at Madame's; it was already a tradition. But how could I as a German and at the same time a guest of the British, and later the Swedes, share in the daily lunch without disclosing my nationality?

John Howard found the answer.

With the British I was introduced to Madame as "Major van Luck," and with the Swedes as "a Viking from Sweden." Over all the years Madame had responded with the words, "I like the English" and "I like the Vikings," accompanied by a kiss on either cheek. Although it was reassuring that Madame had never discovered my true nationality, I was nevertheless far from happy about this white lie.

While Steve and I went on signing copies of his book, the Swedish commandant and John Howard were still sitting in Madame's sanctuary, the little back room with all her photographic mementoes.

Suddenly John Howard came out.

"Hans, for Madame the 6th of June 1984 will be the high point of her life. The celebrations for the fortieth anniversary of D-Day will be attended by Prince Charles, who will also be coming to Pegasus Bridge and the Cafe Gondrée, and will meet Madame. She is very ill and is only keeping herself going for that day. I think we should finally tell her the truth. She ought not to die with our white lie. I'll speak to her."

I waited outside, anxious about how Madame would react.

Then she came out, with her arm hooked through John's. She stopped in front of me; her expression was kind.

"Monsieur Hans, John has told me everything. I know now that today you are close friends, and John's friends are also my friends. Let us forget and forgive everything. God protect you!" And this time her little kiss was legitimate.

The reconciliation with this patriotic woman meant more to me than many other encounters.

A few weeks later John called me from England.

"Hans, I shall never forget the meeting between Prince Charles and Madame. Before the eyes of the world's press and TV cameras, this wonderful woman kissed the hand of the British heir to the throne and expressed her gratitude for 'liberation from the Nazis.'

"She died a few days ago, happy, as her daughters told me."

The following year I went with John to the little village cemetery and laid some flowers on her grave. I also laid a bunch on the grave of Lieutenant "Den" Brotheridge, the first man to fall in John's company. They had a claim to my respect.

In *May 1987* I was invited by the French consul, Monsieur Kieffer, to Rittershoffen in Alsace. Not far from this village, which had been so hotly contested in January 1945, a one-time casemate in the Maginot Line was to be inaugurated as a museum. French and German youngsters had worked there voluntarily for months, a wonderful sign of reconciliation.

On Monsieur Kieffer's initiative a monument had already been inaugurated the year before between the two villages of Rittershoffen and Hatten. On it were inscribed the names of the divisions that had fought against each other in the last phase of the war. Under the fluttering flags of America, France, and West Germany, former enemies shook hands, in the knowledge that they had no intention of ever fighting each other again.

In *July 1987* I was invited to deliver a lecture at the University of Innsbruck in Austria to some twenty-five students, male and female, who were members of Steve Ambrose's class on a study-visit to Europe. Quite a number of them were Jews. Before we all traveled to Normandy for a long weekend, we sat together each evening in a little restaurant and talked. I knew that many of them had been highly sceptical as they listened to the lecture of a "former officer in the Nazi army." I was able to satisfy them that the term "Nazi officer" was incorrect and a generalization, and that the vast majority of the German army realized, after the invasion of Russia and the lost war in North Africa and France, that the ideology of the "Thousand-Year Reich" was false and had plunged not only our own people but the whole of Europe into misery.

I also said, however, that I was still a German, and would stand by that.

On the train journey to France I tried to give them an idea of Rommel's personality, which interested them greatly, and to make clear to them that the black-and-white portrayal of the Russians as nothing but evil and us in the West as nothing but good was mistaken and led us nowhere.

They also wanted to know whether we former soldiers had not, after all, known something about Auschwitz and the other extermination camps and done nothing about them. I was able to satisfy the students that this had not been the case; until I heard that my future father-in-law had been killed in Sachsenhausen concentration camp, I had known nothing about them. That for me had first opened a chink in the door to the appalling events.

The fact that they believed me is for me the clearest evidence that the youth of today is trying to see things objectively.

In their examination papers and in their personal letters to me it was evident that they had received a new picture of their former opponents, us Germans, for which they thanked me.

The youth of the Western world, the new generation, has long since built bridges to each other and thereby unconsciously and without difficulty effected a reconciliation between former opponents.

Glasnost and *perestroika* will make it possible, one hopes, for resentment toward our former Russian opponents to be broken down and for a hand to be extended also to them.

This is something that not only the politicians of East and West are called upon to do, but all of us.

One wish would be fulfilled for me if I could meet that blond Russian lieutenant again who protected me from the Mongolians when I was captured; or if I could shake the hand of my "breakfast colonel," who displayed such humanity toward a captured former opponent. I would even be prepared to down a full glass of vodka on an empty stomach with that Russian tank colonel, who greeted me with respect after my capture.

I have often felt that in the first half of my life I was, in a double sense, a prisoner of my time: trapped on the one hand in the Prussian tradition and bound by the oath of allegiance, which made it all too easy for the Nazi regime to misuse the military leadership; then forced to pay my country's tribute, along with so many thousand others, with five years of captivity in Russian camps.

As a professional soldier I cannot escape my share of the collective guilt; but as a human being I feel none.

I hope that nowhere in the world will young people ever again allow themselves to be so misused.

Selected Bibliography

Ambrose, Stephen. *Pegasus Bridge*. London: G. Allen & Unwin, 1984.

Botting, Douglas. *In the Ruins of The Reich*. London: 1984.

Buffetaut, Yves. *Rommel en France 1940*. France: Edition Heimdal, 1985.

Hastings, Max. *Overlord*. London: Michael Joseph Ltd., 1984.

Haupt, Werner, and J. K. W. Bingham. *Der Afrika Feldzug*. Podzun Verlag, 1968.

Kortenhaus, Werner. *Die Geschichte der 21. Panzerdivision 1943–1945*. Forthcoming.

Liddel Hart, B. H. *The Rommel Papers*. New York: Harcourt, Brace, 1953.

Rommel, Feldmarschall Erwin. *Krieg ohne Hass*. Verlag Heidenheimer Zeitung, 1950.

Name Index